Losing the Atmosphere

A Memoir

A Baffling Disorder, a Search for Help,
and the Therapist Who Understood

Vivian Conan

Afterword by
Jeffery Smith, MD

Losing the Atmosphere

A Memoir

A Baffling Disorder, a Search for Help,
and the Therapist Who Understood

Vivian Conan

Afterword by
Jeffery Smith, MD

GREENPOINT PRESS
NEW YORK, NY

Copyright © 2020 by Vivian Conan

All rights reserved.

Losing the Atmosphere
A Memoir
A Baffling Disorder, a Search for Help, and the Therapist Who Understood

by Vivian Conan

No part of this book may be reproduced or transmitted in any form or by any electronic or mechanical means, including photocopying and recording, or by any information storage and retrieval system without the express written permission of the publisher, except where permitted by law.

ISBN Paperback: 978-1-7346740-1-9
ISBN eBook: 978-1-7346740-2-6

Library of Congress Control Number (LCCN): 2020944730
LCCN Permalink: https://lccn.loc.gov/2020944730

Book Designer: Robert L. Lascaro
LascaroDesign.com

Greenpoint Press
A division of New York Writers Resources
greenpointpress.org
200 Riverside Boulevard, Suite 32E
New York, NY 10069

New York Writers Resources:
- newyorkwritersresources.com
- newyorkwritersworkshop.com
- greenpointpress.org
- prisonwrites.org

Printed in the United States on acid-free paper

Praise for *Losing the Atmosphere*

"Vivian Conan has written a real-life medical mystery that is as resonant and profound as an Oliver Sacks case study—but in her case, we see it from the inside. ***Losing the Atmosphere*** is, at its heart, a book about what it is to be an imperfect human (as we all are) walking through an imperfect world."
—**Dawn Raffel**, author of *The Strange Case of Dr. Couney*

"In razor-sharp prose, ***Losing the Atmosphere*** traces one woman's lifelong journey to mental wellness. Afflicted by two complex disorders and misdiagnosed time and again, Vivian Conan tells her story with poignancy, determination and fierce intelligence. You will cheer for this survivor."
—**Sally Koslow**, author of *Another Side of Paradise*

"A compelling story of a woman struggling to find her identity as she battles a baffling psychological condition that has plagued her since childhood. In this beautifully written memoir, Vivian Conan gives a fascinating account of a woman who, despite having grown up in a close, extended family in Brooklyn, creates a complicated imaginary world to cope with a demanding father and a distant mother. ***Losing the Atmosphere*** will haunt you well after the last page has been turned."
—**Joy Behar**, co-host, *The View*

"Vivian Conan's ***Losing the Atmosphere*** gives a powerful, personal account of how recurring childhood trauma can fracture one's identity and result in a deep loss of self. Conan illustrates the little-understood but very real role multiple identities play for children and adults living with MPD and DID. This beautifully written memoir is a testament to a woman's intelligence, tenacity and courage to find herself and make peace with a turbulent, oppressive past. In a world in which we increasingly rely solely on biochemical solutions, Conan proves that education, self-advocacy, and hard therapeutic work can lead to self-discovery and true healing."
—**Christina Chiu**, author of *Beauty* and *Troublemaker and Other Saints*

"A potent, heartfelt life story."
—*Kirkus Reviews*

"Vivian Conan's memoir is what self-help, genuine self-help, feels like. Sensing the problem. Grasping the problem. Grappling with the problem. Overcoming the problem. This is quiet heroism."
— **Mark Goldblatt,** author of *Twerp and Finding the Worm*

"*Losing the Atmosphere* is an engrossing and highly informative memoir about how a child faced with an environment that is incomprehensible, sometimes terrifying, and psychologically unmanageable creates an illusory world to sustain her and develops different identities as a way of coping. It is first the compelling story of how this all began, then the uplifting narrative of how Ms. Conan learned to process and integrate experience that had been overwhelming—to mourn, forgive, and finally re-engage with the world as a full person. As a window into the experience of a person who developed dissociative identity disorder and found ways to heal, *Losing the Atmosphere* is a must-read for mental health professionals. It is a remarkable story and a fascinating read for everyone else."
— **Elizabeth F. Howell, PhD,** author of *Understanding and Treating Dissociative Identity Disorder* and *Trauma and Dissociation-Informed Psychotherapy*

"*Losing the Atmosphere* is a heartbreaking account of life with a rare psychological disorder and the events that broke a budding mind to pieces."
—**Claire Foster**, *Foreword Reviews*

"*Losing the Atmosphere* by Vivian Conan is a very fascinating and at times very disturbing book. I don't think I can put words to how much it touched me. It's the kind of memoir that will resonate a long time with readers and show that it is possible to find a road to survival. I'm glad she wrote it, glad I read it."
—*The Bookish Elf*

"Highly recommended for personal reading lists as well as community, college, and university library Contemporary American Biography collections as an intensely personal, exceptionally informative, engagingly written, expressly thoughtful and thought-provoking memoir."
—*Midwest Book Review*

To my mother,
who opened a new chapter in our lives
when she said, "It's love at second sight."

And to Emily,
who kept the kernel of me safe for all those years.

Life, too, is like that. You live it forward,
but understand it backward.

—Abraham Verghese, *Cutting for Stone*

AUTHOR'S NOTE

THESE EVENTS ARE TRUE to the best of my memory and the memories of my mother and aunts, who were generous in sharing them with me. There are no composite characters or altered details, but some names have been changed: all boyfriends; all doctors and staff at Mount Sinai Hospital; all patients during my first Mount Sinai stay; all patients at Albert Einstein Hospital; my Bronx apartment mate, Karen; and Catskills hotel owner Mrs. Comitor. I have also changed the names of some of my therapists—Dr. Sacker, Gerald, Marybeth, and Dr. Blum—and the names of Dr. Smith's children. Excerpts from letters and hospital records are verbatim. Dialogue has been created by me to bring scenes to life.

CONTENTS

Prologue—1

PART ONE: BEGINNINGS

1. Two Mommies—5
2. Two Daddies—13
3. The Gentle Slap of Cards—21
4. Cookie—31
5. A Little Closer to Nebraska—39
6. Sweet Sixteen—53

PART TWO: ANALYSIS

7. Appointments—61
8. The Rush of the River—75
9. Beethoven's Fifth—85
10. Lost Child—95
11. Sailboat—105
12. Ultimatum—111
13. Nine Credits—121

PART THREE: MOUNT SINAI

14. T.U.B.E.—133
15. Dry Mouth—143
16. The Flute Plays the Violin—151
17. Susan Has a Secret—163
18. Sleep—171
19. No Refuge—179

Photo Album: 1942–1965—197

PART FOUR: EINSTEIN

20. Rose Garden—209
21. Psychodrama—217
22. Picasso—227
23. Vagabond—241

PART FIVE: LATE BLOOMER

24. Overing Underground—257
25. Rum Raisin—265
26. Rebecca—271
27. Horizontal—277
28. The Right Choice—285

PART SIX: ALTERS

29. Adulthood—293
30. Flight Lessons—299
31. Mommybeth—307
32. An Explanation—313
33. Meeting Myselves—321
34. Believing, Doubting—329
35. Being Seen—339
36. The Left Back Burner—347

Photo Album: 1966–1997—357

PART SEVEN: HEALING

37. The Saddest Present—365
38. Object Permanence—377
39. Windchill—387
40. The Same Dog—397
41. My Mother's Keeper—409
42. Water Doesn't Flow Uphill—421

Epilogue—429

Photo Album: 1998–Present—433

AFTERWORD *Jeffery Smith, MD*—441

ACKNOWLEDGMENTS—453

ABOUT THE AUTHOR—455

Prologue

MY OWN SCREAM WOKE ME, but I couldn't open my eyes. My flesh was without form, liquid drained into the mattress. My brain said not to worry, this sucked-out Hades feeling was just the morning routine; in an hour I would be reconstituted, able to get up and go to work. There was no way to hurry the process. I started to shake, as if I were having a seizure. The trembling stopped and a keening howl filled the room.

Footsteps. My neighbor passing my apartment door. Had he heard? I would feel awkward if I ran into him that evening in the lobby.

The task: to get my body back.

I concentrated on my right index finger, willing my substance to exude from the mattress and fill it. The shakes returned. Stopped. I could move my finger. It usually happened this way, slowly at first. A few fingers I had to focus on individually until, with a rush, everything filled at once. FingersHandsArms. Torso. ToesFeetLegs. The shaking became continuous, like chattering teeth, except it was the whole length of me. My eyes opened. Daylight at the edges of the window shades. I kept my gaze anchored to the long-necked Modigliani lady in her frame on the far wall until the shudders played themselves out and the howling turned to whimpering. I got out of bed and walked to the bathroom.

In the kitchen, I put up water for tea and turned on the news. It was still 1982. Another bombing in Beirut. Bridges destroyed. But

I was prepared. Weeks back, when I'd first heard of the bombings, I signed up for flying lessons at a small airport in New Jersey so I would have a way to escape. No matter that the fighting was thousands of miles from my home in Manhattan, or that I didn't own a plane. With eight hours on my flight log, I felt capable of getting into any Cessna 150 parked on a rooftop and soaring over damaged bridges to safety.

My colleagues at work thought it was cool that I was learning to fly. "You're so brave," they said. I smiled. It had nothing to do with bravery.

I KNEW THAT, FROM THE OUTSIDE, my life seemed unremarkable. Anyone who stood behind me on a supermarket line or sat next to me on a bus would probably have forgotten me seconds after we went our separate ways. Yet for decades I had been dealing with a tangle of symptoms I didn't understand. In high school and college, I scoured books about abnormal psychology, looking for any label, however scary, that would take away my feeling that I was an alien species of one. None fit. Even in the abnormal world I was a freak.

It would take many years, several wrong turns by professionals, and several suicide attempts and hospitalizations before I learned what was really going on. Then came the hardest task of all: healing. This is my story. ■

PART ONE

BEGINNINGS

CHAPTER 1

Two Mommies

NONA FED US LUNCH the same way every day. White kerchief tied over the coiled gray braid at the nape of her neck, small gold earrings bouncing gently, and lips sucked in over toothless gums, she carried a delicious-smelling pot from the stove to the table. She dipped in a spoon and loaded it with a flavorful mush of potatoes, meat, tomatoes, and string beans. Holding her hand under it to catch any spills, she brought it toward my face. I opened my mouth and she slipped it in. While I chewed, she refilled the spoon and ferried it to my cousin Jerry's mouth. Next was my cousin George's. If food dripped down our chins, Nona scraped it upward with the spoon and guided it into our mouths.

All the while, she told us stories. "De farmer, he work hard to plant ta vegetables," she would begin. "He put water and take out alla ta weeds."

My turn for the spoon.

"He no see de horse what come in de night to eat ta vegetables."

Jerry's turn.

"An' he tink to himself, Why alla ta vegetables dey disappear lak dat? What's happen?"

George's turn.

"An' he say, I gawn fine out who take ta vegetables."

The farmer hid in the field with his gun. There was a loud BAMM! Nona always timed it perfectly. Just as the horse was running away, spinach dangling from his mouth, the pot would be empty.

After we got up to play, Nona walked to the sink, swaying from side to side on her bowed legs, and washed the pot and spoon. She stopped at the stove to lift the lids from the supper pots and give a quick stir. Then she took my baby brother, Marvin, out of his playpen. Carrying him in her arms, she went back down to the basement to sew.

I loved staying in my grandparents' house, where we had been living for the past three months, since my father left for the war. During the day, my mother and aunts were at work, and Papoo peddled aprons and pillowcases to housewives in Brighton Beach. Nona, the lone adult at home, sewed aprons and took care of the children. Sometimes we played in the backyard, sometimes in the basement, where we crawled in and out of the empty cartons next to Nona's sewing machine and Marvin's playpen, or climbed up the mountain of fabric scraps and slid down.

Though not yet three, I sensed that the rules were looser here in Brooklyn. When my parents and I had lived in Knickerbocker Village on the Lower East Side of Manhattan, I hadn't been allowed to put anything into my mouth if someone else's mouth had touched it. Germs. There had been no stories at the table. Most of the mealtime talk had been Spanish practice—if I wanted bread and butter, I had to say, "*Quiero pan y mantequilla, por favor*"—or my father reading aloud to my mother from the newspaper. And punishment at Nona's wasn't really punishment. Once, when Jerry and I did something we weren't supposed to, Aunt Mollie said, "You naughty children!" but she was smiling.

I would find out years later that my mother also felt freer away from my father's control. When she had brought me home from the hospital as a newborn, he'd forbidden her to use baby talk with me. No coo-cooing. She was permitted to speak English, but he spoke to me only in Spanish. To him, I was a grownup in miniature, one step away from the harsh realities of the job world, and it would be useful if I knew another language.

My father had also appointed himself the guardian of my health. Every evening, he demanded a report from my mother. *Where did you go with her today? It was chilly out; did you put a sweater on her? It was hot; did she sweat? How much milk did she drink?* When I caught my first cold at nine months, he berated her. She hadn't dressed me properly, he said, hadn't opened the window wide enough when she put me to sleep. My mother said she began to feel like hired help.

MY PARENTS MET IN MARCH, 1941, at a foreign-language conversation club in Manhattan. Both were first-generation Americans whose parents—hers, Jews from Greece and Turkey; his, Jews from Russia—had come to America through Ellis Island early in the century. Bea, my mother, whose husband of three years had divorced her, was 26. A graduate of Brooklyn College, where she had majored in French, she came to the club because someone told her it was a good place to meet men. My father, Jack, 32 and also divorced—he'd gone to Reno to end a four-year marriage—was a regular who spoke several languages. He was self-taught, having dropped out of high school to support his younger brother and two sisters when both his parents died of cancer.

Sometimes I imagine their meeting. Jack saw a pretty, soft-spoken woman with long brown hair combed into a stylish upsweep. Bea saw a serious, handsome man with dark curly hair and a mustache over full lips. Chatting in French, they told each other where they worked: she, sewing in a garment factory, the only job she could get in the lingering Depression; he, at the post office, where he used his linguistic proficiency inspecting customs declarations.

Their three-month courtship included many strolls along the Coney Island boardwalk. Bea was captivated because Jack liked classical music, studied languages, and played chess, but mostly because he showed an interest in her. She told me her self-esteem had been badly damaged by her divorce, and also that she wanted to be married again to please her mother. The fifth of nine children—eight of whom lived to adulthood—she knew, as did all seven girls, that Mama wished the best for them. The best was a husband. When Jack proposed one May evening on a long walk from Coney Island back to her family's home on 74th Street in the Bensonhurst section of Brooklyn, she accepted. They were married by a Justice of the Peace on July 4, 1941. I was born ten months later, on May 7, 1942.

A MONTH OR SO AFTER MY BIRTH, my mother told me, she arrived home from grocery shopping to find my father giving me a bath in the kitchen sink. To her horror, after he lifted me out of the basin of warm water, he filled it with cold and plunged me in. "Warm water opens her pores," he explained over my shrieks. "If you don't close them right away, she'll get sick." After that, my mother bathed me herself, when my father wasn't home.

Another day, sometime during my first six months, my mother's younger sister Sophia came to visit. According to the routine my father had established, my mother put me into my crib after my evening feeding and closed the bedroom door. She and Sophia were about to leave for the movies when I let out a piercing howl. My mother started toward the bedroom. My father blocked her way.

"If you go in," he said, "she'll learn that all she has to do to get her way is cry."

"You know I don't usually go in," my mother said as my wails continued, "but this isn't her normal cry."

"Don't interfere! *Go to the movies with your sister!*"

They returned several hours later to find my father playing chess against himself in a silent apartment. The incident was never discussed.

WHEN I WAS TWO AND A HALF, my father began to worry about being drafted. Until then, he had been exempt from military service because of an enlarged heart. Now, with the war raging in Europe and the Pacific, the Selective Service was calling up men who had previously been deferred. Rather than wait for their letter, which would almost certainly have meant being sent into combat, he used his typing, stenography, and language skills to secure a civilian position in the Army. He was to ship out at the end of October, but when he said his wife was expecting a baby soon, Army officials allowed him to wait a few weeks.

My brother, Marvin, was born on November 10, 1944. A week later, my father sailed for Italy, and my mother, Marvin, and I moved into Nona and Papoo's house. Its four apartments were already occupied, some by family, some by other tenants, so we added ourselves to Nona and Papoo's apartment. With our arrival, its three bedrooms were crammed with ten people, including Aunt Mollie, whose husband was also in the war; her one-year-old son, my cousin Jerry; and my unmarried aunts, Rae, Sophia, and Diana.

IN THE BEGINNING OF MY PARENTS' MARRIAGE, my mother had deposited her factory salary into their joint checking account, but after she made a small purchase without asking my father beforehand, he'd taken her name off the account. Now, with Nona caring for Marvin and me, my mother found a job as a substitute teacher at P.S. 128, a ten-minute walk away, and opened her own bank account. She also passed the Board of Ed test to become a permanent teacher and, in February, three months after our move to Brooklyn, was offered a fifth-grade class at P.S. 54 in Bedford-Stuyvesant, much farther away. She accepted, even though it meant she would get home more than an hour later.

At about the same time, Aunt Sarah and Uncle Sam, who also lived in the 74th Street house, told my mother about a vacant apartment around the corner, above a dry goods store on 20th Avenue. Though hesitant to move out on her own with two children, my mother liked the idea of having privacy and went to look at it. The small living room and bedroom faced the back. It was winter—no leaves on the trees—and she could see the fences and clotheslines in all the backyards of the houses on 74th Street, right down to Nona's. She decided to take it.

I was miserable at my sudden banishment—from Nona, my aunts, my cousins. On 74th Street, if one grownup was busy, another was glad to pay attention to me. Here, there was just my mother, who was always busy. "I'll look at it later," she said if I tried to show her a drawing.

Every morning while she dressed Marvin, I dressed myself. Then I asked her to tie my shoelaces. "I'll be happy when you learn to tie them yourself," she would say in an annoyed voice. "Hold still!" After we dropped Marvin off at Nona's, she and I walked to the JCH—Jewish Community House—on Bay Parkway, where she had enrolled me in nursery school.

My mother was rushed when she picked me up in the afternoon, too. "That's lovely," she would say, tucking my painting into her bag. "Now get your hat." We walked the quarter mile to Nona's. Still in our coats, we hurried through the upstairs hall and down the side steps to the basement, where my mother lifted Marvin out of his playpen.

Back home, she peeled potatoes and cooked lamb chops and canned peas, washed the dishes, wrote lesson plans, cleaned the bathroom, and darned socks. She hardly smiled anymore. Marvin was too young to play with, so I amused myself, either indoors or on the sidewalk in front of the dry goods store owned by our landlady, Mrs. Feigenbaum. Sometimes I asked permission to walk around the corner to Nona's. My mother usually said yes and might add, "Tell Nona I'll be over in a half hour to use the washing machine."

I was invariably cheerful at Nona's, where I got lots of love and attention, but with my mother I began to whine.

"Mah-*meee,* I can't find my *sweeea*ter," I complained one morning.

She stormed into the bedroom in her suit and her new short haircut that I was still getting used to—"I have no time for long hair," she said soon after we moved—and pulled out all the dresser drawers. "*Here!*" She flung the sweater onto my cot. Feeling like a worm you poke with a stick, I put it on quickly so we could leave.

Spring came, and the two trees in Mrs. Feigenbaum's backyard burst into flowers that pushed against our windows like pink ruffles. "They're cherry trees," my mother said, smiling. She opened a window, glanced down to make sure Mrs. Feigenbaum wasn't in the backyard, and leaned out over the clothesline to cut some branches.

"Aren't they beautiful?" she asked.

I wasn't sure she was talking to me, but I said yes just in case.

In May, days before my third birthday, a package arrived for me from Europe. My mother and I opened it to find the smallest record I had ever seen.

"Hello, Viv. This is Daddy, talking to you from across the ocean in Italy." The voice on the Victrola was scratchy, but unmistakably my father's. "Do you remember how I used to lift you high in the air and say, '*Uno, dos, tres, arreeeeeba*'? And do you remember how you didn't want to go to sleep when I put you back down in your crib, and you used to say, '*No quiero dormir*'?" I did remember.

Soon afterward, on a day my mother was particularly annoyed at me, I said, "Why don't you pack me in a carton and mail me to Daddy?"

My mother smiled, then said, in her teacher voice, "That wouldn't work, because when they sealed the carton, there wouldn't be enough air for you to breathe. You can never send living things through the mail." It made sense.

"M AH-*MEEE,* MY *LEGS* HURT," I whined as I trudged alongside her one day, holding the handlebar of Marvin's stroller while we walked for what seemed like miles. To the dry cleaners on 75th Street. The grocery store on 73rd Street. The shoe store on Bay Parkway. "When are we going *home?*"

She stopped suddenly and slapped my face. "Get out of my *sight,* you fucking bastard! Go *shit* in your *hat*! Your name is *mud*!"

When she screamed like that at home, I went to my room to color until she was in a good mood again. How could I get out of her sight here, when I had to hold onto the stroller?

We kept walking, in silence now, looking straight ahead, so I couldn't see her face. But our hands were holding the same handlebar. I felt her loathing seep through it and into me, circulating in my veins. For a minute, I felt like the worm you poke with a stick again. Then a picture came into my head of a silly man taking off his homburg, placing it upside down on the sidewalk like a pot, and squatting over it to have a bowel movement. I laughed out loud. A moment later, I stopped laughing and began sucking the thumb on my free hand.

After that day, the picture of the squatting, shitting man came to me whenever my mother screamed, "Go *shit* in your *hat!*" I always laughed, even when she slapped me.

It was as if I had two mommies: a love mommy and a hate mommy. The one who loved me hung my paintings on the wall. She let me lean against her when she read my Little Golden Books on her bed in the living room and gave me orange slices to suck when I was sick and threw up, to take away the bad taste. When the mommy who loved me was there, I didn't know about the mommy who hated me, and when the mommy who hated me was there, I didn't know about the mommy who loved me.

FINDING IT INCREASINGLY DIFFICULT to balance work and motherhood, my mother applied for maternity leave when the school year ended in June. The Board of Ed denied her request. Leave was for new mothers only, they said. Marvin was eight months old. Seeing no other option, she quit, even though the principal wanted her to stay and leaving meant she would lose her permanent license. Her plan was to look for a substitute job closer to home in September.

With the summer off, my mother was more relaxed and didn't scream as much. Almost every day, she tucked a pail and shovel, a towel, and my bathing suit into the stroller alongside Marvin for the three-block walk to Seth Low Park. Often my cousin George came, too. My mother would read on a bench while we played in the sandbox or cooled off under the sprinkler in the wading pool. Sometimes I could even get her to push me on the swings.

She did find a substitute job in September, teaching English at Seth Low Junior High, and I went back to nursery school.

Then, in November, exactly a year after he had gone, my father wrote to say he was coming home from the war. His ship would be sailing into Newport News, Virginia, and from there he would find a train or bus to New York.

We were all at Nona's one afternoon when an upstairs tenant came rushing in and said, "I just saw your husband walking on Twentieth Avenue!"

"Go! Quick!" Nona urged my mother. "So you be there before him to say hello." ∎

CHAPTER 2

Two Daddies

MY FATHER WAS TEACHING ME to tie my shoes. He placed them on the kitchen table, on top of old newspapers, then sat down beside me. We each took a shoe, and I copied him. First we made a loop with one end of the lace and held it in place with a thumb while we wrapped the other end around and pulled it through to make a second loop. Then we pulled on both loops to make it tight. "*Bueno,*" my father said.

Another day, the lesson was how to say "Open it" and "Close it" in Spanish. My father unscrewed the lid of an empty jar and held one part in each hand, arms spread wide. "*Abrelo,*" he said. He screwed the lid back on. "*Cierralo,*" he said. After several repetitions, he handed me the jar. I opened it and closed it over and over, saying "*Abrelo*" and "*Cierralo.*" My father's eyes never left me, and there was a little smile under his mustache.

But I soon came to fear him. My mother had few rules. As long as I kept out of her way, I could do what I pleased. My father had many rules. No coloring books. They stifled creativity. I was allowed to draw only on plain typing paper. Don't leave anything in the middle of the floor, where a blind person could trip on it. Don't put your glass down too close to the edge of the table. By the time Marvin was able to talk, he, too, was expected to obey. If we did everything right, my father would be in a good mood. But over the course of a day, we inevitably broke rules. That always meant yelling, sometimes hitting, or worse, tight squeezes on the back of the neck. My father used to be a boxer. His hands were strong.

He would hit if he *thought* we had broken a rule. Like the one about feet.

At night, even in winter, my father opened the window in the room Marvin and I shared, because, he said, fresh air was good for you. "Keep your feet under the covers," he ordered after we were in our beds against opposite walls. We were permitted to talk for ten minutes. Then he came to the door and said, "Face the wall." That meant no more talking. I turned, curled up to keep warm, and traced the paint bumps on the wall until I fell asleep.

My father had to get up early for his post office job, and it was still dark when his alarm rang in the living room, where he and my mother slept. On the way to his closet, which was in our room, he slid his hand under each of our blankets to feel our feet. They were usually icy. "I told you to keep them under the covers," he would say in his angry voice, then hit us through the blankets. I'd try to explain that I *had* kept my feet covered, but he would say I was lying, so by the time I was in kindergarten, I stopped explaining.

There were rules for my mother, too. For one, she wasn't allowed to turn on the radiators. If it was very cold and my father wasn't home, she would sometimes turn one on anyway, making sure to turn it off at least an hour before he got back. The only times that didn't work were when my father came home earlier than expected. Then there would be a lot of yelling about how hot it was while he opened all the windows and stripped down to his underwear. The yelling eventually gave way to muttering, which could last an hour, and we all knew to keep out of his way.

But even with the radiator knobs completely closed, a tiny bit of heat came out.

One Saturday, when my mother was at City College—she had started taking courses for her master's in education soon after my father returned from the war—he sat with his toolbox on the floor beside the living-room radiator. After a long time, he was finally able to pull it away from the wall. All that was left in its place was a pipe sticking out of the floor. He dragged the radiator into the hall and wriggled it to the top of the staircase.

"Keep back," my father said as he started to carry the radiator down. "Stay at least four steps behind me." Marvin was only three years old, so I counted, to make sure we were doing it right.

Outside, my father dragged the radiator across the sidewalk to the curb. I saw our landlady, Mrs. Feigenbaum, peek from behind the curtain of her dry goods store. A second later, she was in the street.

"Vat do you tink you're do-ink?" she said. The apron she always wore was tied over her housedress, and her short brown hair was in tight curls, the way hair looks when you get a beauty-parlor permanent.

"I'm throwing out the radiator," my father said, the same way he might have said, "I'm throwing out some old newspapers."

"You're nut allowed to do thet!" Mrs. Feigenbaum said, stepping forward.

Marvin and I moved closer to my father.

"Oh, yeah?" It was my father's angry voice. "Who says?"

A man walking down 20th Avenue with a grocery bag stopped to watch.

"*I* say!" Mrs. Feigenbaum shouted.

"Who are *you*?" my father shouted back.

Two ladies with bakery boxes were passing. They paused.

"I'm the *lend*lord!"

"What has *that* got to do with it?" The veins popped out on the sides of my father's forehead.

I wished Mrs. Feigenbaum would stop. You weren't supposed to yell back at my father. If you were a grownup, you were allowed to answer him in a low voice. If you were a child, you weren't allowed to say anything. She should have let him throw away the radiator so we could go upstairs.

"Thet's my property!" Mrs. Feigenbaum screamed.

"I don't care *whose* property it is!" My father's face was red. "I don't want it in the house!"

More people gathered, forming a circle around the four of us. Marvin and I kept close to my father's legs. Whenever he moved, we moved with him.

"You hef no right to throw it out!"

"I have a right to do whatever I want!"

"Take thet rediator beck upstairs!"

"DON'T TELL ME WHAT TO DO!"

"CALL THE POLICE!"

"I'll call, lady," a man said. He went into the candy store near the corner, where they had a pay phone. Another man told Mrs. Feigenbaum to calm down, the police would be here soon.

All at once, my father smiled at Marvin and me and started to shadowbox. He showed us uppercuts and how to block with one hand while we pretend-punched with the other. I felt funny playing with people watching, but my father was having a good time, so I started having a good time, too.

Two policemen came, and my father stopped boxing. His smile went away, but he didn't shout. "Look," he said to them, "I don't want the radiator in the apartment." The people moved back into a circle, and Marvin and I kept close to my father again. Mrs. Feigenbaum didn't shout. She just said, "Thet's my property." There was a lot of talking. Finally, Mrs. Feigenbaum agreed that my father didn't have to take the radiator back. She would keep it in her store for as long as we lived there. The policemen carried it in for her.

Marvin and I went upstairs with my father. "Get ready to go to the park," he said as he put his toolbox away.

SOME THINGS MY FATHER DID WERE FUN. He read to us from *A Child's Geography of the World* and showed us how to make a magnet out of a screwdriver by wrapping one end of a wire around it and plugging the other end into a wall outlet.

Tennis was not fun.

Saturday mornings, when the concrete baseball field in Seth Low Park was empty, my father would position me on the field and show me how to hold my special child's racket. "If you stand *this* way, the ball will go *there*." Gripping my shoulder with his left hand, he swung my arm with his right. "See? But if you stand *this* way"—he tightened his grip and pivoted me—"the ball will go there." After several repetitions, he pitched a ball to me. If I swung correctly, he said, "Atta girl!" and pitched again. If I made a mistake, he repeated the gripping and pivoting. The supposedly light racket felt heavier and heavier, but I wasn't allowed to stop until my father said it was Marvin's turn.

Sunday mornings were better. My mother was home and, even though she didn't actively do things with us, the apartment seemed like a gentler place. While she studied, my father brought a chair over to the stove so we could take turns standing on it to stir the orangey-yellow mixture of lox and eggs. "Easy, now," he would say. "Just move the fork across the bottom of the pan. You don't want it to go over the sides." When it turned from soupy to tight, he would say, "OK, Viv. You can tell Mommy the feast is ready."

I was careful not to talk with my mouth full, but sometimes Marvin forgot. Whenever he did, my father got the angry forehead crease and yelled, "How many times do I have to tell you not to talk with food in your mouth!" It was a good meal when no one got hit.

I now had two daddies as well as two mommies: a love daddy and a jail daddy. The love daddy was happy with me when I was learning and obeying. When the love daddy was there, I felt special inside, much more than I did with my mother. But when the jail daddy was there, it was my mother I went to for solace. Even though she couldn't do anything to stop him, she understood how I felt, and that helped.

Once, when I was in kindergarten, my mother went with me to a classmate's house for his birthday party. The cake was sliced, and I went to where she was sitting with the other mothers to ask whether I could have a piece.

"You know Daddy doesn't allow cake," she said.

I'd been hoping that since he wasn't there, she would say yes, the way she sometimes broke the radiator rule. "Doesn't Daddy want me to ever have any fun?" I asked, retreating to her lap so I wouldn't have to sit with the children in my shame.

"He just wants what's best for you," my mother said, but I could tell from her tone she was sorry and wished I could have cake, too.

Watching the other children eat, I wondered how it happened that I came to have my particular father and they had theirs—as if there were a pool of fathers and you were assigned one when you were born. I concluded I was less deserving, somehow deformed inside, where it didn't show. With sadness, and with a pain in my chest that felt like a hole, I accepted this.

IN SCHOOL, I TRIED TO TELL MY TEACHER, Mrs. McCullough, about the hole. It came at the same time every day, when our chairs were arranged in front of her piano for singing and she looked around at all of us with her kind face. A longing woke in me then that made my insides hurt. Every morning, I walked up to her piano stool and whispered in her ear, "I have a stomachache." Hands on the keyboard, she would lean toward me and say gently, "Sit down and try not to think about it, and it'll go away." The stab of disappointment always took me by surprise. She didn't see the hole. As I walked back to my seat, my insides hurt so much I thought they would break. Then, just as Mrs. McCullough said, the ache would go away and I would start singing with the rest of the children.

Outside of school, I daydreamed that I had a sore throat. It was so bad that when Dr. Dalven came to the house to examine me, he sent me to the hospital. I had my own special room because I was the sickest little girl there. Not even my mother and father were allowed to visit. Doctors conferred in whispers at the foot of my bed. Nurses in white caps smiled as they leaned over to smooth the fold of my top sheet and slip a thermometer into my mouth. I lay still and looked up at them—only my eyes moved—and they understood that I couldn't talk because it hurt too much.

Day by day the story grew, until it came to feel like an actual, secret part of my life. One of the nurses brought me a doll with white lace around the collar of its pink flannel pajamas. She lifted the sheet to slide it in next to my burning-fever face and stroked my cheek. The hospital world vanished when I was playing in the street with other children, but when I was alone, it started up from where it had left off—the nurse who had lifted my head from the pillow now held a glass of water to my lips.

Soon, in my secret world, I was sometimes another little girl, not in the hospital but walking around doing regular things, like going to school. No one could tell I had a big hurting hole inside me except a different set of doctors and nurses. These weren't in bodies. They were loose molecules floating in the air, all mixed together. I knew about molecules. If you cut something in half, then in half again, and kept doing it, you would eventually get the smallest piece of whatever it was. The molecule doctors and nurses saw everything that happened to me and knew everything I thought and felt. They couldn't make the hole go away, but I didn't need them to. It was enough that I wasn't invisible to them.

I wasn't invisible to the YellowSweaterLady, either. I met her the day my mother brought me to City College to lend me to a classmate who needed practice giving IQ tests to children. It was winter, and I was wearing a yellow sweater and green leggings.

"That's a pretty sweater," the lady said. "Is yellow your favorite color?"

"Green is." I didn't mind that she had gotten it wrong. No one had ever asked what I preferred before.

I arranged colored blocks into designs. "Good!" the lady said. Then she asked whether I was cold and whether I wanted her to shut the window. This was new, too. My father acted as if being cold was my fault.

That afternoon, while my mother read her book on the subway ride home, I looked at my reflection in the train window: a little girl with dark brown hair parted on the side, held in place with a barrette. I didn't turn away, because I felt the YellowSweaterLady looking down on me from above, her molecules mixed in with those of the doctors and nurses, and I wanted to keep seeing what she was seeing.

MOST OF THE TIME, the doctors and nurses and the YellowSweaterLady stayed in the background. But whenever I really needed them, they were right there.

One day when I was six, I was walking on 20th Avenue with my father and tripped on a sidewalk crack.

"Fuck!" I said.

"Where did you learn that word?" My father had the angry crease in his forehead, but his voice was regular.

"Mommy says it."

"Mommy never uses that word. Where did you hear it?" Now his voice was angry.

"From Mommy."

We reached Mrs. Feigenbaum's store, and my father opened the door to the hall. His voice got nicer as we walked up the stairs. "I just want to know where you heard that word. If you tell the truth, I won't hit you." He unlocked our door, and we went in. "I'll give you one more chance."

"I told you. Mommy says it."

My father grabbed my arm and lifted his other hand high in the air. It came down hard on my tush. He did it again on my back, and again on my side, and-again-and-again-and-again. The whole time, while I cried, he kept saying, "I'm hitting because you lied, not because you said that word." When he finished, he said, "What are you crying for?" as if he were angry about the crying, too. You were supposed to answer when my father asked a question. I tried to, but I couldn't talk, so I went into my room.

For a long time, I couldn't stop crying. Not because it hurt. That was before. Now I cried because it wasn't fair. I took out my crayons and paper. I made a red tulip with green leaves, a brown tree with red cherries sprinkled all through, a yellow sun, and a blue sky. I went inside the picture and stopped crying.

A while later, I heard the hall door open. My mother was home! Now she was talking to my father in the kitchen. I snuck into the foyer to listen.

"Bea, do you ever say 'fuck'?"

"Yes."

"You do?" He sounded surprised.

"Yes. Why?"

"Vivian said it today. She told me she heard it from you. I didn't believe her."

"Well, I'm sorry to say it's true."

I was glad my mother said that. Now my father would apologize. I went back to my room to wait for him.

I waited a long time—five drawings. He didn't come.

A few hours later, the four of us were sitting at the kitchen table, eating meatloaf. My father was the only one talking, reading out loud from the newspaper about Joe Louis and boxing. My stomach was tight and I couldn't chew, even though the rule was that you had to finish everything on your plate.

Then, all at once, I was in the hospital at the same time that I was sitting at the table. The doctors and nurses knew how much my stomach hurt and how hard it was for me to eat. They watched me pick up my fork and bring a piece of meatloaf to my mouth and agreed that I needed extra medicine today. ■

CHAPTER 3

The Gentle Slap of Cards

"HERE JACK," MY MOTHER SAID when the sewing machine stopped. "See if the pocket is where you want it."

"Yup," came my father's voice. I pictured him trying on his shirt. "Good work. Can you put another one here?"

Pockets made his trip seem real. He always asked my mother to add extras to his shirts the night before he left. Lying in bed after face-the-wall time, I was happy knowing we would be without him for eight days.

In summer, the four of us usually went for a week to Villa García in upstate New York, but during the school term, my father traveled alone to places where he could practice speaking a foreign language. That year, when I was eight, it was Cuba.

Early the next morning, he filled his new pockets with money, passport, and the little pieces of paper he always carried with him for studying: vocabulary words in different languages, math formulas, chess moves. He kissed us all goodbye and walked down the stairs with his suitcase.

Drinking the eggnog that was breakfast—my mother put a raw egg and some sugar in a glass of milk, added a splash of vanilla, and stirred it with a fork—I didn't feel much different than on days my father left to go to work. His body was gone, but his aura hung in the air. After school, I changed into pants and told Mrs. Norris, the woman who walked Marvin home from school and cleaned our apartment, that I was going down to play with my friend Maxine. Her parents owned the candy store on the corner.

I always felt free when I played in the street—games like potsy and A-my-name-is—but I was aware of that feeling only when I was going back upstairs, about to lose it. Once I entered our apartment, the memory of my liberty vanished and I became a guard soldier, monitoring every building creak. The door? My father coming home? When he arrived, I tracked minute changes in his voice, listening for any sign that an explosion was imminent. Hours of calm might pass indoors, but I never relaxed.

When I left Maxine that day, I felt my usual hallway dread. But by suppertime, my stomach didn't feel bunched up, and Marvin and I told riddles while we ate. At bedtime, my mother left the window closed. She let us talk a bit, then came to the door and said, "Face the wall." It sounded funny, as if she were rehearsing for a play. "OK," we called, then continued our game of 20 Questions. When it was over, I moved around in my bed as if I owned it. I lay on my back, then on my left side facing Marvin, then with my head down where my feet should be.

The second night, my mother forgot to say, "Face the wall," and by the third day, I didn't feel a shift in the hallway when I came upstairs. That evening, I approached my mother as she was grating carrots for tuna salad. "Mommy," I said to her back, "why don't you get a divorce?" A girl in my class lived with only her mother.

Hand still on the metal grater, my mother turned to face me. "I thought about it, but I decided not to."

That was the most grownup thing she'd ever said to me. "Why?"

"I'm not going to give you my reasons." She went back to the carrots. "This discussion is over."

The next afternoon, Maxine and I were squatting on the sidewalk with her new ball and jacks. We were up to threesies when she said, "Here comes your father."

"It can't be," I said. "He's in Cuba."

"He's not. He's across the street."

I looked where she pointed and saw my father walking on 20th Avenue with his suitcase. He waved. Feeling my body shrink, I waved back and watched him check for cars before he crossed.

"Hi, Dad," I said as he bent to kiss my forehead. "You're home early."

"I decided not to stay," he said, then went into the house.

Maxine bounced the ball to continue her turn, as if nothing had changed. But everything had.

THE NEXT YEAR, WHEN I WAS NINE, my teacher sent home a note saying I did poorly on the E chart vision test and should be checked by an eye doctor.

"What gives her teacher the right to interfere?" my father screamed. "If she starts wearing glasses now, before you know it she won't be able to see without them!"

"Jack," my mother said in the low voice she used when he raised his. "I've been wearing glasses for years, and they haven't made my eyes worse."

For 15 minutes, I listened to their voices, alternating loud and soft, from the room I shared with Marvin. When my father's yelling subsided and I heard him go into the living room, I went into the kitchen, where my mother was getting supper ready.

"I'll make an appointment with the eye doctor tomorrow," she said.

Two weeks later, I tried on my glasses and felt as if I had discovered a new world. The face of the woman looking at frames across the room was in sharp focus. I hadn't known something like that was possible.

"Take those off!" my father shouted when we got home. "I don't care *how* much they cost!"

I hid the glasses in my sock drawer.

My father demonstrated eye exercises and made me practice them in the living room. After he released me, my mother called me into the kitchen. "You can wear the glasses in school and when you play in the street," she said. "You can also wear them in the house when Daddy's not home."

For a month, my father never saw me with my glasses on. Then, one day, he came home from work and I said, "Hi, Dad," in my usual way before I remembered I was wearing them. I was about to take them off when I realized he seemed not to have noticed. "Is it still raining out?" I asked.

"Letting up," he said.

Wow! I went into the kitchen to tell my mother.

"Good," she said. "Now you can wear them all the time."

WHEN I TURNED TEN, WE MOVED BACK to Nona's house on 74th Street, this time into our own apartment, upstairs rear. With three bedrooms and a living room that could actually be used as a living room, it seemed palatial. Also, the block was prettier: no stores, lots of trees, and driveways—we called them alleys—between the houses. Our house, which Papoo had built in 1926, was brick with a small garden of forsythia and roses. Six steps, perfect for playing stoop ball, led up to the green front door. They were flanked by pillars topped with flowerpots.

I loved having my own room. As long as I didn't do anything to upset my father, like play my radio too loud, he rarely came in. I felt luckier than Marvin. He, too, had a room, but his wasn't closed off; I had to walk through it to get to mine. To give him privacy, my mother had an accordion-folding partition installed, creating a hall-like passageway along one side.

Whenever our apartment felt too stifling, all I had to do was walk into someone else's apartment. It wasn't necessary to knock. I simply opened the door. Across the landing at Aunt Mollie and Uncle Bill's, I played with my cousins: Jerry, Annie, and baby Robert. Aunt Mollie would often offer me half a stick of Juicy Fruit chewing gum. "I'm economical," she would say by way of explanation. Still, it was a treat, something I wasn't permitted in our apartment.

In the downstairs front, where we had lived when my father was in the war, were Nona, Papoo, and Aunt Sophia, the only one of my aunts not yet married. If Nona was baking *koulouria,* she would give me a piece of the sweet dough so I could roll it into a snake, join the ends to make a cookie-sized circle, and place it in a corner of her baking pan. I also spent many evenings in Aunt Sophia's room, watching her get ready for dates. As she put on makeup, I held her many lipsticks up to the dresses in her closet to see which matched. All the while, she listened to my stories about friends and school, or we planned our next outing: another Broadway show, or a trip to Poughkeepsie to see the house President Roosevelt lived in when he was a boy.

Downstairs in the rear were Aunt Sarah, Uncle Sam, and their daughter, Beattie, who was more like an aunt than a cousin. No matter what the day of the year, there was a fat white *yahrzeit* candle burning in the darkened living room, for my cousin David, who had died of complications from heart surgery in his twenties. But Aunt Sarah's kitchen was a cheerful place, where she dispensed homemade cheese-and-spinach *calzonia*.

In the back basement, Nona and Papoo sewed. The front basement was for storage, with discarded clothes, furniture, toys, and books organized against the walls. Any relative, whether or not they lived in the building, could swap items in and out. The center of the floor was free for playing. Jerry's Lionel trains were set up on a gigantic table in one corner—a miniature world of trees and mountains, tunnels and bridges, houses and lakes. The front basement was also where Nona and Papoo held Passover seders, with long tables laid out end-to-end. There were always 30 or more relatives; the house seeming to expand to absorb them as they went freely up and down the stairs and into all the apartments except ours, borrowing chairs, collecting ice cubes, and lying down on any bed to rest.

Ours was the one apartment with a locked door, by order of my father. Whenever one of my aunts wanted to talk to my mother, she had to knock. I was often the one who answered. "Is your father home?" an aunt would whisper. If I said yes, she'd say, "I'll come back later." The only one of my mother's sisters not afraid was Aunt Rae, but she never tried to come in. My father had barred her permanently years before, when he had forbidden me to participate in something my cousins were doing and she'd said, "Oh yes she can!"

For Marvin, settling in meant getting a puppy. I was surprised that my father didn't object when he asked for one, just said it would be good to have a watchdog. Papoo brought us a mutt from one of his Brighton Beach customers, and we named him Brownie.

For me, settling in meant a trip to the basement with my mother to pick out furniture for my room. I chose a desk, a mirror that Uncle Bill hung on a gold upholstery braid hooked over the molding near my ceiling, and an armchair, for which Aunt Mollie sewed a tan slipcover. A small end table functioned as my vanity, holding a brush and comb. I'd never experienced privacy before and luxuriated in reading fairy tales curled up in my armchair without worrying that my father would yell, "What good is it going to do you in the future to find out whether a frog turns into a prince? It's not even *real*! You could be spending your time doing something *useful*."

He'd started teaching me typing when I was eight, and when I was ten he added Gregg stenography, "so if Mommy and I die, you'll be able to earn a living."

Each day I had to do one of the business letters in the maroon Gregg Shorthand book. First I translated the words into squiggles on a piece of lined paper. Then I rolled an unlined sheet into the typewriter and translated the squiggles back into words. *We are in receipt of your invoice of March 16.* I sometimes wondered where you were when you were *invoice* or *in receipt,* and why *invoice* was one word instead of two, but I didn't care enough to look anything up. All that mattered was handing my father two sheets of paper after supper and standing next to him while he checked them. Then I could return to my room and crochet or do an art project while I listened to classical music on WNYC.

Though I suspected my father had long since forgotten, he'd banned all other stations when I was in second grade and we still lived on 20th Avenue. It was shortly after he had come home from work one evening with two identical radios: brown plastic, AM only. He set them on the dresser in the room Marvin and I shared and demonstrated how to use the volume control to make them so soft we could each hear only our own. In the days that followed, I listened all around the dial. One day, the announcer described a doll with eyes that opened and closed. You could give her a bottle of real water, and when you held her up it would trickle out. She could be yours if you mailed in $5.00. I already had two dolls, but this one sounded special. I wrote down the address.

I didn't ask for the doll. My father would have said it wasn't educational. My mother would have told me to use my allowance. I had saved $4.50 from the 25 cents she gave me each week. Marvin, younger, got ten cents. After I swear-to-god promised I would pay him back, he lent me five dimes. In my neatest printing, I wrote a letter, Scotch-taped one dollar in coins to the bottom, and folded the paper over the four bills. I took a stamp and envelope from my parents' desk in the living room, then went down to the street to drop my letter into the corner mailbox.

On a Saturday morning a few weeks later, the mailman rang our bell. Something was too big to fit into the box! I followed my father downstairs and watched him sign for a package.

"What's this?" he said when the mailman left. He opened the box, and there was my beautiful doll, lying with her eyes shut. He lifted her out and shook her in front of my face. "Where did this come from?"

"I sent away for it," I said, watching her eyelids bounce open and closed. "I used my allowance."

"Where did you hear about it?"

"On the radio."

"You sent away for something you heard about on the *radio*?"

I thought he was going to hit me, but he started up the stairs, muttering about "people advertising to children." He walked into the bedroom, where he set the doll on the dresser between the radios. He turned mine on and began adjusting the dial. Voices unafraid of him flitted by.

"There," he said in his instruction voice. "This is WNYC. There are no advertisements on this station. Keep it here all the time. Is that clear?"

"Yes."

My father set Marvin's radio to WQXR, also a classical music station, and told him, too, never to change it. That didn't make sense. Marvin hadn't sent away for anything, and, besides, WQXR had advertisements. But when my father walked out, I stopped wondering about the stations. He hadn't taken the doll!

Now, two years later and in my own room with the door closed, I still honored my father's decree. Whenever the tuning on my radio started to drift, I adjusted the dial the tiniest bit, careful not to stray onto adjoining stations, as dangerous as Communist territory. Marvin was less obedient. Sometimes, walking through the passageway to my room, I heard a baseball game.

MY PARENTS, TOO, WERE ALWAYS PREPARING for the future. While my father copied bits of information from books onto pieces of paper at his bridge table in the living room, my mother worked with her education books in the kitchen, copying whole sentences or even a paragraph onto index cards that she kept in flip-top metal boxes.

After supper, my mother moved her books and cards to her bedroom, because I would be in the kitchen doing the dishes, a chore I hated. I wouldn't have minded if I could have used my own method: wash and rinse each dish under running water the first, and only, time I touched it. But I had to follow what my father called "a system," which took over an hour. Scrape the plates onto several layers of newspaper. Fold the paper into a tight packet to keep flies from smelling the food, then place it in the garbage pail. Rinse each dish under running water and stack it on the drainboard. Fill the sink with soapy water. Put in all the dishes, wash them, and restack them on the drainboard. Empty the sink of the soapy water. Fill it with clear water. Dip in each dish before putting it in the rack to dry. I couldn't skip any steps because I never knew when the door between the living room and kitchen would open and my father would look in. During the intervals between checks, he stayed at his table in the living room so he could supervise Marvin's piano practice. The future, for my brother, was Concert Pianist.

I had begun piano lessons when I was five, at the home of a local teacher, with the understanding that I would practice a half hour a day on Nona's old black Pianola. Marvin had begged for lessons, too, and when he was five my mother started him with the same teacher. By then, the Pianola had been moved to our apartment on 20th Avenue, and we both practiced at home. It quickly became apparent that, while I was proficient, Marvin was gifted, so shortly after we moved back to 74th Street, my father decided the Pianola was no longer good enough and we got a new blond spinet. When Marvin was eight, my father took him to the Chatham Square School of Music in Manhattan, which awarded him a scholarship.

My father gradually increased Marvin's practice time until, by the time he was nine, it was two hours every afternoon and two hours more after supper. According to my father's rule, if Marvin made a mistake, he had to repeat the measure over and over, until he got it right many times. Marvin followed that rule in the evenings, when my father was home, but in the afternoons he played all his pieces straight through. Roller skating outside with girls on the block, I could hear the music coming through the window. It sounded as good as a concert.

Marvin's playing made washing the dishes a little less boring, as did the company of Brownie, who watched me from his corner in the foyer. My pleasure in the music never lasted long, though. Marvin might be playing Liszt's Hungarian Rhapsody No. 2—I especially loved the end, with the left and right hands chasing each other up and down the keyboard—when I would hear a thud and the music would stop.

"Ow!" Marvin's voice.
"What do you do when you make a mistake?" My father's.
"Go back and play it over."
"Then why did you continue?"
"Because I really knew it. My hand just slipped."
Crack.
"What did I do this time?" Marvin would be whimpering now.
Another thud. "That'll teach you not to be fresh!"

I could picture Marvin, shoulder throbbing, cheek inflamed, wiping his eyes with the back of his hand. His face was always streaked at the end of his practice.

I was glad I wasn't talented. Glad, too, that my mother had recently switched me to guitar, saying only, "It's time you learned another instrument." No one cared how long I practiced, and I liked being able to accompany myself while I sang "Swanee River" and "My Old Kentucky Home" alone in my room. I also enjoyed being able to play guitar at the two or three musicales my parents organized. Held in our living room, they were for any of my friends or Marvin's who played an instrument. Each event was a combination party and recital, with the children performing, their parents clapping, and everyone eating my mother's tuna salad and coleslaw.

The parties were fun. Listening to Marvin's evening practice wasn't. I never understood why he persisted in answering back, not only about the piano, but other things, too. Occasionally my father got so enraged he beat Marvin with a strap, and once I saw him bunch Marvin up and kick him down the foyer like a football.

The most afraid I ever was for my brother was the day, shortly after he got a tool kit for his ninth birthday, that I saw a sprinkling of sawdust on the olive-green carpet and a gash in the piano leg above it.

"Daddy's going to kill you," I warned. Marvin seemed unconcerned.

When my father came home, he looked at the piano leg for a few long seconds but said nothing. Nor did he speak about it during supper. The tension was so great I would have preferred his yelling. After Marvin and I left the table, my father spoke quietly to my mother in the kitchen, an occurrence so rare I worried even more. Then he called Marvin into the living room and spoke quietly to him. When they came out, Marvin told me his practice had been reduced to three hours a day.

The number of hours changed. The procedure did not. Screaming and hitting mixed with beautiful music remained a part of every evening. Sometimes, when I finished the dishes, I went to my room to lose myself in a book. More often, when I couldn't ignore the sounds, I waited for my father's yelling to get so loud he wouldn't hear the door opening, then slipped into the hall and went downstairs to Nona's.

I often found her in the kitchen playing Canasta with my aunts—not only those who lived in the building but any who happened to be visiting. My mother was frequently there, too, though I never knew when she had left our apartment. She looked relaxed here.

"Hi, Vivvy," Aunt Sophia would say. "Will you join us?" And when I sat down: "Now we can play partners."

Our cards competed for space on the red checked tablecloth with coffee cups and a plate of koulouria. Nona would bring me a glass of milk. Aunt Sophia might ask whether I would take her pumps to the shoemaker after school—leather lifts, no taps. Aunt Rae, who made and sold jewelry in addition to her teaching job, sometimes fished in her large bag and presented me with a necklace. No one mentioned the backdrop of music, yelling, and thuds we could all hear. For me it was unreal, like the sound of a TV program coming from a neighbor's house, so I was able to concentrate on the game.

At some point the music stopped, and there was only the gentle slap of the cards. The quiet was harder to ignore than the piano practice had been. "I guess we'll be going up," my mother would say, tension back in her voice. "It's getting late." ∎

CHAPTER 4

Cookie

I BOARDED THE BUS along with Ronnie and Iris, friends from school and my Girl Scout troop. We didn't know any of the other campers, but those who had been to Quidnunc before told stories and sang camp songs, and by the time the bus wound its way up the dirt road two hours later, we were all bellowing: "We're here, because we're here, because we're here, because we're here!"

I had always loved the country, and that summer, when I was 12, I looked forward to escaping the Brooklyn heat and being away from my family. My mother had no objection when I asked to go. Girl Scout camp was not expensive. My father didn't involve himself in the discussion, which meant it was OK with him.

After the director's welcome speech in the parking lot, we followed our counselors to our units. Ivy, the head counselor of mine, read our tent assignments from her clipboard—five girls to a tent—and told us to get our trunks from the pile near the campfire circle. As we paired off to help one another, the camp magic began: two girls, strangers when they each took the side handle of a trunk, stumbled together over tree roots on the narrow path and were friends by the time they hoisted their burden onto the wooden tent platform and started back for the other trunk.

It was the tradition at Quidnunc, which means *What now?* in Latin, that everyone, campers as well as counselors, had to choose a nickname. I decided on Cookie. Ivy wrote *Cookie* on the chart of morning chores that hung from a nail on a tree, and Ginger, the waterfront counselor, painted *Cookie* on my bathing cap in red, the color denoting my swimming group: Beginners.

Our daily routine seldom varied. The counselors woke us at 7:00, when it was sometimes so cold we could see our breath. Breakfast could be hot cereal, eggs, or pancakes—sometimes in the dining hall, sometimes around the campfire. All the girls helped with cleanup, drawing lots for wash, Brillo, rinse, dry, and put-away. We sang camp songs while we worked, told jokes, and teased the counselors. Next came housekeeping: making our cot-beds, sweeping the tent platforms, unrolling the canvas side-flaps to shake out spiders and leaves, then rerolling them. By 10:00, we were ready for swimming, boating, arts and crafts, and hiking.

Iris and Ronnie missed electricity, flush toilets, hot water, and television, but I loved everything about Quidnunc: singing around the campfire; trudging up a mountain to watch the sun set; going on overnight hikes, when we slept in bedrolls on the ground and looked up at the stars. Most of all, I loved being Cookie in a world where the same rules that applied to me applied to everyone else.

I even liked hating swimming. The lake was cold, and we all begged Ginger, who stood on the dock with a sweatshirt over her dry bathing suit, to let us come out of the water. "Sorry, but y'all have to stay in," she drawled in her Southern accent, which she didn't mind that we imitated. Between laps, we compared fingernails and teeth-chatter to see whose were bluest and loudest.

Hating the food was fun, too. You had to eat everything on your plate, including the milky-green mash that was supposed to be a vegetable. But as the counselor served each item, she asked whether you wanted a yes-thank-you or a no-thank-you portion. The no-thank-you was a teaspoonful.

When the four weeks were over, most of the girls on the bus back to Brooklyn, me among them, alternated between sobbing and singing the camp song.

AFTER MY TASTE OF GIRL SCOUT CAMP, I found the apartment on 74th Street more oppressive than ever. I asked my mother if we could do things the Quidnunc way, like having no-thank-you portions. She thought it was a good idea but said my father would never deviate from his rule that Marvin and I had to eat the full portion of everything on our plates, no matter how much we disliked it. I knew she was right.

In September, I started seventh grade at Seth Low Junior High, where the students came from several elementary schools, and I added Carol, Diane, and Susan to my circle of friends. I didn't think about camp when I was out with them, but at home I pined for it so viscerally that I felt what the *sick* part of homesick meant, a concept I had understood only intellectually before, from reading *Heidi*. When we studied Shelley's "Ode to the West Wind" in school, I copied the last line into my notebook: *If Winter comes, can Spring be far behind?* I asked my mother whether I could go to camp for six weeks the following summer, and she agreed.

My mother was my ally, but she could also be unpredictable.

The previous year, a few days before my 11th birthday, Aunt Sophia had knocked on our door, ascertained that my father was home, and thrust a gift-wrapped box into my hand, whispering, "For you, an early present."

I opened it in my room to find a white blouse with eyelet trim—the most beautiful blouse I'd ever owned. I tried it on and went into the kitchen.

"Mommy, don't I look pretty in my new blouse?" I pirouetted so she could see front and back.

My mother said nothing, just looked angry and slapped my face.

For a second, I was so stunned I couldn't move. Then, cheek burning, I returned to my room.

If I had left drops of milk on the table, I could have laughed this off as an absurd reaction. My mother often screamed if Marvin or I didn't wipe off the table, sometimes hitting us with a wooden hanger because "it hurts me when I use my hand." But this time I'd done nothing wrong. It was almost as if my mother couldn't tolerate my very existence. I had the same feeling I'd had a few months before, when she brought me to the doctor because I had a vaginal infection. "You're disgusting!" she'd said when we got home and she was helping me apply the medicine he'd prescribed.

I put the blouse back in its box and laid it on a shelf.

But the love mommy was still walled off from the hate mommy, and, despite what had happened, I was able to enjoy being with my mother the following Tuesday for our prearranged Time.

When I was ten, she'd gotten the idea from one of her child psychology books to schedule an hour a week with each of us, to do whatever we wanted. My Time was Tuesdays at four. I looked forward to it all week. Sometimes I asked my mother to sit in my room and watch me work on an arts-and-crafts project while I talked about my friends or things I did in Girl Scouts. Once, I wanted to show her the apartment house on Avenue P where Pat, a girl in my class, lived. My mother and I walked to Avenue P, looked at the outside of the house, then walked back. I chatted the whole way—about the girls in my class who were friends with Pat and why I thought she might want to be friends with me. My mother never screamed or hit during Time, which started and ended like a regular appointment.

She continued with Time until the school term ended. I would have liked it if she had started again in September, but she didn't, and I didn't ask. For a week in October, though, when my mother used me as the subject in a study for one of her education courses, I enjoyed something similar: each day, for an hour, she read me questions and wrote down my answers. I felt close to her during those sessions, not only because she paid attention to everything I said, but because I liked knowing I was an asset to a part of her life that was important to her.

I had gotten a glimpse of that life a few days before the blouse incident, when we were walking on Bay Parkway and I heard someone shout, "Dad! There's my teacher!" Seconds later, a boy stopped in front of us and said, "Hi, Mrs. Conan." He looked excited to see her.

"Hello, Henry," my mother said in a formal voice that I supposed she used in her classroom. I was jealous of the way she smiled at him.

"Hello, Mrs. Conan," said a man coming up behind the boy. "I'm Henry's father. It's nice to meet you. He talks about you all the time."

"It's good to meet you, too," my mother said, shaking his hand. Then she looked at Henry. "Are you going shopping today?"

"I got a new pair of sneakers." He held up a bag.

"Very nice," my mother said. She put her arm around my shoulder and drew me forward. "This is my daughter, Vivian. We just bought a locket for her birthday."

Henry said, "Hi," and his father said, "Happy Birthday, Vivian."

I felt proud that they saw I belonged to her.

My mother also tried to stand up for me where my father was concerned.

Ours was the only apartment in the building without a television set: my father didn't approve of them. So the day my teacher assigned a TV program to watch for homework, I arranged with Aunt Mollie to see it in her apartment. When my father learned of the plan, he forbade me to go.

"Jack," my mother said in her quiet voice, "it's for school. It's about Abraham Lincoln."

"I don't care *what* it's about! The teacher has no right to tell her what to do at home!"

When it became apparent that my mother couldn't get him to relent, I was distraught. She asked whether I wanted her to write my teacher a note explaining why I wasn't turning in a report. That would be embarrassing but better than getting a bad mark. I told her to write it.

SPRING EVENTUALLY DID COME, along with my mother's announcement that it was time to redecorate my room. It had never occurred to me that you could redo a room, especially when nothing was broken, but it gave me something to look forward to besides camp.

My mother didn't ask my father's permission. She'd stopped doing that when we still lived on 20th Avenue and she wanted to get a phone. My father said we didn't need a phone and relented only when she became a day-to-day substitute teacher and had to wait for a call each morning. Now, my mother earned more as a teacher than he did in the post office, and she had her own checkbook.

"Jack," she said one evening, walking through the living room with a pile of laundry, "the carpenter's coming tonight to measure Vivian's room."

"What carpenter?"

"The one I hired to build some furniture."

"What's wrong with the furniture she has?" His voice was beginning to rise.

"She's going to be a teenager soon. She needs a place where she can bring her friends, and a place to study and keep her clothes."

"What's wrong with her closet?"

My mother answered his protests, one by one, in a dead voice. My closet, the little portable one he had kept his own clothes in when we lived on 20th Avenue, was too small, she said. My desk was shabby and didn't have enough storage space. Then she continued on her way with the laundry.

The carpenter's knock came moments later, putting an end to my father's muttering. He remained in the living room, while, in my room with my mother, I watched the carpenter sketch plans for a wall unit that included a closet, desk, and shelves. Work was to begin as soon as I left for camp and would be finished by the time I returned.

THE MOMENT I BOARDED THE BUS and greeted the girls I knew, some of whom I'd been writing to all winter, I felt I had truly come home. Now *I* was part of the group that told camp stories to the newcomers and led the singing, and when the director gave her welcome speech in the parking lot, I knew everything she was going to say before she said it.

I was in the next-to-oldest unit, Neppies Nook, named after Neptune because we were closest to the lake. Without Ronnie and Iris, I had no ties to my Brooklyn-Vivian life. The girls and counselors in Neppies Nook were my only family, Camp Quidnunc my only world. I was completely Cookie, completely happy.

Jinx was my favorite counselor. The other two were funnier, but not as soft. I contrived to sit at Jinx's table in the dining hall and get into her group whenever we divided up for activities. Within days, she became like the doctors and nurses whose molecules floated in the air: I felt her watching over me, knowing what I was thinking and feeling every moment.

The YellowSweaterLady had been the only other real person to become part of what I now thought of as the Atmosphere. For several years after I'd met her with my mother, I'd been certain that one day her hand would reach down through the air, scoop me out of my world, and take me to hers, where I would live in her house and be her little girl forever. The longer that took to happen, the more the YellowSweaterLady faded from the Atmosphere, until, by now, she was no longer in it.

Unlike the YellowSweaterLady, whom I had met only once, Jinx was part of my everyday life. I could be feeling her disembodied Atmosphere presence while I walked down one of the paths, maybe to hang my bathing suit on the line, and her in-person version would chance to come toward me from the opposite direction. "Hi, Jinx," I would say in the most surprised voice I could muster, as if she were the last person I could have been thinking of.

The only time her Atmosphere and in-person versions came together as if they belonged together was when we sang around the campfire at night. Jinx was usually at the back of the circle, so I couldn't see her face. The faces I could see were noses or eyes that flickered orange then disappeared, giving way to others. In this magic place Jinx's voice, blending with yet separate from everyone else's—she was the only one singing harmony—seemed to be coming from another dimension.

Every night after campfire, we snuggled under our blankets, under the canvas, under the trees, under the stars. The counselors, standing near the dying fire, sang "Taps." When their last note faded, the only sounds were from crickets and the occasional snapping of a twig.

One night, lying under my blankets in the safety of everything that was familiar—alone, yet not alone—I began to feel vaguely uneasy. I listened to the regular breathing of my tentmates and the murmuring of the counselors sitting on logs by the embers. The leaves rustled. I felt something shift inside me and rustle along with them. *Eeeeeee-naaaaaaah.* The wail was loud inside my head, but I knew I hadn't made an outside sound.

The breeze blew through the tent, taking a layer of me with it as it passed over my face. The forest was suddenly menacing, filled with writhing shapes I could barely make out. *Nah-SAAAAAH-koh-meh!* The wail was louder this time. I felt myself leaking out of my skin into the shapes, felt the shapes flowing back into me. To keep from dissolving, I buried my face under the blankets and held onto the sides of the mattress.

"Get away from me!" Oh god. That was an outside scream.

"Cookie, wake up!" my friend Lolly called from her cot. "You're having a nightmare."

I was glad she thought I was sleeping.

Footsteps. A hand on my back through the blankets. "Cookie, what's the matter?" It was Jinx.

I wanted to say, *Nothing. I'm Cookie, here in the tent with my friend*s. But I was also not Cookie. I was part of the howling forest and the undulating mass of scary shapes sucking me in.

"Get away from me!" I shrieked, throwing off the covers and sitting up.

I squinted into the beam of Jinx's flashlight. She pointed it toward the floor. "It's me. Jinx."

I began to sob. I choked, coughed until I caught my breath, howled into the night. My tentmates offered me tissues and tried to take my hand. The safer I felt with everyone around me, the more I let myself slide into the terror without holding back. I pulled my sheets, clutched my blankets, and kicked. It was a relief to let the fear well up and take over my body. I knew I was acting crazy, but I didn't feel crazy. I felt an enormous release, and though I really was frightened, I knew there was nothing to be afraid of.

My animal cries had a momentum of their own and kept escalating until they crested with a long howl. When it ended, I whimpered softly, coming back into my body, into Cookie. Exhausted but calm, I sat on the heap of tangled blankets and let Jinx put her arm around my shoulder.

"Hi," I said, smiling weakly at my tentmates as they came into focus.

"Hi, Cookie. That was some nightmare."

I nodded.

"OK, girls, it's almost eleven," Jinx said. "Back to your beds."

As she helped me straighten my blankets and tucked me in, I felt calmer than I ever had, as if something wordless that was trapped inside me had finally come out, been heard, and gone back inside. ■

CHAPTER 5

A Little Closer to Nebraska

IN COMPLIANCE WITH MY FATHER'S RULE of quiet-activity-only after 9:00 p.m., our apartment was silent. He was at his table in the living room, my mother in bed with a book. Marvin, finished with piano and flute practice—he now had a second instrument—was in his room. I was in mine, studying for a geometry test.

There was a faint click from my phone extension, the click all telephones made just before they rang. Another rule was no calls after 8:30, even incoming ones. I sprang from my chair and picked up the receiver.

"Hello?" I whispered, cupping my hand over my mouth.

"You always pick up so fast," Carol said. "It didn't even ring. Are you studying?"

I settled on the floor and talked softly into the desk well, my hand still covering my mouth. "I'm up to isosceles triangles."

"I just finished those. Isn't Mr. Krulick cute?" She giggled.

I could never conceive of anyone in authority as cute, but most of the girls had a crush on our math teacher at Lafayette High School, and I wanted to sound regular.

"Yeah."

"Too bad you didn't make cheerleaders."

"I didn't really expect to."

At 15, I was the only one of my friends who had tried out, and I'd actually been terribly disappointed. I had bought a baton and practiced on the sidewalk in front of the house for weeks. I thought I was good until I saw the girls on the tryout line ahead of me. I could do all the baton flips and finger-twirls, and my outfit was perfect—black wool skirt, red crew neck sweater accented by the collar and cuffs of the white shirt beneath it, ponytail high and bouncy—but I knew I would never be able to match their proud struts and beaming smiles.

We talked a few minutes more. Then Carol said, "See you at the bus stop, the usual time," and we hung up.

I returned to geometry but couldn't concentrate. I felt like a prisoner, buried alive in the tomb of my room, which was encased in the larger tomb of the apartment, while, outside, life was going on. I knew Carol would watch the Jack Parr show, as she did every night, even though it came on after 11:00. Ronnie watched it, too; on our walks home from school, they often talked about his guests. We had a television set now, but I was allowed to watch only the two programs my father decreed mandatory: *You Are There,* because it was educational, and *The Steve Allen Show,* because he liked Steve's humor and musical talent.

I hated my father for the daily struggle I had to go through to juggle his world, with its crazy rules, and the world of my friends. Fingering a lock of my long brown hair, I wondered what accident of fate had given me my particular father. At least my friends didn't know what he was really like. Whenever any of them came over and said, "Hello, Mr. Conan," on their way to my room, he would look up from his papers and say hello in an ordinary way. If he was in a good mood, he'd smile, too, and say something like, "Pretty windy out there." My friends knew I wasn't allowed to watch what they did on TV or eat certain foods, but those were things they understood. "Your father's very strict," they said.

I twisted the hair around my finger then released it, watching it fan out. I lifted another lock and slid it around in my fingers. Back and forth. It made a silky sound. Back and forth until, soon, the entire universe was reduced to a clump of hair in a hand. Part of me let myself get pulled into the void, and I dissolved into a comfortable nothingness. Another part panicked. I needed to attach my hair and hand to my body before I vanished. I raised my eyes as far as they could go, to see where the hair connected to my head. I couldn't. I lowered them, followed hair to hand, hand to elbow, elbow to shoulder. I strained until my eyes hurt but I couldn't see past the shoulder to my neck.

Holding the hair and hand straight out, I walked to the mirror and was relieved to find a girl's face in the oval frame. Though I could see only from her head to her knees, it was enough to place her in the room: the armchair over her shoulder, the dresser behind the chair. I tilted my head to the left. The head in the mirror tilted. I tilted my head to the right. Again the head tilted. Now it was safe to release the hair, and I opened my hand.

The mirror girl smiled, turned serious, smiled again. She was me, but not me. She existed—she had a body I could see. As long as I stayed in front of the mirror and could see her, I could exist through her body, and as long as I was in a body, even a borrowed one, the Atmosphere people would be able to watch over me.

The original doctors and nurses were still in the Atmosphere. Jinx was there, too, her molecules mingled with theirs. I felt them looking down on the girl in the mirror and play-acted to stay connected to her. "I'll meet you after school," I said, watching my words come through the moving lips of the girl in the mirror. "We can go to the movies. Do you want me to ask Beverly, too?"

I didn't know a Beverly, but I was used to the mirror-version of myself talking about friends I didn't know or things I didn't do. While the general circumstances of our lives were similar, the specifics were different. We even had different parents, though hers were as difficult as mine.

When the mirror girl paused and waited silently for a few seconds, the Atmosphere people knew she was getting a response from her classmate. Neither they nor I could hear what it was.

"Oh, that'll be fine," the girl in the mirror continued.

Another pause.

"No, don't worry. I'll make all the arrangements."

The Atmosphere people knew how hard her life was and marveled that she was able to maintain a normal exterior. They couldn't rescue her, but she didn't need them to. All she needed was for them to know. Their knowing gave her dignity. It made her real and gave her the strength to go on with everyday life.

I locked eyes with the mirror girl. Our eyebeams made a bridge, and the Atmosphere people looking down on her saw that we were connected. Now they knew about *my* hard time, also, and would continue to know if I walked away from the mirror. I was real again.

Craving a snack, I left my room, hugging the foyer wall to avoid floor creaks. I opened the refrigerator door so slowly it didn't make a sound and managed to make a cream cheese and jelly sandwich and spirit it back to my room without getting caught. If I had been, I would have had to look attentive during my father's five-minute lecture: "A person should take care of all food needs earlier.... A person should wind down in preparation for bed...." Then I would have been free to return to my room, without the food.

My father had no control over the other apartments, though. He would get upset if he even *thought* he heard a radio. One night, he walked into the hall and put his ear against Aunt Mollie's door, then came striding back, to tell my mother to tell her sister to get Jerry to turn down his radio. My mother put on her bathrobe, and I followed her.

Annie and Robert were drinking hot chocolate in the kitchen. Uncle Bill was in the living room watching television with the sound low. Jerry was doing homework in his room, his radio only slightly louder than the TV.

"Would you please lower your radio?" my mother said in her dead voice. "It's disturbing Jack." My father's ranting could be heard through the walls.

"He's *always* upset, and it's *never* loud," Jerry griped but he turned down the volume.

"Thank you," my mother said.

Another night, when the sound of hammering came from the downstairs rear apartment, things didn't go so smoothly. Aunt Sarah and Uncle Sam had recently moved to a house they bought nearby, and Aunt Diana, Uncle Eddie, and my cousins Barbara and Elliot had moved in. Uncle Eddie was installing shelves.

BANG, BANG, BANG, BANG.

My father sent my mother down. She returned a few minutes later and said, "Eddie says he works during the day, and the only time he has to fix up his apartment is in the evening."

"So tell your *sister* to get him to stop."

"I did, but she refused."

The conversation ended, and I figured my mother had gone back to bed with her book.

BANG, BANG, BANG, BANG.

Muttering, my father opened the apartment door. This was so unusual—he preferred letting my mother confront her family—that I went into the hall to watch. So did my mother and brother. Downstairs, my father knocked on Aunt Diana's door. Even in his anger, his obsession with privacy wouldn't let him walk in unannounced.

"Stop that hammering!" he demanded when Uncle Eddie opened the door.

"I have a right to do whatever I want in my apartment," Eddie shot back.

"You have no right to disturb others!" Spittle flew from my father's mouth. His face was red, and the veins on the sides of his forehead stood out.

By this time, everyone in the building was in the hall, standing back.

"Don't tell my husband what he can do!" Aunt Diana spat from behind Uncle Eddie.

"You keep out of this!" my father screamed.

"Don't talk to my wife that way!"

My father grabbed the wooden kitchen chair Nona kept next to her hall pantry. Holding it with the legs facing out, he took a step toward Uncle Eddie.

I was scared. My father had never hit a grownup before.

Uncle Bill came forward to stand between them. "Why don't you do this on Saturday?" he asked Eddie in a calm voice that sounded strange after the screaming.

"He can't tell me what to do!"

"If you wait until Saturday, I'll help you."

"Well—OK."

My father put down the chair and turned toward the stairs. Everyone moved to let him pass. My mother, brother, and I went up after him, but not before I saw Nona catch my mother's eye in sympathy.

Now, taking a bite of my cream cheese and jelly sandwich, I felt a heaviness that seemed to come from nowhere. Nothing bad had happened this evening, and I was sitting in a room I loved. There was the new wall unit: a combination desk, shelves, and closet that could have been in a magazine picture. The rust-colored carpet. The champagne wallpaper with designs that picked up the carpet color. The brown convertible sofa that had replaced my bed. My very own phone extension so I could talk to my friends in private. I began to cry. What good was a room I loved when I hated my life?

It wasn't any specific incident that was so bad. It was the fact that no one acknowledged how bizarre it was to live this way. The day after my father's fight with Uncle Eddie, no one mentioned it.

Except for Nona's sympathetic look, no one gave any indication that they knew how stressful it was to live in this apartment, even when my father was not erupting. I knew my mother knew, because her face was grim most of the time, but whenever I asked why she tolerated all my father did, she would say, "I'm surviving," or "I'm coping," as if she had met her goal. She didn't realize I was asking why she tolerated it for the whole family, not just herself.

My crying turned to sobs. I muffled them with a pillow. When they didn't stop, I got up from the armchair to look at my reflection in the mirror. My mouth in the glass was twisted from trying to choke back the sounds, and snot was dripping from my nose. I was too disgusting even for the Atmosphere people. They weren't there.

I pulled a tissue from the box and wiped my nose, then began brushing my hair, tilting my head slightly with each stroke, watching the hair fan. As I brushed, the gulps became weaker, then stopped. There in the glass was a pretty girl with a serene face. The lashes under her brown eyes were wet, but no sound escaped her lips. Slowly, she began to smile, a brave, tentative smile. I put down the brush, locked eyes with her, and took control of the smile, making it stick. Now I was presentable enough for the Atmosphere people. They came and looked kindly down on me, admiring me for bearing my pain with quiet dignity.

That wasn't hard, because I no longer felt the pain. I had only a memory of it, as if it belonged to a me of the past. The present me, the smiling girl in the mirror, had just become an orphan and would never feel the pain again.

Conscious that the Atmosphere people were waiting to see what I would do now that I had no relatives left in the world, I walked to my closet and took my red-and-white scarf off its hanger. Back at the mirror, I arranged it around my neck, then pantomimed getting money out of my bag.

"One way, no return," I said aloud to the bus driver. I handed him some money and took my ticket. The Atmosphere people admired my pluck.

I rode for days until I saw a town that looked perfect: small shops, picturesque houses, winding streets with lots of trees, people dressed as if for church even though it wasn't Sunday. Still watching myself in the mirror, I adjusted the scarf, then turned sideways and lifted my arms. The Atmosphere people knew I was taking my suitcase down from the overhead rack.

I got off and watched the bus pull away, then asked some people what place this was.

"Nebraska," they said.

Nebraska. So far from Brooklyn it was in another galaxy.

And somehow, just as I knew that Nebraska was where I would start my wonderful new orphan life, I knew my name was Ellen Willow.

In the days that followed, I spent a good deal of time in front of my mirror, enlarging the story. I rented a small house in Nebraska all for myself and found a job as a maid for a kind, rich, middle-aged couple, Mrs. and Mrs. Robinson, who lived on the other side of town. I bought a typewriter, wrote books under a pseudonym, and mailed them to a publisher in far-away Boston who didn't know my real name or that I was just 15.

At first I added details to my Nebraska life only when I was looking into the mirror in my room, but soon I began embellishing the story whenever I was doing something that didn't require concentration: walking by myself in the street, washing the supper dishes, or working at my after-school job in Aunt Sarah's pajama factory on 20th Avenue. It was like coming back to a book I had read many times and never tired of. I could open to any page and go forward from there.

Just as the reader of a novel doesn't know every particular of the heroine's life but only those the author chooses to share, I didn't know everything about Ellen Willow. I knew she was a novelist who used a pseudonym but not what the pseudonym was. I knew she quickly learned the names of the streets in her Nebraska town but not the names themselves. And I knew bad things had happened to her before she became an orphan but not what the bad things were.

Though I often felt completely immersed in Ellen Willow's life, I understood that it was just a story. In between the periods of relief it provided, I still lived my 15-year-old life as Vivian in Brooklyn: I walked home from school with my friends, went to my factory job, and did homework in the evening.

AUNT SARAH STRODE OVER to where I sat at the buttonhole machine and dumped a batch of pink flannel pajama tops onto the floor to my left. She went back to the long table that ran through the center of the factory, scooped a batch of greens from the trough, and tossed them on top of the pinks. The pile was higher than my seat.

"OK," she said in a voice that rang out over the din of the machines. "The pinks are size ten. The greens are twelves. Get to work!"

My job was to make four buttonholes in each pajama top. Speed counted. So did accuracy. Each pajama top took five seconds. *Dzzzz-chop, dzzzz-chop, dzzzz-chop, dzzzz-chop.*

Aunt Sarah waited until I finished the first, then went back to her own machine, one of ten that lined the long table, five on each side. Those were for regular sewing, a different job at each machine: putting rickrack on the edges of collars, attaching sleeves, sewing elastic into waists. The trough ran like a communal ditch through the center of the table. Though the women on one side of it faced those on the other, they couldn't talk over the drone and vibrations. I was glad the button and buttonhole machines were in the front of the shop. It was only slightly less noisy, but there was a window. Every once in a while, I looked through the grimy plate glass at women pulling shopping carts filled with grocery bags.

I was bored making buttonholes, but soon I wasn't making them anymore. They were making themselves. I was Ellen Willow in Nebraska, and the Robinsons had told me they were having company for dinner. They hadn't given me any other instructions because they trusted me to know exactly what to buy and how to cook and serve it. I had planned a menu of roasted chicken, mashed potatoes, and string beans. Salad would be first, coffee and pastries last. I would stop at the florist on my way home from the bakery. Mr. and Mrs. Robinson would be pleased when they saw fresh roses on the dinner table between the lighted tapers.

"Mary!" Aunt Sarah's megaphone voice brought me back to Brooklyn. "Vivian made enough for you to start now. I'll finish those hems."

Mary left her machine at the long table and walked toward the front of the shop.

"Sam!" Aunt Sarah called. "Vivian needs more work. Bring her the size fourteen yellows from Jenny's machine."

The only man in the shop, Uncle Sam took orders from Aunt Sarah the way the rest of us did. He got up from his machine, scooped the yellows from the trough, and carried them over to me.

Mary sat down at the button machine on my right. "Hi, Vivian. How are you today?"

"Fine."

Within seconds she started her own work, and I slid back into Nebraska.

"That's Ellen Willow, the new maid who works for the Robinsons," I heard the florist whisper to another customer as I walked into his shop. "She's only fifteen, but she's more capable than any of the grownups they had before. They're very happy with her."

I felt a delicious warmth inside. Maybe, if I did everything perfectly and made myself indispensable, Mr. and Mrs. Robinson would love me and ask me to call them by their first names. Then I would tell them about my books. They had no idea that the little maid who poured coffee in their elegant dining room was really the bestselling author they had been reading about in their newspapers. Would they be surprised! They might even want to adopt me.

I reached for the last pajama top in my pile. *Dzzzz-chop, dzzzz-chop, dzzzz-chop, dzzzz-chop.*

"That's it for today, Vivian!" Aunt Sarah called out. "Come tomorrow as soon as you get home from school."

"OK." I stood, stretched, and cleaned my glasses on my skirt. It wasn't flannel dust I wiped from them, but dust that had blown out when I swept under the divan in Mr. and Mrs. Robinson's parlor.

Taking my jacket from the back of the chair, I glanced at the large wall clock: 5:30. I'd been here two hours. Another two dollars in the envelope Aunt Sarah would give me on Friday. I would spend most of it Sunday, when Carol, Ronnie, Diane, and I went to the Wollman Memorial Rink in Central Park—on the ice-skate rental, the steaming cups of hot chocolate we sipped at the side of the rail, and the hamburgers, French fries, and lemon Cokes we would have before taking the train back to Brooklyn.

The cool air was refreshing after the machine-oil smell of the factory. I crossed to the bakery on the other side of 20th Avenue. My mother's study group was coming over that night; she and several other teachers were preparing for the assistant principal's test. She'd asked me to pick up bread and cookies.

"A large rye, no seeds, sliced," I said to the man behind the counter.

He laid a loaf in the slicing machine and waited for the rows of metal wires on one side to rise out of their grooves, pass through the bread, and come to a shuddering halt in the grooves on the other side. "Anything else?" he asked, balancing the bread stack on its end in the palm of one hand and slipping a wax-paper bag over it with the other.

"One pound of these." I pointed to the jumble of small cookies under the glass counter: round pink ones with dark jelly fillings, tan squares with nuts poking through, mint-green leaf shapes with chocolate icing. They would look attractive when I arranged them on the Robinsons' oval platter.

Holding my bakery box by the string, I walked the two blocks home, not past small houses separated by narrow alleys but past white churches with spires, and two- and three-story gabled houses, each with a wraparound porch and a garden. I had lived in Nebraska for some time now and knew my way around the winding tree-lined streets. I even exchanged nods with some of the Robinsons' neighbors as I passed.

My mother was standing at the kitchen table, an apron over her suit, studying an index card propped against a teacup while she made tuna salad.

"Here are your bread and cookies," I said, laying both on the table next to her bowl. "And your change."

"Put it on the cupboard." She didn't look up. "I'm working here."

"Mommy," I said as I moved everything. "I'm going skating with Carol and Ronnie and Diane on Sunday, and I want to go shopping at A and S Saturday for—"

"Can't it wait?"

"IWantToGetASkatingSkirtLikeRonnie's," I said quickly, to get it all in before she chased me away, "TheKindThat'sShort,AboveTheKnee."

"If you're asking for money," she said, adding a spoonful of mayonnaise to the bowl, "take ten dollars from my purse. Don't involve me in the details."

Victory, but bittersweet. "OK. Can I have some tuna?" It smelled good.

"Take it to your room."

I made a sandwich, poured a glass of milk, and carried them past Marvin's closed partition to my room. I liked eating alone. My stomach didn't tighten the way it did when we all ate together. I knew my father would eat alone, too. As soon as he got home, any minute now, my mother would bring a sandwich into the living room for him so the kitchen would be free for her friends. He didn't object to them. They were trying to get ahead in their careers, something he approved of.

I placed my food on the tray table next to my armchair, alongside *Pride and Prejudice,* and settled into my idea of perfect contentment: reading while I ate.

The novels I wrote as Ellen Willow were like Jane Austen's, in which society people were *presented* and said things like "the former" and "the latter" when they spoke. They never raised their voices. If they were annoyed, they expressed their displeasure with cold civility—so elegant—or witty sarcasm. But most of the time in Jane Austen's books—and mine, too—people had ordinary conversations as they sat around in drawing rooms or walked through country lanes, the ladies wearing long dresses and carrying parasols.

I finished my sandwich just as Elizabeth was consoling her sister Jane on Mr. Bingley's sudden return to London. I would take the plate and glass back to the kitchen when my mother's friends were gone. For now, I set them on my desk, in front of the 5"x7" index card I had tacked to my bulletin board when I started taking French. *JE SUIS MOI!!!!!* it proclaimed in green ink and my neatest handwriting. *I AM ME!!!!!*

My eyes strayed to the gray clothbound notebook on the shelf above my desk, my most treasured possession. Whenever a poem pushed up from inside me, I wrote it first on a lined pad, discarding sheet after sheet until I was satisfied. Only then did I copy it into my notebook. I was going to be a writer one day, and this volume held the beginnings of my literary career.

I took the notebook back to my chair, opened to the first page, and read the title I had printed in block letters the year before.

> Bad Poems
> with bad rhymes and meters,
> but with
> Good Thoughts
> (also other stuff besides poems)
> by one
> ELLEN WILLOW

The Ellen Willow who lived in Nebraska was already a published author, but I knew she was only a fantasy. The real Ellen Willow—me—lived in Brooklyn with my parents and was a sophomore at Lafayette High School. It wouldn't be long before a publisher discovered me, though, and when he did, this handsome, clothbound notebook would be ready to present to him.

With a surge of pride, I fingered the pages—seven poems that *I* had written. The rest of the book was blank, but I hoped to fill it soon. I stopped at a poem about my father.

> *I live with a stranger; I know but his name.*
> *We live together by the rules of a game:*
> *You don't annoy me; I won't annoy you.*
> *Both of us are a little bit fou.*
>
> *Strangers we are—in a house, not a home.*
> *Sometimes I have a great urge to roam*
> *Far, far away and be all by myself,*
> *Perhaps live in the woods like a little old elf.*

I hadn't mentioned my father specifically—merely alluded to him. All my poems had riddles like that, because they were going to be published. When they were, the outside world would finally know what only the Atmosphere people knew now. About the hand that could come down any second and try to drag me away from being human, and how I had to hide inside myself until it let go. About how hard it was for me to do ordinary things when everything could be shattered at any moment. But if I didn't tell it in delicate words, people would flinch and stop reading. So I had to write about my pain in code, to make art and beauty out of it, the way Emily Dickinson did.

Even my name, Ellen Willow, was code. Ellen was from Scarlett O'Hara's mother, Ellen O'Hara, in *Gone With the Wind*. She was only 15 when, after an unhappy love affair with her teenage cousin, she married the 43-year-old Gerald O'Hara and moved from Savannah to north Georgia, "a world that was as strange and different as if she had crossed a continent." She never let anyone see her heartache but assumed her duties as mistress of Gerald's plantation with dignity, gentleness, and "quiet grace." My last name, Willow, was from weeping willow trees: sad, yet beautiful in their sadness.

ONE DAY, WHEN I WAS WALKING in the street, something different happened. I felt just like the Nebraska Ellen Willow: calm, confident, special. Yet I wasn't in Nebraska. I was in Brooklyn. And I wasn't an orphan. I had the same parents and life I did as Vivian. I knew every detail of my life, not just what the author chose to put down on the page: every street name, every bad thing that had ever happened to me. Unlike Vivian, though, I didn't feel miserable or angry. Nor did I feel the reason for all the bad things was that I was deformed inside. I felt proud of being able to live an ordinary life under such difficult conditions. Only an extraordinary person could do that.

From that day on, in my Brooklyn world, Ellen Willow often alternated with Vivian. We went into and out of each other. I could be Ellen Willow one minute and Vivian the next. I wasn't even aware of the changeovers. I/we functioned smoothly in one life. Whenever I wrote a poem, I signed it Ellen Willow. Vivian would never have felt entitled to tell the world what our life was like, even in code. When I wrote ordinary things—a note to my mother saying I would be home late, a birthday card for my cousin Annie—the signature sometimes came out Vivian, sometimes Ellen Willow. No one questioned it. Annie occasionally called me "Miss Willow." My mother and aunts thought Ellen Willow was just a pen name.

Whenever I was the Ellen Willow in Brooklyn, I knew with certainty that one day, I would actually escape to Nebraska, where everything would happen the way it did in the story. Each poem I added to my notebook brought me a little closer. ∎

CHAPTER 6

Sweet Sixteen

I WAS THE ONLY ONE OF MY FRIENDS to have boys at my Sweet Sixteen party. The others had parties in theme restaurants, usually Hawaiian or Mexican: girls only, no dancing, just eating a fancy meal in an exotic setting. It was my mother's idea to have a coed party in the basement. I knew this was because it would be cheaper than a restaurant, but I was thrilled. During the month we spent planning every detail together—the invitations, the menu, the decorations, the cake, the corsage—I felt as if I had a real mother.

I invited 14 girls: friends from school, friends from camp, and cousins. To balance us, I would need 15 boys. But I knew only three well enough to ask. So my mother called *her* cousins—most of whom I knew only as some of the many friendly faces who had trooped in and out of Nona's kitchen when I was young—and asked them to ask their sons to come and to bring friends.

My father couldn't have helped overhearing us talk about the party all month, but he went on with his regular routines as if nothing special was happening. I didn't think that was strange. It was tacitly understood that though he chose not to participate in the rituals of ordinary life, like celebrating birthdays or paying condolence calls, he tolerated the rest of the family's participation as long as we didn't try to involve him.

ON THE NIGHT OF MY BIG EVENING, I checked my stocking seams to make sure they were straight, then put on my tan and white sheath dress and dyed-to-match high heels.

I had gone to the beauty parlor that afternoon to have my hair done up in a French twist, so all I needed to complete my outfit was eye shadow, lipstick, and jewelry—small hanging gold earrings, my gold charm bracelet, and the choker of white cultured pearls my mother had given me as a Sweet Sixteen present. Feeling glamorous and sophisticated, I walked into the kitchen.

My mother was at the sink emptying ice cube trays into a bucket, an apron over one of her good dresses. "You look very nice!" she said, smiling, as she dried her hands on the dish towel and went to the cupboard to get the florist box. She lifted the corsage out of the tissue paper and pinned it to the left side of my dress near my shoulder: 16 sugar cubes nestled in a bed of pink ribbons. "Perfect," she said, standing back to get a good view.

I didn't go in to show my father, who was at his table in the living room practicing chess moves from a book. Since his return from Brighton Beach, where he'd gone to escape the party preparations underway since morning, he'd made no acknowledgment of the activity going on around him, and I thought it best not to call attention to it.

I glanced at the clock above the refrigerator: 7:30. The invitations were for 8:00. I told my mother I was going to the basement, then made my way down the two flights of steps. At the bottom, I paused in the doorway to survey the room. Everything looked beautiful, especially the twists of pink and white crepe paper that crisscrossed the ceiling, dipping down in graceful arcs. Uncle Bill had hung them in the morning, moving his ladder from place to place under my direction.

I made some adjustments to the arrangement of forks and napkins on the long table against the wall and moved the vase of daisies, my favorite flower, to the exact center. Then I placed the assorted kitchen chairs we had borrowed from Nona and my aunts along the sides, so the middle of the floor would be free for dancing. I turned on the table lamps my mother had let me bring down from our living room and turned off the overhead fluorescent light. The room was bathed in a warm, yellow glow. I clicked the thick spindle into place on the portable record player, took a small 45 from the stack my friends had lent me, and started it spinning. A slow, dreamy song filled the room, Pat Boone's "Love Letters in the Sand." Just like a nightclub, I thought. The evening's magic had begun.

My guests began arriving a few minutes after 8:00. Bearing gifts, they came down the outside steps that led directly from the street to the basement. The boys wore sport jackets and ties; the girls, sack dresses and high heels. Feeling like a hostess in a play, I stationed myself at the door to greet each one.

"Hi, I'm Stew," said a boy in a neat crew cut. "Richie asked me. Is he here yet?"

"No, but please come in."

"This is for you." He handed me a gift-wrapped package.

"Thank you," I said, taking it and turning to whichever of my friends was near. "Carol, this is Stew, a friend of Richie's." I handed her the package.

While I stayed at the door to greet my next guest, Carol led Stew in, introduced him around, and added his present to the growing pile on the gift table.

By 8:30, my party was well underway, with kids dancing the Lindy to the records. Everyone loved the food. My mother had made coleslaw and her famous tuna salad—fresh lemon juice and grated carrots were the secret ingredients—and Nona and my aunts had contributed homemade calzonia, koulouria, and sweet, syrupy *baklava*. Store-bought cold cuts and bakery-fresh rye bread rounded out the menu, with plenty of soda and potato chips, replenished periodically by my mother.

Everything was going smoothly, and I should have been happy. But now that I was no longer in my greeter's role at the door, I had to circulate and talk to people. I felt strange, as if I were watching someone in a movie say things like, "Thanks for coming," and, "This is my friend Lolly from Girl Scout camp." Mature words were coming out of my mouth, but inside I felt like a little girl dressed up in her mother's high heels, eating and drinking forbidden foods like potato chips and soda. I didn't belong with these big teenagers, who laughed easily as they joked with one another in small groups.

I was working hard at pretending, hoping no one would see I was an imposter, when all at once I saw the room in a different way. These kids were having fun at *my* party. *I* was the guest of honor, the one wearing the corsage of 16 white sugar cubes. I felt my round shoulders straighten and my neck lengthen, heard my voice become more assured. I felt taller, beautiful, sexy, 16. It was as if a completely different person had emerged from within me and taken over my body, stepping naturally into the role I had been trying to play. I kidded around and even flirted, something I'd never done. Most of the boys hadn't met me before, and this poised, outgoing, lithe and pretty girl was their first and only impression of me. They flocked around and asked me to dance as if I were Cinderella at the ball.

The evening whirled by. I danced, opened my presents to an audience breathing *oohs* and *ahhs*, and donned a hat two of my friends made out of the gift bows. I blew out my birthday candles, handed pieces of cake around as my mother cut them, and danced some more. A few times I noticed one of the boys writing down the phone number of one of the girls. At *my* party! This was the best day of my life.

The dance floor was filled with bobbing couples doing the cha-cha, me among them, when, from out of nowhere, my father charged into the center of the room in his gray trousers and white sleeveless undershirt.

"Get out of here!" he screamed above the music. "Go home!" His face was contorted with rage, and the veins stood out on the sides of his forehead. "What do you think you're doing? *It's midnight!*" His bare arms flailed the air. "GET OUT OF HERE! IT'S MIDNIGHT!"

Everyone fled through the door to the street, not even stopping to say goodbye. I alone stood still, back to my round-shouldered self, watching my party scatter. I was unafraid but mortally embarrassed.

Within seconds, everyone was gone except my mother, my father, and me. The cha-cha music played to the emptiness. My mother lifted the arm from the record to still it. My father started back up the inside steps. He was quieter now, just muttering. I remained standing where I was, looking at the festively twisted crepe paper. It all happened so quickly that I didn't know whether my mother had tried to stop him and couldn't, or whether she hadn't even tried.

"I'm sorry, Vivian," was all she said, meeting my eyes for a few seconds before starting to clean up. Numb, I began collecting crumpled paper napkins and bringing them to the garbage pail near the sink.

I WAS IN MY ROOM THE NEXT EVENING at 8:00, when I heard a knock on our apartment door. That meant trouble: by order of my father, 8:00 was too late for visits. He was in the living room, with the door closed. Hoping he hadn't heard, I hurried to the apartment door and opened it. When I saw three of the boys

I had met at my party, I was flattered. Until the previous evening, boys had never expressed much interest in me. But I was also afraid my father might hear them. They were from the normal world and didn't know about the 8:00 rule, or that "strangers" were never allowed to knock at my door without prior notice at any hour. They also probably didn't realize that the madman who had ended my party was my father. They could have thought he was just some crazy person who lived in the building.

For a few seconds, I didn't know what to say. Then, just as she had the night before, the poised girl took over and went out to the hall to talk with the boys, closing the door behind her. While she bantered like an ordinary teenager, I tried to think of a way to suggest that we continue our conversation in the street. But before I could, my father opened the door.

"Get out of here! It's eight o'clock! *What do you think you're doing?* DON'T YOU KNOW IT'S EIGHT O'CLOCK?"

For an instant the boys looked shocked. Then, once more, they turned and fled. The poised girl disappeared, too.

Finding myself standing on the landing with my father, I followed him back into the apartment. Muttering, he turned right, into the living room. I continued straight, past Marvin's room to mine.

I closed the door and sat cross-legged on the floor, scarcely breathing. Head slumped forward, I attached my eyes to a speck of gray lint on the rust-colored carpet and held on tightly. I felt my body become smaller and smaller. The lint became larger and larger. My head dropped down toward it, lower and lower, until it drew me in and closed over me. ■

PART TWO

ANALYSIS

CHAPTER 7

Appointments

"I'MGOINGOUTTOEATCHINESEFOODAtTaengFongWith MyFriends," I said to my mother one Saturday afternoon.

"Have a nice time," she replied, not looking up from her book. In addition to working on her doctorate at Teachers College, she would soon be starting a new job as assistant principal in an elementary school near Coney Island.

Two hours later, head buzzing with everything my friends and I had giggled about over egg rolls and chow mein, I returned to find my mother still studying in the kitchen. She told me she had made an appointment for me with a speech therapist.

"What's wrong with my speech?"

"You talk too fast. Tuesday at three-fifteen."

"I work for Aunt Sarah on Tuesdays."

"Tell Sarah you'll come later."

I was used to my mother's signing me up for things without asking. In elementary school, there had been an activity every afternoon at the JCH—tap dancing, ballet, Girl Scouts, arts and crafts, pottery—so I would be occupied while she attended her courses. When I was 12, she sent me for ballroom dancing lessons, so I could enter my teenage years knowing how to foxtrot, cha-cha, and tango. But speech lessons were different. Like the private modern dance lessons I had recently begun on Saturday mornings to correct my posture, speech lessons meant my mother thought something about me was inadequate. I didn't like the feeling.

The following Tuesday, I sat across from a woman who made me count to six out loud between each word. It was a relief when, an hour later, I slid into my chair at the buttonhole machine, reached for a yellow pajama top, and surfaced in Nebraska.

I DIDN'T THINK OF NEBRASKA as another location. When I was there, it was the only world I knew, just as when I was with my friends in Brooklyn, that was my only world. I felt real and complete in both places. But there were times, when I was neither in Nebraska nor with my friends, that I felt unreal, as if I were in another dimension, observing myself moving among real people like a ghost. I wondered how it happened that of all the bodies on the planet, I came to be stuck in mine, able to look out and see everyone else, but unable to see myself. Real people probably couldn't see themselves, either, but they didn't seem to be aware of that.

When the unreal feeling came over me, the Atmosphere was not present, and I didn't know it had ever existed. If I was away from home—watching my hand move across the page as it took notes in class; or on the bus, looking at the panorama of real people in whole bodies getting on, dropping their coins into the box, sitting down with their packages—there was nothing I could do to make the feeling go away. But at home, I had the mirror.

More and more often, I would look into the glass to reassure myself that I existed. The girl I saw had her own body and face. I didn't. Yet there was a connection between us. I would give the mirror girl real-people things to say, tossing my head the way real people did, watching her head toss in the glass. Within minutes, her moving and talking would wake up the Atmosphere. The kindly doctors and nurses were in it, along with Jinx, and now Mrs. Warshauer, my English teacher, who understood the delicate feelings Emily Dickinson wrote about. As the mingled molecules of the Atmosphere people floated loose, forming an invisible dome that surrounded the mirror-girl, I would pass through the glass and come to life in her body. Then the Atmosphere people would be watching over *me*, knowing everything I thought and felt and did. Once the Atmosphere people knew about me, I became real.

This had been going on for months. Recently, though, it was as if several versions of me were making their own connections with the Atmosphere. Sometimes the mirror girl turned into Ellen Willow, and I said things like, "Your visitors are waiting in the parlor, Mrs. Robinson. I'll bring in the tea right away." Sometimes she was a girl I didn't know, and I spoke in strange syllables strung together into sentences. "Es pook ah-*nee*-nah." They had no English translation, but I could almost feel what the sounds meant from the rhythm and inflection—sense the flavor, if not the details of the story they were conveying. And sometimes the mirror girl was young, with a pain in the center of her chest that hurt so much I could only stare into her eyes. But no matter who was in the mirror or who was standing outside it, with the Atmosphere surrounding me I was real and three-dimensional. Dreading a return to my cellophane self if I walked away, I often remained in front of the glass for more than an hour, talking, watching, listening.

All the while, an Overview-me saw everything from a place far above. The Overview-me knew something wasn't right, especially because there was yet another me who didn't know anything about Ellen Willow or the mirror or anyone in it: a normal teenager who kept three little pots of eye shadow—blue, green, purple—next to her hair brush, to match whatever outfit she put on each morning.

Aunt Sophia was in psychoanalysis. She still lived with Nona and Papoo and had a shelf of books about mental conditions in her room. I often went down while she was at work and pored through the one on abnormal psychology, looking for a category that fit me. Definitely not paranoid: I didn't think people were after me. Other diagnoses, like catatonic and aphasic, were less clear. There were times I got paralyzed in my armchair, and times I couldn't talk, but according to the book, those states lasted a long time while I could flip back and forth within minutes. I concluded I was probably some kind of general schizophrenic, and the mirror people were hallucinations. In one way, that was comforting: if I fit into an officially defined category, I wasn't a freak. In another, it was frightening: schizophrenic was a lot more serious than neurotic.

I needed to talk to a grownup about all this. Not my mother, and not Aunt Sophia, who would probably tell my mother. I chose Mrs. Warshauer. She had praised my papers on *Tess of the D'Urbervilles*, *The Scarlet Letter*, and *Adventures of Huckleberry Finn*, and I felt she liked me. The Atmosphere Mrs. Warshauer already knew about the mirror, but the in-person Mrs. Warshauer didn't. Our conversations had been solely about my work in her class and my job as a monitor in her office; besides teaching English, she was the Dean of Girls.

But on three different days, as soon as I took a step toward her inner office to ask whether I could speak with her, I suddenly felt more like a shy child than a high school honors student. Mrs. Warshauer changed, too, from a woman whose soft dress folds were set off by a Bohemian necklace and whose few extra pounds made her seem motherly, to a massive body sitting behind a large wooden desk. Each time, I was afraid to approach her, and, each time, I was disappointed in myself for letting the opportunity pass.

I decided to tell her in a letter. I wrote that I was worried because I saw faces in the mirror that weren't me, and that I talked to them. It was easier to say I talked *to* them than explain how I said words *for* them. I didn't write about who they were, or how the Atmosphere watched over them, or how they changed me from two-dimensional to three-dimensional. That was too hard to describe.

Early the next morning, I slipped the letter through the mail slot of Mrs. Warshauer's office, then went to my first-period class. I pictured her picking it up from the floor, reading it with concern, and sending a monitor for me.

In third-period chemistry, a girl walked in with a note.

"Vivian," the teacher called after he read it.

My knees buckled and I had to lean against my desk while I gathered my books. As I followed the monitor out, the class looked at me with sympathy and surprise—I'd never gotten into trouble before.

Mrs. Warshauer was sitting at her desk. My letter, angled at the folds, lay on top of it. "Close the door and sit down," she said without a smile.

I sat on the edge of the chair beside her desk, books on my knees, bag on the floor, again feeling like a frightened child.

Mrs. Warshauer picked up the letter and shook the pages. "Is this a joke?"

I hadn't expected disbelief. The little-girl feeling vanished. "Never mind!" I said, snatching the letter. In one motion, I swept up my bag and stood to open the door.

"Don't go," Mrs. Warshauer said, her voice now gentle. Hand still on the doorknob, I turned and saw her softened face. "I thought you were pulling my leg, but I see you're not. Please stay."

As I slid into the chair, the little-girl feeling returned.

"Whose faces do you see in the mirror?" Mrs. Warshauer's eyes, with their warm corner wrinkles, held mine over her half-glasses.

I had thought she would read the letter and automatically know everything the Atmosphere version of her knew. "I don't know," I whispered, unable to say more.

"Do they talk back to you?"

They didn't talk to me, though they did talk. "I'm not sure."

"Does your mother know?"

"No!" The teenage-me was back. "Please don't tell her."

"I won't. But I'd like you to speak with the psychologist. Would that be OK?"

"Yes," I said, though I didn't really want to talk to someone I didn't know.

She asked me to wait outside while she made a call. Then she sent me to an office one flight up.

The woman waiting for me in the doorway was younger and thinner than Mrs. Warshauer, slightly stoop-shouldered, with short brown hair and a loose gray suit.

"Please come in," she said, then sat down at her desk, gesturing to the chair beside it for me. Pen poised above a lined pad, she turned her head sideways to look at me. "Mrs. Warshauer said you see faces in the mirror."

I nodded, glad her eyes didn't know how to penetrate my insides the way Mrs. Warshauer's did.

"Is it affecting your schoolwork?"

What did school have to do with it? "No."

She made a notation and looked up again. "Do the faces tell you to do things?"

Was she dumb! "No."

Another notation. Then, "Is there anything bothering you that you'd like to talk about?"

"No." I realized she was more uncomfortable than I was. I liked that.

"So." She put down her pen. "I guess there's nothing more. You can go back down."

Mrs. Warshauer was hanging up the phone when I got there, no doubt from speaking to the psychologist. "It's already fourth period," she said. "You better go to your class. Here's a note excusing your lateness. Please come back any time you want to talk."

I felt light as I walked through the hall. The worst was over: Mrs. Warshauer knew. The school psychologist didn't even count.

Later that evening, when I walked into the kitchen, I found

my mother rinsing a teacup at the sink. "I got a call from Mrs. Warshauer today," she said, turning off the water and facing me.

Oh god. She told.

"She said you talk to faces in the mirror. What's going on?" It was more accusation than question.

"Nothing." I held onto a corner of the table and looked down at the floor.

"Well, do you or don't you?"

"I don't know. I'm going to my room now."

She didn't say anything.

I closed my door and sank into my armchair. Later, when the Atmosphere came, Mrs. Warshauer wasn't in it.

THE FOLLOWING DAY, I caught Mrs. Warshauer alone for a minute. I felt no longing for her anymore. Just anger.

"You promised you wouldn't tell my mother," I said.

She looked directly into my eyes. "I'm sorry. But you wouldn't talk to the psychologist, and I didn't know what else to do."

My anger vanished as I realized the in-person Mrs. Warshauer had wanted to help me but didn't understand things the way her Atmosphere version did. At least she took me seriously and cared about me. When the Atmosphere came later that afternoon, Mrs. Warshauer was back in it.

That evening, as I was doing homework, my mother knocked on my door. "I made an appointment for you to see a psychoanalyst," she said. "Wednesday at four." She held out a piece of paper. Heart racing, I took it.

Having delivered her message, my mother left. I looked at the paper. *Dr. Sue Hirschhorn*, along with an address.

IN SPITE OF THE WAY it had come about, I looked forward to my appointment with Dr. Hirschhorn. I envisioned analysis as something like the Atmosphere, where everything about me would be understood and accepted. Though I hadn't yet met her, Dr. Hirschhorn was already part of the Atmosphere.

On the morning of my first appointment, I put on my new lavender-and-purple plaid skirt with matching vest and my long-sleeved white blouse with the rows of pleated tucks. I fastened my hairclip high on the back of my head so my ponytail would swing, and put on light pink lipstick and purple eye shadow. The Atmosphere Dr. Hirschhorn already knew and cared about me, but the in-person Dr. Hirschhorn had never met me. If I looked especially pretty, there was a better chance she would like me.

After school I rode two buses to the quiet, residential neighborhood of Midwood, where sun peeked through the leaves of thick maple trees. Dr. Hirschhorn's office was in her three-story corner house—gray stucco with a small garden. On a post, a discrete sign read: Sigmund Hirschhorn, M.D. Must be her husband, I thought as I approached the door, where another sign read: Ring Bell and Walk In.

I found myself in a chandeliered vestibule. Several elderly people in a waiting room off to the side were speaking softly. They sounded European. Following instructions from my mother, I mounted the carpeted wooden staircase and entered the empty waiting room on the second floor.

Afraid to walk in all the way, I took the chair nearest the door and attached my eyes to a flower in the carpet design. My body was rigid but my mind raced. What would she be like, this fairy godmother in human form? Would she know she was watching over me this very minute, seeing how nervous I was to meet her?

Footsteps. I forced myself to look up.

There she was, standing in the doorway, in a skirt and blouse and open toe shoes. About my parents' age, she had short auburn hair and wore dark pink lipstick and mother-of-pearl glasses that magnified her green eyes. She was beautiful and scary, real and not real.

"Hello. I'm Dr. Hirschhorn. You must be Vivian." Her musical voice had a barely discernible foreign inflection.

I nodded, unable to speak.

"Would you like to come in?" She looked right at me. I couldn't hide.

I followed her into the next room, where sheer curtains made a kaleidoscope of the green leaves outside. They tumbled together with the flowered print on Dr. Hirschhorn's long, wide skirt to create an enchanted landscape. I felt as if I were in a dream, my whole body inside the mirror. She sat down in a cushioned swivel chair. On the wooden desk next to her were some papers, a slightly crumpled embroidered handkerchief, and an important-looking black telephone with two push buttons under the dial. I stood near the door, not knowing whether I was supposed to sit in the huge leather chair opposite her or lie on the couch under the window.

"Please sit down." She gestured toward the chair.

I perched on its edge, afraid of being swallowed up if I slid back. Books on my lap and bag on the floor, I froze the way I had in the waiting room.

"Would you like to take your coat off?" she asked.

"No." I could barely move my lips.

"You can put your books on the floor."

That wasn't a question, so I didn't have to answer. I kept them on my lap.

"You look frightened."

Also not a question.

"Do you know why your mother made this appointment?"

A question, but I was too afraid to talk or to move anything except my eyes. I rolled them to let her know I knew.

"She said you see faces in the mirror."

Not a question.

"Can you tell me about them?"

How could I tell her, when I hadn't even been able to tell Mrs. Warshauer? If Dr. Hirschhorn would only say I could write down my answers, I would be able to tell her a lot. But she didn't say it, and I couldn't ask. "No."

"What school do you go to?"

This was easier. "Lafayette."

"Do you have friends?"

"Yes." In a whisper.

"What are their names?"

"Carol and Ronnie and Iris."

"Do you ever have appointments?"

I was having an appointment now, but I didn't think that's what she meant. I didn't know how to answer, so I didn't roll my eyes.

Dr. Hirschhorn picked up the handkerchief and turned away for a few seconds to blow her nose. Free of her scrutiny, I moved my leg to get rid of the pins and needles, but before I could wake it up, she turned back and I froze again.

"Do you ever have appointments with boys?" she asked.

Oh, I thought. She means dates. "A few."

"Do you have a boyfriend?"

"No."

When would the real stuff begin? When would she find the Inside me with the hurting hole who had never talked to anyone and was waiting for her to make it safe to come out? But Dr. Hirschhorn just asked more Outside questions, and I either gave one-word answers, rolled my eyes, or said, "I don't know." I was stiff, hot, and uncomfortable with the weight of the books on my thighs.

At the end of the hour, she asked whether I could come at the same time next week.

"Yes," I said and handed her the check from my mother.

She thanked me and put it on her desk. "There are only two rules. You're not to read anything about psychoanalysis as long as you're seeing me, and you have to tell me everything that comes into your head."

"OK," I whispered.

Dr. Hirschhorn opened the door. I walked out. She said goodbye, went back inside, and closed the door.

She had vanished, even from the Atmosphere. I stood at the top of the staircase, alone in a vast, airless universe. Then my feet began descending, first one, then the other. Passing through the vestibule, I glanced into the downstairs waiting room and was relieved that there were still people there, still a soft European murmuring. Something was the same as it had been a million years ago.

NO ONE WAS HOME. I ate a slice of bread with cream cheese and started a report for my history class.

Later that evening, my mother and I passed in the kitchen. "Did you see Dr. Hirschhorn?" she asked.

"Yes."

"Did you make another appointment?"

"Yes."

"Good," she said and was gone.

FOR PART OF ME, the week passed quickly: speech lesson; buttonhole job; doing my own homework and helping my cousin Annie with hers; bickering with Marvin, who was now just a year behind me in high school, having skipped a grade in junior high; clandestine calls to my friends that my father, occupied with his little pieces of paper in the living room, couldn't hear. But for the part that couldn't stop thinking about Dr. Hirschhorn, time dragged. She was back in the Atmosphere, watching me constantly, but I couldn't say anything directly to her, nor she to me. I longed for Wednesday, when her essence would be in a body and I could talk to her.

Wednesday came at last. Two buses. Small garden. Ring bell and walk in.

As if there had been no intervening week, I stepped into a world I had left only a minute before: European murmuring in the downstairs waiting room, carpeted wooden staircase, silent waiting room upstairs. I sat in the same chair, locked my eyes onto the same carpet flower. Same terror mixed with longing. Same rigid body, chest barely rising to make room for breath. Same racing mind. What if I couldn't talk again? Of course I would talk. Dr. Hirschhorn would know how to make it safe. She would ask Inside questions today.

Footsteps. At least this time I knew what to expect when I looked up.

But the lady framed in the doorway had no connection to the essence I had been so comfortable with all week, up to one second ago. "Hello," she said. I'd forgotten she had a voice. "Would you like to come in?"

Same crumpled handkerchief on her desk. Same swivel chair for her and huge leather chair for me. I sat down on the edge with my books on my lap, then waited while Dr. Hirschhorn settled herself on her cushion and draped her long flowered skirt over her crossed legs. Only her ankles and open toe shoes peeked out.

"Would you like to take off your coat?" she asked, pinning me with her magnified eyes.

"No."

"You can put your books on the floor."

Please, I begged with my eyes, don't let this be like the last time. Please know how to help me talk.

"So," Dr. Hirschhorn said when I didn't move the books. "Did anything special happen at Wingate this week?"

"I go to Lafayette."

"That's right. I see another girl who goes to Wingate, and I got the schools mixed up."

How? Wingate wasn't even *near* Lafayette.

Dr. Hirschhorn said the Wingate girl was afraid to take the express train to Manhattan, because she felt trapped when a station whizzed by and she could see people standing on the platform but couldn't get to them. She always took the local.

What did that have to do with anything?

"Do you ever feel trapped on the train?" Dr. Hirschhorn asked.

Oh. "No."

She swiveled toward her desk, dabbed her nose with the handkerchief, swiveled back. "Do you still see faces in the mirror?"

My heart pounded. She was going to get Inside now.

"Yes." In a whisper.

"Do you still talk to them?"

"Yes."

"What do you say?"

That would take more than a one- or two-word answer, more than I was capable of. I rolled my eyes so she would understand.

Talk to her, one part of me urged another. Don't lose this chance.

I wanted to. Inside was crying for Dr. Hirschhorn. But Outside remained immobile.

"Some girls make believe they're kissing a boy when they put on lipstick," Dr. Hirschhorn said. "They look in the mirror and say, 'You're so pretty I could kiss you.'" She pursed her dark pink lips and made three quick kissing sounds. "Is that what you do?"

Oh god. "No."

"You don't have to be embarrassed. Lots of girls do that. It's normal."

Relief: She was so far off she had broken the spell and my heart stopped pounding. Disappointment: She didn't know how to get Inside yet.

Dr. Hirschhorn said nothing for a minute, just uncrossed her legs, crossed them the other way, then rearranged her skirt, all the while staring at me. I didn't mind my own silence, but hers made me uncomfortable. I shifted my gaze to the leaves outside the window.

"What classes are you taking in school?"

My eyes came back to meet hers. "History, English, math, chemistry, orchestra."

"What instrument do you play?"

"Viola."

"Do you take lessons?"

"No."

"Where did you learn to play?"

"In school."

"Who are your favorite composers?"
"Mozart and Beethoven."
"Which do you like best?"
"I don't know."
"You must have a preference." She said this as if it were a question. I rolled my eyes.
"Why do you roll your eyes?"
That was too hard to explain. "I don't know."

I kept hoping she would look for Inside again, but after more Outside questions, she said, "It's time to stop now. This can be our regular time. Is that good for you?"

"Yes."

She stood. I handed her the check. She opened the door. I walked out. She closed the door.

Once again I was in the empty hall, alone in a world with no air. Feeling not real, I walked down the stairs, past the murmuring in the waiting room and into the street. As they had last time, my feet started walking the two miles home instead of taking the bus. And, once again, after a few blocks, after I concluded that Dr. Hirschhorn hadn't finished catching up to herself, I got her back the way I needed her. No voice. No body. Just loose in the air all around me. Now I was real.

NOTHING CHANGED the next time, or the next, or the next. Each week on the bus from school, I resolved to talk, but as soon as I stepped past the ring-bell-and-walk-in sign, I felt the same jolt, as if my center of gravity had shifted, and I was filled with a longing and fear so enormous they didn't fit inside me. If I moved or talked, they would spill.

Sometimes, while my eyes were stuck on the carpet flower in the waiting room, the confident me came from behind and slid over the scared, longing me. Then I felt sure I would be able to talk. But as soon as I heard Dr. Hirschhorn's footsteps and turned to see her standing in the doorway, the scared, longing me popped to the top again. She had no words to describe her intense feelings. With her occupying my body for most of the session, the competent me could only watch from underneath and slip an occasional answer into my mouth.

One day, when Dr. Hirschhorn did her usual swivel toward the clutter on her desk, she picked up a record album. "I thought you might like *La Bohème*," she said, holding it upright on her lap so I could see the cover. "It's about students, and you're a student."

Was she lending it to me? What for?

"You can have it," she said, leaning forward to hand it to me. "I bought it especially for you."

Oh, no. A present. "I don't want it," I said without moving.

"Don't you like opera?"

"No."

"I could exchange it for Mozart or Beethoven."

"I don't want anything." A present implied a connection I didn't feel.

"It's OK to accept a gift from me. You don't have to do anything in return."

"I don't want it."

She put the album back on her desk.

A week later, Dr. Hirschhorn offered me a wrapped box of fancy chocolates. When I refused that, too, she pulled off the paper. "Try one," she said, walking to my chair and holding the neat brown grid in the air over my books.

"I don't want any."

Her face tightened as she backed into her chair and laid the open box on her desk. "Why won't you accept anything from me? Are you afraid I'm going to poison you?"

How ridiculous. "No." But I had seen that she could get annoyed.

A FEW MONTHS LATER, when nothing had changed, I started bringing letters to the sessions, hoping they would help the in-person Dr. Hirschhorn know what she already knew in the Atmosphere. I wrote about Outside things: my exams, a party, a reprimand from my father. I wrote about Inside things: the pain in the center of my chest, feeling unreal, watching myself from outside myself. I never wrote about the Atmosphere. When it was there, it was so much a part of me that I didn't think to tell her, just as I wouldn't have thought to tell her I breathed in and out. When it was absent, I wasn't aware of its absence, because I didn't know it had ever surrounded me.

Sometimes my handwriting in the notes came out teenage-loopy, sometimes as a child's straight up-and-down printing; but no matter what the style, if I made one mistake, I copied the whole page over. Like a messenger, I always handed Dr. Hirschhorn the letter at the beginning of the session, before I sat down in the huge leather chair and froze. The first time she seemed surprised, but after that it became part of our routine. She would read all eight or ten pages while I sat motionless, then try to talk about what she had just read. It never worked. The me who wrote the letters wasn't the me who sat opposite her, and the Dr. Hirschhorn who read them wasn't the Dr. Hirschhorn I wrote them to.

But no matter how disappointed I was in any one session, on the walk home, I always got Dr. Hirschhorn back the way I needed her to be. Once she returned, I fished an apple out of my bag, took a bite, then disappeared into Nebraska or someplace else Inside. Days later, I came back to find my legs walking on Bay Parkway, the apple in my hand, the same apple I had begun eating on the walk home from Dr. Hirschhorn. The flesh wasn't brown yet, so it had to be the same day. I took another bite, walked a few more steps, and disappeared again. ▪

CHAPTER 8

The Rush of The River

I GRADUATED FROM LAFAYETTE HIGH SCHOOL half a year early, on a cold day in January 1960, along with my friends Susan and Gloria. My parents and Nona watched from the audience as I was called to the stage four times to receive awards, among them the medal for excellence in English. In just a few weeks I would be starting Brooklyn College, which was free except for textbooks and the registration fee. It was also only a 25-minute bus ride away, so there were no room-and-board costs. Most of my friends, including those graduating in June, were going there, too.

Susan and Gloria planned to major in education. As we sat on the floor in Gloria's living room, she read aloud from the booklet of course requirements. "Child Development. Social Studies Curriculum...."

I began to feel uneasy. Those weren't ordinary subjects, like math, English, history, or biology.

"Look at this," Susan said. "Student Teaching."

Something shifted in me and I became terrified, sure that, beginning tomorrow, if I couldn't earn a living, I would have to sleep in the street. Without a bed.

I tried telling myself I was 17, starting college, and for the next four years I would be sleeping on the convertible sofa in my own room. It didn't help. I raised my hands to my eyes. Many times over the years, when I was having a nightmare, I realized, even as I slept, that I could fight my way to a safe world by prying my eyelids apart But my eyes were already open.

"I haven't decided what I want to do yet," I said with a bravado I didn't feel. Susan and Gloria looked up from their booklets. "I know one thing for sure, though. I don't want to teach." I reached for a potato chip and dipped it into the small dish of mustard next to the bowl. "Maybe I'll become a doctor. My grandfather said he'd pay for medical school if I wanted to go."

"A doctor!" Susan said.

"You always were The Brain," Gloria said.

That's what my friends affectionately called me, and I usually did feel capable intellectually. Even when I wanted to color or suck my thumb, I could read Shakespeare, diagram geometry theorems, and understand mitosis.

I opened my booklet to the section for pre-med majors. "Calculus," I read in a clear, strong voice.

I ARRIVED AT MY FIRST CLASS with two sharpened pencils and my new copy of *Analytic Geometry and Calculus*. Though part of me knew I'd never become a doctor—it was a more in-charge profession than I could imagine for myself—I needed to keep up the fiction.

The professor, a woman in drab clothes and no makeup, told us in a monotone how our final grades would be determined. "Homework, twenty-five percent. Midterm exam, twenty-five percent. Final exam, fifty percent."

At the beginning of the next class, she collected the homework, then showed us how we should have done each of the ten problems. I had gotten only two correct. In high school, I'd considered 90 a low mark. This was the first time I'd gotten a 20. Some students asked questions, but I didn't understand enough about what I didn't understand to know what to ask. The professor began a new lesson. "The correspondent of X zero... domain of definition... second derivative is acceleration...."

I was copying a formula into my notebook when it hit me: I'll never understand this, no matter how hard I try.

The professor was still writing on the board. My hand was still copying. But my handwriting was no longer big and open, so firm it made indentations on the page underneath. The second half of the formula was in tiny, cramped letters that left no impression.

When class was over, I walked into the hall, head down, watching my feet connect to the floor after each step. The floor would probably have been there to catch me if I looked up, but I feared losing sight of it. I heard some students exchange phone numbers and arrange to do the homework together, but I didn't feel entitled to talk to them. I was no longer The Brain.

At home, I told my mother I wanted to drop out of college and go back to my buttonhole job—for the rest of my life. She got me a tutor, the son of one of her friends, and for the remainder of the semester, I spent Saturday mornings at my kitchen table with him. He was patient put pragmatic. When he saw that I would never grasp the concepts, he changed his approach and showed me how to work out problems without understanding them.

I was getting by in my other courses—English, French, Economics, and Health—without much work, but I never raised my hand or talked to other students. This was no nightmare from which I could wake myself. It was my permanent state, unrelieved even when I was home. The mirror wasn't magic anymore. I didn't know it ever had been. The me who bravely managed to live a normal life in spite of her difficulties had disappeared. The me who was here in her place had no knowledge that the Atmosphere people had ever existed.

FOR THE FIRST FEW WEEKS of the semester, I still saw Dr. Hirschhorn, but I felt none of the longing before the sessions that I used to, or the disappointment afterward. One evening, I wrote her a note saying I was quitting and gave it to her in our next session.

"Are you sure?" she asked, peering at me through the glasses that made her green eyes seem large.

Sitting on the edge of the leather chair, I drew my jacket closer around me. "Yes."

I told my mother I was finished with therapy, so she could stop leaving a check on my desk every week. I was glad she didn't ask questions.

Several days later, I was riding home on the bus when my nose began to twitch. Two jerks, a pause, two more jerks. I willed it to stop, but it was as if I had no control over it. I wondered what I looked like and checked in my lipstick mirror. I was like a rabbit, each twitch of my nose flaring my nostrils and exposing my upper front teeth. At least no one I knew was on the bus.

My nose was still twitching when my mother came home. "Make another appointment with Dr. Hirschhorn," was all she said.

It was still twitching three days later, when Dr. Hirschhorn came to get me from the waiting room. "*Now* I know why your mother wanted you to come back," she said. "You have a tic." It sounded like, *Ha! I caught you!*

We resumed our routine. I handed her a note at the beginning of each session, then barely moved or talked except to say, "Yes," "No," or "I don't know." In the notes, I mentioned that calculus was difficult but didn't say anything about the effect that had on me, because I didn't know I had changed. I couldn't remember having ever felt another way.

My calculus tutor was happy when I received a C and bought me a record of Vivaldi's *The Four Seasons*. It was no victory for me, though. I still didn't understand calculus.

I received passing grades in my other subjects—the college's definition of passing, not mine: Bs in French and Health, Cs in Economics and English. But at least the semester was over. I sold my textbooks back to the bookstore and replaced the notebooks on my desk with a stack of novels from the library. My tic vanished by itself, and at an end-of-term celebration dinner with my friends at Taeng Fong, I was surprised to find I could have a good time.

I WAS READING IN MY ARMCHAIR the day after the dinner when the phone rang.

"What are you doing for the summer?" asked Rose, the mother of a classmate from Lafayette.

"Nothing," I said, surprised. Her son and I weren't particular friends.

"How would you like to work in the Catskills? The mountains. I have a nice job for you in one of the hotels. In the office."

She went on to say she worked there every summer as the bookkeeper, and her husband came up on weekends. As one of three office girls, I would type letters, register guests, and operate the switchboard. I would work six days a week, alternating between the day and evening shifts, for a salary of $18.00 a week plus room and board. During my time off, I could use the pool and other facilities.

"It's only a three-hour drive," Rose concluded. "My husband will bring you up. I'm already here."

Still shaken by calculus, I didn't feel capable of handling a glamorous-sounding job. "I never worked in an office," I said. "I don't think I can do it."

That evening, when I mentioned the call to my mother, she encouraged me to go. "You'll be in the country for the summer."

My father said, "You'll be able to practice your skills in an actual office. You'll get *experience*." He tapped the table with his middle finger, the way he often did when he was making a point.

A FEW DAYS LATER, while Rose's husband guided his car around rolling hills, past barns and grazing cows, he filled me in about the hotel in an easy, familiar manner, and my worries lessened. Rose was sitting on one of the lawn chairs when we arrived, a knitted white stole over her black evening dress. Behind her was a sprawling three-story building, white with a red gabled roof, that could have been on the cover of a novel. I liked it already.

Rose led me across the carpeted lobby and into a cramped office. She introduced me to the owner, Mrs. Comitor, middle-aged, in a denim wrap skirt, plaid blouse, socks, and sneakers. After we shook hands, Mrs. Comitor turned to a rack of keys and handed me one. "You're on the third floor for now," she said. "After you get settled, go into the dining room. We saved you some dinner. Be in the office at eight tomorrow."

THE NEXT MORNING began what was to be my daily routine. First I went into the kitchen to ask Lou, the chef, what would be served for lunch and dinner. Then I cut stencils for the menus, ran them off on the mimeograph machine, and delivered them to the hostess in the dining room. No one warned me that if an office girl made an error on the menu—*Vegetables Julien*e instead of *Vegetables Julienne*, or the wrong grouping of dishes under *Choice of*—Lou would storm out of the kitchen in his white chef's hat and apron, scream his way past guests in the lobby, and barge into the office. Spittle flying from his mouth, he would inform Mrs. Comitor that "that stupid office girl" was never to set foot in his kitchen again.

I walked into the kitchen the first morning with my pad and asked for Lou. While I waited for someone to get him, I looked around at men chopping vegetables and stirring huge steaming pots. The door to a walk-in refrigerator opened, and a very tall, very wide man with what looked like knife scars on his face emerged.

"Who are *you*?" he growled, glaring from under bushy brows as he wiped his hands on his apron, leaving red meat stains on it.

"I'm the new office girl come to get the menus."

He eyed me as I imagined he would a loathsome insect, but I wasn't afraid. I wrote down everything he spat at me. "Garden Vegetables...Chicken Consommé...Roast Beef *au Jus*.... Did you get that? *Au Jus! J. U. S. JUS!*"

"I have it," I said, holding out my pad. I wasn't afraid, because I expected a man in authority to act this way. I assumed that, like my father, he would be appeased if I did everything the way he wanted.

In the office, I rolled a blank stencil into the typewriter and flipped the lever so my keystrokes would bypass the ribbon and strike the sheet, making sharp impressions of the letters. When I finished typing, Mrs. Comitor showed me how to squeeze just the right amount of thick tube-ink onto the mimeograph machine roller. I turned the hand crank, ran off one copy of the lunch menu, and brought it into the kitchen for Lou to approve before I ran off the rest. With a scowl, he started reading. A moment later, a smile began at one corner of his mouth. "OK," he grunted, handing the menu back to me.

The kitchen steward, Mrs. Comitor's son-in-law, told me a few days later that when he saw me walk into the kitchen that first day looking so young, he was sure I'd quit by evening. "We always lose one or two at the beginning of each summer. But you just wrote down what Lou barked at you. You didn't flinch. That's when I knew you'd make it."

During the next two months, the unspoken respect I felt from the kitchen staff for being the only office girl never to cry did much to restore my confidence, as did praise from Mrs. Comitor for "figuring out what to do without being told." But what made me feel really good was operating the switchboard.

Guests received calls on phone extensions in the common areas: lobby, swimming pool, casino. There were also a few extensions on the lawn, scattered among the shade umbrellas and white wooden deck chairs. Whenever a call came in for one of the guests, I put it on hold, turned on the public address system, and picked up the microphone. "Long distance calling Mr. or Mrs. Abe Cohen," I announced with my best diction. "Will Mr. or Mrs. Abe Cohen please pick up the nearest phone." A few seconds after my voice reverberated from loudspeakers all over the grounds, a small metal flag on the switchboard popped up to indicate that someone, somewhere, had picked up a phone. I flipped a lever and said, "Main Desk. May I help you?" When a man's voice said, "This is Mr. Cohen," I said, "One moment, please, Mr. Cohen." I flipped another lever to connect him to his party, said, "Go ahead, please," then waited to hear them exchange hellos before I clicked myself off.

I loved everything about my job and strove to be the best office girl in the world.

WHEN I WORKED THE EVENING SHIFT, I was free until four. On those days, wearing a bathing suit under my shorts and shirt, I would walk through the vacant meadow beyond the pool until I reached a rushing river. I packed carefully for these outings: crayons and paper, writing pad, pen, novel, buttered rolls from breakfast. I spread my towel under my favorite tree and let myself become part of the river bank: the sunshine-shadow dance that moved over the ground each time the leaves stirred overhead; the dragonflies hovering low near the water's edge, their lacey wings moving so fast they appeared almost still; the occasional plop of a frog jumping into the water. Then I opened my book.

Whenever I felt a tug from Inside, I didn't have to hold it in, the way I did around the staff and guests. Here I could let the book drop and follow the pull. Sometimes it was to suck my thumb while I watched a tiny white butterfly float in the air over a clump of orange and green jewelweed, or color a bright design with my crayons, or compose a poem, or write a letter to Dr. Hirschhorn. Sometimes the tug was the pain in the center of my chest, and I would become paralyzed on my towel, the way I did in my armchair at home. Here, where there was no mirror, I attached my eyes to the rock in the middle of the river, and soon the water filled with the Atmosphere people and pulled me in. I melted into the rock and felt the water foam over and around me, over and around, until the pain went away and my legs and arms could move again. Then my eyes let go of the rock, and I continued reading where I was, under the tree.

Other times, when I wanted to cool off, I left my moccasins at the water's edge and waded into the river, each step on the stony bottom bringing me deeper into the cold water. I stopped when it was up to my neck. Feet planted firmly, I turned upstream and felt the water rush against the front of my body. I turned downstream and felt it rush against my back. The river foamed a little less when it pushed past me than it did when it pushed past the rock, but I was definitely something it recognized. I was real.

THAT SUMMER I HAD A BOYFRIEND, my first. Fred, the curly-haired director of the day camp, doubled as social director for the adults and came to the office window several times a day to ask for the microphone. One afternoon, after he finished his announcement, he leaned over the sill, whistle dangling from the lanyard on his neck, to replace the microphone on the switchboard table behind me. The hairs on his suntanned arm brushed my arm like a feather. As he straightened up, he asked, "Would you like to go to the movies tonight?"

That day set the pattern for the rest of the summer. Fred asked me out several times a week, and I always said yes. Back in the office girls' cabin, I chose one of my fancy dresses and put on stockings and high heels. Fred, in a button-down shirt and sport jacket, would be in the hotel lobby when I got there, mingling with guests in evening dress who were waiting for the dining room to open. He took his leave of them and we drove away in his car. Dinner in a nearby restaurant was most often a sausage hero dripping with tomato sauce for him, and, for me, spaghetti and meatballs, a welcome change from the hotel's kosher boiled beef flanken. Afterward, we went to a movie or the Monticello Raceway, or played miniature golf.

Other than our conversation that first evening—I told him I was 18, a freshman at Brooklyn College, and had one brother; he told me he was 22, a high school English teacher in Englewood, New Jersey, and had one sister—I didn't have much to say on our dates. Most of the time, I had the same little-girl-out-of-place feeling I did the few times I'd sat by the pool with the guests, waiters, and busboys. But Fred had formed his impression of me from bantering at the office window, where, with my switchboard and typewriter props, I felt grownup and sure of myself.

When we gossiped about hotel goings-on I felt competent enough, but I didn't know the names of movie stars, except for Elizabeth Taylor, who was supposed to be the most beautiful woman in the world, and Rock Hudson, the handsomest man. I had no idea what either looked like. Movies were hard for me to follow, because I didn't always recognize faces of people I didn't know well, and if the characters changed clothes, I sometimes didn't realize they were the same person. To camouflage that, I took my cues from the rest of the audience, laughing or sucking in my breath when they did. Miniature golf was easier, because there was something to do.

The only place I was completely comfortable with Fred was afterward, when he drove his car down a deserted road and we necked. Something changed in me then, the same way it had at my Sweet Sixteen party, when it was as if a different person emerged from within me and stepped into the role I had been trying to play. Here, I didn't have to know movie actors or rock-and-roll songs to be part of Fred's world. He guided my hands where he wanted me to touch him, moaned and trembled, and was so vulnerable that I felt protective of him. This was the part of the evening I most looked forward to—when, without words, he held me close, as if he cared about me. After the first few dates, I planned for it when I chose my clothes. A dress that zipped up the back was better than one that zipped up the side, easier for him to get to my bra strap.

IT WAS A GOOD SUMMER: exhausting sometimes, but one that restored my confidence and made me feel I was part of the regular world in a way I never had before. I was especially pleased when, as the Labor Day weekend drew to a close, Mrs. Comitor invited me to return the following summer.

Fred helped me load my suitcases into Rose's husband's car for the ride back to Brooklyn. "I'll call you soon," he said, then leaned through the car window and kissed me. ▪

CHAPTER 9

Beethoven's Fifth

I TURNED UP THE VOLUME on the hi-fi in Marvin's room, set Beethoven's Fifth on the spindle, and raced to the mirror in my room just in time to raise my arms and bring the orchestra in with a flourish. *Da-da-da-Daaah*. Pencil-baton in hand, arms bent at the elbow, I turned my body to cue in the strings, winds, brass, as they tossed *Da-da-da-Daaahs* back and forth before uniting in one so loud the apartment walls quivered.

Weekday mornings, my mother and father were at work, and Marvin, a year behind me in Brooklyn College, left for class earlier than I did. Today, as on most days, I conducted the entire 32-minute symphony: flicks of my wrist in the delicate parts, more elbow in the loud ones, full shoulder for the giant swells—always with the clear beat I had learned years earlier in conducting class at music camp. I made eye contact with myself in the mirror, but it was the orchestra members' eyes that looked back at me. We moved and breathed as one through every crescendo, diminuendo, staccato, and fermata. My muscles and bones vibrated. The hole in the center of my chest filled with majesty and power.

When the last resounding chord faded, I felt full, satisfied, ready to ride my bike the three miles to campus for my appointment with my advisor. It was the second half of my sophomore year, and his letter had said it was time I declared a major.

After my calculus debacle, I'd given up pre-med. Since then, I had been registering for one or two required liberal arts subjects each term, along with whatever literature courses fit around them.

If I could accumulate credits by curling up in my armchair to lose myself in the worlds of Hardy, Austen, Wharton, Twain, and Hawthorne, so much the better. I still cared about grades but was no longer devastated by a B or C.

Scanning the list of requirements my advisor showed me for various majors, I realized I'd already fulfilled many for the English department's American Literature subdivision.

"English with a concentration in American Literature," I said.

"And your minor?"

I hadn't known I needed one. "Can I tell you tomorrow?"

"No later."

That was easy, I thought as I crossed the quadrangle to my French class.

The professor was younger and more fashionable than my other teachers, with dark, pixie-cut hair and a short-sleeved pullover that left the tattooed numbers on her arm exposed. Each time I saw them, I wondered how she'd gotten from a Nazi concentration camp to Brooklyn College. The girl next to me wore a long paisley skirt and silver filigree earrings. I was in my customary black knee-length skirt and black turtleneck jersey, with a necklace of wooden beads and earrings to match. The professor was talking about Molière. *Social satire*, my hand wrote in a notebook filled with many handwritings and an occasional word in Gregg stenography.

The room seemed to change size. Now it was like a miniature stereopticon scene. The pixie professor was smaller and farther away. The chairs in front of me, along with the students sitting in them, were smaller. I glanced to the side. The bohemian-looking girl was close and not smaller. In the tiny room she was grotesque. A hand was still writing in my notebook. It was not smaller, either. I felt unreal, but I wasn't frightened. This never lasted long. "*Examen jeudi prochain*," the professor said. Test next Thursday, the large hand wrote.

The world was back to the right size by the time I met Susan in the Sugar Bowl for lunch. Over a chicken salad sandwich and vanilla malted, I told her I had to choose a minor.

"Take some education courses," she said. "You might want to teach one day. I'll tell you who the good professors are."

I was never going to teach, but it was as good a choice as any.

After my last class, I started for home down Avenue I, easier for bikes than the bus route on Avenue J. I also wanted to avoid passing

Dr. Hirschhorn's house, which was on J. Seeing it even from the outside made her in-person version too real and woke up the pain in my chest. On Avenue I, she stayed in the Atmosphere, where I needed her to be.

Nothing much had changed in the three and a half years I'd been seeing her. All through the week, outside of sessions, I felt the Atmosphere Dr. Hirschhorn watching over me, knowing everything I was thinking and feeling. As soon as I walked into her office, the Atmosphere vanished, and I felt like a little girl sitting across from a big, intimidating lady. I longed for her to care about me the way her Atmosphere version did. That longing, mixed with my fear, virtually immobilized me, and I barely changed position once I sat down. I knew it would help if I talked and always resolved beforehand that this time would be different. It never happened. I was able to answer questions like "What did you do last weekend?" but I had no words for the feeling inside that was so huge I felt I would burst. The bigger it got, the more danger I perceived myself in, and the more frozen I became.

NO LONGER had a boyfriend.

For six months after my first summer at the hotel, Fred had called every other Wednesday. Our conversation was always the same.

"How's everything?" he would ask.

"Fine."

"What's new?"

I would tell him about an activity I thought made me sound regular: the volunteer work Susan and I did through the college's Social Service Club; or something that happened in the college orchestra, where I played viola and Marvin played flute. I didn't have to say much, just a minute's filler before he asked, "Would you like to go out Saturday?"

After I said yes, he'd tell me what time he would come by, and we hung up.

Fred always chose our activity. It was usually in Manhattan: dinner, then either a play or movie. Afterward, we drove to Plumb Beach in Brooklyn, near Sheepshead Bay. There he found a spot in the long row of cars parked at the edge of the sand, each filled with one or two couples.

At the hotel, Fred and I had lived in the same environment, known the same people, had the same boss. The competent office-girl me felt comfortable talking with the head-counselor Fred, so it didn't matter much that when we went out, I didn't feel like his equal. And at the hotel, Fred seemed like a continuous person. I knew the process by which he transformed himself from the sweaty counselor in shorts to the meticulously groomed date who picked me up in the hotel lobby. "Have to shit, shower, and shave," he would say as he leaned in through the office window. "See you in a little while."

In the city, Fred had materialized every other week, as if from nowhere. I saw him only in dress-up mode. About his life I knew nothing except that he lived with his father and sister in Englewood, New Jersey, and taught English in a nearby high school.

Because we spent two hours of each date driving—from my house to Manhattan, from Manhattan to Plumb Beach, from Plumb Beach back to my house—there were long stretches to fill with conversation. Having no common hotel gossip to fall back on, I was happy to let the car radio fill the silences. Fred roamed the dial freely—a privilege I still didn't allow myself—stopping at rock-and-roll, talk shows, and news. I was surprised the first time I realized he didn't consider news an annoying interruption but actually listened to it.

One evening, the newscaster was talking about Lumumba and Kasavubu, political rivals, both claiming control of the newly independent Republic of the Congo. Fred took one hand from the steering wheel to lower the volume.

"Wanna hear this comedy routine I made up while I was driving to your house?" he asked.

"Sure," I said, suddenly realizing there was a process by which Fred materialized at my door. He drove alone in his car across the George Washington Bridge, down the West Side Highway, through the Battery Tunnel, and down the Belt Parkway. It felt like new knowledge, even though I had been the one to give him directions the first time.

"A spaceship lands in the Congo," Fred said. "An alien gets out. He walks up to the first man he sees and says, 'Take me to your leader.' The man starts toward Lumumba. He doubles back toward Kasavubu. He keeps going back and forth, stumbling all over himself. The alien watches in amazement."

Fred stopped. I figured the joke was over.

"That's a good one," I said.

In the restaurant, Fred might tell me something he had heard on Jean Shepherd's radio show, or something about the play we were about to see—*The Hostage* or *The Fantasticks*. I might tell him about a paper I had to write. Once, fork in hand, he said he hoped to become a principal in a few years.

"Don't you have to take a test?" I asked, trying to sound knowledgeable, "and doesn't it take a long time?" My mother had studied for years and was finally an assistant principal. Soon she would begin preparing for the principal's exam.

"No test," Fred said, "and it doesn't take long. All you have to do is get good recommendations. My principal will write me one."

They must have different rules in New Jersey, I thought. "Good luck," I said.

"Thanks."

It didn't occur to me that Fred actually liked the theater. I had never had a boyfriend before and assumed that's what everyone did on dates, whether they liked it or not: the boy showed up with tickets, told you what you were going to see, picked out the restaurant, and paid for everything.

Plays were as hard for me to understand as movies. There was little action, so you had to figure out the story from the dialogue. If there were two actors about the same age with the same color hair, I often couldn't tell who was who when they changed clothes. In order not to seem different, I did what I'd done in the movies, laughed or gasped in the same places the rest of the audience did.

At Plumb Beach, though, I didn't feel different. As soon as we parked, Fred said, "Why don't you find your station now?" While he pushed back the seat, I turned the dial until WNYC's classical music filled the car.

We would remain as we had been for a moment, facing forward, then turn our heads and lean across the space for a first, tentative kiss. I was watching myself have a boyfriend.

Fred slid out from behind the wheel, slipped his arm around me, pulled me to him. I felt the satisfying pressure of his body, his scratchy cheek, his need of me. I was watching from closer now.

Hands on top of clothes, moving lightly, pressing more, slipping underneath. Bodies sliding down to lying down. Fumbling with zippers, hooks, belts, buttons.

We glided against each other. Slowly at first, then faster. Through clothes, not through clothes, but never going all the way. I was still a virgin.

Fred was hard, strong. Then soft, weak. All in response to me. I felt the miracle of it. I was real, a woman, and he was a boy-man, moaning, vulnerable, trusting. My body felt good, too, though I couldn't let myself go the way he did, couldn't put myself in his power the way he put himself in mine.

We lay together quietly, breath fogging windows, classical music—my music—on the radio, soft stickiness still warm between our pressed-together bodies. This was the time I liked best, the only time I wasn't watching at all.

Fred checked his watch but didn't talk. The music held us.

He checked again. "We better go now," he said, sitting up. And I knew it was 1:40. He was diligent about getting me home in time for my 2:00 curfew.

I would find the tissues I'd stowed in my coat pocket and give him half. Privately, no longer together, we each cleaned ourselves. The stickiness was cold now, something messy to wipe off. I was watching again.

We would close zippers, straighten clothes. Fred moved the seat forward, started the car. The only thing left of our togetherness was the radio, still on my station.

Seventy-fourth Street was dark and silent when Fred double-parked in front of my house at exactly 2:00. We kissed perfunctorily, with the motor on.

"Bye," I said.

"Bye." He leaned across me to open my door, then watched from the car to make sure I got into the house.

As I walked up the stairs to my apartment, I knew he had already changed the station, just as I knew it would be two weeks before I saw him again. I would let myself in with my key, slip the chain lock into its groove—my father left it unchained on nights I went out—and tiptoe to my room so my heels wouldn't wake anyone.

I often wondered whether Fred had another girlfriend he saw on the in-between Saturdays.

"Next time he calls, tell him you're busy," Gloria advised after a few months. Of all my friends, none of whom had met Fred, she was the most experienced in love. "You have to shake him up."

When the phone rang two weeks later at his usual time, I lifted the receiver and said hello, nervous sweat pouring from my underarms.

"How's everything?" Fred said.

"Fine."

"What's new."

"Nothing."

"Would you like to go out Saturday?"

"I can't. I'm busy."

I waited for him to say, "Then can I see you next week?" But when he finally spoke, he said, "Have a good time."

"Thanks," I said.

I called Gloria to report. She congratulated me and said Fred would surely call in a few days.

He didn't. Nor did he call in a few weeks. Gloria said some boys took longer than others.

I finally realized Fred was never going to call. I wished I could undo our last conversation, wished I could have our times at Plumb Beach back again, when he held me close and I felt special to him. I called Gloria and cried. "It's better you found out now than later," she said.

"Come with us to frat parties," my other friends said. I did, and a few dates resulted, but nothing lasting. I missed Fred.

It was awkward at the hotel the following summer, with Fred there, too. During July I had another boyfriend and was glad Fred knew, but the relationship lasted only a month. Now I was going to frat parties again. My heart wasn't in them, though. I much preferred staying home and reading novels.

"WHEN ARE YOU GOING to let the pearls drop from your mouth?" Dr. Hirschhorn asked toward the end of the hour.

My 19-year-old brain recognized that she was annoyed. My heart, which felt like a first-grader's, exploded with pain far worse than what I had felt over losing Fred.

"Well?" she prompted.

"I don't know," I managed to whisper.

We sat in silence for a long moment. The disapproval pouring into me from her green eyes turned the yearning little girl into the worm you poke with a stick.

Dr. Hirschhorn looked at her clock. "It's time to stop," she said, her sarcasm gone.

I rose, stiff from not having moved for most of the previous 50 minutes, hugged my books to my chest, and walked to the door.

"I'll see you next week," she said. I nodded.

On my walk home, the Atmosphere Dr. Hirschhorn returned. She knew how bad I felt because of what the in-person Dr. Hirschhorn had said, and her understanding made me feel better. She was with me all through the week, until my next session, when the in-person Dr. Hirschhorn came to get me from the waiting room. I walked into her office with the same hope I'd had for four years: that this time would be different and I would be able to talk. We took our customary seats: I, in the chair that felt too big, my books on my lap; she, in the swivel chair next to her desk.

She picked up the handkerchief, dabbed her nose, and turned to me. "How are you today?"

"Fine."

Dr. Hirschhorn looked at me for what felt like a long time before she said, "What does *fine* mean?"

Her voice was hard. Watch out. "I don't know."

Another pause. "Why do you come here?"

For four years, I'd been certain Dr. Hirschhorn knew I waited all week to see her, that I longed for her to find the me who communicated only with the mirror people and the Atmosphere people, that I needed her to feel the anguish and loneliness and emptiness. I was certain because she was part of me and I was part of her. I was certain even now, so I discounted her annoyance and didn't connect it to the pain I felt.

"I asked why you come to see me."

I couldn't have explained even if she hadn't been scary. "I don't know."

She leaned forward. "If you say, 'I don't know' one more time, you can't come here anymore."

I didn't want to lose her, so I didn't say "I don't know" for the rest of the session. I said nothing, just moved my eyes, through which I tried to talk to her.

"Why do you swirl your eyes?"

I didn't want to say "I don't know," so I shrugged.

Somehow, we got to the part where Dr. Hirschhorn said, "It's time to stop."

I walked out of her office, feeling like a mechanized alien. My robot legs carried me down the carpeted staircase, past the European murmuring, through the door to the street. Only when I was outside did I realize I had barely been taking in air.

As I began the walk home, I saw with sudden clarity that all Dr. Hirschhorn had heard for four years whenever I whispered, "I don't know" was *I don't know*. Up to then, I believed she knew that not every "I don't know" was the same. Each was the specific answer to her specific question, a different cry from my heart to hers. I believed she somehow understood the translation. Now I knew she never had.

For the first time in the minutes following a session, I didn't feel the Atmosphere Dr. Hirschhorn in the air around me. But I didn't need her. I wasn't a worm anymore. Nor was I a yearning little girl. I was a mommy whose job it was to protect that little girl from ever having to sit in that big chair again.

When I got home, I phoned Dr. Hirschhorn. "I quit," I said in a firm voice she had never heard. "I'm not coming next week. Or ever."

"OK," she said, not unkindly. "Good luck to you."

CHAPTER 10

Lost Child

FOR WEEKS AFTER I STOPPED seeing Dr. Hirschhorn, I felt lighter than I had in a long time. With her in-person version gone, there was nothing to puncture her Atmosphere version. It remained pure, watching over me, understanding everything.

Then, without warning, the good feeling disappeared. I began feeling unreal for longer periods, as if I were watching my look-alike go to classes, frat parties, orchestra rehearsals. Inside my head, there was a constant background of low-level noise. I ignored it, the way I did static on a radio station, but it put layers between me and any outside person I talked to.

More often than before, I became paralyzed in the middle of doing something ordinary and remained stuck in an uncomfortable position. To extricate myself, I would concentrate, willing motion into my right hand until the fingers began to move, slowly, like underwater tentacles. Next, I turned my hand palm up, palm down, watching my arm pivot at the elbow. I repeated the process with my left hand and arm, and when they were working, turned my attention to my legs. The whole reconstitution process could take 10 or 15 minutes. I automatically snapped out of whatever state I was in if someone approached or spoke to me, but it was like doing a quick costume change.

By fall, four months after my last session with Dr. Hirschhorn, I was having such a difficult time keeping my Inside world from obliterating my Outside world that I knew I needed to see a therapist again.

I talked to my psych-major friend Linda, who knew, as all my friends did, that I'd been seeing a psychoanalyst. None of them ever asked why. Analysis was fashionable. There was no stigma attached to it. I'd once told Linda I felt I was in suspended animation, stored in a spore, waiting for the proper conditions so I could resume life, and she seemed to get it. Now, when I mentioned that I was looking for a therapist, she suggested her professor, Dr. Sacker, who had a private practice. "I think you'd like him," she said, "but you can sit in on one of my classes and decide for yourself."

THE MURMUR IN THE CLASSROOM quieted, and I turned to see a man—Dr. Sacker, I presumed—hoist himself through the doorway on crutches. He looked comfortably old, definitely in his thirties, handsome in the way President Kennedy was, with a shock of brown hair over a squarish face. His slow pace, together with his charcoal gray suit, light blue shirt, and dark tie, gave him a stately air.

"What happened to you, Professor?" a boy called out.

"You won't believe this," Dr. Sacker said with the warmest smile I had ever seen on a man: a complete smile, spreading to his eyes and forehead. "I was smoking while I was driving and an ash fell onto my pants. I looked down to flick it off and hit a tree. The moral of the story is don't take your eyes off the road, even for a second."

I liked his easygoing manner and his teaching style. He didn't lecture but had a dialogue with the students, illustrating his points with interesting examples from his private practice. That night, I called him to schedule an appointment.

DR. SACKER'S OFFICE was in an apartment house a few blocks from campus. It was a studio, he'd said, with no waiting room. If I came early, I was to wait in the hall outside his door without ringing the bell. I checked my watch when I arrived—five minutes to go—put my books down on the floor and leaned against the wall.

Almost immediately, I felt the same stirring I used to feel in Dr. Hirschhorn's waiting room: a craving to be seen and heard. But this was not a private space, where it was safe to let Inside have free rein. I heard sounds from the apartments around me. A cough. A radio.

The stirring faded and the unreal feeling returned. I wound my hair around my index finger and held onto the coil tightly, to ground myself. A door slammed down the hall, and a woman wheeling an empty shopping cart rounded the bend. She nodded, acknowledging my existence, making me real. She pressed the button for the elevator, then disappeared when it came, taking my realness with her.

The doorknob next to me clicked. I let go of my hair, grabbed my books, and stood to the side, stiff at attention. A sliver of light appeared.

"Good luck tomorrow." I recognized Dr. Sacker's voice.

"Yeah. Thanks." The sliver widened and a boy walked out. Crew neck sweater. Pimples. Books. Probably a Brooklyn College student. He turned toward the elevator.

Dr. Sacker came into the hall on his crutches. "Hi," he said with the same smile he'd given his class, but this time it was for me. "Come on in."

I stepped into a room that seemed flooded with light. Parquet floor. Modern furniture, black and brown. Abstract art, also black and brown.

"I remember you," Dr. Sacker said. "You came to my class."

He'd noticed me! "Right. With my friend Linda."

I registered more details: Black leather armchair, probably for him. Black-and-brown striped couch, probably for me. Between them, a coffee table with a hand-carved marble chess set, whites and blacks set up on an inlaid wooden board. Ceramic ashtray. Pack of cigarettes. Lighter.

"Have a seat," he said, indicating the couch with his chin as he hobbled to the armchair. He laid his crutches on the floor, rested his leg on the coffee table, and leaned back. His informality put me at ease. I couldn't imagine Dr. Hirschhorn ever putting her leg up, even if it was broken.

I slid my books off my lap and stacked them on the couch, something I'd never done in her office, then sat forward on the cushion. Dr. Sacker looked at me with friendly brown eyes, and I wondered how to begin.

"I was seeing another therapist, but I stopped last spring," I said.

"Yeah?" It was a friendly, *go-on* yeah, very Brooklyn, nothing like Dr. Hirschhorn's formal "Yes?"

"I don't know what else to say."

"Why did you stop seeing her?"

"I couldn't talk to her."

"How come?"

"I don't know." Oh god. Please don't let the I-don't-knows happen here. I like this man.

"What made you want to see someone else now?"

I told him about the mirror, easier to describe than the different states I was always slipping in and out of, or the pain in the center of my chest. Dr. Sacker looked at me intently, as if he cared and was trying to understand. I didn't know therapy could feel like this.

"Do you still see faces in the mirror?" he asked.

"Sometimes."

"Who are they?"

"I don't know." This, too, wasn't the Dr. Hirschhorn kind of *I don't know*. To my relief, Dr. Sacker didn't seem annoyed.

"Do you mind if I have a cigarette?" he asked.

"No."

He lit one and tilted his head up toward the ceiling to blow out the smoke. "Tell me a little about your family."

Reporting was easy. My mother was an assistant principal. My father worked in the post office. My brother was a year behind me in Brooklyn College. Through the haze of smoke, we went on to neutral topics, like what courses I was taking. When it was time to stop, I made another appointment.

Dr. Sacker accompanied me to the door. "See you next week," he said.

I tried to ignore the woman who stepped from the shadows as I walked out, and to erase Dr. Sacker's "Hi, Celia. Come on in." I didn't like to think of someone else sitting on the couch I had just occupied.

I DIDN'T WANT TO TELL MY MOTHER I was seeing another therapist, so in order to pay Dr. Sacker, I found a job collating book pages for a man who wrote summaries of textbooks and sold them to college bookstores. I earned a dollar an hour. Dr. Sacker's fee was $15 for a 50-minute session. It was hard to work 15 hours a week and still do my coursework, but I preferred that to the weeks there wasn't enough collating work and I had to dip into the $10 my mother gave me for lunch, bus fare, and small expenses.

I never talked to Dr. Sacker about money. The me who worried about it was separate from the me who sat across from him. That me didn't know I was paying for the understanding in his eyes. I needed to keep it that way. At the end of each session, as we stood at the door and he said, "Bye, Kiddo, see you next week," my hand took an envelope from my bag and handed it to him below the beam of our eyes. I was always disconcerted when he made the exchange official by saying, "Thank you."

As with Dr. Hirschhorn, I had two separate relationships with Dr. Sacker. His Atmosphere version was with me all the time and knew everything I thought and felt. His in-person version knew things only if I told him. But unlike Dr. Hirschhorn, the in-person Dr. Sacker wasn't intimidating, and I was able to talk to him freely.

At first, it was only to relate facts. "My mother got mad because I didn't tuck in my blouse when I went out to eat with her and her friends. I tried to explain that was the style, but she cried and said I always try to embarrass her."

After a few weeks, I felt safe enough to venture beyond facts.

"I don't feel real," I said one day.

"What's that like?" Dr. Sacker asked, looking at me with thoughtful eyes.

Inside began to stir. Outside pushed Inside back down so I could keep talking. "As if I'm watching myself from someplace outside myself. I hate that feeling."

"What makes it happen?"

"I don't know."

The in-person Dr. Sacker seemed so much like the Atmosphere Dr. Sacker that it wasn't long before I began to feel as comfortable in his office as I did in my armchair at home.

"My brother's turning eighteen, and he wants to get a driver's license," I said one day. It was the start of the session, and I was sitting up straight with my feet on the floor.

"Yeah?" Dr. Sacker reached for the cigarette pack while his eyes held mine.

"My mother said he could."

"What about your father?" Still looking at me, he shook out a cigarette and picked up the lighter.

"It's my mother's car. My father doesn't know how to drive. He thinks cars are dangerous."

"Yeah?" He lit the cigarette and exhaled toward the ceiling.

I relaxed into the familiar smoke smell, slipping my feet out of my moccasins and drawing them up onto the cushion to sit cross-legged. "When my mother wanted to buy a car, my father said he would leave if she did."

"So what happened?"

"She bought it without telling him. A fifty-eight Ford Fairlane. She parked it on the street. For three weeks, everyone except my father knew the light-blue car was ours. My grandparents, my aunts, my uncles, my cousins. Then he found out. He yelled for a few days, but he didn't leave. That was four years ago. Now he's used to the fact of the car, but he never rides in it. He takes the bus or train wherever he goes, and if my mother's going, too, she leaves the car at home."

"Your father is a very scared person," Dr. Sacker said.

"He's not scared. He just scares everyone else."

"Only a scared person becomes a tyrant."

Inside heard Dr. Sacker say *tyrant*. He understood.

The pain started in one small place in the center of my chest. I didn't try to push it away. It was safe here. Within seconds, it expanded out to the edges and down into my belly. I slumped forward, head so low it almost touched the striped couch cushion.

"It hurts," I murmured in Outside words. English, for the in-person Dr. Sacker.

"What hurts?" His voice was gentle.

"My chest." The closest word, but not exact.

"Are you sick?"

"No."

"What does it feel like?"

There were no English words to describe the gnawing ache. "Ishpoosh, gunna gunna."

"Vivian?"

"Gunna-gunna. Gunna-gunna-gunna."

Through eye slits, I saw the bottom of Dr. Sacker's sweater and the tops of his knees. I smelled the cigarette smoke that cocooned me into him. It was OK that I couldn't talk. The in-person Dr. Sacker had melded into the Atmosphere Dr. Sacker. He knew what I was feeling.

My head dropped lower. My hair fell forward, making a curtain around my face. There was a piece of white lint off-center on one of the cushion stripes. I stared at it. Became hypnotized by it. Began to merge with it. Now I was embalmed in it. Safely paralyzed. The pain was gone. I didn't blink. If I took my eyes off the lint for one second, I would disappear.

"Vivian?"

I had no way of answering, but that was OK. He knew I was in the lint.

"Vivian?"

I tightened the muscles of my throat and squeezed out a "Yeah?"

"I want to buy a present for my wife, but I don't know how women's sizes run. Can you help me?"

That was a question for Outside. I sprang up, pain-free, pushed the hair out of my eyes, and met his gaze squarely. It was a strange question for a therapist to ask, I thought, but one I could answer.

"There are two systems," I said in my clear Outside voice. "One has numbers like twelve, fourteen, sixteen, and the other has numbers like thirty-two, thirty-four, thirty-six."

Dr. Sacker nodded. The me who did research in the library realized this was a test. He was trying to ascertain my mental state.

Outside continued talking. "Twelve is roughly equivalent to thirty-two. Just to give you an idea, I wear a small size. Twelve."

"That helps a lot."

"Is it all you wanted to know?"

"Yeah. Thanks."

Outside's job was finished. Inside returned. My muscles went slack and I fell against the back of the couch, eyes half closed. The pain was back. I couldn't move or make it go away. I wasn't in the lint anymore.

"It hurts," I said in a voice that sounded far away, even to me. "I need morphine."

"What hurts?"

"I need morphine." I couldn't explain, but I didn't have to. He knew.

THE MORE COMFORTABLE I FELT with Dr. Sacker, the more Inside emerged during sessions. Sometimes all I could do was spout nonsense syllables or moan, yet moments later we could be having a normal conversation. Sometimes I tore a sheet of paper from my spiral notebook and wrote disconnected phrases upside down and sideways, then splashed scribble on top of them. It never occurred to me that Dr. Sacker might be perplexed. I was sure he understood me completely. At home, I wrote him letters, not only facts, but how I felt.

> *My brain is made of orange juice. If I tilt my head, it will spill, so I have to walk very carefully.*

I wrote the letters to the in-person Dr. Sacker, to help him know what the Atmosphere Dr. Sacker already knew. I mailed them as soon as I wrote them, sometimes two or three a week, believing that the second I dropped a letter into the mailbox, it became part of the Atmosphere and he knew its contents, with no intervening time needed for delivery or reading. During sessions, I never wanted to discuss the letters. Each contained what I had felt the moment I was writing it. The session was a different moment. After a few tries, Dr. Sacker stopped asking me about them. He would just say, "I got two letters from you this week," and I would nod.

About three months after I started seeing him, Dr. Sacker said, "Would it be all right if I gave you a Rorschach test?"

I had thought he understood me perfectly and was surprised that he needed a test to figure me out. "I guess so."

He took a stack of large rectangular cards from his desk. "I'm going to give you these one at a time. All you have to do is tell me what you see in them."

He handed me the top card, a modern-art looking ink blot that appeared to have been folded in half when it was wet, so one side was the mirror image of the other. It resembled a hideous butterfly. Outside wondered whether Dr. Sacker, pen and pad in hand, expected me to say something about sex. According to what I knew about Freud, everything that stuck out was a penis, and everything with a hole was a vagina. Oh god.

"I don't see anything," I said.

"Take your time. There are no right or wrong answers."

My heart began to pound, and my breath came in pants.

"What are you afraid of?" Dr. Sacker asked.

"I don't know."

"We don't have to do this." He took back the card.

I felt as if I had failed an exam. Worse, I had disappointed Dr. Sacker.

BY THE TIME I'D BEEN SEEING Dr. Sacker four months, I had used up whatever money I'd managed to save and had to ask for help.

"Mom," I said, coming into the kitchen one day.

She looked up from her papers. "What is it?'

"I just wanted to tell you I'm seeing a therapist."

"Oh?" A pause. "Who is she?"

"He. His name is Dr. Sacker."

My mother put down her pencil. "How did you find him?"

"He's Linda's professor."

I waited for another question, but she was silent. The overhead fluorescent light and all her books and papers made the room seem like an office, in spite of the dishes drying in the rack and the black patch on the sink where years of scouring had worn away the enamel. Finally, she said, "How do you know he's safe?"

"Why wouldn't he be?"

"He's a man."

"So?"

"He might do sexual things to you."

"That's ridiculous. I just wanted to know whether you'd pay for it."

"I have to think about that. I'd like to talk to him first."

She hadn't said no. I gave her his number.

The next time I saw Dr. Sacker, he told me about their conversation. My mother had said the only thing the matter with me was that I was upset because I didn't have a date for New Years' Eve. I was astounded.

"You know," Dr. Sacker said, "I used to think your father was your biggest problem. I'm beginning to think your mother is."

"But he's crazy. She's normal."

"I'm not so sure. I have a theory that when two people stay married, they're equally sick or equally healthy, even if it shows in different ways."

That made sense, though I didn't like hearing it.

But from then on, my mother left a check on my desk every week.

WHEN CLASSES BEGAN in the fall of 1963, a year after I began seeing Dr. Sacker, I focused on my day-to-day assignments as if this were an ordinary semester, not the last before I graduated. I hadn't given thought to a career since I gave up pre-med four years before, but now I had to make a choice. Neither of the customary options for women—teaching and nursing—was appealing.

My mother didn't try to influence me, and my father wasn't around. Since his retirement the year before, he'd taken several trips, each lasting a few months, mostly to places where they spoke another language. This time it was to Majorca. I had accumulated the minimum number of education credits required for a substitute teacher's license, so when my friends urged me to join them in a career seminar for would-be teachers, I did. A seminar was not a commitment.

The professor running it spent a good deal of time telling us how to get hired. "You want the interviewer to feel you'll give your full attention to teaching. If you have long hair and wear it loose, it gives the impression that it needs a lot of care, even though it might not. Put it up in a bun or a French twist." She wrote the address for requesting Board of Ed applications on the blackboard and, in the weeks that followed, spurred us on. "Did you write your letter yet? Have you filled out the license application? Did you receive the date for your oral exam?"

Everyone scrambled to follow her directions, reporting on their progress each time we met. I couldn't picture myself as a teacher—an authority figure—and felt nothing in common with my enthusiastic classmates. Yet I was in an adult body, soon to go on stage and play an adult part. Lacking a script of my own, I followed the professor's: I wrote my letter and received my application. A few weeks later, I found myself sitting across from a gray-haired examiner at the Board of Ed, my hair in a French twist.

"What would you do if you took your class on a trip," he began, "and when it was time to come back, you realized one child was missing?"

"I'd look for him," I said, surprised. I had expected him to ask about teaching theory.

"What if you couldn't find him?"

Was this a trick question? "If there was another teacher with me, I'd send the class back with her. Then I'd go to the police."

"What if it was three o'clock and you had a date with your boyfriend? Would you leave?"

"Of *course* not!"

He pressed me about the lost child for another minute, then said I could go. I walked out certain I had failed.

A week later, I received a letter telling me I would become licensed as a substitute teacher upon getting my bachelor's degree. ▪

CHAPTER 11

Sailboat

AUNT RAE, A GUIDANCE COUNSELOR at P.S. 16, in the Williamsburg section of Brooklyn, said her school had an opening for a second-grade substitute, filling in for someone on maternity leave, and she could get me the position if I wanted it. I told her I did. Mrs. Newman, the principal, hired me sight unseen. When I met her a few day later, she said the class had been "a bit wild" since the teacher left three weeks before, in early January. No sub would return for a second day, so they'd had a succession of teachers. My coming would bring stability. The idea of teaching was still so unreal that I didn't understand the implication.

For my meeting with Mrs. Newman, I'd taken two trains and a bus and saw that if connections weren't smooth, the trip to the other side of Brooklyn could take an hour and a half. My mother offered me the use of her car, a stick shift. I had recently gotten my license, having learned on an automatic. On the Saturday before I was to start, she went with me for a practice run. Traffic was light, and we made it there in half an hour.

I left extra early on Monday, anticipating, correctly, that rush-hour traffic would stretch the trip to an hour. When cars behind me honked—I stalled in the middle of a busy intersection as I attempted to coordinate the clutch and gas pedal—I cried. But once I reached the school, it was as if the ride hadn't happened, and I proceeded confidently to the office. The secretary showed me my mailbox, then directed me to the cafeteria, where, she said, my class would be lined up at the far end. I threaded my way through a noisy, undulating mass of children and found them: not a line, exactly, but a bunch of seven-year-olds running around punching one another.

"Hello, class," I said, trying to make myself heard. "I'm Miss Conan, your new teacher."

A few kids stopped to listen. I asked which staircase we took to our room and they led the way. I fumbled with my key and opened the door.

As 30 children surged in, I looked around. Moveable desks and chairs. When I had gone to elementary school, they'd been bolted to the floor. A blotter atop a massive wooden teacher's desk. Blackboard with a chalk ledge along the front wall.

It struck me. *I am a teacher. This is my classroom. This is my class.*

The boys had flung their coats to the floor and were chasing one another, leapfrog style, across the tops of the desks. The girls, most of them seated, were talking in groups. I had only minored in Ed and hadn't done student teaching. I wished I knew what children were supposed to learn in second grade.

"Hello again," I said. "I'm Miss Conan, your new teacher."

They quieted. All the boys took seats except one.

"I know you've had a difficult few weeks, but that's over now, because I'm going to be your teacher until June." I didn't know what to say next.

"Teecha," a girl called out. "You're supposed to take attendance."

"Right," I said, looking toward my desk.

"You wan' me to show you the book?"

"Yes, thank you."

She walked importantly to my desk, took a thin book from one corner, and handed it to me.

Happy to have something teacherlike to do, I called out 30 names and began associating them with faces. I learned that André, the boy walking around, was the only one without an assigned seat. "He's a fighter," the other children explained, so he was allowed to sit wherever he wanted. If someone else happened to be in the seat he chose, that person had to get up. The children seemed to accept this arrangement. I thought it strange but decided to let it stand.

"Teecha, there's a bad word on the board." A girl's voice.

I turned and saw FUCK printed in sloppy letters.

"Who wrote that?" I asked.

No response. I took the black felt eraser from the chalk ledge, wiped off the word, then faced the class. A few children giggled.

"Teecha," a boy called, "there's another bad word."

This time it was SHIT. I'd seen no one get up. How had it gotten there? I asked, received no answer, and erased it.

The room erupted. The boys resumed chasing one another across the desktops. This time, some girls joined them. When one child caught another, they fell to the floor and began fighting. Part of me knew I was supposed to be in charge and wondered what I could to do bring the class under control. Another part felt the terror I'd felt as a little girl when Freddy, the neighborhood bully, threatened to beat me up if I tried to ride my tricycle past his house. Three boys ran out the door. My first impulse was to chase after them, but if I did, I would have to leave the others alone. I stayed in the room.

In the melee, children began tugging at my clothes to get my attention. "Teecha, he pushed me." "Teecha, there's a bad word on the board." "Teecha, he took my pencil."

As the tidal wave rolled over me, I addressed the only thing I felt I could do something about: the bad words. Each time one appeared, I asked who did it, got no answer, and erased it, only to have another appear. I was momentarily relieved when the runaways returned. The class was still leapfrogging across desks, punching one another, and throwing books, but at least they were all in the room.

I felt as if my lungs were filling with water. When it seemed as if I had only one more breath left, I walked over to the girl who had shown me the attendance book and said, with all the authority I could muster, "Go across the hall to the guidance office and get Mrs. Maresco."

A minute later, Aunt Rae came into the room. "What's going on here?" she asked the class with mock severity, smiling at them. "Eugene, when I spoke to you with your mother last week, you said you were going to try to be good." Eugene looked at her sheepishly and slipped into his seat. "Gail, *you* know you're not supposed to do that!" There was love in her voice for the mischievous girl, and Gail, too, sat down. I watched in amazement as one by one, the children took their seats. Then Aunt Rae conducted a lively discussion about how it felt to misbehave. She made the children squirm with what looked like a mixture of pleasure and chagrin as they realized she saw through them. When she left my room ten minutes later, each child was sitting, quiet and attentive. A moment later, pandemonium returned.

During lunch break, I took refuge in the guidance office, not feeling entitled or able to join the conversation in the teachers' lounge. Aunt Rae gave me a few tips and assured me things would get better. All too soon, it was time to leave this oasis of plants and artwork and return to my class.

The children were even more charged up in the afternoon, but something in me had shifted. I felt as if I were watching the wild scene through a pane of glass. Calmly, I sat on the edge of the teacher's desk and began reading a storybook aloud, pretending it was more for myself than the class. It was so noisy that only the children closest to me could hear. They began to follow along. The small quiet zone they created allowed the children behind them to listen. Pretending not to notice the change that was rippling out to the edges of the room, I kept reading, holding up the pictures for them to see before I turned each page. By the time I came to the end, the entire class was quiet and seated, including André.

When the story was over, anarchy returned. I realized it hadn't been me who had calmed them, but the story, and felt helpless again.

"Teecha," one of the girls asked when the room seemed about to detonate, "is it time to get Mrs. Maresco?" I nodded. Again Aunt Rae quieted my class, and again the melee resumed when she left.

At 3:00, I dismissed them, only to contend with the clutch, gas pedal, and traffic.

I told my mother it had been "a rough day" and retreated to my room. It felt more like a foxhole than a sanctuary, a place to shelter until tomorrow's battle. I couldn't curl up with a book or do an art project. I couldn't even call Susan or Linda. I didn't have the wherewithal to say *How was your day?* Looking in the mirror as I took the bobby pins out of my hair, I saw a generic face. No yearning came out of her eyes and pulled me into her. No magic happened.

THE NEXT MORNING at P.S. 16, I found a note in my mailbox informing me it was my class's turn to decorate the bulletin board in the hall. When I showed it to Aunt Rae, she said if I had the children make drawings, she would hang them up for me and suggested wind power as a theme.

I conducted an impromptu discussion on types of wind power. The class seemed mildly interested. Then I instructed the first row to draw windmills, the second sailboats, the third kites, and so on.

Paul, in the sailboat row, came up to my desk. "Teecha, can I draw a windmill?"

"No," I said. "You'll draw a sailboat, like everyone else in your row." When he sulked back to his seat and drew a sailboat, I was pleased. I had maintained discipline.

Although the children were proud that their drawings were posted in the hall, most of the time they were still wild. I survived for three days with the help of Aunt Rae. Then I had my regular appointment with Dr. Sacker.

"Why don't you quit?" he asked

"Quit my *job?*"

"Yeah." The smoke widened around his head as it floated to the ceiling.

That would mean reneging on a commitment. "I can't do that."

"Why not?"

I stared at the chess pieces on the coffee table between us. It was an alluring concept, a way to end the nightmare that only a minute ago I had thought would last forever. "Do you think I could really quit?"

"Sure."

Never before had he given me advice or recommended a course of action. This must be more serious than I thought. "I don't know," I whispered, not raising my eyes. "Maybe. I'll think about it."

On the ride home, I considered the idea. On one hand, I was seduced by the prospect of an easy escape. Nothing inside me felt grownup. My tissue-paper teacher costume was all that stood between me and the chaos inside me, which more than matched the chaos in the classroom. On the other, I felt that work was the most important thing in the world, and I had to stay even if it killed me.

I went to bed undecided. I woke certain. As soon as I arrived at the school, I told Mrs. Newman I was quitting but would stay up to two weeks—no longer—to give her time to find another teacher. She tried to convince me to give it one more chance. When I declined, she said she would find someone as soon as possible.

Once I knew I was leaving, I felt like a different person. The next time I heard, *Teecha, there's a bad word on the board*, I looked to see what it was, then glared at the class.

"It says *fuck*," I said, placing particular emphasis on *fuck*.

Instant silence. Even the fights stopped as each child froze in place. With pink chalk, I framed the word. Those who had been running around inched their way back to their seats. I drew a green border around the pink one, and, with exaggerated mannerisms, stood back to survey my artwork.

"Teecha, aren't you going to erase it?" someone asked.

"No. I don't know who put it there, but whoever did obviously wanted it to be there, so it's going to stay there." I heard my voice and was astounded. It was firm, almost threatening.

The children were all in their seats, motionless, staring at the word. For a few minutes, I savored my absolute control. Then, through the small window in the door, I saw what the children could not, Mrs. Newman's pretty blonde head moving down the hall toward my room.

"OK, Irene," I said to the child sitting closest to the board. "I think it's been up there long enough. You can erase it."

The children's relief was palpable as Irene walked to the blackboard, picked up the eraser, and brushed it over the offending word. Just as it disappeared, Mrs. Newman entered. She said hello to the class, called me to the door, and told me she had found a teacher who would start a week from Monday. ▪

CHAPTER 12

Ultimatum

Thursday
Dear Dr. Sacker,
It seems as if I am very far away from everything and I can't find where I should go. Also, I'm afraid to get a job, because I'm afraid I will do something that's not right....
I told my mother I would probably die in a year, but she told me I shouldn't talk that way....
Sometimes I talk in the mirror again. Only I don't see other people—I see myself. I just imagine the other people are there. It feels like I have no contact with anyone anymore....
If I try very very very hard to talk, could you please try to help me?
I hope your tooth feels better.
Vivian

THROUGH MY MOTHER, I found a temporary position as an assistant teacher in a nursery school at the Sea Gate end of Coney Island, again filling in for someone on maternity leave. My job was to get the children out of gooey aprons when they finished working with clay and listen to explanations of castles and bridges in the block corner. Estella, the head teacher and a young mother herself, was good at "making the children mind," as she put it. Not creative, though. She was glad I enjoyed doing crafts with them. I brought in buttons from my mother's jar, feathers and beads from Aunt Rae, rickrack from Aunt Mollie, and fabric scraps from the pile by Nona's machine.

> *Sunday*
> *Dear Dr. Sacker,*
> *Hello, it's me again, Vivian—the pest, but I won't bother you too much longer so you can please listen to me now. There is no one to talk to and I'm all alone, so could I make believe I am talking to you even though you're not here? ....*
> *I went for a walk on Kings Highway this afternoon, then to the movies....*
> *Do you know what happens to people when they get dead? Do they feel anything or nothing? I used to be very scared to stop living, but I don't think I'm so scared anymore....*
> *You are very nice to listen to me like this when I feel like talking. I am sorry if I ever said you weren't nice. Compared to the rest of the people in the world, you are 100% nice. Now I know why I used to talk to people in the mirror. I had to have nice people to talk to, so I made them in the mirror, but if I can talk on paper like this instead, I don't think I'll need to talk in the mirror anymore. I have no friends. Susan maybe is my friend?*
> *I'm going to finish talking to you in the morning—all right? Thanks for listening.*

I omitted that the purpose of my walk to Kings Highway was to find a drugstore in a neighborhood where they didn't know me, so I could buy sleeping pills. Unable to determine which of two brands was more potent, I'd purchased both. I felt lighter immediately. I had an out. I even felt generous toward my mother, who had been unhappy since my father left on another of his long trips, and I bought her a bag of pistachio nuts, the one thing I knew she liked. Every night after her study session, there would be a pile of shells in a bowl next to her book. When I gave her the nuts, she seemed surprised in a good way and thanked me.

> *It's morning now.*
> *My mother is taking a test to be a principal. The written part is today and tomorrow.... She left early and is going to be away until suppertime. I didn't want her to be upset before she took the test. If I am going to get dead, I will do it Tuesday night or Wednesday or later. I am going to buy her flowers after she takes the test.... Also, I am going to write her a letter to say that I really like her and it's not because of her that I am dead, but because I just didn't want to live anymore and I am not mad at her so she shouldn't feel too bad....*
> *My brother is coming home from his bicycle trip very late tomorrow night. Maybe I won't see him because maybe I'll be sleeping and sleeping.*
> *Could you please hope I'll be happy when I'm dead? Shakespeare made Hamlet very smart when he said to be or not to be, because he couldn't make a decision because he didn't know what happens to you when you are dead.... I have a dog and a bicycle and a viola and a guitar and a book with horrible poems in it that I wrote and a teacher's license and dresses and blouses and shoes and other clothes. I have a radio and pictures and books. But there's no difference between me and some people who live in a leaky tent, because they will die in the end the same as I will.*
> *Time is forever and ever and ever. One life is about 1/100 of a second of all time.*

For this fraction of a second, people go to work all day and kill themselves to be able to live in society and have a "fine" life.

Sometimes people go to horse races and watch the horses go around and around the track like this faster and faster until they all drop dead.

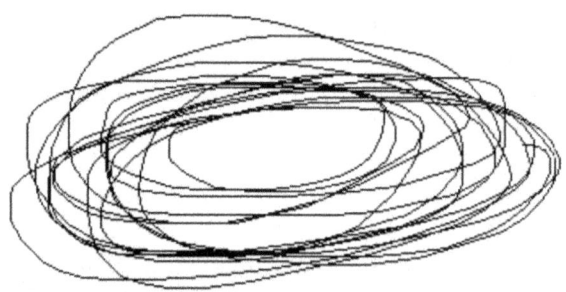

This is a very nice way of talking by writing, because no one can tell you to shut up. I won't bother you anymore, so please don't be too mad that I wasted your time with nonsense now. I am going to mail this so it will really be like talking because you'll be able to hear it too.

Vivian

I was surprised when Dr. Sacker called.

"Should I be worried?" he asked.

"What for?"

"Your letter was a little scary. You wrote—"

"OK! OK!" I didn't want to discuss what I'd written. Atmosphere people were able to see my insides without assistance. The in-person Dr. Sacker was almost-Atmosphere. The letters were my way of giving him information he almost-knew. Their content wasn't supposed to jolt him. "If you're nervous, I can't tell you things anymore."

"I don't want you to stop writing. The letters are sometimes the only way I have of knowing what's going on with you."

"I can't write if you're going to get all funny."

"I won't get funny." His voice was softer. "Just promise you'll keep writing."

This was the Dr. Sacker I thought I had lost. "I promise."

WHEN THE CLASS PARAKEET DIED, the children wanted to bury it. I helped them wrap the bird in fabric and pack it in a shoebox tied with ribbon. We put on our jackets and went outside, under the boardwalk. There, to the sound of the pounding surf, we buried it in the sand.

At Linda's house that evening, after we played four-handed "Chopsticks" on the piano and sang songs from the fake book for her parents' enjoyment, we holed up in her room to knit and talk. Linda was phobic—about crowds and other things—and though she knew phobias weren't my problem, she understood that I was sometimes shaky.

"I'm always amazed that you can be so upset one minute and so fine the next," she said.

"It's easy," I laughed. "I just snap in another cassette."

"I wish I could do that."

I was feeling pretty good when I left to walk the two blocks home.

"Hi, Mom," I said.

"You're here." She looked up from her book.

I stood next to the kitchen table, not knowing what to say but feeling I should stay another minute before I went to my room. Fidgety, I picked up the can opener that was next to a box of tissues and punched a hole in the box. I punched another. It was like doodling, something to do while I talked to her.

"Stop it!" she screamed. "You always know how to spoil it when I'm happy!" She walked out.

I went to my room and began tidying up, not understanding what I'd done wrong. When I returned to the kitchen 20 minutes later, my mother was washing dishes. Her face was wet with tears.

"You didn't help me clean once all day! Just went away with your friend!"

"But—"

"Get out of my *sight!*"

Back in my room, I felt bad, not because I should have helped my mother clean, but because she screamed like this a lot lately, especially since my father left, and I knew I should feel sorry for her but I couldn't.

From what I knew of my father's travels, he was frugal, spending only his pension. He would find an inexpensive hotel, usually in a warm climate near a beach, and keep to much the same routine he had at home. He studied his little pieces of paper, did some exercise or sport every day, and played chess or bridge so he could talk different languages to other retirees from different countries. He took one meal a day in the hotel dining room, also to practice conversing, and ate fruit and cheese in his room for the other meals. I gathered all this from the chatty, journal-type letters he wrote my mother once or twice a week, which she sometimes showed me. I was always glad when my father was away, but my mother, while happy for the first few weeks, soon came to wish he would come home.

Friday

Dear Dr. Sacker,
On Friday, I was feeling very bad and I decided to die that night, but I was afraid the sleeping pills wouldn't work all the way and would give me a stomach ache. I decided to take two of the orange ones, and then, about 45 minutes later, when I was almost asleep, to put a plastic bag on my head and then go to sleep and then I would be dead and I wouldn't even know it and it would be painless. I was very nervous, but I took the two sleeping pills and when I was almost asleep, I put the plastic bag on my head. It got stuffier and stuffier and it was harder and harder to breathe. I wasn't sure I really wanted to die, and anyway, it was getting pretty uncomfortable, so I took the bag off my head and went to sleep. The next morning, I threw all the pills in the garbage truck because I didn't ever want to take them again. Now I decided that it's better to live than to die.
Vivian

I hadn't wanted Dr. Sacker to get funny on me again, so I didn't write that letter until a week after I'd thrown away the pills. I also didn't include the details of how I had prepared for my last night on earth.

I'd washed my hair, set it in big rollers, and sat under the hair dryer. If I was a beautiful corpse, people would love me and care about me even after I was dead. I brushed out my hair and put on makeup, taking extra care with the eye shadow and mascara, so my closed lids would be picture-perfect. I put on my prettiest nightgown—yellow flannel with small flowers—and placed a glass of water on the end table, along with a note to my mother saying it wasn't because of her.

I took two orange pills, lay down on my back, and pulled the covers up to my shoulders. Then I waited, plastic bag in hand. When I thought I was almost asleep, I put the bag over my head. According to my plan, I should have been asleep a second later. That didn't happen, and the bag got uncomfortably stuffy. Thinking the pills needed more time to take effect, I removed the bag and waited, vigilant, trying to catch the last second of wakefulness before I put it on again. I tried this several times.

I was surprised to wake in the morning. Eyes gritty with mascara, plastic bag tangled in my nightgown, I realized I had missed the transition moment. I felt like the living dead, trapped in the life I thought I had left. At the same time, I was relieved. What if it had worked? I had to dispose of the pills in a place where I couldn't retrieve them, so I took them down to the street, waited for the garbage truck to come by, and threw them in. Then I went to work.

WHEN THE NURSERY SCHOOL term ended in June, I said goodbye to Estella and the children as if I really cared. Part of me did.

Out of a job again, I signed up with a temporary agency and worked in several different offices in Manhattan throughout the summer. On days I had no assignments, I went to the beach or strolled the tree-lined streets of our neighborhood with my friends, chatting about who got engaged, how to comb out the teasing from a beehive hairdo, the blouse sale at Rainbow Shops. I didn't think about the future, or the fact that my friends were off for the summer because they had teaching jobs to return to in September, while I had no plan.

Then, in mid-August, my mother said, "If you want to live in this house, you have to get a job or go to school." She wasn't smiling. In the literal way I often took things, I pictured her throwing my bed into the street and piling my clothes on top of it.

I had plans to eat out that evening with Susan and another friend, Louise. I no longer felt like the person who had made those plans but forced myself to get dressed and put on makeup.

We had finished our salads, when I said, in what I hoped was a casual voice, "My mother gave me an ultimatum. She wants me to get a job or go to school. If I don't, I have to move out."

"What are you going to do?" Susan asked in her crisp, practical way.

"I don't know."

"Why don't you go to school to become a librarian?" Louise asked.

I looked at her across the candle flickering in the Chianti bottle. As far as I knew, all librarians did was mark the due date on a slip of paper pasted inside the back cover of the book. "Do you have to go to school for that?" I asked.

"You need a master's degree," Louise said. "I once thought I wanted to be a librarian, and I sent away for library school applications, but I changed my mind. Would you like them?"

"Yes." If I went to school, I could still live in my room.

The next day, Louise gave me packets for Pratt Institute, Rutgers, and Columbia, the only nearby library programs. I rejected Rutgers and Columbia because they required the Graduate Record Exam. Pratt required only a college transcript and the names of three periodicals I read regularly. I listed *The New Yorker*, *Atlantic Monthly*, and *Saturday Review*. I never read them, but they would give the impression I was literate.

Because the term would be starting soon, Pratt agreed to interview me before my Brooklyn College transcript arrived. After a few questions related to my education and work experience, they explained the registration procedure.

"I got in!" I told my mother when I came home.

"Good," she said.

My father, who had returned a few months before, was happy, too. He thought being a librarian was an excellent profession.

DAYS AFTER I STARTED CLASSES, I had a session with Dr. Sacker. "I don't feel real, even though I look real," I said. "But I guess I am. How else could I be walking around?"

He blew out his cigarette smoke, then looked at me. "What would make you feel real?"

"Sometimes I look at my belonging cards."

He regarded me quizzically.

"Want to see them?"

"Sure."

I took out my wallet and handed him my driver's license, Social Security card, and Pratt ID. "This is the newest," I said, pointing to the one from Pratt. "The only one with my picture on it."

"Do they help?"

"Yeah. They're official. You can't get these if you're not real."

"True, but if you need them to prove it, something's wrong."

"I know." ∎

CHAPTER 13

Nine Credits

"IMAGINE YOU'RE THE DIRECTOR of a library that's getting a new building," one of my Pratt professors instructed the class. "Write a paper on what you'll discuss with the architect." The homework for another course was to write a draft of the library's policy on acquiring controversial books. It was as if they were asking a kindergartner to imagine the decisions she'd make as CEO of General Motors. I found it hard to do, even in make-believe.

More difficult were assignments for the two courses that could be done only in the library: becoming familiar with a host of directories, bibliographies, and indices. Each evening of my first week, soon after I sat down at the long wooden library table, I felt the pull of Inside. When that happened at home, I rebalanced by letting myself slide to different places in my head, but here it wasn't OK to talk to myself out loud, crouch on the floor, or become paralyzed. I had to use all my energy to push Inside back and barely got any work done.

The only one of my five courses I liked was Cataloging. All I had to do was take a brief look at a book to determine what it was about, assign a call number from the two-volume *Dewey Decimal Classification* manual, choose one or more subjects from the *Sears List of Subject Headings*, and type a set of catalog cards: author, title, and subjects. I had always been compulsive about putting things in order and found this soothing.

On Friday morning of my first week, I woke feeling overwhelmed.

Also scared I would flunk out. I still took my mother literally and was going to school in order to have a place to live. But by the time I got off the train at Pratt, I had a plan. Instead of heading to class, I went to the office and dropped the two courses for which I had to spend long hours in the library. That left me with three classes totaling nine credits.

"How was your first week?" my father asked when I got home.

"OK," I said, walking through the foyer toward my room.

"What courses are you taking?"

I monitored his voice, the barometer that warned me of impending danger. I recognized that his chattiness wasn't idle, but he was still in friendly mode. I turned to face him. "Cataloging, Selection of Library Materials, and Function and Management of Libraries."

"Only three? Is that all they require?"

The barometer flashed a caution signal. Maintaining eye contact, I took a step backward, toward Marvin's room. "I was taking five, but I dropped two today."

I took another step back. He took one forward, keeping the few feet of space between us constant. I could tell he did it unconsciously, but it unnerved me.

"What do you mean, you dropped them?"

I stiffened. "I was taking fifteen credits, but now I'm taking nine." I didn't move back. I was afraid he'd move forward again. I slipped off my jacket and draped it over one arm. My bag and books were in the other.

"Why did you drop them?"

"They were too much work."

I moved back. He moved up an equal distance.

"I'm sure if you go in Monday and tell them you made a mistake, they'll let you reinstate them."

"I don't *want* to reinstate them."

I felt the doorsill with my foot, the beginning of the accordion divider passageway alongside Marvin's room. If I could get through it to my room, I would be safe. My father rarely came in.

"But you want to be a *librarian*." His voice rose and his eyes burned into mine. "If you're a librarian, you're *someone*. People will *respect* you. If you're not a librarian, you're *no one*."

"I'm *still* going to be a librarian."

I moved. He moved.

"You're taking *fifteen credits*"—he was yelling now—"and you drop three, and you're only taking *twelve*." I inched back. He inched forward. "Pretty soon you drop three more, and you're only taking nine." I took another step. He matched it. We were slowly moving through the passageway. "You drop another three, and you're only taking six. *Six!* That's *nothing!*"

"I'm taking nine credits," I said, softly but firmly.

His voice got suddenly gentle. "If you tell them you want those courses again, I'm sure they'll say OK. Anyone can make a mistake."

"It *wasn't* a mistake." When I moved back, I felt the doorsill to my room. I was both glad and afraid. I had to work it so I got in but he didn't.

"Viv, you want to be *someone*. A librarian is *someone*. You don't want to be no one." His pleading was desperate, almost a threat.

"I *am* going to be a librarian." I stepped back and into my room. He stepped forward, still in the passageway.

"You drop another three credits, and you're only taking *three!*" He was yelling again.

"I'm taking nine credits, and I'm not going to drop any more."

This time, when he stepped forward to match my movement back, he stepped over the doorsill, invading my sanctuary. With a thud, my center of gravity shifted. I grabbed the edge of the desk to catch my balance as my body rearranged itself—the connection my feet made with the floor, the way my arms attached in their sockets. He changed, too. His face became larger, grotesque. Wild energy streamed from his eyes, flowing over me.

"You drop those three, and you dropped out altogether. You're taking *nothing!* NOTHING!" The huge face was between me and the door, blocking any chance of escape.

"I didn't drop out," I said feebly.

"You'll have *no profession!*" the face screamed. "You'll be a *nobody* and no one will respect you." The lips got softer. "If you ask them, you can get everything back. It's not too late."

I laid my jacket, books, and bag on the desk, then folded closed, leaving an uninhabited body standing in front of him.

Nothing...profession...respect... The words penetrated my empty container. I couldn't move or speak, but I had my listening look on. It was safe as long as he thought he was getting his point across. Time passed. Five minutes? Ten? *...mistake...*EXPLAIN...NOBODY....

Something took over my body. Propelled it toward the closet. I pushed the sliding door open, stepped in, and closed it. Jackets and skirts brushed my face. In the darkness, I moved to the back and crouched on the shoeboxes.

"Answer me! Say something!" I could tell he had walked up to the closet. *"Come out of there!"*

I was afraid he would open the door, but when he kept on alternately yelling and pleading, I realized he wouldn't. He was only inches away, but the wooden panel that separated us was like a castle moat. I closed my eyes and curled around the little dot that was left of me, the dot that knew I was taking nine credits.

After a long time, my father's voice stopped, and I heard him leave. I waited a moment before sliding the closet door open a crack. The stillness was eerie. I let my eyes adjust to the brightness and tiptoed through the passageway. Good—the living room door was closed. He wouldn't see me. A second later, I was in the hall, the normal world that was always just on the other side of our apartment door. I ran down the stairs and into Nona's kitchen.

She was standing at the stove, and Papoo was sitting at the table in his worn flannel bathrobe and crocheted woolen cap.

"Hi, Nona. Hi, Papoo," I said, sitting down across from him.

I watched the familiar coffee ritual. Papoo smoothed out the stained dish towel he used for a placemat and readied his cup and saucer. He kept his eyes on the cup as Nona filled it to the brim. He poured in milk from the small ceramic pitcher. The coffee overflowed into the saucer. He added three spoonfuls of sugar and stirred. More overflow. He slurped from the cup, refilled it from the saucer, and heaved a contented, "Ahhhhhh."

Nona brought me some koulouria and tea, which she knew I preferred, then sat down with her own coffee.

"Can I sleep here tonight?" I asked.

"Shoo you can sleep," Nona said. Her eyes spoke her understanding.

"Stay till you go," Papoo said in his jovial way.

A few hours later, stretched out on the green brocade sofa in the living room, watching television with Papoo, I heard, "Hi, Ma. Is Vivian here?"

"Inside mit Papa."

I sat up to make room on the sofa for my mother and told her what had happened. "I *hate* him!" I concluded. "I never want to see him again. And I'm never going back upstairs. You can bring down my toothbrush. And my books and my pajamas and my radio."

My mother looked at me with resigned eyes. "OK, Vivian," was all she said. In five minutes, she was back with my things.

"Thanks."

"Good night, Vivian." Her eyes were pained. I didn't care.

"Good night."

NONA AND PAPOO'S WORLD had changed little since I was a child. Nona still kept her for-weddings-and-bar-mitzvahs false teeth in a glass of water on the bathroom windowsill, and there was still a pile of torn newspaper squares on the hamper. Papoo used them for toilet paper, the way he had in the old country. In the morning, Nona made yellow farina, then sat with me while I stirred in hard bread crusts, butter, and salt.

My mother came down during the day to say hello. I ignored the torment on her face. I planned on staying indefinitely and gave her a list of things I needed from my room. She said, "OK, Vivian," and brought them down immediately, like a deliveryman.

When I got home from Pratt on Monday, my third day at Nona's, my mother gave me a verbal message from my father. "He says if you come back, he won't bother you about school."

I told her I liked it here, where I was in charge of my own life. She urged me to return.

"OK," I said finally, "if he really won't bother me. But if he says just *one thing*, I'm leaving."

There was no fanfare when I got upstairs. My father merely nodded and said, "Hello, Viv," as I passed the living room door on the way to my room. I felt powerful in a way I never had before.

I CONTINUED ATTENDING my three classes, and I continued seeing Dr. Sacker and writing him letters between sessions.

October 15, 1964

Dear Dr. Sacker,
... Sometimes I really want to be crazy, and I don't want to have anything to do with the real world and real people. ... But in truth, I am <u>not</u> crazy, because even if I do crazy things, I <u>know</u> I am doing them.

Many of my classmates were middle-aged women returning to school after having raised children. At first I was on guard, worried someone would discover I was a little girl masquerading as a grownup. Then one of them, Laura, asked me for help. She was warm and motherly, confident socially, but couldn't understand the Dewey Decimal System. When I explained how it worked, she thanked me and said, "You're so smart!" Laura was friendly with most of the other students, and whenever I went to the cafeteria with her, someone would approach our table and say, "May I join you?" With Laura beside me, I felt entitled to be part of the group.

> *October 19, 1964*
> *I auditioned for the chorus at Pratt, but I don't know if I made it. I hope I did.*
> *A man died on my block last week.*
> *Do you get mad when I write letters?*
> *Something is wrong with the way I am living, but I don't know what it is....*
> *Half of me never wants to grow up. It wants to stay young forever.*
> *Sometimes when I look in the mirror and see myself, it's just the flesh that looks like me and that people recognize as me, but my brain is not behind the skin. It is really not me behind that face. I don't know if I look like that.*
> *Vivian*
> *Vivian*
> *Vivian*

I dropped out of the Pratt chorus after two rehearsals—I found the people too earnest and churchy—but continued playing with the Brooklyn College orchestra, which rehearsed every Friday. It was the one place I felt completely full and real. With the horns blasting behind me, the cellos soaring to my right, and my bow moving in unison with those of the other violists, I was an integral part of this huge, vibrating organism.

In other places, I felt either like a phantom, or as if a gale were whirling through my brain. Often I placed my hands on my head, one above each ear, to hold it together.

"Why are you holding your head?" Dr. Sacker asked one day.

"It's spilling. I need string and glue, but I don't have any."

"What would happen if you took your hands away?"

"Probably nothing." Still, I kept them there.

He looked at me for a long moment, and I felt a deep, satisfying oneness with him. Then he said, "I feel as if all I'm doing is holding my finger in the dike, keeping you from getting worse, not helping you get better." The oneness evaporated.

ONE FRIDAY IN DECEMBER, an hour before the orchestra rehearsal, I readied my viola and music folder, then went to the closet for my jacket. As I was lifting it off the hanger, my fingers relaxed their grip, and it dropped back into place.

I turned to face the room. It seemed familiar, yet new. Rust-colored carpet. Crayons on the desk. Throw pillows on the couch. I wandered to the window and looked out at the fences and weeds, bricks and TV antennas, sky and clouds. The telephone pole stood like a dead tree between our backyard and the yard of the apartment house on 73rd Street. Clotheslines from both houses were attached to it, sheets and socks swaying. Outside was big. I turned to the room. There was the mirror, with a little girl in it. I met her eyes and she pulled me into her fear.

At the closet I tried again, but my hand and jacket were like repelling magnets.

The armchair beckoned. I curled up and sucked my thumb.

From somewhere above, I watched Inside and Outside vie for control of my body. It was 2:20 p.m. Orchestra was at 3:00. I dialed Dr. Sacker and got his answering service. Five minutes later, he called.

"Hi," I said with my Outside voice. Then Inside took over. Inside believed Dr. Sacker knew everything, so there was no need to talk. I was silent.

"Is something the matter?" he asked gently.

"No."

"What did you call about?"

"I can't decide whether to go to orchestra."

"Did anything happen?"

"No."

"Then why can't you decide?"

"Never mind. I'll be OK."

"Sure?"

"Yeah. I'm hanging up now."

I went to the rehearsal and forgot about the incident.

Dr. Sacker didn't mention it in our next session, so I was surprised the following day when my mother said, "Dr. Sacker called. He feels you should be in a hospital. He set up an interview for you at Mount Sinai in Manhattan."

"*What?*"

"It's for tomorrow." Her face was as solemn as if she were telling me someone had died. "Do you want me to go with you?"

"*No!*"

I went to my room and called Dr. Sacker. This time, I reached him directly. "Why did you do that behind my back?" I didn't even try to mask my anger.

"I'm sorry," he said, "but I had to. When someone can't decide whether to go to a rehearsal, something is very wrong."

Of course something was wrong, or I wouldn't be seeing him. But it wasn't hospital-serious that I couldn't make up my mind.

IT NEVER OCCURRED TO ME to refuse to keep the appointment, but I didn't want to go alone, so I asked Aunt Rae to accompany me.

We were sitting in the Mount Sinai waiting area when a thirty-ish woman in a white lab coat over a gray suit approached. Her brown hair was short, and she held a clipboard.

"I'm Dr. Wallace, the chief resident," she said with a serious face. "You must be Miss Conan." She extended her hand and we shook.

Aunt Rae introduced herself and stood to come with us.

"Nice to meet you," Dr. Wallace said. "But I'd like to talk to Miss Conan alone. We'll be about fifteen minutes."

We walked down the hall to a small office with no window or pictures. There were a few chairs and a desk with only a phone on it.

"What brings you here?" Dr. Wallace asked when we were seated.

"Dr. Sacker made the appointment."

"Do you know why?"

"I couldn't decide about the orchestra rehearsal."

When I didn't go on, Dr. Wallace asked, "How long have you been seeing him?"

"About two years."

She wrote on the clipboard. "Do you ever hear voices?"

How should I answer? I sometimes heard half of a conversation, like one person's half of a phone call. Or maybe I just thought it. "I'm not sure."

"Do voices ever tell you what to do?"

"No." I was certain of that.

"I'm going to read you a proverb, and I want you to tell me what it means. 'One swallow doesn't make a summer.'"

"You need other things, too, like grass and flowers and trees."

She made a notation. "Did you ever try to hurt yourself?"

Something like punching myself? "No."

She looked up from her clipboard. "You never did?"

I must have given the wrong answer. "I don't know what you mean."

"Did you ever try to take your life?"

Oh. I had been trying to kill myself when I took the two sleeping pills, then put the plastic bag on my head, but that might not count, because I threw away the rest of the pills. Anyway, it was last spring.

"Do you mean recently?"

"Any time."

"Once."

Another notation. "Why do you want to be in a hospital?"

"I don't."

"So why are you here?"

"Dr. Sacker wanted me to come."

After a few more questions, she said, "I'll give Dr. Sacker a call this afternoon. You can go home with your aunt now."

In the waiting area, Aunt Rae put down her magazine. "How'd it go?"

"I guess OK."

"Do you want to talk about it?"

"No."

She didn't press me.

Later that evening, Dr. Sacker called. "Mount Sinai won't admit patients who don't want to be there," he said. "They won't take you, even though you qualify for admission."

"Does that mean we still have our regular appointment tomorrow?"

"Yes."

During the following weeks, I continued going to classes, orchestra, and sessions with Dr. Sacker. He acted as if nothing had happened, and I ignored what I considered his betrayal. I needed to think of him as I always had.

While I wrote papers and studied for exams, I thought about the hospital. *Qualified for admission* was both frightening and comforting. Dr. Wallace had seen that I was in trouble. The idea of not having to pretend was appealing. I imagined the hospital would be like my room, a safe place where I could be who I was underneath. The only difference would be that the Outside people in the hospital, the doctors and nurses, would understand the Inside me. They would be a real live version of the Atmosphere doctors and nurses who had been watching over me for years.

I told Dr. Sacker I had changed my mind. He set up another interview.

On January 25, 1965, a few days after I got my grades—A in Cataloging, B in my other two courses—I was admitted to the psychiatric unit of Mount Sinai Hospital. ▪

PART THREE

MOUNT SINAI

CHAPTER 14

T.U.B.E.

"YOU'RE HERE BECAUSE YOU'RE SICK, and sick people wear pajamas," the nurse said as she walked out with my clothes. I was glad Aunt Mollie's muumuu passed as a bathrobe. With a black turtleneck underneath, and my wooden-bead earrings, which I was permitted to keep, I felt almost dressed.

Alone for the first time since my arrival an hour before, I glanced around at what looked like an ordinary hospital room, with a curtain hanging from the U-shaped ceiling track over each of the four beds. There were no phones or TVs, though, and when I saw my distorted reflection above the bathroom sink, I realized the mirror was polished metal.

I wandered into the hall. It, too, was ordinary, except that the nursing station was enclosed by windows that reached the ceiling. A man in hospital-issue pajamas tapped the glass and held up a cigarette. A nurse opened the door, gave him a light, then went back inside. A woman in a bathrobe and high heels walked down the hall and disappeared through a door.

"Miss Conan?" said a man's voice behind me.

I turned.

"I'm Dr. Abrams, and I've been assigned to this case." He nodded at his clipboard. "I need to ask you a few questions. This way."

When we started our walk, Dr. Abrams was a gangly man in a lab coat who seemed strangely uncomfortable for a doctor. When we ended it ten seconds later, he had acquired Atmosphere attributes. The unadorned room we entered seemed full of possibilities.

He took the chair behind the desk, leaving several for me to choose from. I selected one that revolved.

His first questions were easy: things like age, schooling, and family members. He read them from his clipboard and wrote as I spoke.

"Why are you here?" he asked

"I don't know. I guess because I see faces in the mirror."

"What faces?"

I suddenly felt very young and shy. "I don't know," I whispered, swiveling in my chair. It was the only response I could manage to the rest of his questions, which continued for another ten minutes.

I was relieved when he released me back to the hall. Also disappointed. He hadn't seen me or known how to get Inside. Moments later, however, he resumed his place in the Atmosphere, and my disappointment evaporated.

That evening in the dining area, which doubled as a lounge, three women invited me to play Scrabble. I memorized their names—Marie, black hair; Doris, red; Evelyn, gray—and learned that the first two were my roommates. Earlier, when the nurse had come around with the medication cart, I'd seen all three receive a tiny paper cup of colored pills. I felt a benevolent condescension toward them. They were here because they were sick. I was here because I needed a rest.

Doris put down tiles that formed SLIPERY. I let it go and began my turn.

"Wait," she said. "Is that how you spell slippery?"

"No, but it's OK," I said.

"It's not OK if it's wrong." She took back her tiles and put down a different word, correctly spelled.

Chastened, I began to listen to their conversation with respect. Marie, whose left hand and wrist were bandaged, talked about the four-hour operation to repair the damage but said nothing about why she had tried to kill herself. As for Doris and Evelyn, if I'd met them elsewhere, I wouldn't have guessed anything was wrong. I came away from the game with information about the occupational therapy schedule, daily Group, and weekly Grand Rounds. I also found out the real reason we couldn't have our street clothes. This was an open unit, with no locks on the doors or elevators. It would be harder to escape in pajamas.

At 9:30, a nurse turned off the TV and directed everyone to their rooms. That's when I met my third roommate, Cheryl, a bouncy

15-year-old in pink pajamas. I washed my face and brushed my teeth, then lay on my bed and watched what seemed like an animated painting of three scenes in one frame. Doris wrote in a notebook on her bed, stopping every so often to stare at the air. Marie, also in bed, lifted one area of her bandage, inspected underneath, then moved to another area and lifted that. Cheryl flitted out to the hall and back several times, dragging an enormous plush bunny by the ear. I was in the room and not in it, apart but feeling safe and taken care of.

At 10:00, a different nurse tucked Cheryl in with her bunny. Then she said, "Goodnight, ladies," turned out the light, and closed the door almost all the way.

With no scenes to anchor me anymore, I glued my eyes to the sliver of brightness that came in from the hall and listened to the whir of the ventilation system. The longer I lay there, under a blanket that wasn't mine, the more I felt I was dissolving into nothingness. It helped somewhat that the aide who had done the half-hour census checks before bedtime—marking each patient's whereabouts on a clipboard chart—also did it after lights-out. But she tiptoed in and out and didn't stop to talk.

I realized I had drifted off to sleep only when I awoke to banging. I peeked out the door. An old man whose pajama bottoms were falling down past decency was pounding on the nursing station window with his cane and shouting in a European accent, "Open de door! Open de door." The glass didn't break. It was mental-patient strong. A nurse came out, said, "Go back to your room, Mr. Rosen," then barricaded herself inside. The patient kept banging and shouting.

I slept fitfully, wakened several more times by Mr. Rosen, and was glad when morning was announced by a nurse standing in the doorway. "Time to get up, ladies."

After breakfast, which arrived on individual trays, aides rearranged the lounge chairs into a circle large enough for 25 patients, several nurses, and the chief resident, Dr. Wallace. Though we had spoken in her office a few days before, she didn't acknowledge me except to say, "We have a new patient: Miss Conan." People turned to look at me. I looked down at my feet.

Dr. Wallace announced that Group was a daily forum for discussing issues related to community living. For the next hour, I jiggled my leg and listened to complaints about things like the volume of the TV. The bickering reminded me of my father, except that no one seemed afraid of anyone else. More upsetting than the arguing was a patient with her hair in a bun who said, "May I make a suggestion?" no matter what the problem was, as if only she knew how to solve it.

I was happy when Group was over, happier still to see a volunteer with a library cart. I borrowed *The Mayor of Casterbridge*, one of the Hardy novels I hadn't read.

ASIDE FROM GROUP, which I never stopped hating, my routine was soothing. I read in the lounge, aware of people coming and going in the hospital world while I roamed the English countryside with Michael Henchard, a farmhand who sold his wife and baby daughter to a sailor for five guineas when he was drunk, then went on to become the respectable and prosperous mayor of Casterbridge. When Inside tugged, I walked the halls, sometimes as Ellen Willow in my Nebraska world, sometimes the little girl with the hole in her chest, sometimes an Ophelia-like psychotic, but always with the Atmosphere watching over me. Walking the halls was like making buttonholes: I was fully engaged with Inside, yet I had one ear tuned to what was going on Outside, so I responded appropriately whenever I passed another walker who said, "The soup was pretty good today." I felt calm in the hospital, where nothing was expected of me, and I didn't have to put constraints on my inner world.

My brother visited almost every evening, bringing his guitar. With his long hair and beard, Marvin was like the Pied Piper. Patients who had no visitors followed us into the laundry room, where he perched on top of the dryer and sang "Blowin' in the Wind," "The Sound of Silence," "Love Me Do." They leaned against the wall or sat on the washing machine or the floor. A few sang or hummed. Occasionally, someone requested a song. When visiting hours ended, Marvin said goodbye to everyone individually. During those evenings in the laundry room, with hardly a word of conversation between us, I felt closer to my brother than I ever had before.

My mother usually stopped in to see me for 10 or 15 minutes on days she had an appointment with the social worker, a requirement of the hospital's team approach.

"Do you need anything?" she would ask.

"A tube of Prell shampoo," I might answer. "Not a bottle." Glass would be confiscated.

"I'm writing." She would hold out her pad to show me. "Tube. T.U.B.E."

Then she would report some bit of family news. "I got a letter from Dad. He registered for an accounting class." My father had gone on another of his trips before I left for the hospital, this time to a college in Santa Barbara. I didn't know whether my mother had written that I was here. Nor did I care. I was always glad when she arrived, but equally glad when she left. She seemed relieved to go, too.

THE HOSPITAL HAD an unwritten two-tier system, of which everyone was aware. On the bottom were patients like me, whose bills were paid by insurance. When that ran out after 30 days, if they weren't considered a danger to themselves or others, they were sent home. Otherwise, they were transferred to a state hospital. If they acted out, they were transferred before 30 days. The nurses sometimes used this possibility to encourage good behavior. "If you don't stop kicking the wall, you'll wind up in a state hospital." On the top tier were patients who were paying with their own money. There was no restriction on how long they could stay, even if they tore the place apart, especially if their family had made a donation to the hospital. Mr. Rosen, who banged on the nursing station window nightly, had been there six months.

My interaction with the staff was minimal. The nurses checked my blood pressure every morning. A psychologist gave me tests one day, but when I waved to her in the hall the following day, she was with another patient and barely responded.

I never knew in advance what day or time I would be talking with Dr. Abrams. He simply looked for me in the hall or the lounge, then found an empty office. I had no period of anticipation, the way I did in the minutes before my sessions with Dr. Sacker, when Inside would come rushing to the surface. Once Dr. Abrams and I were seated, Inside tried to push through, so I wasn't able to talk much, but neither did I feel safe enough to make the sounds I did with Dr. Sacker. In 20 or 30 minutes, when Dr. Abrams said, "That's all for today," and released me to the hall, his Atmosphere version returned and all was well again.

Toward the end of my first week, I began to feel I should be registering for the spring term at library school. I asked Dr. Abrams whether I could be transferred to the Day and Night Center, where patients went out to work or school and came back just to sleep; other patients came only for the day and went home at night. He didn't feel I was ready but said he would ask Dr. Perlman, whom I'd heard referred to as The Attending. I wondered why someone who had never met me could make this decision, yet when a no came back, I was relieved. Dr. Perlman had understood that Inside was in need of care. Now he, too, was in the Atmosphere.

I met him in person the following morning. It was the day I was among five patients, selected for our stable behavior, who would be going out to a Chinese restaurant for lunch, accompanied by a nurse and a volunteer. We were to leave as soon as Grand Rounds, my first, was over. A nurse unlocked the walk-in wardrobe and gave us our street clothes. As instructed, I dressed, then sat on my bed to wait. My three roommates, clad in pajamas, were also waiting on their beds. Minutes passed. I tried to read but couldn't concentrate.

"It always takes a long time," Doris said.

After an interminable half hour, I heard the click-click of leather heels, like an army marching out of step. I sat up straight. The sound stopped. I looked toward the door.

"They went into one of the other rooms," Doris said. More clicks. More silence. Four times. "They're coming in here!" she whispered. I smoothed my skirt.

A man in a brown suit entered. Behind him were six white-coated doctors carrying clipboards. The last of them was Dr. Abrams. They formed a semicircle at the foot of my bed. I looked at Dr. Abrams, but he didn't meet my eye.

"Hello, Miss Conan. I'm Dr. Perlman." The man in the brown suit extended his hand.

"Hello." I put out my hand and we shook, as if we were in a play.

"How are you feeling today?"

"Fine."

"I see you're dressed. Are you going someplace?"

"Yes."

"Where?"

"A Chinese restaurant."

"What's the name of it?"

"I don't know."

"What street is it on?"

"I don't know."

"How will you get there if you don't know the name of the restaurant or where it is?"

What a dumb question. "I'm going with everyone else."

He turned to the residents. "She's going to a restaurant, and she doesn't know the name of it, and she doesn't know where it is, but she thinks she's going to get there." They wrote on their clipboards.

I felt humiliated and angry, mostly at Dr. Abrams. He should have at least caught my eye to let me know he knew how ridiculous this was.

Dr. Perlman turned back to me. "Nice to meet you, Miss Conan. Enjoy your lunch."

"Thank you."

He proceeded to Marie's bed, entourage in tow. "Hello, Mrs. Corelli. How are you feeling today?"

I grabbed my coat and went into the hall to find the restaurant patients.

A nurse and a volunteer in a mink coat came with us. The nurse wasn't in uniform, so we looked like an ordinary group. We walked to the restaurant and ordered from menus as if it were something we did every day. On the return walk, we were allowed to go into a store, where one woman bought a lipstick. Being in the street felt a little scary. One week of not wearing regular clothes and not going outdoors made the big world seem intimidating. I was glad when we got back.

Though I felt safe and peaceful in the hospital cocoon, I missed Dr. Sacker and called him every few days from the pay phone. When he said, "Hi, Kiddo, how ya doin'?" I felt it was a real question. I always said, "Fine," and we hung up in a few minutes, but the warmth in his voice was a reminder of what could be.

After the Grand Rounds day, neither Dr. Abrams nor Dr. Perlman was in the Atmosphere anymore. During sessions with Dr. Abrams, Inside stopped trying to push through. That made it easier for me to talk to him, though only about surface things. He said I was making progress, because I was more relaxed with him.

One morning, when I was almost at the end of *The Mayor of Casterbridge*, I was on my bed, reading, finger on the corner of the page, when suddenly, I could comprehend nothing of the story. It was as if a wall had slid down in my brain in the middle of a sentence. I understood the first half of it, but not the second. Similar things had happened for a minute or two in the past, at times when

I was preoccupied. I drank some water, then picked up the book again. Nothing made sense. I tried reading aloud. I was able to pronounce each individual word correctly and knew what it meant, but I couldn't attach it to the word on either side of it to form a concept.

I stared at the room. It got smaller and smaller, until it was the size of a dollhouse, clear and in proportion, including Cheryl's tiny bed with the minuscule bunny on top of her blanket.

I went out into the hall and began walking, but I didn't cross the portal to Inside, the way I usually did on my strolls. It was as if all the activity that comprised Inside was in a compartment the now-me had no knowledge of. I felt detached from everyone and everything, like a fake person.

A matchstick-size nurse walked briskly on black-and-white linoleum squares the size of Chiclets. At the door to the lounge, I looked in at the panorama of people smoking and playing cards and checkers, all in miniature. Some patients were watching a soap opera. I understood each separate word the actors said but couldn't string them together into sentences.

I began to pace. Down the length of the east corridor, through the laundry room to the west corridor, back up to the nursing station, and around again, aware of nothing except the jittery feeling in my body.

I thought I might be able to sit if I had something hypnotic to do, a repetitive motion that didn't require thought. I called my mother and asked her to bring a crochet hook and yarn the next time she came. It wasn't a social-worker day, so I was surprised when she appeared two hours later, a fairy godmother with four crochet hooks of different sizes, along with skeins of wool in pink, blue, yellow, and green. Without taking off her coat, she said she had to get back to work and disappeared as quickly as she'd come.

I draped one skein over the back of a chair in the lounge, sat down in another, and started winding the wool into a ball. The rhythmic motion allowed me to relax.

"May I make a suggestion?" It was the woman with the bun who kept interrupting in Group.

"No."

"If you stretch the wool between *two* chairs, you could pull it tight, and it would be easier to wind. May I show you?"

"I said *no!*"

I snatched the wool and went to my room to finish winding the ball, then began crocheting on my bed. Back and forth in straight rows, no pattern, just the same triple-crochet stitch over and over. I was calm as long as my hands were moving.

That night, when Mr. Rosen's banging and shouting woke me, I walked up to him. "It's hard for the other patients to sleep when you're making so much noise," I said.

To my amazement and that of the nurses, he said, "I'm sorry," and went back to his room.

The next day I still couldn't read, but objects were the right size. I spent the morning pacing and crocheting.

"What's going on?" Dr. Abrams asked when he read my chart.

I couldn't say. My agitation was so much a part of my state of being that I couldn't stand back from it to explain.

Dr. Abrams prescribed Stelazine, which I knew from other patients was for schizophrenia. Now when the medication cart rolled around, I, too, waited in line. "Apple juice or water?" the nurse would ask as she handed me a paper cup with a little blue pill in it. I was officially sick.

Despite the Stelazine, my anxiety increased. I felt as if poison energy were racing through my veins. After one or two more tries at reading, I returned the unfinished book to the library cart.

As my 30-day discharge date drew near, Dr. Abrams asked whether I wanted to see him as an outpatient. I didn't. It wasn't just that Mount Sinai was an hour's car ride or an hour and a half train ride away. I missed Dr. Sacker. But Dr. Abrams warned that I would disintegrate further if I stopped taking Stelazine, and Dr. Sacker couldn't oversee it because he wasn't an MD.

"Couldn't I see you for medication only and have sessions with Dr. Sacker?" I asked.

"The way the hospital works, I can't do that," he said.

I doubted the Stelazine was working but was afraid to stop taking it, so I agreed to see Dr. Abrams. On the morning I left, he handed me a prescription, which I filled in the hospital pharmacy. Feeling much worse than when I had arrived a month before, I got into my mother's car for the drive back to Brooklyn. ▪

CHAPTER 15

Dry Mouth

LYING IN BED, I LISTENED to the morning sounds. Rush of water in the bathroom. My mother flushing the toilet. A trickle. Brushing her teeth. It was still dark out, but light from the foyer created a swath of pale yellow on the wall opposite my bed. I heard Brownie groan and pictured him in his corner, rear raised, front legs straight out in a stretch. I wished I could stay in bed all day. Sleep was my only escape from the jumpiness that had only increased since I came home from the hospital two days before. Footsteps going toward the kitchen. Click of the light switch. Scrape of a match. My mother boiling water for her instant coffee.

Steps approaching my room. My mother's silhouette in the doorway. "It's six-fifteen. I'm leaving at six-thirty. I think you should get out of bed before I go."

"OK."

She walked away.

I turned on the lamp. The orange shade threw a deceptively warm glow over the room. The radiator had barely begun its morning clangs. I slipped my feet into cold moccasins, went into the kitchen, and watched my mother dribble powdered milk into her coffee. A book lay open next to her cup, pencil in the groove. She was dressed in her elegant tan suit with the dark brown velvet trim and her clunky Alan Murray space shoes. Every few years she got a custom-made pair. With their thick wedge soles and molded tops, they looked like miniature mountain ranges, every bump in her toes represented by a corresponding bump on the top of the shoe.

"You should get dressed before I leave," she said. She didn't smile, but her words weren't harsh.

"OK."

I went to the bathroom, then back to my room. The clothes I'd taken off the night before were on the armchair: socks, underpants, bra, turtleneck, dungarees, sweater. I put everything on, including the underwear—easier than opening drawers for something clean—then returned to the kitchen.

My mother was putting her washed cup into the dish drain. "I'll be home at four-thirty. Call if you need anything."

"OK."

She got her car key from her purse, picked up her coat and satchel, and walked out. I looked at the clock above the refrigerator. 6:29.

Brownie fidgeted near the door. I let him into the hall and followed him down the stairs, past Nona's and Aunt Diana's apartments, out into the alley. Cold without my coat, I walked quickly to the backyard, where Brownie would stay for the day, and locked the gate. Upstairs, I checked the clock. 6:33.

I sat on the edge of the plastic-covered sofa in the living room. My jitters escalated. I popped up and half-ran through the living room to my mother's room, turned, and came back through the living room to the kitchen. Still 6:33. I wished I were in the hospital again, where predictable events marked the passage of time: morning medication cart, lunch cart, afternoon medication cart, dinner cart, evening medication cart. In the hospital, even though I was alone on the planet, I wasn't alone in the universe. There were people going about their activities in their diorama, and when I nodded to them from afar, they nodded back. Here, I was alone in the universe. Brownie was outside. My mother was at work. My brother was sharing an apartment with a friend. My father was still in Santa Barbara, getting the college chance he'd always wanted. My mother had read one of his letters out loud the day before—about the hippie girl students who saw him as a gray-haired campus guru and sewed his buttons on for him.

Kitchen, living room, mother's room, turn; back through the living room to the kitchen: that was Route One—past the blond spinet piano, the rose-colored sectional sofa, my mother's unmade bed, the framed oil painting of Huck Finn with his fishing rod that I had copied from a book jacket years before. *Kitchen, foyer, passageway, my room; passageway, foyer, kitchen*: that was Route Two—past the bookcases, the funereal neatness of Marvin's uninhabited room, my desk and armchair, my unmade bed.

Route One, 6:51: I took a hard-boiled egg from the refrigerator, peeled it at the sink, threw the peel into the garbage, and ate while I paced.

Route Two, 6:54: My arms were stiff appendages hanging at an awkward angle. How did people usually hold their arms to make them fit?

I played a game with the clock. Instead of checking every time I passed the refrigerator, I forced myself not to look, so when I finally did, I would have the satisfaction of seeing that five or six minutes had elapsed.

9:47.

Every few hours, I collapsed onto my bed and slept for 15 minutes. The price of that rest was steep: when I woke, I felt the horror of the empty apartment as if for the first time. The intensity of that aloneness was almost worse than the exhaustion. I stopped taking naps.

11:19.

It didn't occur to me that I could go down to the basement to sit with Nona while she sewed, or into Aunt Mollie's apartment when she came home from the factory for lunch. My reality consisted only of the nothingness of isolation and the horrible jumpiness under my skin.

At 4:24, I heard my mother's step on the staircase and opened the door. She looked just as she had when she left 300 years ago—tan suit with brown trim, Alan Murray shoes, satchel filled with books and papers.

"Hello, Vivian." She seemed tired.

"Hi." I followed her to her room and watched her change into slippers and one of Aunt Mollie's muumuus.

"What did you do today?" She hung up her suit.

"Nothing."

Neither of us knew what to say next—we weren't used to chatting—but I was grateful for her presence. In the kitchen, she took the spaghetti pot down from the cabinet above the sink. I rocked back and forth near the table like a pendulum.

"Did you go out at all?"

"No." I watched her fill the pot with water.

She took two plates from the cupboard and got the jar of Ragu spaghetti sauce from the refrigerator. "This'll be ready soon. Why don't you bring Brownie up."

A joyous Brownie greeted me in the backyard. He was old and didn't leap the way he used to, but he wagged his tail, seeming not to mind that I was less than human. I marveled that such happiness existed.

Upstairs, my mother was piling spaghetti onto the plates. I opened a can of low-protein dog food—Brownie's kidneys were bad—emptied half into his dish, and broke up the lumps with a fork. I felt a companionship with my mother. We were doing different things, but we were doing them together. Our flurry of activity over, we sat at the table. She spooned sauce onto her spaghetti directly from the cold jar before passing it to me. I did the same, then twisted the spaghetti around my fork. I was sitting. I felt a little normal.

We ate in silence. My mother always concentrated on her spaghetti when she came home from work, and I had nothing particular to say. I finished in a few minutes.

"I'm going to bed," I said.

"Wait a little longer. Five o'clock is too early."

5:32. Again I announced I was going to bed. Again my mother suggested I wait awhile. I set myself a respectable goal—6:00—and she agreed. I paced and looked at her, paced and looked at the clock. As soon as it was 6:00, I went to bed. The sounds of my mother's activity in the apartment calmed me. Mercifully, I slipped into unconsciousness.

When I saw Dr. Abrams the next day—my mother drove me—I told him I couldn't sit and didn't want to live anymore. He prescribed Thorazine in addition to the Stelazine.

The Thorazine virtually immobilized me, but at the same time, it increased the restless feeling. Now the agitation was trapped inside a body that could hardly move. Yet I was driven to keep moving. My mouth was horribly dry, and my neck didn't pivot. If I wanted to see something to the side, I rotated my whole body.

Kitchen, living room, mother's room, turn; back through the living room to the kitchen. Rigid, stiff, exhausted, thirsty, I walked on. Each minute I thought I couldn't stand one more minute, but then another minute came. I was 22 years old and my life was over. I wanted to die, but the process of killing myself seemed like too much work. *Kitchen, foyer, passageway, my room; passageway, foyer, kitchen.*

A few days after I started taking the Thorazine, I was sitting on the toilet trying to move my bowels. Next I knew, I was lying on the bathroom floor in a pile of shit, and my mother was cleaning the tiles with rags. She told me to get up, but my arms and legs didn't work, and the walls were spinning. With a mixture of annoyance and businesslike efficiency, my mother cleaned me with a washcloth, then somehow got me back to bed and put fresh pajamas on me.

I WAS READMITTED TO MOUNT SINAI ten days after my discharge, again under the care of Dr. Abrams. The object of this second hospitalization seemed to be figuring out what to do with me. One option was a transfer to Hillside Hospital, in Queens, where patient stays were longer than at Mount Sinai. My mother accompanied me to an intake interview. I was impressed with the grounds, which looked more like a college campus than a hospital—some patients were playing ball on the lawn—and I'd heard it was a forward-thinking place. At first, I was disappointed when they rejected me, citing "lack of urgency at this time." Later, I decided that was something positive. It meant I wasn't severely ill.

After two weeks, when no other options were found, I was discharged back to my mother's house, but this time under a different arrangement, which I'd fought for: the Thorazine and Stelazine would be prescribed by Dr. D'Amico, my family doctor, and I would return to Dr. Sacker for therapy.

"HI, KIDDO. IT'S BEEN A LONG TIME." Dr. Sacker smiled a big warm smile that made his eyes crinkle.

I followed him in. Same striped couch. Same chess set. Same coffee table and leather chair. He looked the same, too, in chinos and a blue plaid shirt open at the collar. Yet everything seemed different, as if it were the first time I had been there. He gestured toward the couch. "Would you like to sit down?"

"I guess so." I walked around the coffee table to the couch on which I used to feel so comfortable and sat stiffly on the edge.

I had long awaited this moment, but now I didn't know what to say. Before Mount Sinai, Dr. Sacker's office had been a magic place, where it was safe to let the pain in my chest and the chaos in my head fly loose in the room. It had never bothered me when I couldn't speak because Inside was sure Dr. Sacker knew everything without my saying a word. I used to think I was communicating clearly when I grunted and moaned, or disappeared into a piece of lint on the cushion. Now I was locked in a rigor mortis body and a rigor mortis soul, acutely aware that if I didn't talk to Dr. Sacker in words, he wouldn't know what was wrong.

"I can't sit still," I began. That didn't sound right. "I can't do anything."

Dr. Sacker looked at me kindly and I could see that he wanted to understand. I couldn't help him. I was as stymied and shut out as he was. Yet our eyes were connecting. Across the beam of his steady, caring gaze, on a plane separate from our words, something was flowing from him to me. Only a tiny bit seeped through my dry, caked soil, but that was enough to make me want to keep the connection open. Not knowing how to do that, I began to talk at random.

"I'm on medication. Thorazine and Stelazine."

"I know. I spoke with Dr. Abrams."

I crossed my legs, uncrossed them.

"What's going on at home?" Dr. Sacker lit a cigarette, slipped his feet out of his loafers, and put them up on the table.

"Nothing. My father's still in California, and my mother goes to work."

"So you're home alone?"

"Yeah."

"What do you do all day?" He took a drag and tilted his head back to blow the smoke toward the ceiling, then rested the cigarette in the ashtray groove.

"Nothing."

"Nothing?"

"All I do is walk from one room to another."

"Why is that?"

I wondered at his question. My present condition was a fact. I hadn't considered that it might have a cause. "I don't know." Then, as if my not being able to do anything were of no more importance than anything else, I gave him family news, the way my mother gave me news in the hospital. "Marvin is going on a cross-country trip with his friend Elliot. My mother's giving him the car to keep. She's buying herself a new one. And in September, he's going to

Michigan State for a PhD in clinical psychology." I reported all this in a matter-of-fact voice, as if I found it natural that there were people who chose to go to all the trouble doing those things entailed.

"Vivian?" Dr. Sacker's voice was suddenly serious. So was his face.

"Yeah?"

"How can I help you?" He leaned forward and looked at me intently.

"What do you mean?"

"Well," he said slowly, "I can see how terrible you're feeling, and I'd like to help. What can I do that would be useful?"

I was unprepared for the gratitude that welled up in me. This was the first time anyone had told me in words they knew I was suffering. "I don't know. Nothing," was all I could whisper. I couldn't say he was already helping me, that our talk was just a side-show. The main event was the beam that stretched from his eyes to mine.

His scrutiny made me uncomfortable, even as I craved it. I looked down at my knees, but his gaze still burned into me. I placed my hands flat on the cushion for leverage, leaned forward to lift my weight slightly, then resettled myself in the same position. This new silence was too loud.

To make it quieter, I began talking about my cousins—how one by one, they were all moving away from the 74th Street house. Barbara was already gone. So was George, who had been staying with Nona and Papoo while he was in college. Annie was living with her boyfriend, and Jerry would probably marry Rosanne soon. Before long, only 12-year-old Robert and I would be left.

Soon the 50 minutes were up, and I realized it hadn't been difficult to sit still.

"See you Friday," Dr. Sacker said as he walked me to the door. "Take care of yourself."

I didn't want to leave. "Bye." ▪

CHAPTER 16

The Flute Plays The Violin

OVER THE NEXT FEW WEEKS, the only event I looked forward to was seeing Dr. Sacker. I prattled to him about the here-and-now—my mother got a letter from my father, Brownie was old and slowing down—aware that under his easy manner, he was trying to understand why I felt so bad. The caring itself was healing, and soon I was taking off my shoes, tucking my feet under me, and leaning back against the cushions.

I saw him for 50 minutes twice a week. In between, I still paced, but my pacing was not as empty as before. I would remember the way Dr. Sacker looked, or something he said. At first the thoughts lingered only seconds before they evaporated. Then I began to feel a thin coating of Dr. Sacker around me. He knew how uncomfortable my body felt, because he was inside me and in the air around me. His knowing made my restlessness almost tolerable.

One morning on my rounds, I glanced at the bookshelves above my desk. *Gone With the Wind* caught my eye. I brought it to my armchair. The few times I'd tried to read since my return from Mount Sinai, I'd been able to comprehend the individual words but couldn't string them together. Now, to my amazement, the opening sentence made sense. *Scarlett O'Hara was not beautiful, but men seldom realized it when caught by her charm as the Tarleton twins were.* Hardly daring to believe it, I tried reading more. With no effort, I understood that Scarlett was sitting on the porch of her father's plantation house, flirting with the twins.

I took a blanket from the bed and curled up in the chair, where I remained for almost six hours. When my mother came home at 4:30, I was on page 195. Scarlett had married Charles to spite Ashley, because she was jealous that Ashley had married Melanie. Then Charles had died in the war. Now a 17-year-old widow, Scarlett was tending wounded soldiers in the hospital, hating the lack of fun. Rhett had begun to pursue her. And I had a ringside seat.

That evening began like any other. A little before 5:00, I went down for Brownie, who had to stop every few steps on the way up to rest. I put some food into his bowl, and my mother and I sat down to spaghetti.

"I decided to get a Chevy Nova," she said. "Same car Eddie has. I figure he already did the research."

"What color?"

"Whatever they have. My goal is to make my life easy."

I finished eating and looked at the clock. Forty-five minutes until my 6:00 bedtime. I started pacing. When I circled back to the kitchen, my mother was reading, absently twirling spaghetti around her fork. Watching her, it occurred to me that I could read, too.

Scarlett was just where I had left her at 4:30, when Rhett bid $150 in gold to dance with her at a charity ball. It didn't matter that I had read *Gone With the Wind* before. That was part of its allure. I knew it wouldn't disappoint.

Though I was involved in the story, it was still just a means of passing time until I could sleep. At exactly 6:00, I put down the book and went in search of my mother. She was in her room, looking through her filing cabinet.

"Good night, Mom."

"Good night, Vivian."

Before that day, neither my muscles nor my mind could relax while I lay in bed and waited to fall asleep. Now it felt luxurious to forget about my body and read until my eyes closed by themselves. Waking up the next morning was different, too. There was the pleasantly unfamiliar feeling of having something to look forward to. I reached overhead to turn on the lamp, then fished into the folds of the covers for the book.

"You're awake," my mother said when she came to my door at 6:15. "I'll be leaving soon."

"OK. I'm getting up."

I still felt a terrible aloneness when my mother walked out, but I could open my book any time and have company: Scarlett, Rhett, Ashley, Melanie, Aunt Pittypat, Dr. and Mrs. Meade, Mammy, Gerald, Ellen. They were perfect companions. I could get close to them but didn't have to talk. Their activity didn't depress me. And whenever I needed a rest from them, I could close their world and lay it aside.

I brought Brownie down to the backyard, curled up in my armchair, and read for an hour. Then I got up for some water. On the way to the kitchen, I realized my book was only 1,024 pages long. It didn't occur to me that if I could read one book, I could read another. *Gone With the Wind* wasn't a book. It was a world I was living and breathing in. I formulated a plan: no more than 100 pages a day.

I finished my day's allotment in the morning, then put the book down and began pacing. A few minutes later, like an alcoholic who knows where the bottle is hidden, I went back for just two more pages. The two stretched to 15, the 15 to 30. I abandoned the restriction.

For the next three days, I sat comfortably in my chair while Melanie gave birth to Ashley's child and Scarlett gave birth to Rhett's. In between, Atlanta burned, the war ended, Scarlett ran a lumber mill, and Melanie died. Rhett finally left Scarlett because it pained him that she was still obsessed with Ashley. At first Scarlett was devastated. Then she said, *I'll think of it all tomorrow... After all, tomorrow is another day.* THE END.

I was stunned—not by Scarlett's loss, but by mine. The curtain had crashed down on my world.

DURING THE BLEAK DAYS of February and March, the elements had been in harmony with my misery. Now, all of Brooklyn was bursting with forsythia loudly proclaiming Spring. The profusion of lemony blooms mocked me whenever I went on errands with my mother or on bus rides to Dr. Sacker. Ending my life seemed the only way to end my torture, and I used my pacing hours to devise several methods before settling on what I thought would be the easiest and most painless: take all the Thorazine and Stelazine at once, along with a bottle of over-the-counter sleeping pills, put a plastic bag over my head, then lie down.

But if I were dead, I wouldn't be able to see Dr. Sacker.

To be, or not to be? I wanted to retain both options, so at the same time that I made suicide plans, I tried to figure out what would make my life bearable. I had begun to suspect that at least part of my torment was due to the drugs.

"Do you think I could stop taking the pills?" I asked Dr. Sacker. He wasn't an MD, but I thought he would know better than Dr. D'Amico, who was supposedly supervising my medication. In reality, all Dr. D'Amico did was give me a blood test every once in a while to make sure I wasn't being poisoned.

"Yes."

I was surprised that he hadn't hesitated. "You do?"

"I don't see any problem," he said, leaning back and putting his feet up, "as long as you do it gradually. It wouldn't be good to stop all at once."

"What if I took them every eight hours instead of every four?"

"Sounds like a good way to start. We'll see how it goes."

That was the entire discussion. No dire predictions, just cautious optimism. And he had said, "*We'll* see how it goes." I had a partner. I began to think I might have a future.

Emboldened, I tried another change when I got home: a trip down two flights of stairs to the basement to sit with Nona while she sewed. I emerged into the familiar space that was home to four factory machines, each with several conical spools of thread suspended from metal poles.

Nona was sewing hems across the tops of denim apron pockets, her black kerchief tied in back over her coiled braid. She sang as she worked—"Samiotisa," my favorite of all her Greek songs. I stood in the doorway and watched her peel a pocket from the stack on her left, fold the top edge down, and slip it under the presser foot.

"Hi, Nona," I said, stepping forward.

Her face broke into a smile. "Viviana. How-eye-ya?"

"Fine." I hoisted myself up onto the cutting table and sat cross-legged.

She eyed me quizzically.

"I just came down to visit."

"Dear Gren*daw*da. You know you always welcome."

After she sewed another pocket—in a few seconds—I couldn't sit still and jumped down to finger the pile of pockets on the floor.

"Can I cut these apart for you?"

"Shoo you can." Nona stopped working only long enough to hand me the scissors.

I began cutting the pockets apart and stacking them on the table. Nona continued sewing and singing. I finished in a few minutes.

"Nona," I called loudly, to make myself heard over the machine, "I'm going now. The pockets I cut are over here."

"Thanks you coming, Dear Gren*daw*da. Come again. I wish you only de best. *Meh eeYAH*." Nona said "*Meh eeYAH*" to anyone embarking on a new venture, whether it was going on a vacation, wearing a new dress, or having a baby. It was her all-purpose blessing: wear it in good health, use it in good health, go in good health.

As I walked up the stairs to the empty apartment, I felt a glow, and from then on, I went down for 10 or 15 minutes each day. Sometimes it was pockets, sometimes pillowcases, sometimes pajama collars. I was at home with all of them. I had been cutting, folding, and stacking since I was four.

ONE SATURDAY MORNING a few weeks after I started reducing my medication, when I went to take Brownie down to the backyard he seemed to be asleep. "Brownie," I called. He didn't move. I knelt. "Brownie," I said more softly, inches from his face. He opened his eyes and his tail gave a feeble thump. "Do you want to go down?" He kept looking at me but didn't move. I wasn't too surprised. He had thrown up everything he ate for the past few days. My mother had spoken to the vet, who said there was nothing much we could do. I went to her now and told her he couldn't get up.

"It's time to put him to sleep," she said matter-of-factly.

"When?"

"Today."

"*Today?*"

"He's only going to get worse."

She made a phone call and arranged for someone to pick him up that afternoon. Then she went to the basement with a load of laundry, and I began to pace.

This is momentous, I told myself. I should be feeling something. For 14 years, Brownie had loved us all, even my father, who had sometimes trained him to be a watchdog by praising him when he barked and other times trained him not to bark by thrashing his nose with a rolled-up newspaper. Brownie had loved us even though we confined him to the boring backyard all day. When he was younger, he would station himself at the gate and spring as high as he could off his hind legs. Once or twice a year, he made it over the top, and I would get a call from my friend Carol, who lived on 75th Street. "I just saw Brownie. He's visiting his girlfriend on Seventy-sixth Street." Two or three days later, Brownie would come back and wait on the front stoop for someone to let him in.

He spent his last morning curled in his corner by the closet, where the baseboard molding had long been discolored from the oils and dirt in his fur. I stopped a few times on my pacing rounds to stroke his head and smooth back the strands of fur that flopped forward into his eyes. He looked at me trustingly, and I felt guilty. He didn't know what we had planned for him.

The doorbell rang.

"Get Brownie and bring him down," my mother called from her room. "I can't handle it." I had never heard her say anything like that. I was especially surprised, as she was the only one in our family who never petted him.

I carried Brownie down the stairs. He'd lost so much weight that he was light, but he was warm and molded against my body like a baby.

"His name is Brownie," I told the man waiting downstairs. "He's not feeling well, and he won't try to do anything, so please be gentle with him."

The man nodded noncommittally and handed me a clipboard, saying, "Someone has to sign this." I put Brownie down on the floor and took the pen, but the man stopped me. "Someone over twenty-one."

"I'm twenty-two. Would you like me to get my driver's license?" I wanted to shield my mother.

The man looked at me, then let me sign. I picked up Brownie and handed him over, like a package. The man took him, not roughly, but not compassionately. I longed to ask how they were going to do it and whether he would feel any pain, but I couldn't. The man walked out. I pressed my face to the window in the door and saw him open the back of his double-parked truck and put Brownie into a metal cage. Then he got into the cab and drove away.

I went back upstairs. "It's done," I told my mother. She didn't say anything, but I saw that she had removed Brownie's bowls and damp-mopped the floor. Maybe it was good that I could hardly feel. My deadness had enabled me to spare her, the first useful thing I'd done in months.

TRUE TO MY HUNCH, my intense physical agitation was abating with the reduction in medication, but I didn't feel the relief I had anticipated. Now that I wasn't so distracted by physical torment, I became more aware of the world around me and realized the enormous gulf that separated me from regular people. On the bus ride to Dr. Sacker, I studied them as they talked together, nodding and exchanging looks of understanding. How did they learn that? I concluded I must be intrinsically different, missing some vital human essence.

I began reading again, Louisa May Alcott books I found on the shelves above my desk. *Little Women, Little Men, Eight Cousins.* They were stories I knew well, filled not with epic events, but families and friends, pillow fights and picnics, joys and sorrows. Through them, I eavesdropped on emotions I didn't have anymore: sadness, anger, happiness, disappointment, love. Every once in a while, I felt the release of a few tears.

SUSAN CALLED ONE DAY to ask whether I wanted to go for a walk.

"What for?"

"Just to get out of the house. I could come by and pick you up."

I knew she meant *she* wanted to get out of the house. During the months I'd been in the hospital and at home pacing, Susan had become engaged to a medical student and shopped for a wedding dress. Though she had called every week, I hadn't been able to relate to her world or talk about mine.

"I picked out dishes," she said one time. "Yellow, with a flower pattern."

"That's nice."

"What did you do today?"

"Nothing much."

Then her fiancé broke the engagement.

Intellectually, I understood that Susan was devastated, but I couldn't empathize with her. My own feelings were limited to discomfort with my body and an unease of mind I wasn't able to articulate. I couldn't imagine any other kind of distress. All I knew was that we were both fragile, she wanted to go for a walk, and I had nothing better to do.

Susan and I had been best friends since high school, but when she came to pick me up, I no longer felt like her equal. She was a teacher. She had been engaged. She was attractive, with dark brown hair done up in a beehive at the beauty parlor, large brown eyes, and thick lashes that didn't need mascara. She was wearing lipstick and gold clip-on earrings. In my mismatched clothes, with no makeup or hairdo, I felt too dumpy to walk beside her. But Susan didn't seem to care how I looked or expect scintillating conversation, and I soon felt at ease. By unspoken agreement, we kept our conversation light. When she talked of her broken engagement, it was just about logistics. "I have to return all those gifts." I, too, spoke only of surface matters. "Dr. Sacker is helping me get off medication."

ONE AFTERNOON, MY MOTHER handed me a flyer. "The J is forming an orchestra," she said.

"So?"

"I thought you might be interested."

"Well, I'm not."

"I think you would enjoy it. The first rehearsal is next Monday."

I looked at the announcement from the JCH. "Eight o'clock! That's too late."

"Vivian," she said in her teacher voice, "eight is not too late for ordinary people. It's not normal to go to bed at six."

"Who says I'm normal?"

"I'm only trying to help you. Just consider it."

"OK! I'm considering it. Now let's change the subject."

Six o'clock Monday came, and I surprised myself by not changing into pajamas. At 7:15, I watched myself get my viola out of the closet and open the case. The strings were loose from months of disuse. I tightened them and adjusted the bridge. I checked my rosin cake. Cracked, but usable. At 7:30, I put my collapsible music stand into my shoulder bag. That's when I knew I was going.

The conductor turned out to be an easygoing man in his mid-thirties who was grateful that people showed up at all. We didn't have the correct mix of instruments, so he did things like assign flutes to play the violin part.

During the rehearsal, it was as if I were two separate people. One was a musician who knew what to do when the conductor said, "We need a sudden forte two measures before C. Let's go back and try it from B." The other kept looking at the darkness out the window, wondering what she was doing in this strange place in the middle of the night.

But from then on, I went each week. Though I stuck to my 6:00 bedtime on other evenings, I longed to be part of something again. The orchestra was easy to fit into, because I didn't have to make conversation. There was always a pleasant cacophony when I arrived: a clarinetist tossing off arpeggios, an oboist blowing snorts into his mouthpiece to moisten the reed, the hollow fifths of a cello being tuned. I nodded hello to those around me, set up my stand, and added to the din by practicing a few random measures until the conductor tapped his stand to start the rehearsal.

At the end of May, we gave a concert to an enthusiastic audience of relatives and friends, my mother and Susan among them. Each time they clapped, I felt a tiny spark. They were acknowledging the orchestra, and, by extension, me.

SUSAN AND I WALKED REGULARLY in the late afternoons, after she got home from work. We saw the neighborhood gardens progress from lilacs to azaleas to roses. As the days got warmer, the streets filled with girls bouncing Spalding balls and chanting, "A, my name is Anna and my husband's name is Al," and boys shouting, "Time!" to suspend their stickball game for ten seconds while a car passed.

By the beginning of June, I was off all medication. The only vestige of it was the itchy red blotches I got if I didn't keep out of the sun. I had begun to put a little more effort into my appearance—at first for Dr. Sacker, then for Susan, too. I selected clothes that went well together and occasionally set my hair and wore makeup. My gait was back to normal. But I still didn't feel like a regular person. I was more like someone after a stroke, trying to relearn how to do things that had once been second nature.

Either my mother didn't realize how shaky I was, or she thought I needed another push, but she came home from work one day and suggested that I take a job in the school where she worked. With a month left before the summer break, the assistant teacher in one of the Head Start pre-kindergarten classes had quit.

I was dumbfounded. How could a nonperson teach real children?

My mother told me the head teacher, Sylvia, whom she'd known for years, had already agreed to accept me as her assistant. All I'd have to do was give out milk and cookies, tidy up the block corner, and things like that.

If I had imagined myself working at all, it would have been collating, or stuffing envelopes, or even making buttonholes in Aunt Sarah's factory. Yet my mother thought I could teach. If I looked human, maybe I was, or at least an apprentice human. Maybe that was good enough.

During the month of June, I got up when my mother did and drove with her to school. I quickly learned all Sylvia's routines—the transitions from free play to story time to naptime to milk time. I learned the children's names but had no feelings for them. I was too dead inside. I watched Sylvia intently. She hugged the children as if she meant it. She praised them. She looked into their eyes when she talked to them. Once, I saw her walk over to a scowling girl who didn't look at all pretty to me. "You're so pretty," Sylvia said to her. The girl smiled and did look pretty. Sylvia made those kids feel good about themselves. Even when she scolded them, it was with love and respect, and they adored her.

As inadequate as I felt in the classroom, I felt even more so in the teachers' room. I was so awed by their talk of mothers-in-law and shopping for furniture at Macy's that I couldn't say anything. Once, Sylvia passed out fliers about a demonstration against the Vietnam War. I hadn't even known there *was* a war.

I was still using all my energy to get through one day at a time and never thought about the future, but, as June drew to a close, my mother made her own plans for the summer. She would be taking courses at Plattsburgh State Teachers College in upstate New York. My father would go with her and take a course of his own. Marvin, back from his cross-country trip, had already left for a counselor job at Camp Wel-Met in the Catskills.

"So you'll be alone in your apartment," Dr. Sacker said.

"Yeah."

"That's not such a good idea. Why don't you ask Susan to stay with you?"

"I never thought of that. I don't know whether she'd want to."
"If you ask, you might be surprised."
He turned out to be right. Susan said yes immediately, adding, "I need to get out of my house."

SUSAN PLANNED TO TAKE EDUCATION COURSES at Brooklyn College during the summer. In order to have something of my own to do, I registered for a course at the Pratt Institute Library School, my first since the previous fall. Still, when I went to bed the night before my mother was to leave and Susan was to arrive, I felt my usual deadness inside.

The next morning, I opened my eyes to see sun at the edge of the venetian blind, a golden ray that rippled with the breeze coming through the partially open window. I followed its dance with my eye as I stretched long and luxuriously. Then I bounded out of bed and, with one pull of the venetian blind cord, flooded the room with brightness that matched the way I felt.

I wanted to call Susan, but 6:30 was too early—even my parents were still in bed—so I sat down in the kitchen with a bowl of cornflakes. I felt lithe, comfortable in my body, glad to be alive. I wasn't grateful for this seemingly miraculous change, because it didn't feel like a change. The anguish of the past six months had nothing to do with the me who had just woken up. Right now, my only reality was the sensation of crunch in my mouth and the refreshing shock of cold milk sliding into my belly.

Back in my room, I arranged the throw pillows at jaunty angles. I got dressed, put on eyeliner, and brushed my hair, smiling at myself in the mirror as I turned my head left and right. Then, for the first time in six months, the mirror opened to receive me. As if they'd never left, the Atmosphere people were back, too, watching me get ready for my day. ■

CHAPTER 17

Susan Has A Secret

"I'LL TRADE YOU TCHAIKOVSKY'S Piano Concerto for Judy Garland at Carnegie Hall," Marvin said, pulling an album from his stack.

"No way."

"How about the Tchaikovsky and Schubert's Unfinished?"

"Deal!"

It was past midnight in late August 1965, and we were sitting on the floor of his room, dividing the record collection, our only communal property. We'd started a few hours earlier, alternately selecting one album each from the more than 100 we owned. Now we were bartering. Even as we joked, I felt the solemnity of the occasion. It was the last time either of us would call 74th Street home. Marvin was 20, a long-haired hippie who played guitar much more than piano. He had graduated from Brooklyn College with a BA in Psychology the previous January. Tomorrow, he would stow his records in the trunk of my mother's old 1958 Ford Fairlane, now his, and drive to Michigan State to begin work on his PhD in psychology. I was 23. In two weeks, I would bring my records to the apartment Susan and I had found on Ocean Avenue, a few miles away.

Carrying them to my room in batches, I thought about the summer. Mornings when Susan and I had planned our day over breakfast: the beach, tennis, shopping. Evenings when she came with me to the Pratt library and studied for her course while I did homework for mine. The Saturday we took the bus to visit Marvin at Camp Wel-Met, near the Pennsylvania border, then missed the return bus home. The Sunday we helped each other into our gowns for Linda's wedding, at which I was maid of honor.

Though I'd known all along that the summer would end, I wasn't prepared for the change in the apartment when it did. The loss of the living room bothered me most. I'd been surprised the first time Susan had settled on the couch to watch television. No one had ever relaxed in the living room before. She turned it into friendly territory, and I began going in to play the piano—Mozart and Beethoven sonatas, or songs from the fake book that we sang together. Now my father's bridge table was back in the center of the room, as if he had never left.

Susan, too, had been reluctant to return to her family.

"We could get an apartment to share," I'd said in the beginning of August.

"Maybe," Susan had said.

Now it was really happening. I placed the last of my records on my desk, whispered goodnight to Marvin, and closed my door.

THE RENT FOR THE THIRD-FLOOR WALKUP in Ocean Castles, an apartment complex in the Midwood section of Brooklyn, was $80 a month. We chose it because it had high ceilings and lots of light. There was a large living room that would double as a dining room, a bedroom we would share, a nice-sized foyer, and a long, narrow kitchen. When you opened the oven door, it barely cleared the opposite wall.

"You're not working," Susan said as we left the rental office, lease in hand. "Where will you get the money?" This wasn't the first time she'd brought it up.

I was so glad to be escaping from 74th Street that I wasn't concerned about money. Though I hadn't asked my mother, I assumed she would help if my savings ran out. "I'll always pay my half," I said.

The apartment needed work before we could move in. Cockroaches ran rampant in the kitchen cabinets. The cracked linoleum in the living room and bedroom had insect larvae underneath. The paint was peeling. I had no trouble envisioning it all fixed up, picket-fence cozy, a place where, if I got hungry in the middle of the night, I could cook a hamburger without worrying that the refrigerator door might make noise. I loved washing and scrubbing, seeing the apartment begin to bloom. It was OK with me that Susan was ambivalent and didn't feel like helping. I understood, because her mother didn't think she should move out unless it was with a husband and said, "What are you going to eat?"

My father was still the boss of things like noise and the temperature on 74th Street, but he no longer attempted to control what Marvin and I did outside the house and said nothing about my impending move. My mother told me I could take anything I wanted from our apartment or the basement.

Whatever help Susan couldn't offer was made up for by my family. After I set off a roach bomb one evening and came back the next morning to sweep up the corpses, Aunt Diana and Uncle Eddie painted. Aunt Rae discovered parquet under the linoleum and arranged to have the floors sanded and varnished. Aunt Mollie sewed curtains. Aunt Rae and Uncle Frank hung the framed prints I took from my room on 74th Street: Picasso's *The Old Guitarist* and *The Lovers*, Van Gogh's *Sunflowers*, a Modigliani woman with a long neck. Susan, who had been sharing the expenses, reluctantly admitted that the apartment was looking good, and her mood began to lighten.

The van came to 74th Street first. Movers loaded my armchair and convertible sofa, a bed, a dining table and chairs, end tables, a rocking chair, night stands, dressers, a small desk, the portable stereo and my records, a carton of pots and dishes, an ironing board, bedding and towels, and a bag of cooking utensils. Best of all was my mother's sewing machine, Nona's present to her when she got married, which she was now giving to me. It was the fanciest piece of furniture I was taking, in a dark wood cabinet with sculpted legs and a natural grain pattern that met in an upside-down V on the doors. The next stop was Susan's house, where all her mother would allow her to take was her bed, one sheet and one blanket, and an old television set. Her mother stood on the sidewalk in her housedress, watching the men load the truck. "How are you going to get everything up the stairs?" she asked. In that moment, I felt profoundly sorry for Susan.

At my insistence, we didn't go to bed that first night until all the furniture was in place, the dishes and pots on their proper shelves, and our clothes in the drawers and closets. Then, as if we had lived there for years, Susan lay down on her bed to watch TV, and I lay down on mine with my book. It felt like a real home.

The next morning, I walked to our local train station, on the Brighton line, for the ride to Pratt to register for the fall term. The Sea Beach line, which I had taken since I was a child, ran through Bensonhurst. The Brighton ran through Midwood. This change, too, felt liberating. On the bulletin board outside the library school office was a job posting for a librarian-trainee, to work in the Pratt Reference Department. The salary was just $80 a week, but the benefits included free tuition and medical insurance. I applied and was hired on the spot. As the position was full time, I decided to take only two courses, which would get me to 18 of the 36 credits required for my degree.

"Now you don't have to worry about the rent," I told Susan when I got home.

MONDAY MORNING, I DROVE to campus in the blue Chevy Nova my mother had given me. "I gave Marvin a car," she had said, "so it's only fair that I give you one, too." I was already familiar with the reference room, having spent many hours there doing homework in the summer. Jo, the department head, welcomed me warmly and introduced me to Ruth, the assistant librarian, and Rose, the secretary. Like theirs, my desk was out in the open, with a backdrop of bookshelves and wooden library tables.

On my third day, one of the Pratt trustees called asking for Jo. She wouldn't be in until 1:00, so I took a message: He wanted information about a man who had been involved with the Institute 50 years before. It was 9:20. Ruth wouldn't arrive until 10:00. Feeling that a request from a trustee should be answered immediately, I told Rose to call me if anyone needed reference help, then climbed the stack staircase three levels to the locked archive cage at the top.

The cage was the only section of the department not meticulously organized. Its shelves were filled with dusty papers—some in folders, some not—cartons, and bound volumes with tissue paper between the pages and ribbon tying the flap-covers closed. There were also items like candlesticks and mortarboard caps. Nothing was catalogued, so I decided to look for the man's name on every page of every document. By 10:00, when Ruth came up to check on me, I'd found nothing. She suggested I stop.

"Do you mind if I keep looking?" I asked.

"No, but you're wasting your time."

By noon, I'd found the man's name on nine pages out of the hundreds I'd perused. I brought the documents down to my desk, told Ruth about them, and said I was going to lunch.

The moment I left the library, I felt something shift, as if my organs had rearranged themselves. A wave of chaos and pain rushed up from Inside. To stem it I held my hand straight out and pushed my palms against the air as I walked. "Rehearsing for a play," I would say if anyone asked what I was doing. No one did.

"Osh be-*gon*-ni. *Mak*-ana," I whispered, to calm the screams in my brain. "Ha-*boo*. Ha-*boo*."

Inside went into suspended animation when I entered the student cafeteria. I took a tray and joined the food line, the buzz of conversation around me seeming to come from another world.

"Tuna on a roll with lettuce, tomato, and mustard," I heard myself say. The hairnet woman behind the counter handed me my sandwich, along with a pickle and some potato chips. "Thank you," my voice said.

Inching my tray toward the cashier, I wished the line would move faster. Inside was beginning to wake again. I paid and hurried out through the campus gate to the surrounding residential streets.

I spoke softly as I walked and ate, in a voice that ranged from hissing, to soothing, to pleading, and back.

"I didn't *do* that... Osh be-*gon*-ni. *Mak*-ana... No! Get out of my way... Ha-*boo*. Ha-*boo*."

I was calmer now that I didn't have to squelch anything. I knew I sounded crazy, and whenever I passed anyone, I stopped talking for a few seconds. I probably *was* crazy—I didn't know where the words came from or what they meant—but it wasn't scary. The Atmosphere doctors and nurses, along with Dr. Sacker and Dr. Hirschhorn, whose Atmosphere version had remained pure, were with me.

All the while, another part of me kept checking my watch. 12:50. Time to head back. I arrived at my desk at 1:00 in crisp librarian-trainee mode.

I told Jo, who had just arrived, about the trustee's request and the papers I had found. "You're a natural librarian," she said. "And you were right—it's very important to satisfy the trustees."

Natural librarian! From then on, I was Jo's protégée.

About a month after Susan and I moved in, I came home from work, put Beethoven's Violin Concerto on the record player, and hummed along while I made supper. Susan set the table, and we sat down.

I started on my salad, but Susan didn't pick up her fork. She looked at her plate, then up at me. "There's something I have to tell you."

"What?" I speared a carrot round.

"I'm seeing Ted."

"Ted?" I bit down, enjoying the crunch.

"Dr. Sacker."

I spit out the carrot. "What do you mean?"

"I'm in therapy," Susan said, meeting my eyes.

"You're kidding."

"No." She looked sheepish, then tried a smile.

"When did you start?"

"Last spring. When my engagement broke off. I needed to talk to someone, and you always said nice things about him."

Pain shot though my insides. Dr. Sacker was more than my therapist. He was a major part of the Atmosphere, where his sole concern was me. That he had other patients I didn't know was one thing. But Susan? I felt as if she had robbed me. "You were seeing him *all summer*? While you stayed with me on *Seventy-fourth Street*?"

"Yes." She seemed even more uncomfortable but didn't look away.

"Why are you just telling me now?"

"Ted thought you were too fragile before. He asked me not to say anything. But now you're doing better, and he thought it would be OK." She picked up her fork and put it down. "I had a session with him this afternoon, and we agreed I would tell you tonight."

"You *agreed*?"

"He thought it would be a good time, because you're seeing him tomorrow morning, in case you're upset."

The pain was too big for my chest. I could hardly breathe. "You call him Ted?" was all I could say.

"Don't you dare throw that!" Dr. Sacker's voice was stern. I froze mid-swing. "Put it down." His tone implied *or else*.

I opened my fist and contemplated the marble horse before replacing it on the knight's square. We sat, I on the edge of the couch, he on the other side of the coffee table that held the chess set. Eyes on me, he reached for his cigarettes. The movement no longer seemed familiar now that I knew he could get angry. This wasn't the Dr. Sacker who understood everything. He didn't know about the pain that sliced through my heart as soon as we started talking about Susan. He didn't know the only way to make it go away was to smash something. I jerked my head back and banged it on the wall behind me. It made a loud thud.

"Vivian!" Dr. Sacker sprang to my side of the table, then stood still, looking uncertain.

"I'm OK," I said, pressing my hand to the already-forming bump. The Atmosphere Dr. Sacker would have known that the pain in my head had knocked out the pain in my heart.

"I'll get some ice." He went into the studio's kitchenette and came back with a few cubes wrapped in a dishtowel.

I didn't think I needed ice, but I held it to my head to make him feel better. "Why didn't you tell me about Susan?" I asked.

"I wanted to, but you always seemed too fragile. And it was really for her to tell you, not me."

That made no sense, but I didn't challenge him.

Dr. Sacker spent the rest of the session assuring me it wouldn't make any difference that he was seeing Susan, because when he was with me, I was his primary focus. It sounded logical, yet panic pushed up from Inside. It wasn't only when I was physically in his presence that I needed to be his primary focus. It was the long times between sessions, when he was in the Atmosphere. But I so wanted to show I was a good sport—I didn't want to lose him—that by the end of the hour, his point of view had become mine.

"See you Friday," he said as he walked me to the door. "Take care, Kiddo."

AT HOME EVERYTHING SEEMED DIFFERENT. Susan and I still sat down to supper together but avoided the topic of Dr. Sacker. The second night, we were eating chicken and mashed potatoes when the phone rang.

"Vivian?" said a voice I recognized.

"Yes?"

"This is Dr. Sacker."

"I know. Why are you calling me?"

"Actually, I'm calling Susan. Is she there?"

"Hold on." I held out the receiver. "It's Dr. Sacker."

"I'll take it in the bedroom," she said and walked out.

I hung up when I heard her on the extension, then stood for a few seconds, numb. A car horn outside unstuck me. I drifted to the window and parted the curtain to look down at the headlights moving in opposite directions in the darkness. Susan was in therapy with Dr. Sacker. For real. She was on the phone with him that minute, while I was standing there alone.

I heard a step and turned back to the room.

"I asked him to change my appointment," Susan said as we sat down again, "so he called to tell me the time."

I was glad she thought she owed me an explanation. It was an unspoken acknowledgment that she had encroached on my territory. "Oh," I said, staring at the potatoes I was moving around the plate.

"It's much easier now that you know." She picked up her knife and fork, then held them in midair as another thought struck her. "Remember last week when I told you I was going to the bakery? It was really to use the pay phone. I only bought the Danish so you wouldn't suspect."

I sensed that Susan expected me to sympathize. I couldn't.

"And I could never have a session on a night you were home," she said as she cut into her chicken, "because I couldn't think of an excuse for being out so long. Now it doesn't matter."

"Why are you telling me this?"

"I'm sorry," she said after a pause, meeting my gaze. "I didn't mean to upset you."

"It's OK." She was my best friend. I loved her. I needed her. ■

CHAPTER 18

Sleep

OVER THE NEXT FEW DAYS, Susan sprinkled our conversations with "Ted said," as if she had to tell me everything she'd stored up. This increased my jealousy, as did the fact that she used Dr. Sacker's first name.

In a way, though, the different names made it easier. During the two years I'd been seeing Dr. Sacker, psychotherapy styles had become more relaxed, and some therapists now introduced themselves to new patients by their first names. I was an old patient, going to a traditional therapist. Susan was a new one, going to a modern therapist. We weren't seeing the same person. I could picture her sitting up straight on the striped couch, talking to Ted about marriage or her mother. I couldn't visualize her curled up on it with her shoes off. Ted would never know how to follow her Inside. Only someone with a *Dr.* in his name could do that.

Before long, though, it was hard to remember a time I hadn't known Susan was seeing Dr. Sacker, and we settled into an easy routine. Weekdays, after a quick breakfast, we went our separate ways to work. Evenings, after supper, while she watched TV in the bedroom, I put on a record and read, knit, or drew in the living room. Sometimes I played the piano, a housewarming gift from my mother—she'd asked what I wanted, and we'd gone to a secondhand store. Whenever I felt Inside tug, I went into the bathroom and let myself glide through the mirror. I didn't worry about privacy. I was separated from Susan by two closed doors and the sounds of the TV and record.

Most Sundays, there was a wedding at the East Midwood Jewish Center, across the street. Susan, who yearned to be married, stationed herself at the window to watch the limousines disgorge the wedding party. "That must be the mother," she'd say. "And, look, there's the mother-in-law. They don't get along. You can tell from the way they shook hands... Here come the bridesmaids. Nice dresses."

When the party entered the building, there was nothing more to see, but Susan would still be in wedding mode, so we'd stage one in our living room. I'd drape a sheet around her and improvise a crown from tissue paper. For a bouquet, I'd hand her the piece of white coral my cousin Arthur had brought back from Australia. Susan would march down the length of the living room holding the coral straight out in front of her, while I played "Because You Come to Me with Naught Save Love" on the piano and sang in my most operatic voice. Those mock weddings always ended with Susan's laughter turning to sobs.

But on evenings Susan had a therapy appointment, I couldn't read, draw, clean, knit, play the piano, or slip through the mirror. When I knew specifically what Dr. Sacker's in-person version was doing—sitting in his chair talking to Susan—he wasn't in the Atmosphere. No one saw me or knew I was in the apartment. I felt not-real, a human look-alike sealed in a tomb with lights and furniture but no people. Scarcely able to move or breathe, I just lay on the couch.

I began having trouble falling asleep. When over-the-counter sleeping pills didn't help, I asked Dr. D'Amico, my old family doctor, for something stronger. He prescribed Doriden by phone, no questions asked. The first time I took one, I lay down in bed and waited for something to happen. For an interminable 25 minutes, nothing did. Then, just as I was beginning to think Doriden was no better than off-the-shelf pills, my insides flooded with the most serene feeling I'd ever experienced, as if a fairy godmother had touched me with her wand. It swelled into my belly, spread through my arms and legs, overflowed to fill the hole in my chest. I'd never known such a feeling of peace and well-being existed. I fell asleep floating on it.

The next morning, I woke with a hangover and a dry, fuzzy mouth that toothpaste didn't help. It lasted into the afternoon, but that night, remembering only the good feeling, I took another pill. The high wasn't as intense this time. The third night, I barely felt it. The fourth, I doubled the dose, but even two had no effect, and I worried that I would use up my supply before refill time. By experimenting, I found that if I took Doriden one night, I had to wait a week or two before it worked again.

After our initial discussion, I didn't talk to Dr. Sacker about his seeing Susan. If he thought it irrelevant, I wanted to believe it was. I did tell him about the pills, though, omitting the part about the high. He seemed to think anything that helped calm me was good. Most of the time, however, I didn't bring up concerns like sleeping problems. I spent the better part of our sessions curled up on the couch, melted into one of the stripes, and let Inside moan, whisper, or shriek. Nothing existed except the raw me and Dr. Sacker's comforting presence. "Vivian?" he would call softly. I would answer with another moan, certain he understood what I didn't have words for.

Then one night, Susan said, "Ted's starting a new group, and he asked me to be in it."

I had known for a while that Dr. Sacker ran several therapy groups. They'd never meant much to me because they involved patients I didn't know. This was different.

"He didn't ask me," I said.

"It's for people with relationship issues."

After a few more questions I let the conversation drop, but later that evening I took one of the Doridens, even though I wasn't going to bed yet.

"Can I be in a group?" I asked Dr. Sacker when I saw him next.

"I don't think a group would be right for you."

"Why is it right for Susan?"

"She has different problems."

I was hurt. He favored Susan. At the same time, I was reassured. I didn't have issues to work out with other people, the way normal neurotics did. My problems were more internal. The Atmosphere Dr. Sacker had long known I was in need of special care. I was glad the in-person Dr. Sacker knew, too.

Susan's weekly group sessions were in addition to her weekly private sessions. The six men and women became like a family to her. "The Group feels I shouldn't go out with Jonathan anymore," she reported one day. "He's not ready for marriage."

The Group soon blended into the background of our life, the way Susan's private sessions had. Because I no longer thought of either one minute-by-minute, I didn't connect them to the growing chaos Inside and the feeling that my brain was leaking out through my skull. Pressing my hands to my head to stop the leak, I was sure I was psychotic.

As my internal world expanded, my external world became more circumscribed. In order to make acceptable conversation the few times I went to a party or out on a date, I pushed Inside down so deep that I didn't know it existed. This left me feeling empty and fake, which I hated. I went only because I hoped for the part that sometimes followed, where the boy would hold me and touch me in a world that needed no words and where I didn't feel artificial. But the obligatory conversation that came first was so draining that I eventually stopped going out.

"YOUR MOTHER CALLED ME yesterday," Dr. Sacker said, lighting a cigarette.

"What for?"

"She thinks you and Susan are lesbians. She thought I should know."

"What?"

"I told her I didn't think you were."

"Shit!"

"Your mother's a strange person."

Dr. Sacker had put into words something I'd felt without knowing I felt it. My mother seemed more normal than my father, but she didn't think like most people.

I didn't confront her, but, after that, whenever I went to the 74th Street house, I was wary of both my parents. I had no idea what was going on in my mother's head under her efficiency, and I didn't have the energy to keep putting on the details-of-my-job performance to satisfy my father's questions about my work. At least he would be leaving for Spain soon. For six months, there would be only my mother to contend with.

I soon came to see the benefit of letting her think Susan and I were lesbians. It was better than having her know what I really needed Susan for.

When Susan was awake, she was a living presence in the apartment, even if she was in another room. When she fell asleep, her essence evaporated, and if the Atmosphere wasn't working, which was happening more and more, I was alone. Not temporarily, but permanently, on a distant planet, with no hope of human contact.

One evening was typical. I was crocheting in the living room, with the reassuring sound of the TV barely audible through the closed bedroom door, when the sound ended. I opened the door to see Susan lying on her back, eyes shut, covers pulled up to her chin. It did no good to know that Susan's sleep didn't mean Susan's death, because it felt like death. If I didn't wake her, I would be alone for eternity.

I tiptoed to her bed. Grabbed her feet. She jerked and opened her eyes.

"What are you doing?!" she said, laughing as I began to tickle her. "Sto-o-o-p!"

"I'll stop if you stay up."

"I'm tired," she said between laughs. "I have to get up early. My class is rehearsing the play tomorrow."

"So rest in bed." I took my hands off her feet. "Rest is as good as sleep. Do you want some apple juice?" With a glass in her hand, she'd have to stay awake.

"No. I want to sleep." She sat up to straighten the covers, then lay down.

"Please stay up."

"OK. For a little while."

I started back to the living room to get my crocheting. When I returned, Susan's eyes were closed.

"You're going to sleep!" I headed for her bed.

She opened her eyes. "I'm not. Please, no tickling."

But she did go to sleep, and I was left by myself, trying to patch together some breathable air out of an undependable Atmosphere and Doriden that didn't work.

I'D ALWAYS HAD AN AUTOMATIC CONTROL that kept screams, nonsense words, and slack facial muscles on hold until no one was near, so I managed to limp along without most people realizing I was limping. But that control was being strained. By December, the only place I felt OK was at work.

I had been saving the Doriden for the days I felt the worst, but now every day felt like the worst. I called the Poison Control Center to find out how much Doriden was lethal. They wouldn't tell me, so I began collecting as much as I could—I stopped taking them but refilled the prescription when it came due. This hoarding was calming in two ways. First, I had the comfort of knowing there was a quick out if things ever got so bad I couldn't stand them. Second, I liked the security of having a stash that would enable me to take three or four at a time when a single pill didn't flood me anymore.

I began making frequent emergency calls to Dr. Sacker in the evening. Susan would go into the living room to give me privacy. Lying in bed, I talked to him in non-words and felt even more connected to him than I did in his office. With no body, just a soothing voice coming through the phone, he was more like an Atmosphere presence.

One night in late December, I placed the phone beside me on the sheet and dialed Dr. Sacker's number. After I gave my name to his answering service, I hung up and drew the covers over my head and the phone as usual. A few minutes later, it rang.

"Hi, Vivian. It's Dr. Sacker."

"I'm dying," I whispered from the dark of my tent-world.

"I don't think you're dying."

"I need morphine."

"Why don't you take one of your pills and go to sleep? You'll feel better in the morning."

I couldn't tell him I didn't want to take a pill because I was hoarding them. Besides, something was so wrong that a pill wouldn't fix it. I didn't know how to explain what it was. Then I slipped down a level, and everything was clear. "Lish ka-*ni*-mi. Colla-colla-colla."

"Vivian?"

"Yeah?" I swam to the top to meet him.

"Let me talk to Susan."

"She's in the other room."

"Can you get her?"

I didn't say I was paralyzed and buried under the covers. I thought he saw me and knew. "No."

"Vivian?"

"Mish gouli. Gouli-gouli."

"Are you OK?"

"No."

"What do you want me to do?"

He wasn't helping. "I don't know. I'm hanging up now."

"OK. But call if you need me."

"All right. Bye."

"Bye, Kiddo."

From someplace outside myself, I watched things get steadily worse. On the evening of Tuesday, December 28, as if I were two separate people, one part of me was talking to Dr. Sacker on the phone when another part hijacked the call to say, "I think I need to be in a hospital again."

"When would you like to go?"

I hadn't meant it literally. I'd just wanted him to be aware of my state. "I don't know."

"How about tonight?"

"Right now?"

"Why not?"

"It's nine-thirty. I'm wearing pajamas."

"That doesn't matter. You can go to the emergency room at Mount Sinai. When you get there, tell the resident to call me."

"I'll think about," I said and hung up.

When I got over my shock at Dr. Sacker's eagerness to get me into a hospital, I found I was relieved. I tossed the covers aside and began packing a suitcase.

It was midnight when the night nurse brought me to a room on 8 North with two beds. A girl of about 20 sat cross-legged on the one nearest the window, her red plaid pajamas bright against the white hospital blanket. She had straight shoulder-length hair parted on the side, light brown with a hint of auburn. The radio on her nightstand, barely audible, played rock-and-roll.

"Hi," I said. "Sorry to disturb you so late."

"It's OK. I wasn't sleeping." Her voice was friendly. "My name's Janet."

"Mine's Vivian."

"There's one thing I need to know," Janet said after the nurse left with my sharps and outside clothes.

"What?"

"I smoke."

"So?" I knew smoking was permitted in the lounge.

"In the room. I hate the lounge. Too many people. And I hate asking the nurses for a light." She paused. "Are you going to tell?"

"Of course not."

She smiled. "I think we're going to get along. Do you mind if I have one now?"

"No."

Janet slid her arm into the case of her bottom pillow to pull out a pack of cigarettes, matches, and an ashtray. She lit up, inhaled, and blew the smoke away from me.

Feeling calmer than I had in a long while, I reached up to turn out my light. ▪

CHAPTER 19

No Refuge

DR. SCHWARTZ WAS ABOUT 30, and though his manner was formal, his face seemed approachable, more like a Dr. Sacker face than a Dr. Abrams face.

Sitting at the desk in one of the bare offices I remembered from the year before, he tapped his clipboard twice with his pen. "I see you were admitted through the emergency room last night because you're afraid of hurting yourself." He looked up. "Can you tell me about that?"

Hospital people always said *hurting yourself* when they meant *killing yourself*. "I don't think I would actually *do* anything," I said, to maintain the etiquette. "I don't really want to die."

"So why was it an emergency?"

"I don't know." Part of me did want to die, but I didn't. What bothered me most wasn't being suicidal, but the feeling that I was about to fall off a tightrope into an ocean of insanity. Yet I didn't feel crazy all the time. Right now, sitting in a chair alongside the desk, I felt logical and fine. All this was too hard to explain. "Dr. Sacker wanted me to come. My therapist."

"How long have you been seeing him?"

"Almost three years."

Dr. Schwartz rolled his chair to the side until there was no desk between us. I realized his intention was to remove a barrier, but I wasn't ready for more intimacy. I rolled my own chair back a few inches, slowly, hoping he wouldn't notice I was widening the space between us.

"Is there anything you want to tell me?" he asked.

Inside hardly knew this man. Yet even if I had been more at ease, there was no place to curl up, no cushion for my hands to fiddle with. In an Outside voice, I told him I was afraid to be alone. I didn't say anything about the sealed-tomb annihilation I had felt when I woke during the previous night, unsure whether Janet was sleeping or only lying still. Nor did I describe how I'd waited for the census checker to come around with her flashlight and rescue me from dissolving into the mattress—how, before I had a chance to reconstitute myself to talk to her, she was gone and I didn't think I would last another half hour until she came again. I said, "It was hard to sleep last night."

"Would you like someone to sit with you until you fall asleep?"

"Yes," I said, surprised. It was as if Dr. Schwartz understood what I hadn't been able to say.

"I can also write an order for sleeping medication."

"That would be good."

He moved to easier topics: my job and my classes.

"So," he said after 20 minutes, "that's all for today. We'll talk again tomorrow."

"Would you call my mother and tell her I'm here?" I had already asked Susan to call the library and tell Jo I was in the hospital, and to imply that it had something to do with a throat infection.

"What would you like me to say?" Dr. Schwartz asked.

"That I'm all right, not to worry."

"Sure."

In the hall, I watched his back as he walked toward the nursing station. Feeling suddenly invisible, I took a few steps to the doorway of the lounge. There were patients watching television, playing chess, reading, smoking. Except for the uniformed aide, it looked like an oversized living room decorated with colors you might find in a motel lobby: olive green, brown, and gold.

Crossing to an empty armchair, I felt Dr. Schwartz's presence in the Atmosphere. Conscious that he was watching me, I picked up a magazine and settled against the foam backrest. The piping on the chair was frayed. I played with the stuffing that poked through. "Hash ki-*no*-la," I whispered as the threads began to draw me in. Dr. Schwartz's molecules were mixed in with the molecules from Dr. Sacker, Dr. Hirschhorn, and the hospital-in-general. Collectively, they surrounded me. "Osh-ki pa-*ni*-na," I said from inside the stuffing.

The sound of laughter. I looked up to see a girl who could have been on the cover of *Seventeen:* strawberry blonde hair that fanned when she moved her head, leather boots to match her rust-colored Bermuda-shorts pajamas, dangling earrings, iridescent lipstick, black eyeliner, and eye shadow that picked up the green in her eyes.

"Let's sit here," she said. A boy in hospital-issue pajamas put his cloth bag on the table. The girl was about to take the opposite chair when she noticed me. "I'm Carrie," she said. "He's Stephen. What's your name?"

"Vivian."

"When did you come?"

"Last night."

"Must've been late. I watched *Kildare* till nine."

"Around midnight."

"I'm glad you're here. There's just me, Stephen, and Janet. Everyone else is old."

"Janet's my roommate."

"She's nice, but she stays in bed most of the time. Wanna play Chinese checkers?"

"OK."

Stephen was setting up the marbles in the round wooden board. "Hi," he said shyly.

Cracking gum, Carrie talked as we played. She told me she was in foster care. So were all her friends. "When we get too wild, they lock us up for a few weeks—here or in Hillside."

"Do you go to school?" I wondered what "wild" meant.

"Mostly I cut. Except lately I've been going 'cause there's this teacher I like. But she's leaving to have a baby." All Carrie wanted, she said, was to get her own apartment. Or maybe she would live with her boyfriend. He was 21 and had a motorcycle. She was 16. "What do you think of the nurses?"

"I only met two so far. Miss Weber and Miss Engel."

"Miss Engel!" Carrie made a fart sound with her lips. Stephen stifled a smile.

I wished I were like Carrie: pretty, fashionable, and carefree. I was shocked that she didn't want to go to college or even finish high school, but I wanted her to think well of me, so I didn't mention my Pratt worries—that the term would soon be over and I had two papers yet to write. I was pleased when she said, "It's so cool that you share an apartment with your friend."

That night, a nurse handed me two red gel chloral hydrate pills in a tiny paper cup. The rule was that within 15 minutes of taking sleeping medication, you had to turn off the overhead light and go to bed, though it was permissible to read with your night light. I couldn't concentrate on my book with Miss Washington, the aide assigned to stay with me, sitting against the wall. She was just waiting, I was sure, for me to close my eyes so she could watch TV. I laid my book aside and made a big production of adjusting my pillow so she wouldn't think I was asleep and leave me alone.

The chloral hydrate hit suddenly. One second the world was all edges. The next, everything was wrapped in velvet.

MY EYES OPENED BY THEMSELVES, and I didn't have a hangover. A moment later, a nurse came in, turned on the overhead light, and called, "Good morning, ladies." Janet pulled the covers over her head. I brushed my teeth, washed my face, and put on makeup, then dressed in my alternate muumuu. Janet was still under the covers. I brought yesterday's clothes to the laundry room and started the machine.

The unit was wonderfully alive. Doctors going in and out of the nursing station. Aides walking around with clipboards. A man wheeling the breakfast trolley. The hospital was a living, breathing organism beginning its day, and I felt part of it, ready to begin a regular day in my own life. That meant going to work and school.

I always thought the way I was at any given moment was the way I would be forever. I could remember having felt differently, but only as something that happened to a me who once was. While I knew I had come to the hospital two days ago because I felt crazy and suicidal, that was history. When I saw Dr. Schwartz, I would ask him for a pass to go to work.

After breakfast and Group, I slipped a dime into the pay phone. It was Christmas break. Susan would be home.

"Can you bring my black A-line skirt and my maroon poor-boy sweater when you come tonight?"

"Sure."

"And could you drive my car and leave it in the lot here?"

"Why do you need it?"

"In case there's a transit strike." The radio had been announcing the possibility for days, to start January 1, less than 48 hours away. "I'm going to work soon."

"Already?"

"Yeah. And my money. It's in an envelope in my top drawer."

The only thing left to arrange was a pass. I didn't want to go up to occupational therapy, because I didn't know when Dr. Schwartz would come, so I sat in the lounge to wait. He showed up after lunch.

"So, how are things going?" he asked, rolling his chair to the side of the desk.

"OK." I stayed where I was and met his eyes.

"Were you able to sleep?"

"Yes." I didn't elaborate. I wasn't sure how long our talk would last, and I didn't want to waste it. "Can I have a pass to go to work?"

He looked taken aback. "You just got here."

"I feel fine."

"You weren't fine the other night. How do you know it won't happen again?"

"I just know. If I have a pass and it goes OK, can I be discharged?"

He took an audible breath. "Miss Conan, the reason you're here is so you can forget outside concerns and focus on why you want to hurt yourself."

"I don't want to anymore."

"What happened to that feeling?"

"I don't know. If I can't go to work, can I at least go to the Pratt library to start my papers?"

"You don't need that pressure right now. We have to find out what caused your crisis."

The crisis was gone, and I'd be under more pressure if I didn't work on the papers. Before I could tell him that, he stood and said, "We'll talk about it some more tomorrow."

Walking into the hall, I felt powerless. I was glad Dr. Schwartz was concerned about my welfare but frustrated that he didn't understand how I could be crazy sometimes and also fine, and I was always fine at work.

By nighttime, thanks to Susan, I had my car keys in my drawer and, unbeknownst to the nurses, a set of work clothes in my narrow metal closet. All I needed was permission to use them.

The next day was both Friday and New Year's Eve. Again I asked Dr. Schwartz about going to work. Again he said it was too soon. Though I expressed disappointment, which I did feel, somewhere Inside, I knew the reason I was doing better was that the hospital walls were holding me.

"Can I at least be transferred to the Day and Night Center?" I asked.

"I don't understand what happened, but you do seem different. If you continue this way over the weekend, I'll bring it up at the meeting next week, and if my supervisor agrees, I'll see if the Day and Night Center will admit you."

"I'm already admitted."

"The Day and Night Center is a different department."

I felt my insides shift. I didn't want that information. The hospital-in-general, as one entity, was mixed together with everyone else watching over me. I needed to keep it that way.

Dr. Schwartz stood. "Have a Happy New Year, Miss Conan. I'll see you Monday."

That night, Miss Weber let us stay up late to watch Guy Lombardo welcome 1966. Just before the ball began to drop, she gave out noisemakers, and we blew them in each other's faces. Then she came around with the sleeping medication.

THE DAY AND NIGHT CENTER, where I was transferred right before bedtime on January 5, did not have actual rooms. It was just an open space with built-in seating alcoves along the walls that unfolded into cots at night. With tables and chairs in the middle of the floor and a shelf of board games, the area was at once dormitory, lounge, and dining room. A nurse demonstrated how to convert my assigned seat into a cot. She said that before I left for work the next morning, I was to turn it back into seating and stow all traces of myself—clothing, pajamas, toothbrush, book—in a camouflaged compartment alongside it. My place would belong to one of the day patients while I was gone. Because the transit strike meant extra-long commutes, most of the other overnight patients were already in bed. I, too, would be getting up at dawn, so I made up my cot and took the chloral hydrate the nurse offered me.

In the morning, I said goodbye to a different nurse and went down to the hospital parking lot, which was outdoors. I slipped my key into the ignition and the motor sprang to life. I felt alive, competent, in control. For the next few hours, the surface me negotiated traffic jams unperturbed while, underneath, I let my head go where it pulled. Whenever there was a lull Inside, I turned on the radio, alternating between traffic reports and classical music.

At the library, my coworkers interacted with me the way they always had. If someone asked whether I was feeling better, I assumed they'd bought into the throat-infection story and said yes without elaborating. The strike helped. War stories about getting around were the main topic of conversation.

The evening traffic was worse, and I didn't arrive back at the hospital until 9:00. A nurse I hadn't met gave me the supper tray she'd set aside. The overhead light had already been dimmed for patients who were trying to sleep, so I ate alone in what felt like twilight and went to bed. In the morning, I said goodbye to yet a different nurse.

The previous day, I hadn't stopped for hitchhikers holding up destination signs on the 96th Street entrance ramp to the East River Drive. Now, emboldened by radio stories of strangers helping one another, I opened my door to a woman with a kind face whose cardboard sign read *Brooklyn Bridge*. In the 80 minutes it took us to reach it, she told me about her children, her job of 30 years, and her husband, who had recently died. I told her about library school and the Pratt library. I was pleased to think she had no idea I was a mental patient out on a pass.

Work was again OK, but as the return drive stretched to hours, I felt more and more unreal. In the Day and Night Center, there was another strange nurse. I felt I would dissolve into nothingness and cease to exist if I unfolded my cot and got in. Unable to explain this, the only reason I gave the nurse for wanting to be transferred back to 8 North was that I felt lonely. She suggested I wait until the next day. I insisted on going immediately. She paged the on-call doctor, and by midnight it was arranged.

MY BED IN JANET'S ROOM was occupied by a new patient, so I was put in a room with three older women, all of whom were sleeping. I woke the next day, Saturday, to learn that Stephen was being transferred to Rockland State Hospital. I wondered why. He'd always been well-behaved. I was the only one there to say goodbye to him. Carrie had been discharged, and Janet was on a weekend pass. Nothing was permanent here, either.

On Monday and Tuesday I went to work, a privilege for which I had to negotiate because 8 North was supposed to be for full-time patients. The strike was still on, so I left early and got back late. Even though my toothbrush and book were waiting for me on my nightstand and no one else had used my space during the day, I missed being part of the daily thrum and felt almost as alone as I had on the Day and Night Center. I was not sorry when Dr. Schwartz told me a new rule had been made: no patient could go out to work from 8 North. With as hoarse a voice as I could muster, I called Jo to say my throat infection had come back.

TWO WEEKS INTO MY MOUNT SINAI STAY, Dr. Schwartz told me he would be leaving for vacation the next day, and Dr. Feingold would be taking over. I felt betrayed. Why had he waited until the last minute to tell me? Why had he even been assigned as my doctor if he wasn't going to be here the whole month?

To my surprise, I liked Dr. Feingold. Over the next four days, I didn't talk to him much, but I didn't think I had to. I felt he understood things automatically. Then came the weekend, when I wouldn't be seeing him.

I was feeling more uneasy than usual that Saturday, though I didn't know why. It was as if something cataclysmic had happened in a light-years-away galaxy, and the ripples were only now making their way to me. I began pacing, crossing from the east corridor to the west through the laundry room, and the west corridor to the east through the elevator bank. The other patients seemed like figures gliding by in another dimension. I felt hollow, unreal. If the floor had been sand, I would not have left footprints.

On weekends, the nursing station was eerily still. There were no doctors hurrying in and out, just a skeleton crew of two nurses sitting at the counter behind glass walls, lip-talking like figures on a soundless TV screen—fish-tank scenery that broke the monotony as I passed.

On round three, or four, or maybe fourteen, I paused in the doorway of the lounge. It was nearly deserted. Had more people been discharged, or were they on weekend passes? A man reading a magazine looked up and said hello. From the other side of Real, I returned the greeting.

I stood in the doorway another few seconds, thinking it might be nice to go in and sit. I had often surveyed the room from this vantage point before entering, to see who was there and whether the good armchairs were free. But the lounge looked different today, smaller, as if I were seeing it from farther back and through a plexiglass wall. I felt the way I do in a theater, where I know everything on the stage is fake—the rooms, the actors pretending to be people they aren't—but it's lit up and alive and seems more real than the "real" world where I sit in the dark.

As I stood in suspended animation, something rushed up inside me. Ignited. A Frankenstein spark that shattered the plexiglass and catapulted me into Real. I took a breath, my first in this new world. My body expanded. It was too big to fit in my skin.

My arm shot out. Grabbed the leg of the end table nearest the door. I made a quick sweep with my eye to chart a trajectory free of people, then hurled. The table flew across the room, knocking over a chair near the window before landing.

As fast as it happened, it was over. I still felt real, but now it was a peaceful real.

Though I was calm, the unit was not. The magazine man and the woman watching TV turned to stare at me. Miss Thomas, the aide, ran out and came back with Miss Engel, the nurse on duty.

"Please leave the lounge," Miss Engel ordered the other patients. They did. Then, to me, "What made you do that?"

"I don't know," I said truthfully. I knew my arm had thrown the table, but not why or how. At five feet tall, I weighed 100 pounds. The table was small, but too heavy for me to lift and throw with enough force to reach the other side of the room.

"What do you mean you don't know?" She seemed angry.

I shrugged.

"I'm paging Dr. Feingold. Maybe you'll tell *him* why you did it." She turned to Miss Thomas. "Stay with her."

On weekends, they paged a doctor only in emergencies. I thought Miss Engel was overreacting, but I didn't expect her to understand. She wasn't one of the good nurses.

The television was still on, tuned to *American Bandstand*. I sat down and watched without seeing, conscious of Miss Thomas sitting next to me.

Fifteen minutes later, Dr. Feingold walked in with Miss Engel. "I hear you threw a table," he said, and I knew from his gentle voice that he understood.

"Yes." I waited for him to say something to show Miss Engel and Miss Thomas they were making a big deal over nothing.

"Why" he asked.

Maybe he *didn't* understand. "I don't know." Even if I had known, I wouldn't have been able to talk to him while we were standing in front of the TV, which was still on, and Miss Thomas and Miss Engel were listening.

"Miss Conan," he said in a tone that had changed to pseudo-gentle, "just tell me what made you do it, and everything will be all right."

"I don't *know* why."

"Either you tell me or I have to medicate you." This wasn't even pseudo.

"I really don't know."

"I'm writing an order for medication. If you change your mind and want to talk, let Miss Engel know and she'll page me."

He and Miss Engel left.

Minutes later, Miss Engel returned. With her was a muscular man from Security, over six feet tall. In her left hand she carried two small paper cups, one with four orange pills, one with water. In her right hand she held a syringe and a tongue depressor.

"Either you take the pills," she said, "or I have to give you an injection."

Under three sets of watchful eyes, I reached for the pills, which I recognized as Thorazine, 200 milligrams altogether. The most I had taken at one time last year had been 50. I swallowed the pills.

"Open your mouth," Miss Engel said.

She couldn't be serious.

The Security man took a step toward me. I opened. Miss Engel probed my mouth with the tongue depressor and announced, "She took them."

They left.

Word got out that it was OK to use the lounge again. Five or six patients drifted in, making the room seem friendly once more. I didn't know how long it would be before the pills kicked in, but for now I felt like a lighthearted child. I skipped from chair to chair, stopping in front of each person to say hello with a bow and a giggle. I jumped up and down on the couch as if it were a trampoline, shrieking with glee while I looked at Miss Thomas to see whether she would stop me. She didn't. I marched around singing "Row, Row, Row Your Boat," lifting my knees high and swinging my arms.

The patients turned their chairs to watch me instead of the TV. One tapped her foot to my singing. Others in the hall heard the party noise and came in. They were all smiling. I even saw Miss Thomas suppress a grin.

Every once in a while, Miss Engel stuck her head in the door.

"Hi, Miss Engel," I shouted each time, waving wildly, as if we were a block apart.

"Hello, Miss Conan," she answered stiffly.

My frolic lasted an hour. Then the pills hit. One second I had boundless energy. The next, there were 1,000-pound weights on my arms, my legs, my eyelids. Darkness closed over me.

FROM THE DEPTHS OF MY STUPOR, I felt something shaking me. I tried to open my eyes, but they were glued shut with Duco Cement. I tried to move my arms, but I was strapped to my bed by a pharmacological straitjacket.

Someone was raising me to a sitting position, supporting my rag-doll back. "Miss Conan, wake up."

I couldn't respond.

"You have to take your medication."

More shaking. My eyelids let in a slit of light. There was a horrible taste in my mouth, which was sandpaper dry.

"Can you open your eyes?" I recognized the voice. Miss Galyan, my favorite nurse. The slit widened, and I saw the small paper cup. In it was one orange pill.

"Sorry, Miss Conan, but Dr. Feingold ordered fifty milligrams every four hours." She held the cup to my lips and lifted it. The pill slipped into my mouth. She held up a cup of water. I felt that if I swallowed the pill, I would die. I kept it in the hollow of my cheek while I let the water go down.

I had to do something so she wouldn't check my mouth. "More water," I said, my voice a hoarse whisper. "It got stuck." I drank the refill.

Miss Galyan eased me down without checking and left.

With a Herculean effort, I moved my legs until they hung over the edge of the bed. I slid to the floor and crawled to the bathroom. Gripping the toilet seat for leverage, I rose to a kneeling position, leaned over the bowl, and opened my mouth. The pill plopped in and sank, like an orange M&M. I lifted one hand to reach for the flush handle, steadied myself, and pulled. A rush of water carried the pill away. I got back to the bed on all fours but couldn't hoist myself up against gravity, so I gave in to my stupor on the floor.

Next I knew, an aide and Miss Galyan were bending over me. I mumbled something about having gotten up to use the bathroom. They lifted me onto the bed, and Miss Galyan placed the call button on my pillow. "Press this if you need to go again," she said.

The passage of time was marked by the repeated routine: shake awake, orange pill, second helping of decoy water, trip to the toilet, back to bed, which I now managed to get into myself. It kept getting easier.

There came a time when my eyes opened though no one had shaken me. I lay there registering sounds of ordinary life from the hall. It was dark out the window, semi-dark in the room. Someone walked in and turned on the overhead light. She came into focus as she approached my bed. One of my roommates. "You're up," she said. "We were worried about you. How do you feel?"

"OK. What day is it?"

"Sunday."

I had fallen asleep on Saturday. "Thanks."

"Do you want anything?"

"No."

She walked to her bed.

I still couldn't respond with more than a few words when my other roommates came in, but I was definitely back. I reached for my glasses, which someone had put on my nightstand. With the world in focus, my eyes followed the women. One lathered cold cream on her face. Another brushed her teeth. The third filled her plastic water pitcher. I felt peaceful and content. I had rescued myself from death. But I also realized that the hospital, which I had thought of as a refuge, was no refuge at all.

By the time Mrs. Galyan came in to say, "Good night, ladies," and turn off the overhead light, I was fully awake.

"It's nice to see you up again," she said, coming over to my bed.

"I'm not tired. Is it all right to sit in the lounge?"

"That's up to Miss Weber. I'll be leaving in a few minutes, and she just came on. I'll tell her you asked."

"OK."

It was hard to lie still. To me, it was morning. My eyes were gummy—I hadn't had a chance to remove my mascara before the Thorazine hit—and the horrible taste in my mouth remained even after I drank some water.

I brought my toilet kit to the bathroom and glanced at my smudged eyes in the metal mirror. I brushed my teeth and tongue, washed my face, and combed my hair. Back in bed, I drew the curtain closed along the overhead track and turned on my nightlight. Now everything was reversed. Most of the world was dark and sleeping, while I was awake on an island of brightness. I leaned over to get the bag of afghan squares I was crocheting from the nightstand drawer, settled against the pillows, and wound the rainbow-colored yarn around my index finger.

I was still crocheting 20 minutes later, when Miss Weber came in. "I don't see why not," she said about going to the lounge. "You've been sleeping more than thirty hours. No wonder you're not tired."

"Thanks!" I jumped up before I recalled she didn't know I hadn't been taking the pills. I would have to remember to move slowly.

Miss Weber brought hot chocolate and toast into the lounge, then stayed to play gin rummy. We talked. I crocheted. We played Scrabble. She said it had been snowing while I was sleeping, but because the temperature was above freezing, it had turned to slush, and she'd had a hard time getting to the hospital. It was strange to think the people who took care of us in here did things elsewhere. On 8 North, where the weather never changed, it was too easy to forget that on the other side of the reinforced windows was a world of sidewalks, supermarkets, buses—and library school.

"I'm worried I won't get credit for my courses," I said. "I still have papers to write, and I missed the finals."

"I'm sure your professors will let you finish late if you tell them where you are," Miss Weber said.

"I don't want them to know."

She agreed that was a problem, and I was grateful. I hated it when people said, "Don't worry, everything will be all right," when I knew everything might not be.

DR. FEINGOLD CAME BY after breakfast the following morning. Remembering to walk slowly, I went with him into one of the session rooms.

"How are you feeling?" he asked when we were seated.

"Fine."

"Do you know why you threw the table?"

"No." The whole incident seemed as if it had taken place hundreds of years ago and had nothing to do with me.

"I'm going to continue the Thorazine," he said. "You seem to be doing well with it." A moment's silence. "Is there anything else you want to tell me?"

"No."

"Then I guess that's all for now."

THE NEXT MORNING, ONE OF THE PATIENTS popped his head into my room to say I had a phone call.

"Vivian," my mother said when I picked up the dangling pay phone receiver in the hall. "What's going on?"

"What do you mean?"

"Why do they want to send you to a state hospital?"

"*What?* Who said that?"

"Miss Wycker."

"Who is she?"

"The social worker." My mother told me Miss Wyker had called that morning to say I had "poor impulse control" and was "a danger to myself and others." My status had been changed from *voluntary* to *involuntary*, meaning I couldn't discharge myself at will. It also meant that even though I was over 21, my mother could legally make decisions regarding my fate. Miss Wycker had given her two options. She could sign me out to her own care and supervision, or she could let Mount Sinai transfer me to Brooklyn State Hospital for long-term confinement. Miss Wycker strongly recommended Brooklyn State.

"I don't believe this!" I hissed. "How can she recommend something when she never met me?"

"I have an appointment with her tomorrow," my mother said grimly. "I have to decide by then."

"What are you going to say?"

"I don't know, Vivian. I'm confused. What should I do?"

It was odd to hear my mother unsure, and frightening that she could even think there was a question. "Sign that you'll be responsible for me."

"But they say you need a hospital."

"They don't know what they're talking about."

"I still have to consider it."

Shit! ShitShitShit!

Forgetting about slow motion, I marched up to the nursing station and knocked. "I want to see Dr. Feingold! Now!" I said to the nurse who opened the door.

"I'll page him for you, Miss Conan." She seemed a little afraid of me. Good. I hated them all. Hypocrites! They acted nice to your face while they plotted behind your back.

As I paced in front of the nursing station, I was aware of the four nurses inside pretending to do paperwork but really watching me, and of the aide who had come to the door of the lounge as if by chance, but probably for backup. All at once, I understood why Dr. Feingold had hardly talked with me yesterday, and why he hadn't been around today. The hospital was finished with me. The new policy was: Don't waste any more time on her; just control her with Thorazine until we can ship her out.

I saw Dr. Feingold coming down the hall. "Hello, Miss Conan," he said, as if nothing had changed. "You wanted to see me?"

"Yes!"

"What about?"

He was the biggest hypocrite of all. "I don't want to talk here," I said. The nurses were staring from their window. Other patients were in the hall.

"OK. Let's find a room."

"Aren't you scared to be alone with me?" I couldn't resist that. All the staff except Miss Galyan and Miss Weber seemed nervous around me.

"No," he said in a serious voice. "We know each other pretty well by now."

Bully for you, I thought. You're so brave.

In one of the session rooms, we took our customary seats. For a few seconds, I didn't say anything as I got used to my new perception of this man in a white doctor costume. It was the first time I didn't ascribe magical powers to him or feel like a longing child in his presence.

"What did you want to see me about?" he asked.

"My mother called me." I pinned him with my eyes. My voice was clear and strong. "She told me about the state hospital. Who makes decisions about me, anyway? You or some social worker I never met?"

"Miss Conan, all the doctors discussed your case and felt—" He turned up his palms as if waiting for the right words to drop into them. "You never told us why you threw the table." I realized *he* was getting used to a new perception, too, a firm-voiced me he hadn't heard before.

"I don't *know* why I threw it, so how could I tell you?"

"As I was saying, the doctors met to discuss—"

"Which doctors? *You're* the only doctor here who's talked to me. You're the only one who should make decisions about me. Do *you* think I should be in a state hospital?"

"Yes."

"Well. Then there's nothing more to talk about. You're not on my side, and anything I say will be held against me." I walked out.

WHEN THE FEMALE AIDE, accompanied by a man from Security, escorted me into Miss Wycker's office for a meeting with my mother the next day, I could see this was not some generic office used by any social worker as the need arose. The bookcase was overflowing, and papers cluttered her desk.

My mother sat in a chair, coat draped over the back, purse on her lap. She wore one of her work suits and her Alan Murray space shoes. Facing her from the other side of the desk sat a slightly overweight woman of about 40 with short, dyed-blonde hair and a plain black dress that set off her gold costume jewelry. I got the impression the two had been talking a while.

"Hello, Miss Conan. I'm Miss Wycker." In a parody of gentility, she rose, extending her hand as she leaned over her desk. We shook.

"Hi, Mom." I took the chair next to her. Behind us, the aide and Security man positioned themselves on either side of the door.

"Hello, Vivian." My mother's face looked as if we were in a room where someone was dying.

"Your mother and I were just talking about you," Miss Wycker said.

I nodded.

"I understand you threw a table."

"Yes."

"Can you tell me why?"

"I don't *know* why."

She turned to my mother. "This is the reason we're advising the state hospital."

"You mean if I told you why I did it, you wouldn't commit me?" I asked.

"I didn't say that."

"You implied it."

"Miss Conan, I don't want to get into a semantic argument. This is a difficult situation, and I want to make it as smooth as possible for everyone."

Easy for you to say, I thought.

In a flat voice, my mother said she'd gone to see Brooklyn State yesterday. There were bars on the windows and she'd heard screaming. She didn't like it. "What if I don't want her to go?"

"You can sign this," Miss Wycker said, handing my mother a sheet of paper, "to say you assume full responsibility for her."

"Vivian," my mother said, turning a pained face to me, "I don't know what to do."

"Sign that paper," I spat.

For a few seconds, no one spoke. Then my mother let out a shallow sigh. "OK." She reached for one of the pens on the desk.

"I think you're making a mistake," Miss Wycker said.

"It's what Vivian wants. She's my daughter."

"She may want it, but it's not what's best for her."

My mother didn't bother to wipe the tears on her cheeks as her eyes met mine.

"Sign!" I commanded. At that moment, I hated her, hated that she had the power to decide my fate. I didn't care that she was miserable. All I cared about was my freedom.

"If you sign," Miss Wycker said, "Vivian has to live with you. And she can't drive."

"Will you come back to live with me?" my mother asked.

"Yes," I said, though I knew I wouldn't.

"And you agree not to drive?"

"Yes." Another lie.

My mother placed the tip of the pen on the signature line. *Beatrice Conan*, she wrote. *January 26, 1966*. My father's birthday. He was in Spain and probably knew nothing of this.

"You understand that you can never come to Mount Sinai again," Miss Wycker said, "because you're leaving against medical advice."

"That's fine."

"You can go up to get your things while I process your discharge papers."

Boy, did they want me out.

"One last question," Miss Wycker said as I rose. "You're not a patient here anymore, so you can answer honestly. Have you been taking your medication?"

"No." What jackasses.

"That's what we thought."

The Security man, the aide, my mother, and I rode the elevator up to 8 North, where a nurse was waiting in front of the hall closet. "I hear you're leaving us, Miss Conan," she said, unlocking the door.

"Yes." I grinned and went in to get my coat and suitcase.

My mother sat on a chair in my room while I packed. She already had her coat and gloves on. "Do you need help?" she asked.

"No." I didn't want her touching my things. I wouldn't have wanted her there at all, but without her, I couldn't leave.

On our way back to the elevator, we passed the nursing station. Everyone inside came to the door.

"Bye, Miss Conan," each one said, shaking my hand. "Good luck on the outside." As if making it on the outside were a matter of chance.

In the parking lot, my mother and I skirted icy patches on our way to my car. She walked to the driver's side and waited for me to give her the key. I walked to the passenger side, unlocked the door, and held it open for her.

"Get in," I ordered.

"You agreed not to drive."

"Of course. I didn't want to go to a state hospital. If you want a ride back to Brooklyn, I'll take you. If not, you can go the way you came. By train." I knew I was being cruel, but I was fighting for my life.

She came to the passenger side and held out her gloved hand, palm up. "Please give me the key, Vivian."

I walked to the driver's side, got in behind the wheel, and started the car. "Either get in or close the door so I can go," I called across to her, then turned on the defroster.

She got in.

We waited in silence until the ice on the windshield became soft enough for the wipers to sweep to the sides. Only after I had pulled out of the lot did I speak again. "I'm not coming to live with you. I live with Susan on Ocean Avenue. I'll drop you off on Seventy-fourth Street or at your school. Your choice."

"They said I'm supposed to supervise you," she said weakly.

"I can supervise myself." ■

PHOTO ALBUM: 1942–1965

With my father at age two months outside our apartment in Knickerbocker Village on Manhattan's Lower East Side (July 1942)

With my mother at age three months (August 1942)

A family portrait taken on my second birthday (May 1944)

My mother, brother Marvin, and me in our apartment on 20th Avenue in Brooklyn while my father was serving in Italy (January 1945)

Dressed up for a walk around the neighborhood on Rosh Hashanah (September 1946)

My mother sometimes made me feel like a worm you poke with a stick. (September 1946)

Getting a tennis lesson from our father (Summer 1947)

Marvin (second from left) and me (right) with our cousins Neil, George, and Jerry outside Nona and Papoo's house on 74th Street (December 1946)

At Gravesend Bay in Bensonhurst Park (Summer 1947)

At a sleepaway camp in Kingston, NY, where my mother worked as a laundress so we could attend for free (Summer 1950)

At Brighton Beach Baths, a sprawling beach club just a subway ride from home. We were members for years. (Summer 1953)

At a musicale in our living room, where friends and classmates performed for parents (1953)

Papoo and Nona (center) at a wedding with their eight children: Sarah, Mollie, Rae, my mother Bea (next to Papoo), Jack, Sophia, Esther, and Diana (July 1948)

Marvin performing at another musicale (Circa 1956)

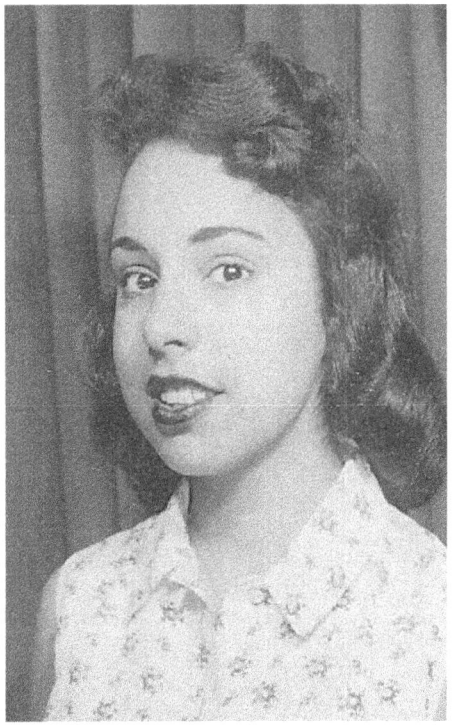

A self-portrait I took in 7th or 8th grade, when photo booths were a popular source of instant images (Circa 1956)

With my Girl Scout troop (bottom left) on a trip to Washington, D.C. (April 1955)

My father and me in front of Lafayette High School on the day I graduated (January 1960)

On my way to Seth Low Junior High graduation (June 1957)

Marvin and me on our way to perform with the Brooklyn College orchestra. I played viola, he played flute. (1961)

With my close friends, Linda (left) and Susan (right), and new friend, Diane (second from right), when we were juniors in college (Autumn 1962)

I graduated from Brooklyn College in January and returned in June for the ceremony and to play viola in the orchestra (June 1964)

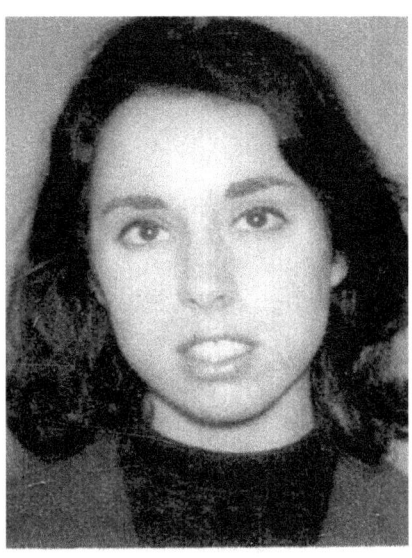

My Pratt ID photo, taken four months before my first hospitalization (September 1964)

PART FOUR

EINSTEIN

CHAPTER 20

Rose Garden

I RESTARTED MY LIFE with three phone calls. To Jo, to say I'd be back at work the next day. To the library school, to check on the status of my fall classes and register for the spring term. To Dr. Sacker.

"You're back?" He sounded surprised.

"Yeah. It happened fast. I'll tell you when I see you. I just called to make an appointment."

"Would you like your regular time?"

"Yes." He hadn't given it away!

I resumed my old life with Susan, too, eating supper with her after work, bringing her tea when she returned, whiny and drained, from visits to her mother, and panicking whenever she went to sleep before I did.

One evening, about a month after I got home, I was sitting cross-legged on my bed, watching her lay out the clothes she'd wear the following day. She draped a baby blue dress over her chair.

"It's only eight-thirty," I said.

"I know, but I'm tired, and the assistant principal's observing me tomorrow." She added stockings, underpants, a bra and slip.

"Please don't go to bed."

"I have to." From her jewelry box, she selected gold clip-on earrings and a dark blue beaded necklace. Only shoes were left.

Suddenly I felt a surge of power. I sprang off my bed, grabbed the bottle of Jergen's lotion from Susan's dresser, and threw back her bedcover.

"No!" she said, racing over. But I was quick and managed to pour some of the creamy liquid onto her sheet. Grinning, I went back to my bed and waited to see what she would do.

With remarkable good humor, Susan wiped the lotion off with tissues and placed a towel over the damp spot. I'd been hoping she would change the sheet. That would have taken more time. Already in pajamas, she slid under the covers, said good night, and closed her eyes.

I watched her for a few minutes, then tiptoed to her bed. Her eyelids were quivering. She was awake. I thrust out my hands, gave her a swift tickle up and down through the covers, then ran, giggling, to the other side of the room.

"Stop!" she laughed, opening her eyes.

Determined to keep her from closing them, I grabbed a pair of scissors and reached into the closet for something from her side.

"No, please!" she said as I held the blades to the pink dress I pulled out.

"Then don't go to sleep."

"Please, that's my good dress. If you have to cut, take the flowered one. I was going to give it to Goodwill anyway."

She was sitting up now. Partial victory.

I went back for the flowered dress and made several cuts in the fabric while Susan looked on with a mixture of amusement and resignation. I tossed the ruined garment to the floor, laughing with glee. I was winning my stay of execution a minute at a time.

Abruptly, as if a switch had been thrown, my power evaporated. I retreated to my bed and sat meekly, waiting for the inevitable. There was no way I could keep her awake.

"Good night," Susan said.

I was unable to answer.

She lay down again and closed her eyes. Soon her breathing became slow and regular.

I looked at my feet. They seemed miles away, but they couldn't be. They were on the bed. I looked out at the room. Walls. Floor. Furniture. Susan's bed with her lifeless form. The universe was vast and empty, yet the room seemed small, with walls close on all sides. I lowered my eyes. They attached to a loose thread on the blanket, held on until the thread became the only significant object in the world.

I didn't know I had disappeared until I emerged from the thread and saw that I was still on the bed. I walked to the bathroom, reorienting myself to the floor. I was dying, but I wasn't in pain. Just empty and unreal. I would have preferred pain. I lifted my toothbrush from its holder and looked at the face in the mirror. The eyes were at once intense and hollow. The mouth hung slack. Like a marionette moved by an external force, I washed off the eyeliner and makeup and brushed the teeth.

Back in the bedroom, I heard Susan breathing, but no essence emanated from her. I was alone on the planet and couldn't rescue myself because I had my own rules. Preventing her from going to sleep was OK. Waking her was not. I changed into pajamas, then was afraid of the stillness of lying down. But I couldn't stay up, or the night would never be over. I took the vial of Doriden from my drawer, ground two to a powder, and swallowed them with warm water, so they would work faster.

All too soon, the alarm clock droned. I heard Susan's radio. *Partly cloudy. Chance of rain.* My mouth was dry and full of cotton. I was tense and jumpy, but alert, the way I always was after Doriden.

I went to the bathroom, then joined Susan in the living room. She was drinking coffee, fully dressed, including makeup. We exchanged good-mornings as I poured myself some orange juice, to wash away the fuzz. Neither of us mentioned the previous night. Not that we were avoiding it. That was last night. This was today.

"I'm going to the laundromat this afternoon," Susan said, "so put anything you want washed in the hamper."

ON SATURDAY NIGHTS, Susan went to dances in Manhattan, hoping to meet someone to marry. At 23, I knew I should be thinking about marriage, too. It was what people did. But though my body responded to men in a mature way, my mind didn't. My insides felt little-girl young most of the time I wasn't at my library job, and I couldn't imagine having a conversation with a husband every evening when he came home from work. What would I say?

One day in June, I brought home an offbeat newspaper I'd picked up near Pratt. Susan and I were laughing over the personal ads, most of which were sexually explicit, when we came upon one that was relatively staid. *Graduate student seeks groovy intellectual chick to share apartment.*

"I'm going to call as a joke," I said.

"No!" But Susan hovered as I dialed.

"Hi," I said when a man answered. "My name is Delores, and I'm calling in response to your ad in *The East Village Other*. I'd like to ask you some questions."

"OK," he said in a pleasant voice.

His name was Nick. He was going to New York University for a PhD in economics and lived on Grove Street in Greenwich Village. I asked what my share of the rent would be.

"Look," I said after five minutes. "I wasn't going to tell you this, except you sound like a nice guy. I'm not interested in sharing an apartment. I have a place to live. And my name isn't Delores. It's Vivian. I'm sorry I did this to you."

"I don't mind," he said. "I'd like to get to know you anyway."

To Susan's horror, I arranged to meet him, suggesting a diner in my Brooklyn neighborhood to test whether he was serious enough to travel an hour by train.

A few days later, wearing my puff-sleeved, red-and-tan checked smock dress, I walked into the diner exactly on time. A man was sitting alone at a table rose.

"Vivian?"

"Nick?"

Tall, big-boned without being overweight, he had a firm handshake. Unlike the long-haired, bearded student I'd been expecting, he was clean-shaven, with short, dark hair combed straight back. In a light blue button-down shirt, he seemed almost like a businessman. Over sandwiches, I learned that he came from a small town in Western Pennsylvania. His parents were Italian immigrants. He'd never been to New York until last year, when he had accepted a fellowship at NYU. This was his first time in Brooklyn, and, he said, his first time meeting a Jew.

The evening was mild, and we continued talking as we walked through the streets holding hands. Soon our sides were brushing and our conversation faded. He asked whether we could go up to my apartment. I said no, because my roommate was there, but suggested my car, parked around the corner. We spent the next hour petting in the back seat, with the windows open just enough to let in a bit of the evening breeze. A tree shielded the car from the streetlight, creating a curtain of darkness that ensured privacy despite the occasional couple strolling so close we could hear their conversation.

Nick said he found everything about me exotic: the Brooklyn locale, my religion, the combination of what he described as "intellectual librarian and seductive little girl." I felt beautiful, delicious, and respectable. He was getting a PhD.

Our subsequent relationship consisted solely of going to bed and going out to eat afterward. That suited us both. Nick was obsessed with sex, and I needed to be held. He talked matter-of-factly about what "turned him on" and how he could "service" me. Except for arguments about birth control—he didn't like my using a diaphragm and insisted that withdrawal was 100 percent safe—it was an easy relationship, unencumbered by feelings.

Nick's apartment was a studio, with high ceilings and parquet floors. He had a monster plant on the table whose tentacles reached the windowsill. There were dirty dishes in the sink and piles of books on the table, chairs, and floor. Sometimes I brought along my homework and did it on the bed, the only uncluttered surface. He would have had to do major reorganizing before a roommate could move in. Nick never saw where I lived. My apartment with Susan was a sanctuary for other parts of me, and his presence would have been intrusive. I was glad there was a train ride and a river between us.

We knew little about each other, though I did tell Nick I'd been in a mental hospital. As he never saw the crazy part of me, he accepted my information at face value, the same as if I had said I'd had my appendix out. Past tense. And it was past. The table-throwing episode felt as if it had happened much longer ago than five months. Nick told me about a paper he'd written with his advisor that had been approved for publication. I wasn't curious about his academic life but congratulated him appropriately. I didn't care to dig deeper, and he didn't seem to, either.

I HAD ALL THE TRAPPINGS of legitimacy—boyfriend, job, apartment—but I still felt like an observer watching a sliver of myself participate in life. A 24-year-old wasn't supposed to feel like a little girl sometimes and a piece of cellophane other times. It wasn't normal to talk to mirror people, or to be terrified of being alone. I began doing research again, looking for a medical label that described me, but found nothing.

I didn't mention my research to Dr. Sacker, because minutes after I took my seat across the chess set from him, I slid into another dimension. My mother had often repeated the story of how when I was two and scraped my arm I'd held it out to her and said, "Touch it, Mommy, and you'll see it hurts." In Dr. Sacker's office, I believed he felt what it was like to get sucked out of existence into a piece of lint. At the same time, he was waiting outside the annihilation place, a harbor to return to when I emerged a few minutes before the end of the session, as if I had an internal clock. We made small talk for those last minutes. "He gave me a C, but I got an A in my other course, so I'll still have at least a B average." I walked out to the street with only the sliver showing, even to myself.

ONE SATURDAY MORNING in September, I was in the stationery store on Kings Highway looking for invitations. My mother had passed the principal's exam, and I was planning a surprise dinner party for her and a few of her teacher friends and their husbands.

I was more relaxed with her now than I'd been eight months before, when we'd driven home from Mount Sinai. That day, I'd dropped her off at the school where she was assistant principal, then gone on to my apartment on Ocean Avenue. For about a month afterward, my weekly trips to 74th Street were more errands than visits, most often to pick up a check for Dr. Sacker. I didn't think of the checks as gifts. They were entitlements. I considered my mother partially to blame for my mental state. Let her pay to undo it. Sometimes I didn't even take my coat off.

Then, one day, my mother and I sat down for a cup of tea. It felt OK, and we continued doing that, even after my father returned from his trip. I would say hello to him at his bridge table in the living room, where he still copied bits of information to memorize onto his little pieces of paper.

I knew how hard my mother had studied for the principal's test and wanted to throw this party for her. Waiting in line to pay for the invitations, I picked up one of the books on the paperback rack near the register. Intrigued by the title, *I Never Promised You a Rose Garden,* and the blurb about a young girl who was a mental patient, I bought a copy.

I began reading it when I got home, legs tucked under me on the living room couch. At first it was just a good story, about a teenager named Deborah on her way to a mental hospital, riding in a car with her parents. The drive was long, and they stopped overnight in a hotel, where, safe in a room by herself, Deborah went to a peaceful place in her head that she called the Kingdom of Yr. The family resumed their trip the next morning. I followed them through the gate, onto the hospital grounds.

A few pages later, I found out that Yr had its own language and inhabitants. Sometimes it was a comforting world, sometimes frightening, but always more real to Deborah than the "real" world. I was no longer reading a story. I was reading about myself, things so raw I had to retreat to the bedroom. I pulled down the shades and took the book under the covers with a flashlight.

For two days, Deborah and I were one. When the gods of Yr warned her not to tell outside people about them and threatened punishments for infractions, they were giving those warnings to me. When Deborah made a suicide attempt and was transferred to Disturbed, I was locked on Disturbed, too. When the nurses wrapped her in an icepack to calm her, I was swaddled in cold.

Deborah's doctor, a woman who understood that Deborah's inner world represented strength because it allowed her to survive, became part of the Atmosphere, her molecules mixed in with those of Dr. Sacker and Dr. Hirschhorn. I wasn't jealous that the doctor watched over Deborah, too, because I *was* Deborah.

I finished the book Sunday evening, spent. Susan, thinking I was physically sick, brought me tea with lemon and honey.

I was able to go to work the next day, but reading *Rose Garden* had unsealed something inside, leaving me so volatile that my world crumbled if everything outside wasn't perfectly ordered. When Susan didn't line up the forks properly in the silverware drawer, or when she left her knitting on the end table in the living room, I berated her until she put things to rights. It was as if, in finding out about Deborah's inner world, I had opened a door wider to my own, and now its dark forest drew me in whenever I wasn't doing something that required my full concentration. Most of the time I was exhausted, having to use all my energy to make sure only the normal sliver was visible to others. I continued going to work, but a week after reading the book, I dropped my library school classes.

My mother's dinner party, planned for October, gave me a brief respite from the rose-garden world. In Ellen Willow mode, I spent several days cooking and freezing veal and eggplant parmesan, the same things my mother used to do when she was planning something elegant for company. My father hated social functions and wouldn't commit to coming, so I went to 74th Street when I knew my mother would be out. I showed him the list of invitees, limited to those of my mother's friends I knew he was somewhat comfortable with, and said it would mean a lot to her if he were there. He said he'd think about it. At least that wasn't a no. If he came, it would be his first time in my apartment.

The morning of the party, I baked a cake and wrote *Congratulations, Bea!* in pink on the chocolate icing. That evening, at the table, opened to seat ten, I presided like the gracious lady of the manor in an English novel, enjoying every minute. Once my mother got over her shock—she thought she'd be eating with just Susan and me—she glowed. I hadn't known my father was coming until he knocked on my door, early, as I had requested, in time for the surprise. He wasn't talkative, but his silence wasn't hostile. I could tell, from the way he looked at one face, then another, that he was following the conversation, and that he was proud of my mother. I knew how hard the party was for him and loved him for coming.

The guests went home, Ellen Willow vanished, and the rose-garden world claimed me again. ▪

CHAPTER 21

Psychodrama

"SOMETIMES I'M FINE," I said to Linda on the phone a few days after the party, "and sometimes I feel I'm staving off a nervous breakdown."

"Why don't you come down here for a visit?" she said. "Maybe all you need is a vacation." *Down here* was Norman, Oklahoma, where her husband was in graduate school.

The idea of going far away was appealing. I arranged for a week off from work, then made airline reservations that included a stop in Fort Hood, Texas, to visit my brother, who'd been drafted after he quit graduate school.

When the normal sliver of me boarded the plane at Kennedy Airport, the unstable rest-of-me miraculously vanished. In Texas, I felt maternal toward my hippie kid brother in his combat fatigues, hair cut short, beard shaved off, Private Conan, always running, on the double. "You're not allowed to walk," he explained. In Oklahoma, I joined Linda and her friends in their coffee-klatch world. I discovered an artsy store and bought scented candles and a pair of wooden earrings with gold engraving. After a week of feeling completely normal, I stepped off the plane in New York and into the waiting rest-of-me. Only the candles and earrings let me know Oklahoma had been real.

But now it wasn't only myself I had to hold together. It was my mother, too. My father had left on another trip, this time to take a language course in France, and he hadn't set a return date. In the week after I got back, my mother called every day, often in tears. I'd never seen her this distraught and decided to write to my father. I told him how lonely she was and asked him to invite her to visit at Christmas, and to think seriously about coming home when his course was over.

> *You are a father to Marvin & me, and you are a husband to Mommy. We need you and we love you, even if we do have strange ways of showing it.*

I did not tell my mother what I'd done.

"THERE'S DAN AND HIS WIFE, CAROL. They're both in Group," Susan said as we made our way to our seats about a week after I mailed the letter. She looked around and waved to other people. I began to feel uncomfortable. Was everyone here a patient of Dr. Sacker's?

Listening to the chatter as the small theater on Manhattan's Upper West Side filled, I was relieved to find they weren't. Some were patients of other therapists associated with the Moreno Institute for Psychodrama; some, simply people who had seen the advertisement and thought an evening of psychodrama would be fun entertainment.

I'd found out about the event when Susan came home one night and announced that Dr. Sacker had invited her whole group to attend. He had described it as a form of therapy that involved role-playing in dramatic scenes. I felt a stab of jealousy. He hadn't invited me. The next time I saw him, I asked why. It would be too destabilizing, he said. I took that as a positive sign. He knew how fragile I was. But when I made one of my increasingly frequent emergency calls to him the next night, he suggested I come with Susan, "so I can keep an eye on you."

There he was now, walking onto the stage in a dark suit, light blue shirt, and tie. He waited for the audience to quiet, then said, "Hi. I'm Ted Sacker. Thank you all for coming out on this cold night." It was disconcerting to see him beam his smile out over a hundred or so people, not aim it exclusively at me. After a brief explanation of role-playing as a form of therapy, he asked, "Who has a relationship issue they'd like to work on?" Several hands went up.

"The young lady over there." He pointed. "First give us your name."

All heads turned toward a young woman in a tent dress, her bangs so long they reached her eyebrows. "I'm Pat," she said.

"Hi, Pat. Can you tell us what it is?"

"My mother doesn't like my boyfriend." Her voice was loud and clear.

"Why not?"

"She says he has no goals. Night after night, all through supper. 'You're throwing yourself away! What kind of future will you have?' She drives me nuts."

I wondered how she could say such personal things to a theater full of strangers.

"Who else is at the table?" Dr. Sacker asked.

Her father, brother, and grandmother.

"Is it all right if we dramatize suppertime at your house?"

She said it was, and he invited her up to the stage.

"Who'd like to play Pat's father?" Dr. Sacker asked as Pat sat down in one of the empty chairs behind him. He picked a volunteer. "Her mother?"

Susan's hand shot up.

"What are you doing?" I whispered.

"Susan," Dr. Sacker called.

"Watch my coat," she said, rising.

I felt a piercing pain in the center of my chest as Susan walked up to the stage. Dr. Sacker had chosen her over me. It didn't matter that I hadn't raised my hand.

"Her brother?" Another selection. "Her grandmother?"

Some force in me lifted my arm, held it high. Dr. Sacker looked around the audience, then made a choice. It wasn't me. He hadn't even tried to catch my eye.

The house lights dimmed, and he gave instructions to the people onstage that I could barely hear. They arranged their chairs in dinner-table formation. He stepped to the side and the drama began.

At first the actors were stilted in their discord, like children in a school play, but after a few minutes, they began yelling at one another in earnest.

"Your father works night and day so you can make something of yourself. And what do you do? You find the biggest bum in creation. And then you have the nerve to bring him to this house."

"Mom, please. He's not a bum."

"Oh yeah? So tell *him* to pay for your college education!"

Dr. Sacker let their tempers rise for a while without intervening. Just when the action seemed to be getting out of control, he stepped forward and said a few words to nudge it in a different direction. Again he moved to the side. Again he nudged. When Pat started to cry, he halted the play, talked to her so quietly the audience couldn't hear, as if they were in a private therapy session, then let the drama proceed.

I slid down in my seat, feeling more and more abandoned. This wasn't the Dr. Sacker in whose office I could disappear into a piece of lint, knowing he would be waiting to receive me when I emerged. This was a master of ceremonies Dr. Sacker who didn't know I existed.

I felt a wail deep within me. The more I watched the stage, the more the wail swelled. In another minute, it would escape through my mouth. I grabbed my coat and hurried toward the aisle, whispering, "Excuse me. Sorry."

As soon as I felt sidewalk beneath my feet, loud moans began spilling out of me on puffs of vapor. I let them come while I put on my coat, tied the belt in a half-knot, and arranged my earmuffs over my shoulder-length flip. The moans turned to sobs as I began walking, feeling around in my bag for my gloves. Not bothering to skirt the patches of ice that glinted white from the streetlights, I passed several people going in the opposite direction before an older couple came up to me.

"What's wrong, honey?" the woman asked. "Do you need help?"

"No," I said, pushing the sounds inside and talking in as regular a voice as I could. "I'm all right. But thank you."

"You sure?"

"I'm sure."

"OK."

I went on walking, crying softly now, wishing she hadn't let me go so easily. Maybe she, too, wished she hadn't. Her companion had a kind face. Maybe they were both standing there, watching me. I resisted the urge to look back. I didn't want to find that they had gone on their way.

I rounded the corner and saw a pay phone, slipped off a glove and took a dime from my change purse. Sometimes when I was upset and the Atmosphere Dr. Sacker wasn't enough to get me through it, I called the in-person Dr. Sacker. Right now, though, he was onstage. If I called, I'd get his answering service.

I wished I knew the number of the couple who had stopped for me, but they probably weren't home yet. There was always Nick. If he was in, I could take a taxi to his apartment. No. Nick wasn't someone who would understand the searing hole in my chest.

I pulled my glove over the dime and walked on. The only way to stop the pain was death. I would take the elevator to the top floor of the tallest apartment house and jump. This plan made me feel better. I stopped crying and wiped my face with a tissue, to avoid alarming any tenants. Then I selected a building.

I hadn't counted on a doorman. "Sorry. I think I have the wrong address," I said when he asked who I was visiting.

At the next building, I was prepared. "Can I come in for a few minutes just to get warm?" Once in, I would wander through the lobby, and, when the doorman wasn't looking, take the elevator.

"I'm afraid I can't let you," he said politely.

I was relieved—part of me didn't want to jump. But with relief came return of the pain. I walked with it up and down the streets. To West End Avenue. To Riverside Drive, my feet getting colder and colder in my nylon stockings and Capezios. Back across Broadway to Amsterdam. To Columbus. Finally, for warmth, toward the theater.

I saw Susan a few feet from the entrance, her striped scarf wrapped around her head and neck. "There you are!" she said. "We were looking all over for you!"

"Who's we?"

"Ted. Who did you think? He's inside, searching with the janitor. I told him you went out, but he wouldn't listen."

"How'd you know?"

"The people next to us said you left in a hurry with your coat."

Inside the lobby, I took a tissue from my pocket, wiped the fog from my glasses, and leaned against the door to the street.

"Come in, so I can tell him I found you."

"I'd rather wait here."

"I don't want to lose you again," she said, her voice turning plaintive.

I realized with surprise that she had been worried and followed her into the theater. All the seats were empty. At the far end, Dr. Sacker stood talking with another man.

"Here she is!" Susan called.

Dr. Sacker came over to us. "Hi, Kiddo. You had me scared for a while."

"I just went for a walk."

"Yeah?"

It was the gentle, probing yeah I knew from our sessions, not the voice that had talked about relationship issues onstage. He was the old Dr. Sacker again, focused on me. "They wouldn't let me onto the roof," I said, certain he knew how bad I felt when I was walking the streets.

"What? Ohhh—"

So he hadn't known. The pain shot through me again. I let out a moan.

"I'm riding back in the car with you," he said to Susan. "Do me a favor. There should be a blue Buick double-parked outside. The driver's name is Steve. Tell him something came up and I'm not going with him." Susan left and he turned to me. "Promise you'll stay here while I get my coat?"

I kept my promise for a few seconds, then felt trapped. I wasn't sure I wanted to die, but I wanted the option. Dr. Sacker wasn't in sight. I opened the door to the street.

"Where are you going?" he said from behind me. I started to run. He grabbed my arm. I tried to break free. "Can you bring your car around," he asked Susan, who had just come back.

"It's Vivian's car," she said, taking in the scene, "but I have a key."

Moments later, while Susan drove, Dr. Sacker pinned my arms down in the back seat.

"Let me *go!*" I screamed, trying to open the door and throw myself out.

"Why do you want to jump?" he asked in a joking voice, dodging my kick. "Don't you know this is what every patient dreams of—being in their analyst's arms?"

In the theater, I had longed for Dr. Sacker's attention. Now I had it, but it was the wrong kind. I didn't need him to hold my body down. I needed him to see how much my insides hurt. I knew he was teasing me to calm me, but it only made me feel more invisible.

"Let me *out!*" I gave another kick.

"Susan, how're you doing up there?" he called.

"Don't worry about me." She met his eyes in the rearview mirror. "Just do what you have to with Vivian."

This was the first time I'd been with Dr. Sacker and Susan in the same place. Knowing they had sessions together was bad enough, but now I was hearing them speak. It was as if they had an understanding, a mutual objective.

I flailed harder. At the same time, the part of me that didn't want to fling herself into the path of oncoming cars was glad for Dr. Sacker's restraint.

We rode like that for 15 minutes, doing battle, when all at once I felt myself go limp.

"Vivian?" Dr. Sacker relaxed his grip but kept his hands in place. His voice came from far away.

"Yeah?" It was a whisper, hard to force out.

"What happened?"

"I don't know."

He let go, and I turned to sit like an ordinary passenger, facing forward, feet on the floor.

Ha-*boo*. Ha-*boo*. I let the sounds soothe me, knowing that no outside person could hear them.

"You're a calm driver," Dr. Sacker said to Susan as we rode through the Battery Tunnel into Brooklyn.

"Driving's easy. You have the hard part," Susan said, as if they were partners.

Nish-koola *mah*-kee.

Watching myself slip deeper into Inside, I knew I was probably more in need of Dr. Sacker's concern now than when I had been trying to jump. But I was quiet, not causing trouble, and he left me alone while he and Susan discussed the two psychodramas that had been played out after Pat's. Eyes closed, I rested my head against the back of the seat and gave myself up to the motion of the car.

"Well, here you are," I heard Susan say as we came to a stop. I opened my eyes and saw the white canopy of Dr. Sacker's building. "Let me know when you have another psychodrama. It was very interesting."

"I will." He turned to me. "You've been pretty quiet. How are you doing?"

"All right," I whispered.

"You think you can handle her," he said to Susan, "or should I come home with you?"

The Atmosphere Dr. Sacker had often been in our apartment, but never the in-person Dr. Sacker. I didn't want him there. It would have spoiled the magic. "I'll be OK," I said, back to my regular voice.

"Sure?"

"Yeah."

"OK. Take care, Kiddo." Then, to Susan, "Call me if you need me."

A WEEK LATER, SUSAN AND I were eating supper when my mother called to say she'd heard from my father and was planning to visit him in France during her Christmas vacation. She sounded almost happy. I didn't mention my letter, just said I was glad for her.

After we washed the dishes, I settled on the couch with the *Yellow Pages*.

"I wish you better luck today," Susan said before disappearing into the bedroom to watch her TV shows.

I slid my finger down the nursing agency listings, stopping just past the ones I had marked with an X the day before, and dialed the number.

"Hello," I said in my formal voice. "I'm calling to inquire whether you have psychiatric nurses who come to the house."

There was the pause I had come to expect, and also the question: "Who is this for?"

"For someone who's fine at work but can't be alone afterward. The nurse doesn't have to do very much, just be there when she gets out of work, ride home with her in the car, be there when she gets ready for bed, and help her leave the house in the morning."

"Does she need assistance bathing and dressing?"

"Nothing like that. Only someone to keep her steady."

Silence for a few seconds, during which I let myself hope this call would be different. Then, "We don't do that kind of thing."

Another X.

After two more calls, I put the *Yellow Pages* away and called Dr. Sacker. "No nurse wants to come to the house."

"I didn't think they would," he said.

"Maybe I should go to a hospital again."

"That's probably a good idea."

"I want to pick it out myself this time," I said, not at all upset that he had agreed.

After work the next evening, I called Payne Whitney, Gracie Square, and Columbia Presbyterian. I was looking for a place that would be good for the part of me that needed to be locked up as well as the sliver that was fine and didn't want to relinquish her freedom. I had a list of questions: Would I be able to keep my car there? How soon before I could go out on pass? What was their policy on medication? I wanted to query the people who would be directly involved in my care. But either I reached an operator who said she would take a message, or I was connected to someone, only to find that they wouldn't talk to me because I was the patient, not the doctor.

"Did you try Albert Einstein, in the Bronx?" Susan asked. Her ex-fiancé, a medical student, had said it was one of the best general hospitals in the city.

"We do have a psychiatric unit," said the Einstein operator in the friendliest voice I had heard all evening. "Would you like me to put you through?"

"Yes, please."

"Five South, Julie speaking," said another friendly voice. When I asked my questions, she suggested I call Dr. Welch, head of intake, in the morning.

"Why don't you come for an interview, and we can discuss all that?" Dr. Welch said when I phoned and asked the questions. He gave me driving directions to the Bronx as if we were two ordinary people having an ordinary conversation.

The following day, Sunday, December 4, 1966, I stepped off the elevator on the fifth floor of the hospital and was about to take a seat on one of the plastic chairs in the waiting area when a tall, lanky man with a springy step walked in from the side corridor. His dark, straight hair, parted on the side, was Beatles-length, just long enough to brush the collar of his black suit jacket. He looked to be in his early thirties.

"Miss Conan?" I nodded. "I'm Dr. Welch." He smiled and extended his hand. "My office is this way."

There was a diploma on one wall and, on another, a framed poster of two hands clasping a bunch of brightly colored flowers that looked as if a child had drawn them. The chairs were cushioned in gray upholstery. The room was permanent and personal, nothing like the generic Mt. Sinai offices.

As if describing someone else who was in trouble, I told Dr. Welch of dropping my library school courses after I read *Rose Garden*, the psychodrama, finding it more and more difficult to get to work. He didn't take notes, just listened, occasionally smoked a cigarette, and asked questions with what seemed like a genuine desire to understand.

"Why do you think everything's coming to a head at this time?"

I wasn't sure, but it was easy to talk to him. I told him about sometimes feeling as if I were on top of a mountain, looking down at the world through the wrong end of a telescope, and other times feeling so terrible that I couldn't move. About the mirror people. About periods when I felt I had to "get wild" and break things or I might lose my identity.

"Do you know what causes these states?"

All I knew was that I was becoming increasingly exhausted trying to keep everything running smoothly on the surface while so much was going on underneath. "I know I should be in a hospital," I concluded after more than an hour, "but I don't want to go."

"Why not?"

How could I explain that if I were no longer forced to use all my energy to keep hold of Outside, I might disappear into Inside. "I'm afraid I'll lose my whole life. My apartment... My job... Dr. Sacker...." My eyes traveled to the poster—something strange about the hands; they didn't match—then back to him. "Do *you* think I should be in a hospital?"

"Yes," he said, stubbing out a cigarette without looking. His eyes were on me.

I was relieved—he had seen my need—but I laid down conditions. First, that he be my doctor. He said he was the one who assigned patients to doctors, and that was fine. Second, that I could have passes immediately and be allowed to keep my car—if I felt locked up, I might try to run away. I used "I," but it was as if I were negotiating for someone else. *If she feels locked up, she might try to run away.* He said patients usually weren't given passes until they'd been there a few weeks.

"A few weeks! I'll be discharged by then!" I explained that all I needed was a place where I could rest until I got calm enough to pick up my life again, a week or two at most.

He said we could try immediate passes, but there would be no guarantee. "If you get worse, I'll have to take them away."

That sounded fair. "When should I come?"

"How about today?"

"*Today?*"

"Why not?" ■

CHAPTER 22

Picasso

CHIN RESTING ON STEEPLED FINGERS, Dr. Welch waited for me to begin. I didn't know what to say. Yesterday I'd been a confident negotiator; today he was my therapist.

"The nurses told me you had a hard time last night," he said before the silence became uncomfortable.

"Yeah."

"Can you tell me about it?"

"Not really." All new patients had to be in a room by themselves for a few days, so the nurses could see what their behavior was like before they were moved to a shared room. I'd been terrified being alone. But right now that was a distant memory. I glanced at the poster flowers. Red, blue, yellow, orange. Four miniature suns with petal rays, looking as if they were about to scatter, prevented by the two hands holding them together at the stems.

"Is there anything else about your stay so far?"

"No." I brought my eyes back to him. "Everything's fine."

"Would you like to hear about my conversation with your mother?"

I drew in a quick breath. "You spoke to her?" I'd asked him to let her know I was here.

"Last night."

"And?"

"She wants to visit. I said I'd have to ask you."

"I don't want to see her."

"Why not?"

I shrugged.

"You don't have to. I'm only trying to understand why she upsets you." When I didn't respond, he said, "I can always tell her she can't come."

"You don't know my mother," I laughed. "She'll come anyway."

"She's not in charge here. I am."

I knew then that I had made the right decision. This place, where the patients wore street clothes and the doctors told you ahead of time when they would see you; this place Dr. Welch called a therapeutic community, where the whole environment was healing; this place, Einstein Hospital, was on my side.

After the session, to exercise my pass privilege and show myself I could leave if I wanted to, I asked a nurse to let me out. Several patients, seeing me in my coat, approached with money. "Could you get me a ham and Swiss on rye from Mike's deli?" "Could you get me a pack of Winstons?" Glad to have a destination, I wrote down their orders.

The deli was within walking distance, but I decided to go for a ride first. It felt good to get into my car and turn the key. I drove up and down a few blocks to see what the neighborhood was like. A gas station, one- and two-family houses, some mom-and-pop stores. I parked in the same spot, went to the deli, then returned to 5 South, all in less than an hour. It was lonely being out by myself.

For the next few days, I followed the same routine: session; a drive and walk outside; deli orders; and several rounds of bid whist, a game most everyone here played and which I'd learned my first evening. When I got tired of cards, I wandered into the occupational therapy shop. One of the patients was building a chair using blueprints he had drawn himself and plywood that Jan, the occupational therapist, had bought in the lumberyard specifically for him. I wouldn't be here long enough for an involved project and opted for quickies: 20 minutes to make a bracelet from beads already on the shelves.

I liked hanging around the OT shop, even when I wasn't making anything. There were plants on the windowsill and popular songs on the radio that patients sang along to, like "Winchester Cathedral." And there was Jan's calm presence as she helped with anything from carpentry to crocheting. She knew when she could handle someone herself—she turned off the radio when the Beatles came on because Nora would fondle her breasts with one hand while slapping that hand with her other, saying, "Stop it, Paul!"—and when she had to call a nurse—when Tammy got into one of her trances and began rocking back and forth, or when Alan started pulling out his eyelashes.

In my daily sessions with Dr. Welch, I sat properly in the gray upholstered chair and talked in a regular voice. He asked about the mirror people. I said I had never thought it odd that I spoke to them until one day, when "I woke up in the middle of doing it." It wasn't that I'd never known about them before, but that was the first time I'd watched myself from outside myself while it was happening and realized how strange it was.

"Do you actually see figures in the mirror?"

I wasn't sure, I said. They seemed real, but I also knew they couldn't be real. I told him about Ellen Willow, and about feeling fake when I was Vivian, but not fake when I was Ellen or Wendy.

"Who's Wendy?"

I didn't know and couldn't say why I had mentioned that name.

Dr. Welch talked to me as if I were someone it was worth trying to understand. Still, I missed Dr. Sacker and called him from the pay phone just to hear his, "Hi, Kiddo, how ya doin'?"

"Please don't give away my time," I said.

"Whenever you come home, you can have your time back," he assured me.

On the third day, I got transferred to a room with two other women and felt much better at night.

On the fourth day, I began my session by telling Dr. Welch about Dr. Hirschhorn.

"Why was it so hard to talk to her?" he asked.

Here in his office, it seemed ridiculous that I could have been afraid of Dr. Hirschhorn. She was just a lady with open toe shoes who used a hanky to wipe her nose. "I wasn't the way I am now," I said. "I was like a frightened little person, and she was a scary big person."

"What made her scary?"

"I don't know."

I really didn't know. But a second later, the longing I used to feel for Dr. Hirschhorn rushed through me. I sat with my head slumped forward, chin on my chest. The hurting hole was growing. I wanted Dr. Welch to know about it, but it wasn't safe to have such a big feeling in front of someone else. When the pain got so strong it couldn't fit inside me, I sprang from my chair and banged my head against the wall. Twice.

Dr. Welch grabbed my arm and pulled me away from the wall. "What made you do that?" he asked as we stood facing one another.

"I don't know, but I'm fine," I said in a normal voice. The thuds had knocked away the pain. "You can let go."

He did, but he revoked my passes.

For a few weeks, I complained about my lack of freedom to Dr. Welch and the nurses, but inwardly I felt more secure. With nothing to lose, I could be the mental patient I had come here to be. If a feeling came over me in a session, I let it. Sometimes I screamed. Sometimes I cowered on the floor behind my chair. Sometimes I lost my ability to talk and pointed to the yellow lined pad on Dr. Welch's desk. When he brought it to me, I printed words in backward writing—maybe *babies die in the spring...*

gniɿqƨ ɘʜƚ ni ɘib ƨɘidɒd

...then scribbled circles over it, around and around, and crossed out everything with a big X. By the end of the session, I usually got back a semblance of Outside, but once in a while, after Dr. Welch walked me back to 5 South from his office on 5 North, he would tell the nurses to "Please keep an eye on her."

Dr. Welch didn't seem worried. He said that often when people started to feel safe they let down their guard, and what had been underneath would begin to come out. He felt that was a good thing. I knew he was right but continued to protest my confinement to keep up appearances, mainly for myself. Once I asked to go on a group trip to the movies organized by the recreation staff. "You don't need to see *Georgy Girl*," he said. "You have enough identity problems." I feigned disappointment, though secretly I was pleased. He knew what was going on inside me.

A BIT OF JUNE SUN threw a bright bar across the flower poster in Dr. Welch's office. That picture—a Picasso, I'd been surprised to learn—had been my anchor since I'd come to Einstein six months before. I looked away from its peaceful simplicity, down at the letter Dr. Welch had just handed me. It was from the Pratt Institute Library School. *Miss Conan has taken too many* leaves of absence, it said. If she doesn't return now—the summer of 1967—and finish her degree by the end of the following term, we will have no choice but to expel her. In addition, we'd like a note saying she's capable of being a librarian.

"They should have written to me, not you," I said.

"True." He swiveled to place the letter on his desk. "But what would you like to do about your degree?"

"I don't want to go back."

"Why not?"

"Pratt hates me."

When I'd returned to work in April, with the required note from Dr. Welch, Jo had let me come in early and leave early to avoid the rush-hour traffic. A week later, she said the head librarian, a man I hardly saw, was uncomfortable with my commuting from the hospital, and, much as she wanted me to stay, she had to ask for a letter of resignation. Now the library school didn't want me, either.

"Why do you care what they think?" Dr. Welch asked. "It would be a shame to lose all the work you put in. I'd rather they gave you more time, but if those are their conditions, I'll give you whatever support you need."

Returning to work had been easy, but in school I'd be expected to contribute to the class discussion, write a paper, and take a final. I didn't feel capable of that. Yet something stirred in me when I heard Dr. Welch's words. This was the first time anyone had looked at me as a whole: competent and crazy parts together.

A week after he sent Pratt a note, I received a registration packet. Listed among the summer course offerings was Fiction for Children. I'd just finished rereading *Little Women* and *Little Men* and was starting *Jo's Boys*. This might be easier than I thought.

The first day of class, I felt like an impostor—*mental patient out on pass*—but knew I looked ordinary. Later, back at the hospital, I reviewed the list of books we were to read and called my mother from the pay phone to ask whether she could get them from the library. She'd been visiting weekly, usually before or after her appointment with Mr. Richmond, the social worker who saw all the patients' families as part of the unit's team approach. We'd started the visits as an experiment, and so far it was working. Mostly, she took pleasure in bringing me things I requested, like shampoo.

There had been only one day, two months before, that I'd been shocked to see her. It was shortly after the hospital installed a receptionist's desk outside the entrance to 5 South. On days when none of the patients was particularly upset, the door was kept open. Patients would usually gather around the receptionist, glad for a change of scenery, asking her about movies she'd seen, her nail polish color, and what she planned to serve her husband for dinner. That morning, I had been among them, momentarily carefree, when the elevator door opened and out stepped my parents.

I froze for a split second, then ducked into the unit, hoping they hadn't noticed me. Why were they here? My mother had told me my father was back from France, but I never expected to see him at Einstein. Then a shade came down and everything was obliterated save the image of two ghosts, freeze-framed in the elevator door. I was still in that state when Dr. Welch came to get me for my session a few hours later. I walked woodenly into his office and sat in the chair.

"What happened?" he asked.

"I saw them," I said in a monotone.

"Who is them?"

I pointed to his pad. He handed it to me. I drew two stick figures and held it up.

"Who are these people?"

I drew a box around them, to indicate the elevator door.

"I don't understand— Oh. You saw your parents?"

I nodded.

"I'm sorry. They had an appointment with Mr. Richmond. I was going to tell you your father was coming. I didn't realize it was today."

The next time I saw my mother, I made no mention of what I'd seen, nor did she tell me my father had met with Mr. Richmond. I couldn't imagine what their conversation had been like, and as far as I knew he never came again. But my mother brought me news about him on each of her visits: "Dad went to Brighton Beach, and Nona says hello."

"Sure," she said now on the phone, when I asked about the books. "Hold on. I need a pencil."

Then I called Susan and asked her to bring my portable typewriter.

Remembering stories I had loved as a child, I looked forward to reading the pile of books my mother brought me. But the first one I tried, about a boy during the Civil War, had dialogue that seemed put on the page just to teach facts about Northerners and Southerners.

The next few were no better, so I picked up *Jo's Boys*, not on the list, and settled back against the pillows. Louisa May Alcott's characters, with their yearnings and foibles, were never boring, even on third or fourth reading. Her stories filled the hole in my chest.

"Would you like me to read to you?" my mother asked when she came with a second batch and I told her I hadn't read the first.

Nothing else was working. "You can try."

She picked up one of the library books and we sat on my bed. "*The Snowy Day*," she began, "by Ezra Jack Keats." After each page, she held up the illustrations. It felt strange to be read to as if I were a child, yet I liked it. When she finished, I didn't know what to write for my critical review, so she suggested some key words—*young boy exploring his world*—and I typed a paragraph.

She picked up another book. "*Island of the Blue Dolphins*," she read, "by Scott O'Dell."

This was long, and it took her several visits to finish. Based on a true story, it's about a 12-year-old Native American girl who is inadvertently abandoned on an island off the California coast and survives alone for 18 years before a ship arrives. While I understood that the book was meant to be inspirational, all I felt was the horror of her isolation. I managed to ignore it while I listened to my mother read and wrote my review. But the next morning, I woke feeling the air had been sucked out of my lungs and my body was sealed in concrete. Head under the covers, I heard my roommates get dressed and make their beds. The sounds were at once near and galaxy-far.

"Time to get up, Miss Conan," came the cheery voice of a nurse. "Breakfast is here, and you have school today."

"I'm not going."

She retrieved my moccasins from under the bed. "You'll feel better after you eat."

"I'm not going." I pulled the blanket over my head and heard her walk away.

Five minutes later, there was a knock, then footsteps. "Miss Conan?"

Dr. Welch! He rarely came into patients' rooms. I pushed off the covers and sat up.

"The nurse told me you don't want to go to school," he said, standing at the foot of my bed in his black suit.

"I don't."

"Why not?"

The Blue Dolphin girl's end-of-the-world isolation had so seeped into me that it had become my own. The book was no longer a story about someone else. I was that girl. "I want to stay here."

"I think you should go to class." He looked at his watch. "I have a meeting in a few minutes, but we'll talk this afternoon, when you get back."

"I'm not going."

"Would it help if someone went with you?"

"Who?"

"Maybe one of the nurses."

"A nurse would go all the way to Brooklyn with me?"

"I don't know. I'll see what I can do." And he was gone.

Within minutes, the head nurse came in to tell me she had assigned Miss Feldman to go to school with me. "What time do you have to leave?" she asked.

"Nine-thirty," I said, getting up. *I'd rather they gave you more time, but if those are their conditions, I'll give you whatever support you need.* He had really meant it.

Miss Feldman changed into street clothes. I didn't question her willingness to go in the car with me. I'd always been able to drive well, even when Inside wasn't OK. At Pratt, she read a book in the regular part of the library while I was in one of the upstairs classrooms, then drove back to the hospital with me. We were gone four hours.

From that day on, a nurse or someone from the recreation staff went with me to class. In the hospital, I spent most of my time lying on my bed, finishing *Jo's Boys*, then rereading *An Old-Fashioned Girl* and *Eight Cousins*. While I read, I was inside the stories, in a world where people were very much connected to one another. My mother continued to help me with the required books on the list, and I turned in all my reviews on time. I typed my final paper, "Louisa May Alcott: Why Her Books Live," in my hospital room and got an A.

In the fall, I registered for two courses, one in library administration, the other in humanities research. Depending on how I felt, sometimes I drove to Pratt myself, and sometimes a staff member came with me.

The surface me was participating in ordinary activities again: sewing, whist, the Tuesday cooking group. But deep inside, in my organs and muscles and bones, I was that Native American girl, separated from the rest of humanity by a wall that stretched from the ground to the sky. No amount of socializing or cards or cooking-group dinners could dispel my feeling that I was a fake, going through the motions, and would never be able to truly connect with another person. I got through each day only by telling myself that if things ever got so bad I couldn't stand them, I would kill myself.

I talked to Dr. Welch about feeling unreal, but not about dying. If he took away my passes, I wouldn't be able to commit suicide when the time came.

I made frequent trips to the Fordham branch of the New York Public Library, a short drive from the hospital, to research poisons. I learned that one of the ingredients in Contac, an over-the-counter cold medicine, was belladonna, which can cause death in large doses. What was "large"? I called the Poison Control Center. They wouldn't tell me. I guessed that each of the different colored dots inside the see-through capsule was a different ingredient. Which was belladonna? I bought many Contac packages, opened the capsules, and separated the colors, so when I found out I'd have enough ready. I kept the piles in the back of my bottom desk drawer, each wrapped in a napkin and stuffed into a paper cup.

One day, another patient was discovered to have several empty plastic bags, which were forbidden, and there was a search of everyone's possessions. When my stash was discovered, Dr. Welch grounded me.

"I just need to *know* I can kill myself," I said. "That way I don't have to *do* it. Don't you see?"

"I do not," he said, and wouldn't give me back my passes.

Now that I had no means of ending my life, I felt desperate. Lying in bed that night, I planned my escape. The next morning, I waited near the back service entrance, taking care to avoid the surveillance mirror. All the nurses knew I no longer had pass privileges, but Helen, the cleaning lady, didn't. When she came in with her pail and mop, using her key, I asked her to hold the door. I took the service elevator up—they wouldn't think to look for me on a higher floor—cut across to the regular bank, and pressed DOWN.

There was a November chill in the air. I had my car keys in my pants pocket but hadn't wanted to arouse suspicion by taking a coat. The only warm, free place I could think to drive to was the library. Once in the reading room, I pondered my next step. I'd proven to myself that I could get away if I wanted to kill myself. That was all I needed. I was ready to return. But they'd only lock me up again. Where else could I go?

The Ocean Avenue apartment was no more. The few times I'd gone there on pass, I'd noticed changes, like new knickknacks, and had gotten upset all out of proportion. I felt Susan was taking over and suggested she get her own place. When she did, I sublet the apartment to my brother's friend until the lease was up, then stored my furniture in Aunt Sophia and Uncle Max's basement. There was always a motel, but that would be lonely, and, anyway, I didn't have much money with me.

I glanced around the reading room for someone from the hospital, sure they'd figured out where I'd gone. I was relieved not to see anyone. Also disappointed. There was a copy of *Cool Hand Luke* lying on one of the tables. I'd heard of the movie and picked it up.

For the next seven hours, I was Luke, a prisoner who runs away, gets caught, is punished. Again and again. On his last escape, a guard finds him in a church and shoots him. I reached the final page, tears in my eyes, just as a voice came over the loudspeaker. "The library is closing." I left *Luke* on the table and went out into the street.

It was dark, cold, and I was hungry. I found a pay phone.

"Miss Conan! Thank god!" said the nurse who answered. "Where are you?"

"In a phone booth."

"Where?"

"I'm not saying, but I'll come back if I can have my passes again."

"Give me your number. Dr. Welch said to call him as soon as we heard from you."

When the phone rang, it was Dr. Welch, from home. I stated my condition.

"I'm not bargaining with you over the phone," he said, more sternly than I'd ever heard him speak. "I'll see you in the morning, then decide about passes."

"I'm not sure I'm coming back." But I knew I would.

Everyone was glad to see me, staff as well as patients. I loved their attention, even the ridiculousness of having my temperature taken. "Standard procedure," the nurse said.

The next morning, when Helen came in to clean my room, I told her I hadn't meant to get her in trouble. She said she understood and was happy I was OK.

It was more complicated with Dr. Welch, who wanted my assurance that I would be honest. If I thought about suicide, I had to tell him.

"You'll just take my passes away," I said.

He said not if he felt I wasn't going to act on it.

We talked four times in four days before he let me out again.

Despite having missed a week of classes, I got a B in both courses and received my Master of Library Science degree in January. The cooking group made a celebratory dinner for me from *Joy of Cooking* recipes. Before we sat down to eat, they sang "For She's a Jolly Good Fellow" and placed a homemade graduate's cap on my head, complete with tassel. The card, also homemade, was addressed to *Vivian Ann Conan, MLS.*

I smiled and thanked them, but I didn't feel like a librarian or a graduate. I felt like a misfit.

TWO MONTHS LATER, in OT, I was making myself a gown to wear as the maid of honor at Susan's wedding. Linda, whom I hadn't seen in a year and a half, would be there, too.

I was much less volatile than when I'd arrived at Einstein 16 months before, but along with my calm had come a hollow feeling that was different from Inside's hurting hole. This was Outside emptiness, something I'd never felt before. It was as if I'd just woken up and found that there was more to getting along in the world than competence and politeness. There was a dimension to the way people related to one another I'd encountered only in books, some invisible energy that connected them. Never having experienced it, even in my relationship with Nick, whom I went to see on pass every once in a while, I wanted to understand how it worked. I started watching soap operas in the hospital and going by myself to local theaters to see movies like *Valley of the Dolls*, *Planet of the Apes*, and *The Graduate*. From the safety of the dark, I studied the way people spoke with one another and how what was said in one scene had an effect on what happened in the next. I longed to be part of this rich new world, but I didn't know how to enter.

In sessions with Dr. Welch, I was somber as we talked about my eventual discharge. The plan was for me to get a job, go to work from the hospital for a while, then look for an apartment. I'd already sent out résumés for nearby office positions, but the thought of living by myself terrified me.

The only way I could face living on my own was by knowing I could end my life at any time. One day I would kill myself, not necessarily this month or this year, but eventually. I didn't tell Dr. Welch, but I think he knew. He probably also knew it wasn't imminent.

"WHY DON'T YOU COME to Norman?" Linda asked, straightening the rainbow-colored bows that ran down the front of her white minidress.

"Move to Oklahoma?" I blotted my lipstick, then stood back from the mirror to get a better view of my pink, floor-length gown.

"I know it sounds crazy, but you could stay with us until you find a job and an apartment. It's not only for you. Steve's hardly home, and I'd love the company."

It was April 11, 1968, and we were in the ladies' room in the synagogue in Brooklyn where Susan was getting married. I'd been looking forward to her wedding and being her maid of honor until the day before, when I found out the billing department at Einstein wanted me discharged by the end of the week because of an insurance mix-up. Dr. Welch had gotten a postponement to May 1, but it was all I could think of. Where would I live? I didn't want to go back to 74th Street.

When we'd first come into the ladies' room, Linda had offered me one of her tiny yellow Valiums. "One pill can't hurt," she'd said. "It'll make you feel better." Now, as we stood before the mirror, the Valium hit. One second I was consumed with worry; the next, confident everything was going to be OK. From my new vantage point, the idea of going 1,500 miles for a safe place to land didn't seem preposterous.

"You're really serious?" I asked.

"Hundred percent."

"All right."

"You'll come?"

"Yes."

THREE DAYS LATER, I looked through my hospital window at my car below, parked under a streetlight. It was crammed with everything I'd need in my new life, including my bicycle, viola, and an AAA TripTik. My brother's army leave from Fort Hood was ending, and he'd offered to drive to Oklahoma with me on his way back to Texas if I could leave sooner than originally planned.

I was to pick him up in Brooklyn the next morning at 7:00, so I said my goodbyes before I went to bed. There were wishes of luck from the patients and staff; a letter of recommendation from Jan, in case I wanted to apply for a job as an occupational therapy assistant; assurances from Dr. Welch that it was OK to write to him; and several prescriptions dated ahead: chloral hydrate for the nights and Valium—the stronger blue ones—for the days. The goodbyes didn't feel like real goodbyes, because when they were over, I went to sleep in the same bed I'd slept in for 16 months, with my same two roommates just yards away.

The night nurse woke me at 5:30. At 6:00, she walked me to the elevator. I was on my way. ■

CHAPTER 23

Vagabond

"**G**ET *OUT!*" I GROWLED at the army of demons racing around my brain. "Leave me alone!" I opened the broom closet door and shoved them in. "Stay there or I'll kill you!" I slammed the door and turned to face the living room, where the convertible sofa bed was made up with pillows and blankets.

It was 11:00 at night. Upstairs, Linda and Steve were in their bedroom. I heard their door open, then footsteps coming down.

"Hi, Steve," I said, composing my face.

"I was thirsty. Hope I'm not disturbing you." He was wearing pajamas.

"You're not." Still dressed, I followed him into the kitchen.

He opened the refrigerator and took out a Coke. "Want one?"

"No, thanks."

He set the can and a glass on the table, then sat. "I thought I heard a noise."

"I didn't hear anything."

Taking the opposite chair, I watched him pull off the tab and pour. "Linda played the record of the '2000 Year Old Man' this afternoon," I said.

He smiled. "Did you like it?"

"Pretty funny."

"We love Mel Brooks. Sorry I had a meeting. Linda said you went to the university placement service."

"Yeah. I registered with them."

"You know you're welcome to stay here until you find something."

"Thanks." I knew this was temporary but tried not to think about it.

We talked another minute. Then Steve pushed back his chair. "Will you be able to sleep?"

"Yeah." I stood. "Do you mind if I put on Tchaikovsky? I'll keep it soft."

"Not at all."

After his feet disappeared up the stairs, I placed one of the kitchen chairs against the broom closet door and started the record player. The lilting strains of the violin concerto filled the air. I swallowed a chloral hydrate with hot water, changed into pajamas, and got under the covers.

What had thrown me off balance that day was the mail. I'd been writing to Dr. Welch every morning since my arrival four days ago—about how the conductor of the university orchestra had allowed me to join them, and how I made eggplant parmesan for a potluck dinner with Linda and Steve's friends. Minutes after I finished each letter, I dropped it into the mailbox around the corner. Part of me knew it would take a few days for Dr. Welch to receive it. Another part believed that as soon as it left my hand, he knew its contents. This morning, before I let go of the letter, I noticed the sign on the box: Weekly Collection. The magic came undone. I drove to the post office so my letter would go out immediately. Then I realized he would get this one before the others. He wouldn't be with me in the proper order. I felt myself slipping back into craziness.

AS IF UNAWARE that Inside was unraveling, Outside pressed on. I applied for a job in a small, grant-funded business library loosely connected to the university: a one-room collection of pamphlets and statistical reports housed in a storefront. The budget covered one person's salary—I would be the sole employee. I gave Jo's name as a reference. A few days later, on my 26th birthday, I was offered the position, to begin the following Monday.

The birthday flowers from my mother were still fresh that weekend, when Marvin and one of his army buddies came to visit. They arrived just after my first orchestra concert. Linda and Steve had been in the audience. Maybe I could have a life here.

On Monday morning, I let myself into the library with my key and turned on the lights. During the interview, I'd been so excited by the prospect of getting a job that I hadn't been alarmed when the woman said the library wasn't used much, "but we're hoping to turn that around." Now, while I waited for someone to come in, I looked through catalogs and sent for pamphlets.

The university mail courier stopped by for a minute every afternoon. In three days, only one other person entered the library. This job was like being on the Island of the Blue Dolphins. At least after work, I was with Linda and Steve. Next week, in the furnished room I'd just signed a lease for, I would be alone.

On the morning of my fourth day at work, all I could think about was being alone. I didn't see it as a temporary state but one that would last for eternity. As usual, Steve left for work first, then Linda. I took out my car keys in preparation for the drive to the library, but as I was walking toward the door, a gloom so thick rolled over me that I turned back. Death was preferable to what lay ahead.

I brought my shoulder bag to the kitchen, emptied the contents onto the table. Four bottles of prescription pills, two nonprescription. Was that enough? I turned on the hot water and opened the first bottle.

Oh my god! What was I doing? Once you were dead, you couldn't undo it. Did I really want to die?

Yes.

No.

Yes *and* no.

Shit!

I threw the bottles back into my bag and turned off the faucet. I got out the *Yellow Pages*. Called the airline. There was a flight to New York in six hours. I booked it.

I made a collect call to Dr. Welch. Could I could see him as an outpatient? We set up an appointment for Monday.

Five hours left to close up my Norman life. A call to the woman in charge of the library. "I'm sorry to give such short notice, but I have a family emergency. My friend will return the key." Calls to the real estate agent, and the gas, electric, and phone companies to undo my apartment. A drive to UPS to ship my bicycle to Aunt Sophia and Uncle Max's. A call to arrange a limousine ride to the airport.

My last call was to Linda. "I feel bad telling you over the phone, but I have no time to come to your office. My flight's in two hours."

"I'm sorry it didn't work out, but I understand. I know you've been having a hard time."

"The only thing I'm leaving is my car. Could you advertise for someone to drive it to New York?"

"Sure. I'll ask Steve."

"Thanks for everything."

"Write and let me know how you're doing."

"I will."

I was still in do-mode when I got to the airport, checking my luggage and finding my gate. But once I boarded the plane and fastened my seatbelt, Inside came rushing back. I wasn't prepared for the sudden pain in the center of my chest or the screams in my brain. While the people around me were stowing their carry-ons, I took a Valium. Soon I felt the relief of the float. It faded. I took another. Float. Fade. Another. Another.

"Coffee or tea?"

I opened my eyes to see clouds out the window. When had we taken off? "Tea, please."

I stirred in some sugar and picked up the cup. My eyes closed before it got to my mouth. They opened when I heard the clatter. "Sorry."

"At least it didn't burn you," the stewardess said as she knelt to wipe up the mess. "Looks like you need sleep more than tea. Would you like a blanket?"

I let her tuck me in.

"I GOT A LITTLE DANGEROUS," was all I told Dr. Welch of my suicide fright. I was staying with Aunt Rae and Uncle Frank in Brooklyn and had driven to his Einstein office in Susan's extra car, which she was lending me until I got mine back.

Dr. Welch leaned forward. "What was upsetting about the thought of moving into your own apartment?"

"Being alone, I guess." I uncrossed my legs and recrossed them.

"Can you say more about that?"

"Not really." It seemed ridiculous now. With Dr. Welch at the helm again, everything was all right.

Sort of. As the session neared an end, we arranged for me to see him three times a week. Then he said, "I want to let you know I'll be going on vacation soon."

"When?" I asked, in what I hoped was a normal voice.

"The end of June. We still have a few weeks."

He walked me to the elevator, then let himself into the 5 South unit with his key. I wished I could go in also.

In the two days before I saw him again, no matter what I was doing—stringing beads to kill time while Aunt Rae and Uncle Frank were at work, listening to their opinions about the Japanese restaurant where they cooked the food at the table—I felt an undercurrent of unease. What if some catastrophe struck Dr. Welch while he was on vacation and he never came back?

"I'll only be gone four weeks," he said when I next saw him. "I'm definitely coming back."

"You *intend* to. You don't *know*."

We talked about my worry for a few minutes. Then he said, "I think you should see someone while I'm away."

SO MUCH HAD HAPPENED since I'd last walked through the lobby of Dr. Sacker's building a year and a half before that I was surprised to find nothing had changed. As if I were watching an old movie, I saw myself take the elevator to the third floor and put my bag down on the hallway carpet near his apartment. The soundtrack was familiar: a ringing phone behind one door, a TV show behind another. I leaned against the wall to wait for the patient before me to leave. The ringing stopped, and a woman said, "Hello...? Gertie!" Close, yet miles from the stillness in the hall.

That stillness wrapped itself around me and began to fill with Dr. Sacker. His essence permeated the air, just as it used to, flowing around and through me, until I was part of him and he was part of me. He knew I had just brushed a strand of hair from my eye. He knew about my fear of losing Dr. Welch, that I had been sleeping on the living room couch at Aunt Rae and Uncle Frank's, that I wished I were back at Einstein. Soon he would open the door and step into himself with his body and say, "Hi, Kiddo."

I'd never felt this magic from Dr. Welch. Until Oklahoma, I hadn't needed it to keep him alive in the in-between times, because there hadn't been any. Throughout my 16 months at Einstein, I'd had a session with him five days a week. On his days off, the nurses had been there, charting everything, so when he came back, he knew all that had happened in his absence. When he went on vacation, I'd had the continuity of Jan, the nurses, the hospital walls. I never doubted that he'd return. Now he was gone, and nothing was certain except Dr. Sacker.

The door opened.

"Hi, Kiddo."

"Hi." He looked the same.

"It's been a long time."

It hadn't. He'd been with me in the hall. "I guess so."

Everything else was the same, too, including the coffee table with the hand-carved chess set. I took my old seat on the black-and-brown striped couch. He took his on the black leather chair and lit a cigarette.

He exhaled toward the ceiling in a movement I knew well, then looked back at me. "So, what's been happening?"

"Didn't you talk to Dr. Welch?"

"Yes, but I'd rather hear it from you."

Best to help him get back into the script. I sat up straight, feet on the floor, and told him, in one summary sentence, about being discharged, going to Oklahoma, returning, and living with Aunt Rae.

There was a moment's silence. Then, "What are you working on with Dr. Welch?"

I never came to therapy to work on anything. I came because I needed to have a caring, understanding presence with me when I went Inside, the way it used to happen on this striped couch. But now it was clear I was only a visitor here, a favor Dr. Sacker was doing for a doctor he'd never met: his last patient before the Fourth of July weekend. "Just talking about his vacation."

The rest of the session was filled with facts. How a student had driven my car back from Oklahoma last week. How Aunt Rae, Uncle Frank, and I had moved to their country house in Peekskill for the summer. Dr. Sacker listened with his feet on the coffee table, asking questions to prompt me. With each answer I gave, I felt more abandoned.

"Well, Kiddo, time's up." He smiled, stubbing out his fifth cigarette.

Feeling cheated, I gathered my things.

"Have a good weekend." He opened the door. "See you next Wednesday."

"OK."

The door closed and I was alone in the hall. Really alone. No Dr. Sacker in the Atmosphere. Only the sound of a man clearing phlegm behind another door.

The pain hit as I was walking to my car, right where it always did, in the center of my chest. I slid onto the seat, took a Valium from my bag, and mashed it into wetness with my teeth, so it would kick in faster. I turned on the radio and pulled away for the two-hour drive to Peekskill.

The relief, when it came, didn't last. Keeping one hand on the wheel, I ferried another Valium to my mouth. When that wore off, another—until I finished the ten that were in the vial.

I felt myself nodding and slapped my cheeks. What time was it? I turned up the radio. How had I gotten onto this narrow country road? Probably took the wrong exit off the parkway. I nodded again, jerked my head up, opened the window wider to let the wind blow full on my face. When had it become dark? Must be close to Peekskill. Look for a sign.

I was asleep when the road curved. I woke when the car hit the boulder.

RECUPERATED FROM MY FRACTURED right clavicle on the porch of Aunt Rae's antique store across from the firehouse on Route 6, wearing a foam shoulder brace and playing Telemann on the recorder while she attended to customers. I went with Uncle Frank to the auto repair shop, where he negotiated with the mechanic who was fixing my car, and to the mall with Aunt Rae, where she bought me a bathing suit so I could sit at the lake and read under a tree. Back at the house, I watched Uncle Frank cut the grass with his tractor and asked him to teach me to ride it. "As soon as you're better," he said. My mother wrote to give me news: my father was playing paddleball at Brighton Beach; my cousin Neil was going to teach in the school where she was the principal so he wouldn't get drafted. She also sent a check for the mechanic.

Twelve days after the accident, I had an early morning appointment with Dr. Sacker. Because Peekskill was two hours away, Aunt Rae drove me to the 74th Street house the night before. It would be my first overnight visit in the three years since I'd moved out.

Before going to bed, I arranged my blouse on the floor in my old room. In the morning, I would lie down on it, slip my immobilized arm into one sleeve, then roll over to snag the other sleeve with my good arm before I stood up. Though no one else would be using the room, I lay the blouse down in the farthest corner, knowing my father didn't like what he called "obstacles" in the center of the floor. I placed my shoes next to the blouse, then went to the bathroom to brush my teeth. When I returned, the shoes were on a high shelf, and the shirt was hanging on top of the door, where I couldn't reach it.

Damn him, I thought, and walked into the living room. My father was sitting with his books and papers. He had his muttering face on; he'd probably just stopped when I came in. For a moment his anger frightened me and I turned to go. Then I realized he had no power over me anymore.

"All my life," I said slowly, as if talking to a child, "I never minded that the house was arranged for a blind person. It didn't bother me that the blind person didn't exist. I figured that was your thing, and as long as it didn't put me out, I went along with it to keep the peace."

"I don't know what you're talking about," my father said in a testy voice.

"The blind person. We kept the milk on the left side of the top shelf of the refrigerator, so he would always be able to find it." For years, if any of us didn't position the milk properly, my father would demonstrate the blind person's distress by closing his eyes and groping on the top shelf. "Well, *I* have a handicap now. People with broken collar bones can't reach up high."

"A person could trip on things left in the middle of the floor."

"A *seeing* person? Or a *blind* person?"

"*Any* person." His voice was rising.

"Look. It's all right to arrange a house for a blind person when a blind person lives there. It's *not* all right to arrange a house for a blind person when a person with a broken collar bone lives there."

"Who's arranging things for a blind person?" He was yelling now. "I just don't want your things on the floor!"

I was glad I would be returning to Aunt Rae and Uncle Frank.

BY MID-AUGUST, I WAS HEALED and drove to the Bronx to look at the housing listings on the Fordham University bulletin board. My brother, still in Texas, was about to be discharged from the army. He would be finishing his graduate degree in psychology at Fordham and had asked me to find him an apartment.

I got him a furnished basement in a private house near the school.

For the rest of the month, I swam in the lake, went out to eat with Rae and Frank and their friends, and rode the tractor lawnmower. A few days before the Labor Day weekend, I drove to 74th Street for an afternoon visit.

"Hello, Viv," my father said, rising from his bridge table to give me a hug. I heard the affection in his voice, though our conversation was limited to his satisfaction with the weather. "Drops down to fifty-eight or sixty at night."

"Yeah. It's been getting cooler." I left him to his little pieces of paper and joined my mother in the kitchen.

She was standing at the table, making her signature tuna salad. I sat down across from her, watching her grate the carrots, squeeze a lemon over them, and add mayonnaise. "I'm moving my files into your room," she said as she worked, "and I'd like, after we eat, if we could go through your things, and you'll tell me what I can throw out."

"OK."

I set the table. Same color-coded plastic glasses for my mother and father. Marvin's and mine were no longer on the shelf above the sink, so I took a company glass.

The three of us ate in a comfortable silence. But I was used to mealtime with Aunt Rae and Uncle Frank now, which was always lively and playfully argumentative. The night before, the talk had been about the protestors and police at the Democratic Convention in Chicago. This lunch was not only boring, but surreal. Neither my mother nor father mentioned the fact that I was living with Aunt Rae, or even that I had been in a mental hospital. Nor had they on my previous visit. It was as if I'd just plopped down from nowhere for a while and would be returning to nowhere when I left.

Within 15 minutes, we were finished. My father returned to his table in the living room, and my mother and I went into my old room. It looked like an office. A filing cabinet. A bookcase with education books, loose-leaf binders, and boxes of index cards filled with writing. On the desk, packages of blank index cards in several sizes and a mayonnaise jar of pens and pencils. The only indication the room had ever been mine was the sign still thumbtacked to the bulletin board: *JE SUIS MOI!!!!!*

My mother had everything she wanted me to look through in a pile: clothes, college notebooks, art supplies, old eyeglasses, jewelry. Most if it was throwaway. I'd taken all I really wanted when I'd moved out with Susan. We were done in ten minutes.

"I guess I'll go now. I'll say goodbye to Dad."

"Wait."

I turned.

"Do you have a winter coat?"

What did it matter? This was August. Where was my coat, anyway? Aunt Sophia's basement? Last I remembered, there were bare patches where the fake fur had worn away. "No."

"You're going to need one. Let me give you some money."

I tucked the $100 into my wallet, said goodbye, and drove back to Peekskill.

The next morning, I drove to Manhattan to shop and found a matching coat, skirt, and pants set for $75 at Lord & Taylor. That afternoon, back in Peekskill, I modeled it for Aunt Rae in the living room. Without comment, she turned and walked into the kitchen.

"Don't you like it?" I asked, following her.

"You went for a coat," she spat, spinning to face me. "What did you need the skirt and pants for?"

I was puzzled by her anger. "The whole set was cheaper than any of the coats by themselves."

"Did you have to go to Lord and Taylor? What's wrong with Orchard Street? You have no idea of the value of money! You don't care where it comes from!"

"My mother gave it to me."

"She gives you money for a coat, but she doesn't give me anything for keeping you here."

Oh my god. I thought Aunt Rae loved me. All the caring she had lavished on me—taking me out to eat, driving me to my orthopedist appointments, even closing her store to drive me to Brooklyn—meant nothing now that I knew she thought she should have been paid for it. I ran back to the living room and grabbed my bag.

"Where are you going?" she called through the window as I hurried across the lawn.

"I don't know."

The air inside my car was stifling, heated by the summer sun. I took off the coat and rolled down the window. Within minutes, I found myself on the southbound Taconic, and then I knew. Marvin's apartment.

"You're lucky you caught me," he said when I told him what happened. "I usually stay at Mara's." My brother and Mara were engaged. "I just came for some clothes."

I had been planning to hang around a few hours, then return to Peekskill, but when he said, "Why don't you live here?" it seemed like the perfect solution. I called Aunt Rae.

"Where are you?" she asked.

"At my brother's."

"I'm so glad you're safe! Frank's starting the grill. Should we wait for you?"

"No. But I'll come tomorrow for my things."

THE PHONE WAS RINGING as if it had always been ringing and I was just becoming aware of it. I reached my hand out from the blanket and brought the receiver back under.

"Hello?" A hoarse whisper.

"Good morning, Vivian. It's Jan."

North Vietnam using Cambodia as a sanctuary... The TV, still on from last night.

"What time is it?"

"Seven-thirty. Is your head out of the covers?" Her tone was gentle.

"No."

"Can you push them off?"

...Prisoner of war camps and supply depots...

I pulled the blanket down to my chin. "My head's out," I said in a stronger voice.

She walked me through sitting up, putting on my glasses, sliding my feet into my moccasins, standing.

"I'm all right now. Thanks."

"Good. Take care. I'll call you tomorrow."

I turned off the TV, switched on my brother's stereo, and lowered the arm to the album already on the turntable. Leonard Cohen's tortured-but-soothing voice singing "Sisters of Mercy" followed me as I walked past Marvin's empty cot on my way to the bathroom, as I peed, washed my face and brushed my teeth, took two aspirins for my headache.

When I first came to live in Marvin's apartment, I had nothing to do all day. After one of my sessions with Dr. Welch, I asked to go onto the unit, just to say hello and wound up staying all day, playing whist, eating lunch, and spending time in the OT shop. That's when I told Jan I kept the TV on all night so there would always be a talking face, and how hard it was to get out of bed in the morning with no one there.

I went back to the unit every day for a week. Then Dr. Welch told me of a new rule. The nurses felt it was upsetting to the inpatients to see someone who had been discharged and still needed the hospital. It was decided that former patients couldn't be on the unit unless it was visiting hours, and then only if they were visiting someone specific. He apologized, said he didn't agree with the rule, "but I was outvoted."

One good thing came of my time on the unit, though: I reconnected with Annette, an old roommate. She was working part time in an office in the medical school, where they had no idea she was a patient in the hospital next door. A week after my banishment, Annette called to say she'd given notice because she was starting school. They'd asked her to find a replacement. The job was two hours a day and paid minimum wage: $1.60 an hour; $16.00 a week. Was I interested? Yes!

Now I spent two hours a day processing membership applications for a scientific society. My desk was in the back of an office next to a research lab. It was rare that any of the white-coated scientists came into the back office. That suited me. They were hello-friendly, and I liked knowing they were there, but I didn't feel capable of carrying on a conversation.

The two hours were of my choosing. That day, as usual, I went in right after Jan woke me, to get myself out of the house. And after work, as usual, I went to the Fordham branch of the library to do research on poisons that would kill you without pain, and that you could get without a prescription. But I'd recently started a simultaneous quest: looking for a place to live where there would be other people around and some type of minimal supervision, something like a halfway house. Dr. Welch agreed that I needed a more stable living situation. He and the Einstein social worker had been looking for one but hadn't been able to come up with anything suitable.

Now, having exhausted all the directories, I began looking through periodical indices. Two hours into my search, I came across the citation for an article in the *American Journal of Psychiatry* entitled, "Follow-Up of a 'High-Expectations' Halfway House." I requested the microfilm and threaded it into the machine. The abstract read: "The authors describe the first year's experience of Overing Apartments, a halfway house in which tenants are challenged to accept a full range of responsibilities early in their stay...." An imaginative name for a halfway house, I thought, then looked up the address. Not imaginative at all. The house was on Overing Street—right here in the Bronx. I checked a map. Only a mile from Einstein! ■

PART FIVE

LATE BLOOMER

CHAPTER 24

Overing Underground

"'M LEAVING AS SOON AS HAROLD comes," said Neal, as he stubbed out his cigarette.

Michelle shot him a scornful look. "Don't be such a scaredy-cat. It's not against the law to publish a newspaper."

It was 11:00 p.m., and I was sitting in the kitchen of my apartment at Overing House with Neal, Michelle, Linda, and Angie, current and former tenants. We were talking softly, not only because Renee and Carolyn had gone to bed, but because we were listening for Harold's tap signal on the door to the street, two flights below.

There were four apartments at Overing: one for men and two for women, each accommodating up to five tenants; and one for Jaqui and Don, the husband-and-wife staff. By now, two months after I moved in, I was used to this drab kitchen—a disappointment at first after my intake tea with Jaqui. When she'd told me all four apartments were exactly like hers, I'd pictured them with gauzy curtains and copper-bottomed pots hanging above the stove. Then she'd walked me up here, and I'd seen cigarette burns on the Formica counter, the crusted remains of macaroni and cheese in a battered aluminum pot in the sink, and a pizza box atop the lid of the garbage pail. Her walls were a cheerful yellow. These were olive green and dirt-smudged. Her kitchen smelled of the fresh-cut roses on the table; this one smelled of stale cigarettes.

I no longer minded the kitchen, because I spent little time in it. I kept my food, labeled with my name, in the refrigerator and brought it to my room to eat. Still, I loved knowing that whenever I wanted company, there would likely be someone out here.

"Shhh!" Angie cupped her hand to her ear. "It's Harold!"

We all listened. *TapTapTap...Tap*. Three shorts and a long.

"I'll let him in on my way out," Neal said, then raced down the stairs. A moment later, he reappeared with Harold, each of them carrying a stack of pale blue mimeograph paper.

"I thought you were leaving," Michelle said.

"Harold needed help."

"Yeah, yeah." She pushed back her chair. "More like you didn't want to miss the action."

"Let's bring everything to my room," I said, getting up.

The room I shared with Angie had also been dingy when I moved in. I'd asked permission to paint, and Don had let me choose colors from the half-used cans in the basement. Angie, who spent most of her time in bed with her cat, had been glad to have the space spruced up, as long as she didn't have to do any of the work. The room we walked into now had three yellow walls and one orange.

"Use both beds," I said, closing the door. "Make a pile of page ones, a pile of page twos, threes, fours, and fives. Michelle, don't read! Wait till it's collated." I gave them pencils and showed them how to pull off one page at a time with the eraser end. Linda was the first to hand me a batch. I stapled it and began a new pile: the inaugural issue of the *Overing Underground*.

Of the 14 tenants at Overing, the six of us were the in-crowd. Michelle, whose boyfriend often slept over, was in her twenties and worked for the Welfare Department, even though she was on Welfare herself. Angie, 19, did temp work as a file clerk and would be moving out soon, into an apartment with her sister. Linda, 20, was a college student whose inner arms were covered with cutting scars; when she was feeling OK she spoke English, but at times she spoke only French, which she'd learned in school. Neal, who I guessed was 28 or 29, attended the day program at the community mental health center across the street. And Harold, a car-service driver whose age was hard to tell, was a former tenant who lived in the neighborhood; he'd moved out because he'd exceeded the one-year limit for a stay here and was now on the mental health center's waiting list for a permanent group home.

This bunch had been hanging around my room since I moved in, one or two at a time, first to watch me paint, then to sit in my rocking chair or on the edge of my bed to chat. As I got to know them, I understood why no one at Einstein had heard of this place. Overing and Einstein were in different orbits. I was the only one here who'd come from a private hospital and had a private doctor. The others had come through government hospitals—Bronx State, Harlem Valley, Creedmoor—or a public clinic or mental health center. Except for Linda and me, no one had gone past high school. A good number of the tenants who worked were employed at Altro, a sheltered workshop. I'd once asked Renee what her job involved, and she told me she put tubes of toothpaste into boxes. I tried not to show my horror at the thought of doing that all day, every day, but she didn't seem to mind.

Despite our different backgrounds, I felt a bond with the other tenants. We were all trying to find a way to fit into the world. They were as tolerant of my "states," as Michelle called them—times when I got paralyzed and couldn't talk—as they were of Carolyn's, when her usually sunny face turned tortured and she opened the living room window and shouted obscenities to the street below. If one tenant could calm down another without Jaqui's help, they did; if not, they called Jaqui from the pay phone in the kitchen and asked her to come over. As soon as the upset tenant was OK again, we treated him or her as before. There was nothing residual.

My fellow tenants knew I'd arrived at Overing through a different route than they had. When they complained about the halfway house administration I felt they were talking to me as part of their family yet outside the system, almost as if I could do something for them.

"Why don't you bring up these things in the Monday meetings?" I'd asked.

Run by Steve, the social worker who oversaw the house but didn't live there, the meetings were held in the basement rec room. Attendance was mandatory. There were announcements, such as plans for the special Christmas dinner, and discussions of issues related to group living: complaints about someone "borrowing" someone else's food, playing the TV too loud, leaving hair in the bathroom drain.

The tenants were afraid to voice complaints about Jaqui and Don in the meeting. I, on the other hand, was happy with them. On my worst nights, Jaqui would settle me in with my portable radio next to my ear, tuck the covers around me, and sit with me until my sleeping pill kicked in. I sometimes smelled alcohol on her breath, but it didn't bother me the way it did a few other tenants, who worried that she might not be able to respond if someone had an emergency. I even liked it when she'd been drinking because then she'd sing me a lullaby.

I'd gotten the idea for the newspaper after several grousing sessions during which I saw that despite people's minor complaints, they generally liked Overing, and Jaqui and Don, too. Except for the six of us, most of the tenants came together only on Monday evenings for the meeting and the optional group supper that followed. A newspaper would unite us more, I told them. It could have a Dear Abby-type column, jokes and riddles, and a roving-reporter section—"What's it like for you living at Overing?" Tenants would be able to say whatever they wanted, and they could put their names on it or not.

The idea took hold. We decided that this first issue would be produced in secret. Harold knew the secretary in the mental health center and asked her for stencils and correction fluid without telling her what they were for. I cut the stencils on my portable typewriter, but when Harold said he was going to sneak into the center through a window at night to run them off on the machine, I got nervous.

"You ain't doin' it. I am," he said, looking at me with his intense, dark eyes. "I ain't scared. I been arrested before."

Now, though, with 30 copies ready to distribute to tenants, former tenants, and Jaqui and Don, I was thrilled. The cover page read:

OVERING UNDERGROUND
Volume 1, Number 1
Editorial Board
Vivian Ann Conan, Editor-in-Chief
Mitch, Black Beauty
Harold, the Beard
Ellen Willow
Winifred Stone
Dorothy Emily Quinn
Laura Emily Mason

Harold and Michelle, nicknamed Mitch, were the only ones beside me who had wanted to be listed. All four names under Harold's were mine. No one objected or asked where they came from. Nor did I.

Before parting for the night, each of us took a copy, promising not to show it to anyone until official distribution time, which we agreed would be after Jaqui and Don saw it. I would give them copies tomorrow, as soon as I came home from work.

WHEN I GOT TO the medical school the next morning, there was a pile of mail on my chair, left there by Sylvia, the secretary for Dr. Jim Spiro, who was my boss. I began sorting it, checking to see that each applicant for membership in the society was sponsored by two members whose dues had been paid. If the members were in arrears, I sent them a letter requesting payment. If everything was in order, I sent the applicant a welcome letter.

I'd been working half an hour when Milton, from the mailing service, called to ask how many copies of the brochure we wanted. I hadn't known a brochure was in the works.

"Sylvia's not in yet," I said, "but I'll look for Dr. Spiro."

I went to the door of the lab. "He's at a seminar in Manhattan," one of the white-coated scientists called out, looking up from her microscope.

I asked Milton whether Sylvia could call him back. No, he said. The presses would start rolling in five minutes. We'd ordered 200, but it had just occurred to him that we might need more at a later date; printing them now would save repeat layout and typesetting costs.

My brain clicked into executive mode. What was the brochure about? I asked. Had he ever printed something similar for the society? How much did it cost to print 200? How much for a larger run?

"We'll take a thousand," I concluded. If more copies weren't needed, well, the additional $40 wasn't that terrible for the society to lose.

When Sylvia came in, I told her what I'd done.

"You had no right to spend money," she said. "Dr. Spiro will be very angry."

I didn't think so. I'd heard the letters he dictated to her. They were to senators and even the president, asking them to support funding for basic research. He did things in a big way.

No one was in my apartment when I got back to Overing, usual for midday. I picked up two copies of the paper and was about to take them to Jaqui and Don's apartment when I heard a knock. It was Jaqui and her Irish setter, Brandy.

Jaqui's face was sterner than I'd ever seen it. "The director of the center just gave me this," she said, holding up blue pages that matched the ones in my hand. "In the future, never give out anything across the street before I see it."

"I didn't give it out."

"Your name is on it."

"It was supposed to be only for you and Don and tenants and former tenants. I was just bringing you copies now." I handed them to her.

"I believe you," she said, softening, "but someone did it."

I supposed it was Harold but didn't say so.

Funding for Overing came from a private foundation, with the mental health center across the street having some kind of supervisory oversight. I never understood the nature of the relationship, but even if the director was Jaqui's boss, there was only one line in the paper she might have objected to. In the "Life at Overing" section, Michelle, writing anonymously, had said, "...and with the breath of alcohol, puts us all to sleep."

It turned out no one need have worried. An hour later, Harold stopped by to say the director loved the paper, and from now on, we didn't have to break into the building; the secretary would run it off for us.

BY THE TIME the second issue of the *Overing Underground* came out a month later—with contributions from most of the tenants and a column by Don titled "From the Pen of Alex Pope"—I'd come to think of the halfway house, and the Bronx, as home. Jaqui had had the rec room piano tuned especially for me, and I often went down to play Mozart sonatas or Stephen Foster songs. I was even playing viola in the Bronx Symphony Orchestra.

I seldom went to Brooklyn, not only because someone had rear-ended me on the parkway, totaling my car, but because nothing drew me there. My cousins all had their own lives now, my father was in Florida for the winter, and I didn't feel my mother understood anything about me.

She knew the building I lived in was called a halfway house and had even come to visit, but she acted, in her twice-weekly phone calls, as if I were sharing an ordinary apartment with some women

I just happened to know. I felt she saw the daughter she needed me to be, not the daughter I was.

Apart from Dr. Welch's fee, which my mother continued to pay, she seemed to think that because I had a job, I was self-supporting—despite my once having told her I was working ten hours a week for minimum wage. It was Jaqui who sat down with me to work out a weekly budget for the $16 I took home:

- $14 for rent
- $1 for the Monday night supper
- $1 for everything else: food; laundry; tampax; shampoo; toothpaste; fabric to make an occasional dress; bus or train fare, which was 20 cents

It was Jaqui who helped me apply for Welfare; now I was receiving a monthly check of $60. And it was Jaqui who noticed I'd sprouted a few stray grays and suggested I dye my hair. She went with me to the store to pick out a Miss Clairol kit and helped me apply it.

TENANTS AT OVERING were responsible for filling their own prescriptions and taking their own medication. To numb the pain in my chest and the storms in my brain, I'd been digging into my new pill stash, sometimes taking seven or eight Valium a day instead of four, and occasionally supplementing those with barbiturates—Seconal and Nembutal—which I took not to sleep, but to get calm enough to go about my activities. My body was so used to the drugs that they had almost no effect unless I took a lot.

One night, as I was falling asleep in the pitch-dark room, I saw a butterfly with psychedelic green, orange, purple, and yellow wings glowing on the wall, like a spectacular museum jewel. A moment later, it vanished. Nothing like that had happened to me before, and I told Dr. Welch about it the next day.

"When was the last time you went two weeks without taking a pill?" he asked.

"*Two weeks?!*"

He nodded.

"Sometimes I go two hours."

"It would be a good idea to cut down."

"Are you saying I'm an addict?"

"I'm saying it would be good to cut down."

On my way home, I decided to cut out pills altogether. I didn't want to be an addict.

The next morning, I managed to get through my two hours of work, but by the afternoon, my hands had started to shake. The following day they were still shaking, and now I was sweating and my heart was racing. I called Sylvia to say I had a cold and wouldn't be in.

"I didn't mean for you to go cold turkey," Dr. Welch said when I saw him that afternoon. "I meant for you to cut down gradually."

But I'd already started and was determined to see this through.

The next day, feeling worse, I slid a dime into the kitchen pay phone and dialed.

"Dr. Spiro's lab," came the nasal Bronx accent.

"Hi, Sylvia. It's Vivian. Is he in?"

"Anything I can help with?"

"I need to talk to *him*."

"Hold on." She sounded annoyed.

Dr. Spiro had thanked me for my decision on the brochure printing, saying I showed good judgment, and though my main dealings continued to be with Sylvia, I felt he liked me. I dragged a chair over with my foot and sat, glancing at Michelle's breakfast dishes in the sink.

"Hello!" Dr. Spiro always sounded as if he were looking forward to whatever might come next.

I took a breath and exhaled the speech Jaqui and I had rehearsed. "I'm sorry to give such short notice but there are some things going on in my personal life and I can't work anymore."

"Are you saying you're quitting?"

"Yes."

"Why?"

"There are some things going on in my personal life."

"You already said that. What things?"

"I—"

"I don't accept your resignation." He laughed, as if at a shared joke. "Let's talk about this," he continued more seriously. "I'm late for a meeting now. Are you free for lunch tomorrow? Around twelve?"

I felt dignified by his assumption that I might have other things scheduled. "Yes."

"Good."

After we hung up, I called Jaqui to tell her, then went back to bed. ∎

CHAPTER 25

Rum Raisin

CARRYING THE TRAY with our lunches, for which he'd paid, Dr. Spiro steered through the crowded employee cafeteria. He was a commanding presence, with dark, wavy hair, a short mustache, and skin that looked tanned even on that early spring day. His clothes were formally informal: plaid sport jacket, light blue shirt and tie. Greeting people as we looked for a table, he introduced me as someone who worked for the society. I smiled and shook hands, knowing I looked good in the outfit I'd worn for my job interview: miniskirt suit that I'd made—gold corduroy sprinkled with ruby-colored flowers—and ruby turtleneck.

"So what's going on in your personal life?" Dr. Spiro asked after we were seated and he'd seasoned his hamburger with pepper. "Boyfriend problems?"

I had no boyfriend. I just had Nick, whom I'd seen once or twice when I was on pass from the hospital and a few times since I'd come to Overing. He knew where I was living, and I knew he had another girlfriend now, but neither of us asked questions, which was fine. There wasn't any stress of closeness.

"No boyfriend problems," I said, then bit into my tuna sandwich.

"How old are you, if you don't mind my asking."

"Twenty-six."

His age was hard to tell—he was older than me and younger than my parents. There were no gray strands in his hair, but he had lines around his eyes even when he wasn't smiling.

"So what problems *are* you having?"

"Well—" I looked down at my plate. "I'm living in a halfway house."

"A halfway house." It was a statement. No tone of shock or judgment. "What's it for?"

"Ex-mental patients."

"Are you an ex-mental patient?"

"Yes." I met his eyes.

"Where is it?"

"About a mile from here."

Dr. Spiro seemed genuinely interested, and I was beginning to feel at ease. I wound up telling him about finishing library school while I was at Einstein, about hearing of this job from Annette.

"This explains a lot," he said, lifting his coffee cup. "There was always something about Annette. Don't get me wrong. She was good at what she did. But she never looked me in the eye. You're not like that. You relate well."

I supposed it was a compliment. "Thanks." I sipped my 7up.

"Tell me, what's the difference between you and me?"

"Excuse me?"

"I get depressed, but I've never gone to a hospital."

"You get depressed?"

"All the time. What makes you different?"

"I don't know."

"What are you going to do all day if you quit? Sit around the halfway house and mope?" Before I could answer, he added, "I think you should come back. What can I do that would make it easier for you?"

His concern both embarrassed and gratified me. I shrugged.

"How is it working with Sylvia? She can be bossy, I know."

"She's not too bad. Only I don't like it when she gives me advice, like telling me how to dress."

"Would you rather work from home? You could stop by every so often for the mail and keep a record of your hours."

"Really? Actually, I think I would."

"Good. That's settled. How much are we paying you, by the way?"

"One-sixty an hour."

"My gosh. That's not very much. Let me call Tom"—the society's executive treasurer—"and see if we can give you a raise."

Amazing, I thought on my way back to Overing. He knows the truth and still wants me.

MY ATTEMPT AT WORKING from home left me feeling so isolated—the other tenants were out during the day—that I became virtually immobilized and fell behind on processing membership applications and answering correspondence. I alternated between anxiety about things I should have been doing but couldn't—society business, putting out the next issue of the *Overing Underground*, making a dress to wear to my brother's upcoming wedding—and feeling that nothing mattered, because we were all on this planet for less than a second of cosmic time. The Valium I started taking again helped, though not enough.

There was a no-alcohol rule at Overing, with expulsion as the penalty, but it was generally ignored. When I'd first arrived, I didn't drink much. If I needed immediate relief from psychotic rumblings, or the pain, or the screaming in my brain, and I couldn't wait for a pill to kick in, I banged the back of my head on the wall by my bed. That usually knocked the feeling away, at least for a while. One day, Michelle, whose room adjoined mine, had barged in. "Stop that! You'll hurt yourself." She held out a glass. "Take a sip. It's gin. It'll make you feel better." It tasted terrible, but she was right. From then on, I kept a pint of gin in my underwear drawer and a huge bottle of tonic in the refrigerator, to mask the taste.

But now, as my immobilization and anxiety increased, not even Valium mixed with gin helped. Feeling there was no way I would ever get everything done, one night I became suicidal, got scared I might do something, and without waking anyone, took myself to the Jacobi Hospital psych ER. The next morning, I felt better and asked to be discharged. "It's too soon," a nurse said. I took advantage of the fact that I looked more like staff than patient in this bustling city hospital, and when the shift changed, I slipped into the elevator and went home to Overing.

Jaqui and I talked when I got back. She convinced me it was OK to quit my job, and I wrote a resignation note. When Dr. Spiro received it, he called to say he could get someone else but didn't want to. He suggested I try working in the office again, taking a day off whenever I didn't feel up to coming in. And from now on, he said, I would bypass Sylvia and report directly to him.

THE FIRST TIME DR. SPIRO dictated a letter to me, it was because Sylvia was out. I took it down in a combination of the Gregg stenography my father had taught me and fast longhand, and felt a surge of pride when I typed my initials next to his at the bottom and presented it to him for his signature. After that, even when Sylvia was in, if the letter involved society business, he dictated it to me.

In this way, I became aware of some of the activities of the organization. Most interesting was the Public Policy committee, whose members were contacting writers of soap operas to ask them to slip mention of the importance of basic research into their scripts. The aim was to get voters to tell their congressional representatives to support NIH funding. Both the writers and members of Congress were being sent copies of a pamphlet that explained the science in laymen's terms—the very copies I'd authorized printing!

I still had evenings I got through by drinking gin, and nights when Jaqui had to sit with me while I fell asleep, but all that seemed distant while I was at work, and now that I was doing more than processing membership applications, my job had become interesting.

My most pressing external concern was money. Even with my salary increase—I was currently making $2.00 an hour and occasionally worked more than ten hours a week—I was always short. Once, Michelle asked me to treat her to a slice of pizza, which was 25 cents. I couldn't and felt terrible when she called me a cheapskate. So when I saw a posting from the medical library seeking a circulation clerk for Sunday evenings, I applied, attaching a letter of recommendation from Dr. Spiro. Soon, I was spending one evening a week checking out books and periodicals, accepting returns, flagging overdue items, and sending out bills for fines. One Sunday, I came across a bill for Dr. Welch—he owed $30 for books on schizophrenia and depression—and tore it up. In my next session, I told him what I'd done. "Thank you!" he grinned. "It's good to know a librarian!"

In the summer, I became involved with the company making arrangements for the society's November annual meeting, to be held in Detroit. There were abstracts to be printed, exhibitors to be signed up, council meetings to be scheduled. Whenever I had to ask Dr. Spiro something, I walked into the lab instead of just standing in the doorway, as I'd done previously. I expected the slides and microscopes that were on the counter and wasn't too surprised by the remains of a dissected research cat on the table in the corner, but I wasn't prepared for the way the scientists talked, not only about grant applications and blood-brain barriers but the war in Vietnam. They were against it. Nixon. They didn't like him. They discussed hypothetical questions, too: If you were the only person left on the planet, would you continue your research? That was creepy—too much like *Island of the Blue Dolphins*. Yet I found the conversation fascinating.

What used to be a blur of white coats was now a group of individual people, with names and personalities. One day, in the beginning of the summer, Jeanne came into the back office to ask whether I'd like to be part of the ice cream club. We'd all chip in, she said, and, every day, someone would go to Baskin-Robbins to get surprise flavors. Pleased to be included—and happy that, with my additional job, I could afford it—I gave her $2.00.

The next day, when Ritchie came in with containers of Cookies 'n Cream and Rum Raisin, I joined everyone around the lab counter with my spoon and bowl, feeling the wonder of it all: I belonged to something normal in the regular world.

CHAPTER 26

Rebecca

I DISCOVERED ST. PETER'S churchyard a few months after I moved into Overing, on a day Caroline was having one of her screaming fits and even Jaqui couldn't calm her. To find some peace, I went out for a walk. Spotting greenery on the other side of Westchester Avenue, I headed toward what I thought was a park, but after I crossed under the elevated train tracks I saw gravestones. Intrigued, I tried the gate. It opened, and I stepped inside to find myself in a scene that could have been the frontispiece of a novel by Nathaniel Hawthorne.

The church was storybook old, with arched windows and a pointy spire. A few of the stones were just tips sticking out of the ground, their names and stories long covered by earth, but, on most, inscriptions were visible.

Jemima Watson
Born in West Chester May 19, 1770
Died July 31, 1847

An ordinary woman who had been alive during the Revolutionary War!

Emmeline Paul,
who died Sept 6, 1866,
age 25 years, 7 months, and 10 days

A year younger than I was. I wondered what caused her death.

Henry Clinton Overing

So that's how the street got its name.

During the next few weeks, I visited the churchyard often. Rarely was anyone around. I spread my blanket on the grass, wrote Ellen Willow poems, and watched squirrels chase one another up and down trees. I ate a Swiss cheese and tomato sandwich while I read *Middlemarch*. I brought paper and crayons, and when I came across an inscription so worn it was hard to read, I made a rubbing and was sometimes able to make out the words on my sheet.

One day, passing a grave I'd seen many times, something made me stop.

Mother
Rebecca
Wife of Lewis Doty
Born Feb 1, 1792
Died Nov 1, 1849
Entered into rest

I looked at Rebecca's stone, slanted from years of wind and rain, and felt a sadness start to grow from the place in my chest where I usually felt the pain. Beckie was what everyone had called my mother before a teacher told her during her first year of school that it wasn't respectable and she had to choose between Rebecca and Beatrice. Though she didn't understand why, she didn't question the teacher's authority. Seven years old, she preferred Rebecca but could never remember whether it had two Bs or two Cs, so she chose Beatrice, which eventually became her official name. To the family who had known her before that, though, she was still Beckie.

Rebecca, my mother, was dead. Entered into rest. I placed my palm on her name and closed my eyes to keep the sadness. It was sweet, almost holy. A tear ran down my cheek. I caught it on my finger and licked the saltiness.

The following day, I brought a candle to Rebecca's grave, lit it, and waited for the sadness. Strange, I thought, watching myself cry. I didn't feel crazy when I was sad. My insides were calm.

Each time I visited the cemetery, I knew with certainty that my mother was dead. Back at Overing House, I knew she wasn't dead in real life, just in my cemetery life. But my cemetery life gradually grew stronger, until one day my mother was dead even when I wasn't in the cemetery.

"When did she die?" Dr. Welch asked as we sat in his office, which was now in Manhattan.

"Maybe a few weeks ago."
"But I saw you since then."
"I know."
"Why didn't you say anything?"
I shrugged.
"Is it that you just *feel* your mother is dead?"
"She really *is*."
"How come I got a check from her last week?"
"I don't know."
"Does your brother know she died?"
"I'm not sure."
"Was there a funeral?"
"I guess so. I went to see her in the cemetery."
"Which cemetery?"
"The one near Overing."

By the session's end, part of me was still sure my mother was dead. Another part was glad Dr. Welch didn't seem convinced.

I CONTINUED TO VISIT Rebecca's grave and draw comfort from the sadness. At the same time, I made noncommittal conversation with my Brooklyn mother.

"I'm calling to say hello and see how you are," she would say.
"Fine. I went to the orchestra rehearsal last night."
"Good. Did you enjoy it?"
"Yeah. It was OK."

One day, reading on my bed, I heard the pay phone ring. "Vivian, for you," Renee called. "Your mother."

I walked into the kitchen and picked up the receiver. "Hello, Mother." Since her death, I no longer called her Mom.

"Vivian, I never bought you a ring," she said, as if we were already in the middle of a conversation. "It's time." As if buying a ring were on the schedule of what every mother was supposed to do.

"I don't need a ring."

"But I want to give you one. I'd like to meet you tomorrow, so you can pick it out."

How could she meet me? She was dead. "What time?"

The next morning, I walked up and down Lexington Avenue with a lady who thought she was living. I didn't have the heart to tell her she was a ghost. From someplace outside my body, I watched myself talking to her and thought how bizarre this was.

Eventually I saw a ring I liked: gold with opals in a hexagon setting. The ghost took out her wallet to pay for it, then wanted to go to a coffee shop for lunch. Sitting across from her, seeing her take bites of hamburger, I wondered what happened to food once it was inside a dead person. Maybe it just stayed there, undigested, like stuffing.

Before we parted—she, to ride the Sea Beach train to Brooklyn; I, the Pelham Bay line to the Bronx—she said, "I'm so glad we did this, Vivian. I love you, and now you have a ring from me."

I settled into a window seat on the train back to Overing and fingered the ring, an heirloom my cemetery-mother had left behind when she died.

IN THE FALL, MY MOTHER enrolled Marvin, his wife, Mara, and me in a folk-dance class she was taking at Brooklyn College. She paid the fee for the four of us, but it was an inconvenient gift, forcing us to go to Brooklyn every Tuesday evening—an hour by car from Overing, two hours by train. Marvin and Mara, who lived near Yankee Stadium, also in the Bronx, drove me each week. I hated this forced family togetherness but felt obligated to go. Once there, though, I did enjoy the dancing.

The class started at 8:00. One Tuesday evening, I woke suddenly in my bed at Overing and looked at the clock. "Five after seven! Shit!" The sounds of the *I Love Lucy* show drifted in from the living room. "My brother will be here any second."

"He came ten minutes ago," said Joan, who had become my new roommate after Angie moved out. She was lying on her bedspread, flipping the pages of a magazine. "Peter told him to go without you."

"What?!"

Peter was the intern who had recently come to work with Jaqui and Don. The last thing I'd said to him was, "Wake me at a quarter to seven." He'd assured me he would.

I rushed into the kitchen in my rumpled blouse and underpants, the clothes I'd been wearing two hours earlier, when Peter held my hair back as I retched into the toilet bowl. He was sitting at the table, sipping coffee and reading a book.

"Why didn't you call me?"

"After a pint of gin, I didn't expect you up till morning."

"*How am I going to get there?*" I shrieked.

"You'll just have to skip tonight."

"*I can't! You don't understand!*" Generally I liked Peter, but right now I hated him.

I raced to my room for a dime, then dialed a car service. The ride would cost a lot, but I couldn't disappoint my mother. I still felt repulsed whenever she tried to get close to me, and I still took comfort from the dead version of her when I visited the cemetery, but her living and dead versions were so separate by now that they had nothing to do with each other. I knew this class was important to my Brooklyn mother, even though she was casual about it on the surface.

She would invariably be there when we arrived, her face beaming as she offered us Fig Newtons, as if the gymnasium were her home, and she the hostess. "Hello, Vivian. Hello, Marvin. Hello, Mara," she'd say, awkward-kissing each of us. There was usually time for a quick mention of my father—"Dad says hello"—before we took our places in the circle. For the next two hours, we were an ordinary family, united by "Yemenite left, grapevine to the right," and other steps the instructor called out as we moved in patterns to the music.

Minutes after my phone call, having Listerine'd away the vomit taste, changed my clothes, and put on fresh makeup, I went down to the waiting car. I gave the driver directions, then leaned back and began to relax, absently fingering my ring, thankful I didn't have a headache. "She can't hold her liquor," I'd heard Michelle say to Peter from the bathroom door. "That's why she never gets a hangover."

I gazed out the window at the red taillights ahead. The Brooklyn-Queens Expressway already. This car was like the Starship Enterprise, hurtling through space on its way to a galaxy where my mother wasn't involved in a lawsuit with Einstein Hospital about the bill, and her daughter wasn't living in a halfway house for the mentally ill.

"You're such a lovely family," a woman in the class once said to me. "You live near here?"

"My mother does," I answered. "We live in the Bronx."

"How nice that you all do this together. I'm going to ask my daughter and granddaughter for next term."

What would she have thought if she'd known that, each week, I was there only because the plastic bag I spread under my pillow every night didn't just happen to move while I was sleeping, and my face didn't just happen to turn in such a way that the bag covered my nose and mouth. I'd set it up so it would look like an accident, which technically it would be. It was only a matter of time.

I paid the driver and entered the gym. 8:15. They were already dancing. I spotted my mother's coat on one of the chairs lining the wall—the one with the Fig Newtons on top—and left mine alongside it. Then I walked up to the undulating circle and slipped between my mother and Mara.

"You made it!" my mother said, smiling.

I fell into step, feeling the pressure of the ring as she squeezed my hand. ▪

CHAPTER 27

Horizontal

DR. SPIRO SAT NEAR MY DESK in the back office while he chose the food to be served at the society's upcoming annual meeting in Detroit.

"Let's see," he said, scanning the sample menu the convention-planning company had sent. "Assorted pastries—"

I wrote it down.

"You know, people are very fussy about the way they want their eggs. I worked in my uncle's restaurant when I was in college, and breakfast was the hardest meal. What do you say we avoid problems and get French toast and pancakes?"

"OK." I wrote again, trying not to show my surprise that he was sharing part of his life with me, and also asking my opinion. "Should we do the lunch menu now?"

"Sure." But he didn't go on.

"Dr. Spiro?"

"It just occurred to me. We'll need someone to take minutes. I certainly can't do it." He laughed. "Any chance you'd be able to come?"

Startled, I put down my pen. If anything, he should have asked Sylvia. She knew more about the society's business than I did. But I could definitely take minutes.

"I guess so."

"That's great!" His smile was warm. "You'll be a big help."

I was determined to justify his confidence in me.

But at home a half hour later, I began to have doubts.

"He wouldn't have asked if he thought you couldn't do it," Jaqui said. "You know more than you think. It's only four days, and you can call me collect anytime."

A week later, she lent me a suitcase and sat with me while I packed: clothes and makeup; folders from the office; and, to keep me steady when I wasn't working, a novel, my recorder, and some Bach and Telemann sheet music.

AT THE EXECUTIVE BOARD MEETING on my first morning in Detroit, Dr. Spiro introduced me to the scientists whose secretaries I had been talking to for the past few months. They all seemed to know one another, even though they were from different parts of the country, and they made me feel welcome. I sat beside him and took notes.

As the meeting drew to a close, Dr. Spiro addressed the whole group, suggesting dinner in a Greek restaurant he knew. Then he turned to me. "You'll come too?"

I was flattered but hesitated.

"Unless you have something else planned," Dr. Spiro said when I didn't answer.

Was he being sarcastic? I didn't think so, and if I didn't go, I'd be alone. "OK."

"Great!"

By evening, the party had grown—wives, husbands, other scientists—and at the restaurant we filled three large round tables. I sat next to Dr. Spiro, wearing the royal blue dashiki I'd sewn, my eye shadow matching the blue, and my red tights picking up one of the colors in the embroidery around the hem and neckline. With the wooden earrings I'd bought in Oklahoma and my hair fastened in a clip and hanging down my back, I knew I looked good and no one could tell I felt out of place.

This was Dr. Spiro's turf. The others were happy to let him order. He talked to the waiter in Greek, and, though I understood only a little, the conversation was in the cadence of Nona's kitchen. I began to feel more at ease.

Platters kept arriving, as did drinks and wine. I had orange juice—I considered myself working—and remained clearheaded while some of the people who had seemed so proper at the meeting got drunk. There were loud voices, jokes I didn't get, and shushes whenever someone stood unsteadily to make another toast. I was most surprised by Dr. Spiro. He was in high spirits, but his speech was becoming less and less distinct.

"Have another drink, Jim," someone called out.

"Good idea," Dr. Spiro said, holding up his glass for the fifth or sixth time. "Waiter, another Scotch, please."

Suddenly, I felt his hand on my leg, fumbling for my hem. He pulled it up and began squeezing my thigh. I pushed him away, hoping no one had noticed, but a second later his hand was back. I threw it off again, grateful for the low-hanging tablecloth.

"Why are you pushing me away?" he said in a sotto voce that came out loud. All heads turned toward us. "I'm not terrible. Don't you know you're beautiful? What do you do for sex?"

I felt myself blush and looked down at my plate. This was wrong—Dr. Spiro was married—yet I was aroused. At the same time, I felt I should prevent him from embarrassing himself in front of his peers.

The meal seemed to go on forever, with the squeezing escalating to fondling. I would push him away. There would be a moment's reprieve when he was distracted by conversation, then a repeat. All the while, everyone pretended to ignore what they couldn't help hearing and seeing.

One couple at another table hadn't joined the chorus encouraging Dr. Spiro to keep drinking. I got the impression they'd known him a long time and were friends of his family. For a while now, they'd been looking concerned, as if they wanted to stop him from making a spectacle of himself but didn't know how to buck the merriment. To my relief, they finally took charge, getting both of us back to the hotel in a taxi, then supporting him, one on each side, up the elevator and down the hall to his room, which was next to mine.

I opened my own door and went inside, thankful the evening was over. Washing off my eye makeup, I could hear Dr. Spiro's friends getting him to bed, their voices soft, his loud and slurred. After a few minutes, they left. I put on my nightgown and got into bed with my book.

Moments later, there was a knock. It was on the door between our rooms, not the hall door.

"Yes?" I called.

"It's me."

"Go back to bed."

"Please let me in."

"Go to sleep."

When his pleading continued, I opened the door to a Dr. Spiro in boxer shorts, a sleeveless undershirt, and socks. I had just a second to get over my surprise—and also to register that he was trim but not muscular, with shoulders that were narrower than they looked in his sport jacket—before he took a step in and tottered. I managed to support him until he got to my bed, where he collapsed into a sitting position, feet on the floor.

"I can't sleep," he said. "Please let me stay." It was the voice of a little boy who needed comfort, in keeping with his uncharacteristically apologetic stance.

"I guess it's OK." I helped him swing his feet onto the bed, then covered him and walked around to the other side.

Exhausted but wide awake, I curled up with my back to him, pulling the edge of the blanket over me, leaving a wide space between us.

"Why are you so far away?" he said. "I won't hurt you. Come closer."

I turned to see him lying on his side, facing me. "Dr. Spiro, you're married."

"Jim. Please call me Jim. I'm not happy with my wife. We have problems."

Surprised again, I sat up cross-legged, knees and feet tucked under my nightgown, and looked down at him.

"I love you," he said. "I've loved you for a long time. Last night I was lying on my bed, listening to you play Bach, and I was rubbing myself."

He said this so openly, with no touch of shame, that I couldn't be embarrassed. Rather, I felt special.

"Come lie down over here," he said.

I did.

He put his arms around me, and I snuggled against him, spoon style, feeling enfolded and secure. A moment later, when he began to raise my nightgown, I didn't stop him.

He turned me onto my back. "Look at you. You're a beautiful woman. He stroked my stomach, then kissed it. "Do you know that?"

At 27, I had never thought of myself as a woman. I was a girl. And though I would have described myself as pretty, with long dark hair, small but adequate breasts, and legs that looked good in a miniskirt, I never thought I was beautiful. But at that moment, I felt both womanly and beautiful.

He was clumsy. I didn't care and let his fingers and lips explore while he told me again that I was beautiful, apologized for his "little thing" that wouldn't do what it was supposed to, thanked me for letting him be with me, asked me what I liked. Nick may have been more deft, but sex was never personal with him. This was the first time I felt cherished. I let his finger slip inside me, and when I began to tremble, I felt connected to him in a way I'd never felt with anyone before.

I rested peacefully in his arms a while, then began stroking his chest and stomach, moving my hand lower and lower. "Rub me," he pleaded. I did.

I SLEPT INTERMITTENTLY, awakened sometimes by Dr. Spiro's snoring—I still couldn't think of him as Jim—sometimes by his hands and kisses. In the morning, I was tired but happy. He was tired and had a headache and a white-coated tongue.

The door between our rooms was still open, and he asked me to get the bottle of aspirin from his toilet kit. As I was coming back with it, the phone in his room rang.

"Let it go," I said when I saw what a hard time he was having getting up.

"I can't."

He reached it on the ninth or tenth ring. "Good morning..." His voice was deep, as if he had a cold. "I was in the bathroom... I was out—we went to a Greek restaurant... How are the girls?"

The conversation didn't bother me. It was with someone I couldn't picture.

We each got ready in our separate rooms. He shaved and dressed. I put on makeup and collected my folders for the day's meetings. With the connecting door open, it felt like a normal morning in a regular house. Then he closed and locked it—for the chambermaid, he said—and took the elevator down. I was to follow five minutes later.

I used the time to call Jaqui.

"I'm not surprised," she said when I told her what had happened. "Just surprised that you're surprised."

"His name is Jim."

"I'm very happy for you."

HE DIDN'T CORRECT ME when I called him Dr. Spiro during the breakfast and lunch meetings, but now, when his colleagues called him Jim, I heard it differently and felt closer to him, knowing we shared a secret.

After the last meeting, he told them he needed "to get horizontal" for a while. They seemed to understand that meant he was going to take a nap. We went upstairs in separate elevators.

With the connecting door open, he lay down on my bed fully clothed, and asked me to play some music for him. I propped a Telemann piece against the pillows and sat next to him in my minidress. He listened with his hands clasped under his head, elbows wide. I liked feeling his eyes on me. "Thank you," he said when I finished.

"I didn't know you like classical music."

"Oh, yes." He told me a joke, something about when the angels in heaven are on duty they play Bach, but when they're off duty they play Mozart.

I chuckled.

"I'm thirsty," he said.

I offered to bring him a glass of water.

"Wait." He got up. "I have something better. Come. I'll show you."

I followed him into his room, where he opened a drawer, and, with a conspiratorial wink, unrolled a shirt to reveal a bottle of Scotch. I smiled, though I thought it strange. Why did he have to hide something in his own room? He went to the bathroom and returned with two glasses.

"I don't want any," I said. It wasn't only that I didn't like Scotch, or that I still considered myself working. I was feeling calm and didn't need alcohol. He poured himself a glass and brought it back to my room.

For the next hour, we alternately napped, snuggled, and talked, while every so often, Dr. Spiro/Jim took a sip of his drink. He told me about his parents, immigrants from Greece, and asked about my family. I found out that he was 43 and had two children. I told him about my money worries. He said there was a part-time lab technician job that had just become open. It involved taking care of a colony of axolotls, aquatic salamanders that Pat, one of the scientists, used in her research. He said he would talk to her about hiring me. This was a different kind of intimacy from last night's, also satisfying. I'd never spoken with Nick this way.

We came to a lull in the conversation and were lying quietly together, when he said, "I can't have dinner with you tonight. I'm sorry. Some people invited me to eat with them, and it wouldn't be appropriate to bring you."

I tried to ignore the stab in my chest.

"Why don't you take yourself out to a nice restaurant, and I'll see you later."

He'd only yesterday come into my life as Jim, I reasoned. What did I expect?

"I'm sorry," he repeated when I still didn't answer.

"It's OK." But it wasn't, not just because he was going, but because he'd waited until now to tell me, after I'd felt so close to him for the past hour.

As if taking me at my word, he relaxed, and his eyes closed. Soon he was breathing regularly.

I slipped off the bed without waking him and sat on the chair with my book. It remained on my lap, unopened, while I watched his chest rise and fall. For a very long time. The room felt empty. I missed Overing, the cemetery, Dr. Welch.

"What are you doing over there?" he said when he woke.

"I couldn't sleep."

He looked at his watch. "Oh my gosh. I have to make a call."

He went into his room but didn't close the door, and I heard him phone home. The conversation sounded impersonal—his schedule and the names of the people he'd be having dinner with.

After he hung up, I went into his bathroom and watched him brush his teeth, trying not to let him see I was upset.

"Have a good time," I said as he was leaving.

"You, too. I'll see you around ten."

The door closed. He was gone.

I called Jaqui. Then I ordered a tuna sandwich from room service. I didn't feel secure enough to leave the hotel and look for a restaurant; nor did I want to go to one alone, even the lobby coffee shop. I prepared for tomorrow's meetings. I took a Valium, read, played my recorder. I made a scribble drawing, put it in an envelope, and addressed it to Dr. Welch. I would mail it in the morning, and when he got it, he would come back in time to be with me now. Ellen Willow wrote a poem.

At five to ten, I began straightening the room, putting my things away.

At ten after ten, I started to doubt I was real. Had last night even happened? It had. The door between our rooms was open.

At twenty after, I went to bed.

It was past 11:30 when I woke to his calling my name. Dr. Spiro/Jim was drunk, but not as much as the previous night. "Vivian. Vivian." He ruffled my hair and smiled. "There you are! What-cha been doing all evening? There you are! I'm so glad to see you!"

In a second, I was real again. He held me and told me how beautiful I was. And as if the past few hours had never happened, I bloomed the way I had the night before.

He again lamented his "little thing" and told me he'd give up his professorship, his education, everything he had, if he could be macho, like a truck driver with a hairy chest. He gnashed his teeth and tried to talk like one, grabbing my hair and mock-throwing me against the pillow. "Get ovah heah!"

I laughed and told him I didn't care. He was fine the way he was.

He may have been 16 years older, but now I was a woman and he was a little boy—Jim—baring his vulnerabilities, looking to me for love, comfort, and acceptance. No one had ever trusted their soul to me before.

WHEN IT WAS TIME TO GO BACK to New York, Jim said, "I can't promise you anything. I'm not going to leave my wife. But I want to see you."

I told him that was OK, but only if each time we were together he told me when the next time would be.

He said he would. ▪

CHAPTER 28

The Right Choice

"**Y**OU'LL DO FINE,**"** Jim said as he pulled the car to the snow-crusted curb. He cut the motor and turned to face me. "Just remember. You're a valid person. You have to know that."

"I do." He'd said that often in the year since Detroit, and there were many times I believed it.

"Good! Don't worry about me. I have the *Times*." He gave my hand a squeeze and I got out.

Though I was doing well with my patchwork of part-time jobs—secretarial work for the society, Sunday library clerk, and lab technician caring for the axolotls—I felt I should be looking for a job as a librarian, the profession for which I had trained. Jim had encouraged me. "I don't want to lose you from the lab," he said, "but you have to think about your future. There's no advancement for you here."

My first interview had been with the New York Public Library, where they asked how I felt about working in a depressed area. Inspired by Jim's leftist leanings, I said I would prefer it, and they told me I'd hear from them shortly. This was my second interview, in the library of a company that manufactured industrial cleaning products.

An hour later, I emerged into the sharp air to see exhaust vapor coming from Jim's car. He'd probably had to turn on the heater.

"I'm glad it went well," he said as I got in. It was toasty, and Schubert was playing on the radio.

"How do you know?"

"You were in there a long time."

I unwound my scarf. "He told me not to make any decision until I spoke with him. I'm not sure what that means."

"That he liked you." Jim tossed his newspaper onto the back seat and put the car into gear for the 20-minute ride to my apartment. Once upstairs, he busied himself in the kitchen while I changed into clothes for the lab and took Zorbie, my white German Shepherd, down for a walk.

TEN MONTHS EARLIER, when my year at Overing was coming to an end, I'd given myself two requirements: I wanted to live nearby, and I wanted a roommate. I had felt lucky to find this apartment—the entire top floor of a two-family house a block away, close enough to still go to the Monday dinners—and lucky that Karen, another Overing tenant, wanted to share it with me. Before we moved, I came over to clean and fix up, and when I needed a hammer, I took one from Don's toolbox, knowing I wasn't going to return it. I didn't consider that stealing, just incorporating a piece of my old home into the new, to help me get started.

Karen's obsessions, mainly around food and germs, hadn't bothered me at first. Nor did my upset times appear to bother her: getting paralyzed, not being able to talk, or holding my head with my hands because it felt as if my brains were spilling out. She was usually at work when Jim came over, but if she wasn't, she didn't seem to mind that he and I locked ourselves in my bedroom. When we came out, Jim kidded around with her, made her smile, and sometimes sat with her in the living room while she watched TV. Karen knew more about politics than I did, and they discussed the book she was reading, *The Strawberry Statement*, about the student protests at Columbia University.

But as I became more comfortable being out and about in the world, I began losing patience with Karen. One day, five months after we moved in, she was mumbling about a run in her stocking, and I snapped that I was tired of hearing her make a big deal over little stuff. She was visibly hurt. Things became more chilly between us, and we decided to split up. Jim felt I had been too hard on Karen. It was only after she was gone that I realized he was right.

It had been Jim's idea that I get a dog after Karen left—specifically, this dog, who had been at the Animal Institute at Einstein, in the pool to be used for research. The Institute attendants liked him and didn't send him out when they got requests from scientists for a dog. Jeanne, one of the neuroscientists in Jim's lab, adopted him but brought him back after three days. He was a wonderful animal, she said, but he'd lunged at her baby. She announced that she would keep him in the lab for a few hours, in the hope that someone else would want him. If no one adopted him by afternoon, she would return him to the Institute.

I was in the cold room where the axolotls were housed, feeding them thin strips of liver that I dangled through the water from a forceps, when Jim came in.

"Viva,"—his name for me—"why don't you take the dog?"

"Me?"

"I wish I could be with you every night, but I can't. He'll be company for you."

"I'm not set up for a dog."

"Just come talk to Jeanne."

I lay the forceps on the wooden cutting board and went into the lab.

The dog was lying serenely under the counter, unaware his fate was hanging in the balance. Close by were bowls of water and dry food. When I knelt to stroke his head, he looked into my eyes and his tail thumped against the floor.

"He's great with adults," Jeanne said. "Children, too. It's just babies he doesn't like."

The dog was gazing at me. "Hi, doggie," I said, still stroking his head. I'd forgotten, since Brownie, how satisfying this could feel.

Jeanne put a shopping bag down on the floor. "This'll last a few days. You can keep the bowls and leash."

"I'm not sure I'm taking him."

"In case you do."

I gave the dog a final pat and went back to the axolotls. When I finished feeding them—60 large salamanders in individual plastic bowls of water—I left them to digest for several hours while I did office work for the society. But first I stopped in at the lab to see the dog again. This time, when he locked eyes with me, I knew.

NOW I LEFT MY SNOWY BOOTS in the hall and went upstairs with Zorbie to the snack Jim had waiting: Earl Grey tea and an English muffin for me, coffee for him. He kept his own specially ground brand in the freezer and a stock of Melitta filters in the pantry. I liked having his stuff around: coffee, Scotch, and the jars of herbs I'd been accumulating because he enjoyed teaching me to cook new dishes. In our first kitchen session, we'd made a casserole of baked thyme rice with onions, parsley, and butter.

"Given the choice of the cleaning company or the public library," Jim said as we took our seats and Zorbie settled under the table with a biscuit, "you should take the cleaning company."

"Why?"

"The salary's higher, and it's a smaller library. Once they see you're a good administrator, you'll go places."

"But there's hardly anyone around. It's creepy."

A week later, I had offers from both and accepted the one from the public library, where I would be working at a branch in the South Bronx.

"If that's what you want," Jim said.

I wondered why he wasn't more enthusiastic. "It is."

ON MY FIRST DAY, when I was banished upstairs to the children's room to file catalog cards, I began to regret my decision. The library didn't open until 1:00, and the staff—three librarians and two clerks—used the morning for behind-the-scenes work. I would have preferred to stay on the first floor, where everyone was working silently in the office—Mrs. Brown, gray-haired and matronly, was the head of the branch and didn't allow talking. On the second floor, I would be alone.

"Can I file the adult cards instead?" I asked. The adult department was on the first floor.

"You were told to go upstairs," Mrs. Brown said, "and that's where you'll go."

Shopping bag of cards in hand, I made my way up the broad staircase, feeling the silence of the building close in on me. At the top, I put the bag on a chair near the freestanding catalog and reached in for a card. I found the proper place for it in the catalog but didn't remove the rod at the bottom of the drawer to let the card drop down, because Mrs. Brown would be up later to check on the placement of each card before it could be officially incorporated. Standard procedure in all 87 branches, she'd said. I thought it was a waste of time. I didn't make mistakes.

For the next 40 minutes, the only sounds were the soft slide of the oak catalog drawers, the ticking of the wall clock, and the intermittent clang of the radiator. I glanced into the bag. At least another hour's worth of cards. By then I'd be shrunk to nothingness. I went downstairs.

"Finished already?" Mrs. Brown asked.

"I came for a tissue."

"There's a box in the children's room."

"I didn't see it," I lied.

One of the clerks looked at me with what I thought was sympathy. I opened a drawer in the desk that had been assigned to me, took a tissue from my bag, and went up again.

I filed the last card a few minutes before noon and joined everyone in the office, where we ate brown bag lunches; there was no place to eat out in this neighborhood of tenements and abandoned or burned buildings. Talking was allowed now, but we had to use last names. I learned that Mrs. Brown and the clerks had been with the library for more than 25 years; Miss Stevanovic, the adult librarian and assistant branch head, had arrived more recently. The central administration periodically rotated staff among the branches, and no one had been at this one more than a few years.

At one o'clock, Mr. Thomas, the uniformed security guard, arrived and stationed himself at the door. Mrs. Brown and one of the clerks ascended to the children's room. I stayed downstairs in the adult department with Miss Stevanovic and the other clerk.

Only a handful of people came in, not counting the boys Mr. Thomas barred because they should have been in school. The first was a man who requested *Down These Mean Streets*. After he left, I picked up another copy and looked at the cover. It sounded interesting: the true story of a man who'd grown up in Spanish Harlem, been in gangs, done drugs, and wound up in jail. I checked it out for myself.

Ten minutes later, a woman came in wanting something to help her prepare for the high school equivalency exam. Shortly after she sat down with the test-prep book I gave her, she asked whether I could explain a grammar question. Miss Stevanovic motioned me aside to say Mrs. Brown wouldn't want me to, because "this isn't a school." I said that if someone else came in, I'd get up to help them. Miss Stevanovic didn't look happy but she didn't stop me. As one multiple-choice question led to another and the woman kept thanking me, I began to think this might not be such a bad job.

At three o'clock, Miss Stevanovic said, "Go upstairs now and help Mrs. Brown."

No sooner had I reached the silence of the second floor than an army of kids swarmed up behind me. The air, dead only seconds before, vibrated. I felt a tug on my skirt, another on my hair, my sleeve.

"Miss, do you got the book of *Sleeping Beauty*?"

"Do you got butterflies?"

"Do you got...."

Fifteen minutes later, when the children were settled at tables, I had a chance to look around for Mrs. Brown. Our eyes met and she said, "You got baptized by fire."

"Is it like this every day?"

"As soon as school lets out."

A girl thrust a book into my hand. "Read this."

We sat down on the low wooden chairs. I had barely said, "Once upon a time," when three other children came to hang over my shoulder and squeeze against my sides.

"Now me!" a boy said as soon as I finished. He handed me another book. I was definitely going to like it here.

"You're like the Pied Piper," Mrs. Brown said when I was finally able to get up. She didn't sound pleased, and I became aware that she hadn't been reading stories herself. "You shouldn't encourage them. They'll take all your time." She didn't expressly forbid my reading, though, and I didn't refuse the next tug.

At one point, a boy who couldn't have been more than five approached me with his hand in his pants pocket, finger poking the fabric from inside to make it look as if he had a gun. "Give me some money!" he demanded in a voice at odds with his baby face.

"Honey, I don't have any," I said. "Why don't you ask your mother?"

"I did. She won't give me any." A tear rolled down his cheek.

I sat him in my lap and read him a story.

At six, when the library closed, we had to tell the children to leave. I watched nine-year-olds collect five-year-olds, noticing that no one checked out any books. The library had just been their babysitter. Some kids had keys hanging from ribbons around their necks, and I wondered what they would face when they got home.

On the half-hour bus ride back to my safe, working-class neighborhood, less than three miles away, I opened my book. The story took place in Manhattan, and I was working in the Bronx, but it was about a slum. I wanted to understand the world these children lived in. ■

PART SIX

ALTERS

CHAPTER 29

Adulthood

"*PASSAGES*. EVER READ IT?" Marybeth held up a book.

"By Gail Sheehy. Yes." I didn't see the connection.

She leaned forward. "You're thirty-five, evaluating where your life is going and the choices you've made. Classic midlife crisis."

It was 1977, and I had just spent half an hour summarizing my past for this new therapist. I was here because I'd started to feel a vague internal rumbling, an uneasiness so indefinable that if I didn't consider my history I would have ignored it. But if any craziness was returning, I wanted to catch it before it mushroomed. I liked my now life—a sunny one-bedroom apartment on Manhattan's Upper West Side, a job as director of a suburban public library—and didn't want anything from my before-life to disrupt it.

I felt at ease with Marybeth. Probably around 40, she wore a sweater with asymmetric blocks of bright colors, like a modern painting. Her office was an extension of her style: colorful abstract art and sleek furniture, the whole lit by afternoon sun streaming through sparkling 37th-floor windows on the Upper East Side. I had begun by telling her how I'd worked at various branches of the New York Public Library for six years, advancing up the administrative ladder to become head of a branch; then, when citywide budget cuts led to my being laid off and rehired twice, had found my current job as director of a village library an hour's drive north of the city. Only after I felt I had established myself as someone substantial in her eyes did I outline my mental history, ending with my last long-term therapist, Dr. Welch.

"When did you stop seeing him?" Marybeth asked.

"Five years ago. He died."

Her eyebrows shot up in a question.

"While he was on vacation in Europe. Of anaphylactic shock. His friend, Dr. Harris, called to tell me."

"How did you process that?"

"I was pretty upset."

DR. HARRIS'S CALL had come on an August day in 1972. I'd seen him a few times in the past, when Dr. Welch was away, but we hadn't spoken in a year.

"Something happened to Dr. Welch," he said. "I'd like to set up an appointment so we can talk about it."

"What happened?"

"It's better if we meet."

"Is he going to be OK?"

"No."

Pause. "Is he living?"

Pause. "No."

When I didn't reply he said, "I think you should come in to see me."

I made an appointment and we hung up.

It took a while to absorb that Dr. Welch was no longer on vacation. He was gone permanently. The person who had seen potential in me when I was my craziest. Who had been there as I progressed, knowing when I was sliding, making sure I didn't descend so far I couldn't get back. Who understood the mix of reality and magical thinking that was part of me even now. His impish smile. The twinkle in his eye. I would never see them again. I was pretty shaken.

When I met with Dr. Harris, he suggested I see him for a year, not for any deep work, just to get over Dr. Welch's death. I thought that was a good idea.

"IT'S IRONIC," I SAID to Marybeth. "After I got out of the hospital, whenever Dr. Welch went away, I thought I would never see him again. That was the first time I was sure he'd be back. I think if he had died when I still wasn't sure, I would have fallen apart. But for the past four years, after I stopped seeing Dr. Harris, I've been fine. Unless something's happening now."

"You seem fine to me. What you're going through is developmental. Remember, you just became director of a library. You're a full-fledged grownup. It can be disconcerting to change your perception of yourself."

Her theory made sense. It sometimes amazed me that a staff of 17—librarians, clerks, pages, and custodians—reported to me.

"We have to stop now," Marybeth said, slicing into my reflection.

I gathered my bag and jacket. "Can I come back once or twice more, just to be sure?"

"Of course." She opened her appointment book.

On my way out, I felt lighthearted, as if I had come in worried about cancer and found all I had was a wart.

"WHAT ABOUT RELATIONSHIPS?" Marybeth asked in our next session. "Would you like to get married?"

"Eventually."

Actually, I'd been thinking a lot about marriage. I was still seeing Jim Spiro. He encouraged me to go out with other men, saying he didn't want to stand in the way of my finding someone to spend my life with, but every time I had a date, he asked me how it went and whether we had slept together. I'd had one relationship that lasted a year. When it started, Jim said he wanted to make sure the man would "be good to you," so he made inquiries among friends who had other friends who knew my boyfriend's family and pronounced him OK. I didn't consider that intrusive. It made me feel taken care of. It was the same way I'd felt when Jim and I had first started our relationship and he'd asked his colleagues in the psychiatry department at Einstein what they thought of Dr. Welch, then reported to me that they spoke highly of him. At the time, I'd been surprised he would do such a thing without asking me first, but I also liked it. It meant he cared about me over and above our sexual relationship.

So far, I'd never felt with anyone else the way I felt with Jim. Only he saw all of me, and all of me was OK with him. He would steady me when I started to disintegrate, replacing my hands with his when I tried to keep my brains from spilling out. He rejoiced when I got my new job. Because of him, I was venturing out more into the world. His involvement in liberal causes sparked my interest in social issues. And I had begun to travel. I visited my cousin Annie in Jerusalem, where she was now living; went to Ioannina, the city in Greece Nona came from; and worked in a library in a suburb of Paris on my vacation from the New York Public Library.

It was Jim I had turned to when I thought I might be having a relapse and should see a therapist. I'd asked him to help me find someone not connected to my hospital life, preferably a female comfortable with the Women's Lib movement and clinical enough to evaluate whether anything pathological was going on. He'd asked around, then recommended Marybeth.

Now I gave her a summary of our relationship.

"You're not ready to let go yet," she said.

"I guess not. But he's moving to the Midwest."

"Oh?"

"For a job. Nothing he applied for. A search committee found him. He asked my opinion. I don't want him to go, but it's a better situation for him, so I said I thought he should accept."

"How do you feel about that?"

"Maybe it will be good for me. Force me in another direction."

It struck me that Marybeth and I were speaking as one adult to another, something I'd never done with a therapist. Whether this was because she had introduced herself by her first name, or because I was conscious that we were both professionals, I felt it was further evidence that what I was going through was just a midlife crisis. If something from the past were resurfacing, I would have been in awe of her, unable to talk. At the end of that second session, we agreed there was no need to make another appointment.

WHEN I BEGAN MY JOB as director, my dream was to make the library the jewel of the town. I scheduled chamber music concerts featuring my musician friends, hired staff to run programs for teens, and spoke to community groups about the library.

Though I missed seeing Jim regularly after he moved to the Midwest a year later, he was still very much a part of my life. In our frequent phone calls, we talked about anything and everything, both personal and job-related. And we were able to get together whenever he came to New York for a meeting.

All in all, things were going well. While I knew about the mental patient I had been barely ten years before, it was as if that had happened to someone in another world.

Three years into my tenure as director, the cooperative library system of which we were a member began exploring the possibility of replacing the card catalogs in each of its 38 independent libraries with a comprehensive computerized catalog. That meant getting 38 independent library boards to agree. Feeling I needed to learn about computers in order to advocate for this change with my village's board, which was reluctant to participate because of the cost, I enrolled in an introductory computer class at The New School in the fall of 1979. One of my fellow students was Mike. We spent a few coffee breaks together, then began to date.

I had taken the course only to better do my job, but, to my surprise, I found computers fascinating. The following term, I signed up for BASIC programming, even though the computerized catalog had now been approved by my board; and the term after that I took COBOL programming. Though I still liked my work as a librarian, I wasn't as fired up as I used to be and toyed with the idea of changing careers. To better position myself, in the spring of 1981 I started a master's program in computer science at Baruch College. I also began answering ads for data processing positions.

All this while, Mike and I had been seeing each other. I enjoyed spending time with him but never felt the same connection I did with Jim, with whom I continued to talk often.

In July 1981, almost two years after I began my first computer class, I accepted a junior programming position with a nonprofit organization in Manhattan. The library trustees and staff were stunned. They tried to get me to change my mind, and when they couldn't, threw me a party. Gratified by their warm sendoff, I felt a whole new world was opening to me.

To my dismay, I soon found that it wasn't easy to come into a new career at entry level. I hadn't realized how much my well-being was tied to my accomplishments and the esteem in which I was held by the board, the staff, and the public until I didn't have that anymore. It helped that my new colleagues immediately made me feel part of the team, and that I had Mike to talk to at the end of the day.

But a few months after I started my new job, Mike told me he had rekindled a relationship with a woman he'd known before. "When I'm with you, I'm happy all the time," he said, "but when

I'm not with you, I never think of you. When I'm with her, I'm miserable all the time, and when I'm not with her, I can't stop thinking about her." He said he wanted to give things with her a chance, but he didn't want to lose his friendship with me. I told him that wouldn't work, and we stopped seeing each other.

Shortly after that, I discovered I was pregnant.

My mother, retired as an educator, was now working for the Social Security Administration. She had become an avid reader of self-help books and often attended meditation and New Age therapy groups. When I told her I was considering an abortion, she urged me to weigh my decision carefully. I was 39, she said, and might not get another chance to have a child. If I wanted to have this one, she would help me.

I told Mike I was thinking of having the baby without involving him financially or emotionally.

"I might want to have children in the future," he said, "and I wouldn't like knowing they had a half-sibling running around somewhere."

It was an arrow I wasn't prepared for. I said I'd let him know when I made a decision.

For the next seven days, I alternated between feeling discarded and feeling the wonder of the life growing inside me. Was it a girl or a boy? Would she be shy or outgoing? What foods would he like? I planned how I would rearrange my living room furniture to create a baby alcove in one corner.

Ultimately, though, I felt I wasn't entitled to ruin the future Mike saw for himself. ▪

CHAPTER 30

Flight Lessons

FOR A WEEK AFTER the abortion, I felt relief. Then I wished I could undo it and began grieving. For my dead baby. For Mike. For something indefinable having nothing to do with either.

I woke each morning to howls that seemed to be coming from the other side of the room. It felt as if my body had been liquefied, sucked into a black hole of annihilation. All that was left was disembodied pain. Watching from someplace outside myself, knowing I would eventually be able to get up, I wasn't afraid. As the howls continued, I focused all my energy on one finger until substance began to ooze up from the mattress to form it. Then another. Then the hand. When I finally had all my limbs, the shakes began. Sometimes my body jerked so violently I felt I was having a seizure.

By the time I was able to get out of bed, the howls had turned to sobs. I stood at the kitchen sink in my pantyhose and slip, rinsing soap off a dish, stacking it in the drain, keening with sounds so horrendous that if I'd heard a neighbor making them, I would have called 911. I knew that once I left the house, the crying would stop, so I let it play on a side track while I went to my closet and selected a suit to wear to work.

Though I always seemed OK when I was outside my apartment—with colleagues, friends, or family—my heartache never abated. The crying was merely on hold and began again as soon as I got home. Day after day. Week after week.

On some level, I knew my state had to do with more than the abortion and Mike. They were triggers that had awakened something hibernating deep inside me. What it was, I couldn't say. All I knew was that the world as I had known it was no longer safe. I had to equip myself for a quick getaway and checked the *Yellow Pages* for flight schools.

The flying lessons helped: they gave me a sense of control over my environment. On the ground, there was the preflight visual inspection: walking around the plane to check for loose or missing rivets and looking inside the engine for bird nests. Airborne, I used the horizon to orient myself in space. I learned how to regulate pitch (raising or lowering the nose to gain or lose altitude), roll (dipping a wing), and yaw (turning left or right). Everything had to be coordinated: a turn was accompanied by a corresponding dip, the angle of which depended on the speed of the plane. It was scary at first, but with my copilot-instructor—a retired marine—patiently explaining what to do and why, I soon gained confidence.

Learning to fly made me feel less vulnerable, but it didn't take away the sense that I had fallen through a chasm into another dimension. My isolation felt real, even as I walked through crowded streets with people all around me. One day, I saw a group of Hare Krishnas sitting on the ground in their orange robes, swaying as they chanted and tapped small drums. I longed to be absorbed into their oneness and was about to sit down with them when part of me said that wasn't a good idea. I felt myself being dragged away, as if a hand had actually grabbed me.

It wasn't just the Hare Krishnas I was drawn to but anything I could belong to in an elemental way. A kibbutz in Israel. A husband. Once, on a bus, I scanned the men, deciding which of them I was destined to marry. I picked one sitting across from me, then spent ten minutes wondering how to explain that we should skip the dating preliminaries. The end result was a given, so why not just come home with me right now? I was mustering the courage to approach him when he got off.

The only impulse I did give in to was my desire to see Jim. Though our phone calls always gave me moments of comfort, now I needed to be in his physical presence. When I told him I wanted to take a morning flight, have lunch, then fly back that afternoon, he cleared his calendar. We ate in a restaurant, went to a museum, and talked. About my dead baby. About feeling that my heart had been ripped out, even though I hadn't been in love with Mike and knew all this wasn't about him. About how my flying lessons made my mother nervous but impressed my friends and coworkers. For the first time since my collapse, I felt the relief of being completely connected. It helped to see that Jim needed me, too. It was important to him that I get a sense of his new environment, so he drove me around and pointed out landmarks. I felt at peace when we were together, but as my plane took off for the flight home, my agony returned.

THREE MONTHS AFTER the abortion, I was still waking up screaming, still crying so much I sometimes wondered whether it was possible to become dehydrated from the water loss. My mother, who never saw me cry but knew how depressed I was, invited me to go with her to a Gestalt therapy weekend in the Catskills. There would be two groups, she said, so we wouldn't be together, and if I didn't want to participate, I could just enjoy the scenery. I wasn't interested in a therapy group, but the idea of being in the country appealed to me.

I went to the opening session on Friday evening just to see what it was about, not intending to return. What I saw astounded me. A woman related an incident that took place when she was a toddler, in which her mother had left her feeling unprotected. The event didn't sound like a scary situation to me, and I was surprised it still bothered her. More surprised when she began weeping. Even more when Gerald, the session leader, took her in his arms as if she were that baby and rocked her. Her weeping turned to sobs. The other group members seemed to understand something I didn't. They supported the woman by coming closer and remaining there silently for the 20 minutes it took her crying to ebb. When she quieted, Gerald released her but kept a palm on her arm and motioned to all of us to lay on our hands. Everyone but me came forward and placed a hand on the woman's shoulder, arm, or leg. She smiled as if she had found inner peace. "Thank you," she said. I didn't feel I should be included in the general thank you, but I knew I was in the presence of something special.

I abandoned the idea of country walks and attended the rest of the sessions. One by one, the members of the group came forward with whatever their issue was. With each, I felt the power of the healing that seemed to come simply from everyone witnessing. By the end of the weekend, all but me had had a turn. Gerald asked whether I wanted one. I did but was frightened of unwrapping myself, even in this receptive group, and shook my head no.

A month later, in February 1982, when my howls and shakes still hadn't stopped, I called Gerald in his Manhattan office and made an appointment.

GERALD HAD A DEEP VOICE and slow way of talking that, along with his gray hair, imparted an aura of wisdom. I told him about Mike, the abortion, the crying and howling, relating everything without emotion, as if I were talking about someone else.

"Sounds like a panic attack," he said and asked whether I'd ever tried deep breathing.

Disappointed, I blamed myself. I hadn't given him the clues he needed to get behind my wall. Next week would be different.

But it wasn't.

Winter turned to spring, and still I hadn't shown Gerald where the gate was. I didn't know myself.

During a session in July, after I repeated what I'd said many times in the five months I had been seeing him—"I don't know why I still feel so bad"—I was surprised when tears suddenly welled up and began rolling down my cheeks. Though I had long wanted to cry in his office—the reason I had chosen him as a therapist—now that it was happening, I felt self-conscious and kept my body rigid, to stop sounds from escaping. When the silence lengthened, he walked the few yards to my chair. His proximity charged the air, and I couldn't look up. He placed the tip of his index finger on my bare arm. Something unlocked, and I began to weep. He removed his finger but remained near. It was the first time since my breakup with Mike, almost a year before, that crying brought relief.

Ten minutes later, when I was calmer and Gerald was back in his chair, I apologized for my strong reaction.

"It's easier to cry about new stuff," he said. "It's fresh. Old stuff from childhood takes longer. It'll happen in time."

His words confirmed what I had long believed: my devastation had less to do with Mike and the baby than something else.

Tears didn't come again in Gerald's office, but for the next six months or so, I was able to talk to him more openly. Then, one day, during a quiet stretch, my shoulders started to shake, the way they still did when I woke in the morning. I pressed my arms to my sides to make them stop.

"Let it happen," Gerald said.

Permission.

I allowed the shakes to run their course, and when they subsided, I was calm in a way I didn't feel after I shook alone at home.

In the sessions that followed, the shaking traveled from my shoulders and arms to my whole body. Soon I was sliding off the chair and onto the floor, feeling I was communicating something to someone for the first time. Yet I was still holding back, ashamed to let the howling escape.

As if he could read my mind, during a session in the early fall of 1983, Gerald said, "Can you let a sound out?"

Embarrassed for him to see me, I threw my jacket over my face and moaned softly.

"Good. Can you do it louder?"

What came out was a cross between a gurgle and a deep-throated growl. It went on and on, and when it finally played itself out, I felt a peace that went deep, to the center of my insides.

Several weeks after that, Gerald began to hold me while I shook and howled. I felt cared for, safe, and understood. During the traditional parts of the therapy, we talked while sitting in chairs. I told him I felt as if a sealed container of toxic waste had been buried in me long ago. Mike and the abortion were catalysts that had caused a leak, and poisons were circulating through my blood. I likened the sessions to kidney dialysis. They got rid of whatever toxins accumulated between times.

I couldn't afford to fly anymore, nor did I have time to. In addition to my data processing job, I was working as a reference librarian in the suburbs on weekends to pay for therapy. The sessions were now the highlight of my existence. Everything else took a back seat, including occasional dates with a man I had known before I met Mike.

One day about a year after Gerald started holding me, he began shaking and making guttural sounds himself. I reacted automatically and, in a reversal of roles, held and comforted him.

"What's happening with you is bringing up my own stuff," he said after his shakes stopped. In the moment, I felt privileged that he could be so open with me. But over the following year, as we took turns being OK and not OK, I began to feel I was losing my therapist. I wanted to talk to someone about all this, so in 1985, when Gerald left for his summer vacation, I went to see Marybeth, the therapist who had suggested I read *Passages*.

I brought her up to date on what had happened since we met eight years before. When I came to my almost three and a half years with Gerald, I paused, wondering how to phrase my concerns without making him sound unethical. I described my own shaking first, saying I felt better afterward, then mentioned his shaking and the mutual holding.

"Do you ever talk?" she asked.

"At the beginning and end of the session."

She raised her eyebrows in a question, a mannerism I remembered from our first meetings.

"Maybe what's bothering me is that I don't feel the therapy has a direction," I said, "but I don't want to stop. It's the only thing that makes me feel better."

"So why are you here?"

"I guess to make sure it doesn't go off course."

After three sessions, we agreed that I would keep seeing Gerald, but if anything became more disturbing, I would call her.

When Gerald returned, our sessions grew more intense. He asked me to press down on his stomach because that would help whatever was in him come up more. I complied, and his guttural sounds got deeper, as if he were releasing his own toxins. In subsequent weeks, he asked me to press harder and lower, which I did. Often, he loosened his belt. During the times we talked, he told me about his difficult relationships with his mother and wife. I listened but didn't respond. I didn't want to know details about his life.

One day in early winter, I smelled fresh cologne. This wasn't the faint scent he usually had, probably from a morning application, but strong, as if he had applied it moments before. When I smelled it again the following week, I made another appointment with Marybeth.

"He's not the only game in town," she said.

I knew she was right, but I didn't want to give him up. The release I got in my sessions with Gerald was still the only thing that gave me any peace, however temporary.

We made a new arrangement: I would see both Gerald and Marybeth and keep her informed about what went on in my sessions with him—and I would let Gerald know that's what I was doing.

At first this worked well. I got talking and logic from Marybeth, and a primitive connection and release from Gerald. But as the months wore on, Marybeth became increasingly critical of Gerald's methods and said the only reason she didn't report him was she knew I would stop seeing her, which she felt would be worse for me.

The more the therapist-patient boundary between Gerald and me blurred, the less peaceful I felt after seeing him. I also resented that I was paying for the time. In July 1986, four years after I began seeing him, I told him I thought I should stop therapy with him because it wasn't really therapy anymore.

"That's exactly what I was thinking," he said with a warm smile, as if he had my best interest at heart. "I was going to say the same thing tonight."

You should have said it long ago, I thought. ▪

CHAPTER 31

Mommybeth

I DETOURED ON MY WAY TO WORK to leave a letter with Marybeth's doorman. The moment the envelope passed from my hand to his, I felt calmer, as if she had already absorbed its contents.

Nine years earlier, when Marybeth talked to me about *Passages*, I'd seen her as an equal and appreciated her no-nonsense manner. Now, six months after I stopped seeing Gerald, I was smitten with her in the way a child has a crush on an adult and found her direct manner intimidating. This made it difficult to talk in a session, but at home, where I felt her presence in the Atmosphere, I was able to write. The entries, often in different handwritings, were labeled with the hour and minute, so when Marybeth read them, she could travel back in time to be with me while I was writing. In this way, I was never without her.

The Atmosphere had been dormant during the years everything was going well. It hadn't returned after the abortion, probably because there had been no major presence to fill it. For a while after I started shaking and moaning in sessions with Gerald, I felt him in the Atmosphere outside of sessions. But his Atmosphere version vanished when I made a phone call to him on a day I felt particularly shaky and he sounded distant, not at all like the therapist he was in his office. Now the Atmosphere was back, with Marybeth its dominant presence. My letters were a way of imparting to her in-person version what her Atmosphere version already knew. I left notes with her doorman a few times a week, even on days I didn't have a session.

This day, though, I would be seeing her after work.

ATE THAT AFTERNOON, I took a seat on the couch across the room from Marybeth. The chair opposite her was closer, but recently, I'd been preferring the distance. Perched on the edge of the cushion, I waited for her to talk. Depending on whether she was the soft-voice Marybeth or the crisp-voice, I would know which part of me was safe to let out.

"Why don't you say something?" she asked. Crisp.

"I need to know who you are first."

"You *know* who I am." She sounded exasperated. "We go through this every week."

I withdrew my eyes from her face. They landed on the see-through wastepaper basket. There was my letter, out of its envelope, unfolded. Pain shot through my chest. She had thrown me away. The pain grew. I banged the back of my head against the wall behind me to still it.

"Stop that!" Marybeth snapped. Then, a little softer, "Use words. Tell me what's going on."

I jumped off the couch and hid behind a chair. I couldn't let her see my face when I hurt so much.

"Come out of there! Respectable people don't cower on the floor."

I returned to the couch, unfurled the afghan lying on one of the cushions, and threw it over my head.

"What's going on?" It sounded like a real question.

"The letter."

"I can't hear you. Take the blanket off your head."

"The letter," I said a little louder from the semidarkness of my tent.

"What about it?"

"You threw it away."

"Yes, after I read it."

"Do you throw them all away?" I was sorry as soon as I asked, afraid to hear the answer.

"Yes."

The pain spiked. Without thinking, I banged my head through the afghan. It made a dull thud.

"Stop that!"

My hand went to the bump that had already formed from the first bang. I took in a breath of my own humid air. Its warmth was comforting.

"What's wrong with throwing them away?" Marybeth asked.

Watch out. Don't let her know you're bleeding because she discarded your insides. "You didn't even rip it up. Anyone who walks in can see it."

"Would you feel better if I tore it up?"

That wasn't what I had intended, but I was stuck. "Yes."

Through the woolen weave, I saw her walk to the wastepaper basket, tear up my letter, and drop it back in. I fought the impulse to bang my head.

"Better?" she asked, her voice softer.

"Yes," I lied.

DESPITE MY TUG-OF-WAR with Marybeth, at times I felt the release with her I used to feel with Gerald.

"Can I go on a trip?" I would ask if she was the soft-voice Marybeth, and she would nod.

I would lie on the couch and cover myself with the afghan, leaving my head out. For a moment I would remain still, feeling the security of Marybeth's presence. Then, as layers began to peel off me, my eyes would close.

"Leave me alone," I might hear myself say in a very young voice. "I don't want to."

"Who's making you do something?" Marybeth would ask.

"No one." Feeling slightly older, I'd open my eyes. "I'm just on a trip."

Sometimes a gnawing hunger traveled through my body, and I moaned. Other times I pulled the cover over my head and talked in nonsense syllables. "Ish po-*mi*-na. Po-*li* na *ni*-na."

"I didn't catch that," Marybeth said the first time it happened.

Without removing the afghan, I found a place in my brain that was a bridge to her. "Not English."

"What language is it?"

"No language."

It was as if I were a conduit for messages being passed to Marybeth, and I didn't have to know their contents to fulfill my mission. Despite her question, I felt she understood everything perfectly.

All the while, another part of me moved my arm every so often, letting enough light under the cover to see my watch. Marybeth ended sessions exactly on time, without winding down and helping me prepare for re-entry. In the middle of whatever was happening, she would announce, "We have to stop now." After a few weeks of walking out feeling as if I had no coating over my insides, I took control of the time. Ten minutes before the end, I pushed the cover off my face and started talking about something from the now-world: friends, family, my new job as a systems analyst at MetLife. As I talked, I sat up, swung my legs to the floor, and folded the afghan.

Three minutes before the end, I would gather my bag and coat. "I'm leaving," I would say.

"We still have a few minutes."

"I know, but I want to go anyway."

In this way, she hadn't dismissed me—I had chosen to leave—and her presence stayed with me in the Atmosphere after I walked out.

FEELING MORE FRAGILE than usual one day, I called Marybeth to ask for an extra session. Her schedule was tight, she said, but if I came to her house in the suburbs, she could fit me in.

The Marybeth I had known until then existed only in her Upper East Side office and the Atmosphere. In both places, she had but one concern: me. On some level, I knew she had a home, but that facet of her existence wasn't real for me.

I arrived at her house ten minutes early. Sitting in the waiting room outside her basement office, I heard the clang of a pot and smelled coffee. I checked my watch. Two minutes until my session.

Footsteps descending a staircase. I looked up, expecting to see Marybeth come from around the bend. Instead, I heard the click of a dial being turned. A rush of water. She was doing a laundry.

Marybeth appeared, mug of coffee in hand. "You can come in now," she said, unaware that the world had just imploded.

This office had no couch, only chairs. We sat. I looked at her. She looked at me. Through the closed door, I heard the faint rhythmic pulsing of the machine.

The pain in my chest erupted. I let out a piercing scream. When my breath ran out, I took another and continued the scream. Across the small room, Marybeth watched with a stern face, her mug on the table beside her.

As suddenly as it began, the scream stopped and I was free of pain.

"Hi," I said, in the manner of a normal greeting.

"Do you know what just happened?" Marybeth's voice was colder than I had ever heard it.

"Yes." Not a smart question, I thought. If I hadn't known I'd just screamed, I would have said yes anyway, thinking she was referring to the last thing I did remember.

"What was that all about?"

I was ashamed to say I was upset at discovering I was only a 45-minute slot in her day, sandwiched between a wash and a dry, that when I left, her life would go on without me. "I don't know."

"Try to explain it in words. It's the only way you're going to get better."

It wasn't to *get* better that I was coming to see her. It was to *feel* better. I was a bad patient, in therapy for the wrong reasons. "I really don't know."

The session ground along. When I heard the machine stop, the pain in my chest crept back. I tried to ignore it. As usual, I left a few minutes early, but this time, Marybeth's presence didn't come with me. She was busy putting her clothes in the dryer.

THE MORE MY RELATIONSHIP with the in-person Marybeth soured, the more perfect the Atmosphere Marybeth became. Rather than seeing her in her office, I preferred talking with her on the phone. That way, she was an essence-voice without a body. I felt connected to her the moment I began dialing her number.

"Hello?" she would say in her regular voice, neither crisp nor soft.

"Hi, Marybeth."

"Hi, Vivian." Instantly soft. I never knew why it changed so quickly—perhaps because she could tell from my own voice that I wasn't testing her. Feeling that she was Mommybeth with Atmosphere qualities, I spoke in a mixture of wispy child's words, whimpers that sounded like those of a baby, and nonsense syllables. She would respond by probing in a gentle way, and I felt her caring.

One April morning, about three months after I saw my letter in Marybeth's garbage, I left a message on her answering machine. "I'm not sure whether I'm coming to your office or I'll call you. It depends on how I feel when I get out of work."

Neither of our last two sessions, both in her office, had gone well. I knew I would be risking her disapproval if I opted for a phone session—she'd recently told me she didn't think they were useful—but when I left work, I had an overpowering yearning for the phone Mommybeth.

It normally took ten minutes longer to get to my West Side apartment than to her East Side office. If I ran the four long blocks to the train and made every light along the way, and if the train came exactly when I reached the station, and if I raced up the three flights of stairs to my apartment, I would make it on time.

I began running as if my life depended on it.

Out of breath. Running. Wheezing.

Red light. Keep going. I can get across—

"I FOUND THE DRIVER'S LICENSE. Her name's Vivian." A man's voice.

"Vivian? Can you hear me?" A woman's.

I fought my way up through the blackness.

"Vivian, can you open your eyes?"

With great effort, I did. A woman in a white lab coat was leaning over me. Everything around her was blurry.

"Where am I?"

"Bellevue Hospital. You were hit by a car. Is there anyone you want me to call?"

"Marybeth. Please tell her I'll be late." ▪

CHAPTER 32

An Explanation

"DON'T DO ANYTHING RASH," my mother said as she unwrapped the Wendy's baked potato and placed it on my bed table. She brought me one every day because my weight had plummeted from 105 to 78 pounds and it was the only thing I could digest. Behind her, a month's worth of get-well cards were crammed, parking-lot style, on the windowsill.

"It's not rash," I said through tears. "It's the first good thing I'm doing. But I need your help."

"OK, Vivian." She looked weary. "I can't refuse you."

The world went from black-and-white to color. "Thanks! It won't be as hard for you as you think."

Bellevue had done its job well: removed my ruptured spleen, replaced several pints of blood, inserted a rod into my fractured femur, closed my scalp wound, immobilized my broken arm. All within the first week. Since then, I had been lying on the orthopedic ward, sinking ever deeper into depression, unable to concentrate on reading even a short magazine article. My days were punctuated by a half-hour physical therapy session during which, with the help of a four-footed cane, I was learning to walk; a 20-minute visit from my mother; and occasional visits from others.

The idea had come to me that morning, when I opened my eyes from a sleep that wasn't a real sleep to a life that wasn't a real life and recalled the physiatrist's words from the previous day: "It'll be another month before you're ready to leave." In another month, I would undoubtedly be in less pain and my body would be in better shape, but the last of my brain and heart would have trickled out. I had to leave now.

My mother sat near my bed, a look of consternation on her face, as I began making arrangements to go to her house. First, a call to Dr. Drapkin, my regular, outside internist, to ask whether he would take over my care if I got my own physical therapist. He said he would. Used to my tears, my mother seemed not to know what to make of this new, executive me. Still, she did my bidding and went to call a nurse so I could inquire about the discharge procedure. The nurse paged the physiatrist, who, after failing to dissuade me, suggested that I wait two days: enough time to get my medical records ready to take to Dr. Drapkin, order a cane of my own, and remove the metal staples that ran from my breastbone to below my navel. I agreed.

For the first time in a month, I didn't cry when my mother left. She had taken with her a shopping bag filled with my cards. The empty windowsill looked beautiful. An hour later, I told the occupational therapist I had two days to learn how to get on and off a toilet, move from lying to sitting in a bed that didn't crank or have side bars, and get into and out of a car. We set to work.

MY 45TH BIRTHDAY WAS MAY 7, a few days after I arrived in Brooklyn. I reveled in the novelty of sitting around a kitchen table with Aunt Mollie and my friend Susan, and of being able to change scenery by going into the living room, where I tried on the four running-shoe options my cousin Ilana brought. "I figured if you were learning to walk, you would need new shoes," she said.

My father was there, too. He had learned of my accident on his return from Europe, a week after it happened; my mother hadn't wanted to upset him by telling him while he was away. He'd called me the day he got back and visited once, the next day. "These things take time," he had said. I'd felt his caring and made an effort to speak cheerfully, as if he were the fragile one and I had to reassure him I was OK. Now, though never comfortable at gatherings, he had a piece of cake with us before leaving for the park with his tennis racket.

As one day followed another, I felt I had a whole community behind me. Aunt Mollie made me loose pants with a drawstring closure that was kind to my abdominal incision. Susan drove me to a local physical therapist. My father carried a chair down to the street, so I could sit outside. At first I just watched the activity from the stoop: children riding tricycles, women wheeling shopping carts. Then I began walking up and down the block with my quad cane; I couldn't use crutches because my left arm was in a sling.

But I was still thin and weak. Dr. Drapkin discovered the reason for my nausea and inability to gain weight: I had hepatitis, caused by trauma to my liver from the accident. Managing it necessitated several car-service trips to his Manhattan office, which was near Marybeth's. Initially, my mother accompanied me, but the first time I was steady enough to go myself, I went to see Marybeth as well.

While I was in the hospital, we'd had brief conversations during which I tried to mask my hunger for her by reporting milestones: discontinuing painkillers because I didn't want to go through yet another withdrawal experience, getting my hair washed after the stitches were removed from my head. During those calls, she hadn't been an Atmosphere essence but a person I pictured in a body sitting in her chair by her office window; and when we hung up, I felt no continuing connection.

Now I limped into her office leaning on my cane. "Hello!" I said, grinning, unaware that my emaciated appearance was at odds with the joy I felt at seeing her until a look of shock flitted across her face.

"Hello!" she replied, recovering and matching my smile. "How are you feeling?"

"Fine." It was true. I felt shiny. New. I related how my mother was shopping for food and cooking under my direction so I would gain strength, and how she was otherwise taking care of me. "At first it felt strange to be in the same house I grew up in. I haven't lived there for twenty-two years. But we're getting a chance to do it over, and this time, we're doing it right."

Marybeth nodded.

I told her how moved I was by the many cards I'd received, some from people I hadn't seen in years. What I didn't explain, because I felt it only on a nonverbal level, was that it wasn't the individual cards that had affected me but the collective mass, an outpouring from a world that said, *We know you're there, we know you're hurt, we care*. This accident was like a miracle in disguise, connecting me to humanity in a way I never had been before.

My connection with Marybeth felt different, too, as if I were beginning fresh, getting to know her from another point of view. She seemed to feel the newness, too, because when our time was up, she walked me to the door, something she had never done previously.

We had one more session, during which I felt the same newness. Then I left Brooklyn to spend the month of June recuperating with Aunt Diana and Uncle Eddie at their country house in northern Westchester. As Marybeth would be away for a good part of the summer, it would be fall before I saw her again.

BY THE TIME WE RESUMED our regular sessions in September, I was back in my own apartment and also at my MetLife and library jobs. I was up to 93 pounds and walking without a cane or a limp. But as the outpouring from the world receded, the mental state I'd been in before the accident returned. In sessions, I again banged my head when the pain in my chest got too big, moaned and shook with the afghan pulled over me, and hid behind a chair.

Sometimes Marybeth probed gently. "Did you bang your head when you were a child?" I hadn't. "Did you shake when you were a child?" I hadn't.

Sometimes she was impatient. "Get off the floor! You're just like the homeless people on the sidewalk. They have no self-respect."

In the Atmosphere, though, she remained a caring presence that understood everything about me. At work, my logon password was her name.

A year after the accident, in April, I had surgery to remove the hardware from my left leg and asked the surgeon to save it for me.

"I cleaned it up as best I could," he said, handing me a silver-colored rod.

I was surprised at how heavy it was, and also by the bone fragment coated with dried blood clogging one end of the tube. How strange to have had such an intimate relationship with this piece of metal, yet never to have seen or touched it until it was no longer part of me. The next time I saw Marybeth, I brought it with me.

"What's this?" she said when I pulled the rod from my backpack and handed it to her.

"From my leg. Look. There's still a piece of bone in it."

She recoiled and laid it on her telephone table. "Why did you bring it here?"

"To show you." Because she was Mommybeth. Because it was my trophy from the war.

"Well, I saw it. Now put it away."
Feeling ashamed, I complied.

"YOU'RE A PUZZLE," Marybeth said in July. "Nothing bad is going on in your life, but you're always upset. Why do you think that is?"

I realized she was right. The breakup with Mike had been more than six years before. It was 15 months since the accident, and I'd largely recovered. My jobs were going well. Yet I lived with a hurricane inside me.

I had just read an article about past-life regression therapy, in which people who were troubled without any seeming cause were hypnotized and recovered memories from previous lives. "Maybe I'm reincarnated, " I said. "If you hypnotize me, we could find out."

"That's nonsense," Marybeth said. "There's no such thing as reincarnation. Anyway, I don't know how to do hypnosis."

I was disappointed, though not surprised. Maybe she was right. But there was definitely something pushing and pulling me from Inside that had nothing to do with what was going on Outside.

A few days later, I was browsing the aisles of a video rental store when *Sybil* caught my eye. I'd read the book ten years before, about a woman with 16 personalities, and found it interesting. It was worth a try.

At home, I brought a plate of food into the living room, slipped the cassette into the video player, and put my feet up on the coffee table.

From the opening scene, it was clear that something was wrong with this girl-woman. Sybil had her own apartment, was getting her master's in art at Columbia, and worked as an assistant teacher in an elementary school. She also became inexplicably upset by ordinary events, like the sound of a swing in the park; had amnesia for blocks of time; and found drawings in her apartment she didn't remember making. Most riveting was the relationship she had with her therapist, who cared about her and understood her, and who helped her come to know the personalities inside her who were causing her such distress.

The movie stayed with me while I was cleaning up in the kitchen and washing my hair in the shower. The way Sybil often talked in a little-girl voice. How sometimes what she said made no sense. How she didn't believe it when her therapist told her the explanation for the drawings and missing blocks of time was that she had other people in her.

I was walking from the bathroom to the bedroom when it struck me that Sybil's inside life was chaotic, though nothing bad was going on in her outside life. I stopped in the middle of the living room.

It couldn't be.

I had never lost time or found myself in places not knowing how I got there. Nor did sounds trigger me.

But my letters to Marybeth were in different handwritings. And sometimes when we spoke, my voice was like a little girl's.

No. That was as ridiculous as reincarnation.

Having multiple personalities would explain a lot, though. Talking to faces in the mirror who weren't me. My feeling of otherness, of not being real, of watching myself from outside myself. How I could function well at work and be almost psychotic outside of work, all in one day. Why I could believe something as preposterous as Marybeth being able to know the contents of a letter as soon as I gave it to her doorman, while at the same time, I knew that was impossible.

But multiple personalities? Me?

It couldn't be.

Yet maybe it could.

I was horrified.

Then exhilarated. Yes, me.

I was standing in the same spot I had been standing in a second ago, but I felt larger, more substantial, almost regal. And when I continued on to the bedroom, it was with a respect for myself bordering on awe. There was a whole world inside me.

WHEN I SAW MARYBETH, I told her about the movie and asked whether she thought there could be other people in me.

She appeared surprised by the question, then said yes.

This was almost too bizarre a concept to have confirmed. At the same time, I was gratified.

In our next session, I hooked up the video player and portable TV set I had brought from home, happy Marybeth had agreed to watch Sybil with me. As soon as she pressed PLAY, however, I became anxious. What if she didn't get it? What if she did?

In one of the beginning scenes, Sybil is tormented by disjointed images and sounds flashing through her head. In her agitation, she has thrown clothes, art supplies, food, even a chair all over her apartment and smashed her hand through the window. Seconds afterward, she doesn't remember doing these things. She sees only the mess and the blood.

I was inside the movie and outside it, a part of the story as well as a viewer. At the same time, I felt abandoned by Marybeth. Though she was sitting alongside me, she was more involved with the girl on the screen. I began rocking back and forth.

"Should I pause it?" Marybeth asked.

I needed her to keep watching. "No. I'm OK."

Sybil is in the emergency room to have her hand stitched. A kind doctor gives her a neurological exam because she seemed confused when she arrived. In the voice of a small child, Sybil asks the doctor whether she has a little girl all her own.

"Turn it off!" I pleaded.

Marybeth pressed STOP and went back to her chair. "What part did you find upsetting?" she asked from miles away.

I lay down and pulled the afghan over my head, then started to shake and moan.

IN OUR TWO SUBSEQUENT SESSIONS, Marybeth and I continued watching, never getting through more than 15 minutes before I asked her to turn it off. I finally told her I didn't want to finish, but she could keep the equipment if she wished to view it herself.

When I next saw her—our last meeting before her summer vacation—she said she'd reached the end. "What part of the film did you identify with?" she asked.

There was no specific part, just an overall feeling that this was the story of someone who also felt pushed and pulled by mysterious inside forces, who had the same yearning for her therapist that I did, and who was trying to figure herself out. For so many years I had felt like an alien species of one. This film let me know I wasn't.

"All of it, I guess." ▪

CHAPTER 33

Meeting Myselves

I WAS 46 YEARS OLD, and things were finally starting to make sense. While Marybeth was away, I spent my evenings in the library perusing *Index Medicus* and reading articles. I acquired a new vocabulary. *MPD*: the abbreviation for multiple personality disorder. *Multiple*: a person who has MPD. *Dissociation*: detachment from one's surroundings that can range from mild to severe. *Alter*: an alternate personality. At any given moment, one of the alters might be *out*, meaning in control of the body, with that particular alter's unique way of interpreting and interacting with the world. A *switch* occurs when the alter who is out is replaced by another. An alter is said to be *co-conscious* when that alter is aware of one or more other alters. *The host* is usually the alter most often in control and who manages functioning in the world.

I discovered that some clinicians feel MPD—which would be renamed dissociative identity disorder, or DID, in 1994—is a bogus diagnosis. Others have done studies demonstrating that different alters in a multiple have correspondingly different physiological reactions to a given stimulus, offering this as evidence that MPD/DID is real.

I learned that the dissociation that happens with MPD/DID is similar to what happens when someone becomes numb during a disaster: his thinking is detached from his feelings. This allows him to take whatever actions are necessary to bring himself to safety. Only when he is no longer in danger do his emotions return. The dissociation in MPD/DID differs in that it is usually caused by repeated childhood trauma: physical, sexual, or emotional. A child cannot escape her external environment, so she escapes internally. Some parts of her are aware of the abuse; other parts, unaware of it, carry on what appears to be an ordinary life. Dissociation is not something the child does consciously. It is automatic, like an immune system response kicking in. When it happens repeatedly, the parts become solidified and can seem like separate selves. Most people—nonmultiples—have varying moods and show different sides of themselves at different times, but they don't have dissociative barriers between these sides, so they are able to conceive of all their behaviors and ways of thinking as "me."

Only one thing I read gave me pause: the abuse causing MPD/DID is usually sexual. I'd often been unhappy as a child, but I hadn't been sexually abused and never doubted that my parents loved me. Nothing in my past was remotely as horrific as some of the trauma I read about.

The causes weren't my chief interest, though. I was looking for descriptions of what it *felt* like to have MPD. Most of the literature was by clinicians and researchers, so I was glad to find *When Rabbit Howls*, a memoir by Truddi Chase. She, too, talked in a little-girl voice at times and had different handwritings. Much of what she wrote about, however, was foreign to my experience—in particular, her bouts with amnesia, her estrangement from her family, and the severe sexual abuse she'd suffered as a child. Though I'd read that most newly diagnosed patients don't yet know their alters—they become aware of them through therapy—I couldn't imagine having anywhere near the 92 Truddi did, so many she called them *The Troops*.

I wondered whether Ellen Willow was an alter. I remembered having written her name on the masthead of the *Overing Underground*, the halfway house newspaper, and dug out an old issue.

OVERING UNDERGROUND
Volume 1, Number 1
Editorial Board
Vivian Ann Conan, Editor-in-Chief
Mitch, Black Beauty
Harold, the Beard
Ellen Willow
Winifred Stone
Dorothy Emily Quinn
Laura Emily Mason

The last three names had flowed from the tips of my fingers after I'd typed Ellen Willow. I found it interesting that two of them had Emily as a middle name. It brought to mind Emily Dickinson, and also a book I'd read years before: *Emily of New Moon*, the story of an orphan who burned to write about everything that was bubbling up inside her but couldn't because her aunt took away her notebooks.

For several days, the girl in the story kept popping into my head. I borrowed a copy from the library to refresh my memory. There were two of her: Emily-in-the-glass, whom she talked to whenever she saw her reflection in a window or a pool of water, and Emily-out-of-the-glass, who she was most often. She believed in fairies and had the magic Wind Woman watching over her, whispering in the breezes all around her, "cooing, friendly, lovesome."

Gradually, in a quiet way, as if I had always known, I recognized that there was an Emily inside me. She was different from the Emily in the book: younger, around six, somehow connected to the pain in my chest. And I knew she had come into being when I was very young, without a name, adopting "Emily" only later on.

WHEN MARYBETH RETURNED in September, I still lay on the couch with the afghan over my head, but I was no longer self-conscious if my voice sounded young, and I often referred to myself as *we* or *she*. It was as if I had been talking a foreign language to her before, and now I was free to speak in my native tongue. Outside the sessions, I continued my research, turning next to my own medical records, curious to see whether they contained MPD/DID clues. Neither Mount Sinai nor Einstein would release copies to patients, so Marybeth sent for them. When they arrived, she suggested we read them together.

I wasn't surprised to find both hospitals had given me a diagnosis of schizophrenia. It was the conclusion I'd come to myself at the time. The Mount Sinai records were disappointingly short: only a few pages stating I was manipulative, suicidal, and lacked impulse control. The Einstein record was longer: 15 single-spaced pages written by Dr. Welch at different times during my 16-month stay. As Marybeth and I read through it, I realized, once again, how much he had seen and understood.

> The patient has made use of a combination of depersonalization, derealization, and fantasy in an effort

> to defend herself against overwhelming feelings of loneliness and rage. Her family situation provided a kind of training in the denial of reality and the acceptance of an idiosyncratic world view that helped make it possible for her to develop such defenses. These defenses not only kept her free from painful experiences, but also inhibited the development and integration of her emotional life. She experiences anger as the feeling that she is "going to kill someone" and experiences being emotionally alone as a physical pain inside her which may resemble the experience of a hungry infant when its mother is not in sight....
>
> At times she felt that she had a different real identity, sometimes she was Ellen Willow and sometimes Wendy. She also described a possibly hallucinatory experience which she frequently had in which her "insides hurt." When she felt that way she would have the urge to "act crazy" and break things to make the feelings go away. She also described at other times the feeling of nothing inside, as though she were dead, and sometimes "being away" and experiencing "nothing at all"....

"Who's Wendy?" Marybeth asked.

I shrugged. "The only ones I know are Emily and Ellen Willow." We continued reading.

> She experienced various altered ego states and changes of identity, as well as transient somatic and paranoid delusions. This acute phase resolved partially after three months and she was able to resume work while living in the hospital. She retained, however, the delusional and almost hallucinatory idea that she was surrounded by "mirror people"....

Multiplicity wasn't prominent in the psychiatric consciousness in the mid-sixties. The diagnosis probably hadn't occurred to Dr. Welch, though much of what he wrote described it.

I was so glad to have this new and seemingly perfect explanation, that I didn't consider it might not account for the Atmosphere and it was possible I had a secondary condition. The Atmosphere was not a problem for me. It was soothing. I spoke of it to Marybeth, but almost as an aside, and never told her I had two versions of some people, herself included. Part of me was intimidated by her in-person version and thought she wouldn't understand, and if she did, she wouldn't approve. The closest I got to letting her know was, "I think about you all the time." I was secretly hoping she would realize that meant she was actually *with* me all the time—that her molecules were in the air, that I breathed them in and they circulated through my blood, that I was both surrounded by her and filled up with her. But she seemed to take my words at face value, and I didn't elaborate.

IN THE SPRING OF 1989, ten months after I watched *Sybil*, Marybeth began discouraging my "trips" under the afghan, saying I was skirting my feelings by not talking in a regular way. In her crisp voice, she suggested I read *The Words to Say It*, a novel about a woman who frees herself of her suffering through psychoanalysis. The book made me feel like an inadequate patient. Not only did the heroine talk the way she was supposed to but she was coming to therapy for the right reason: to get better. I was coming because I craved the connection with Marybeth, something I felt I had to hide because she wouldn't approve.

The more I felt I was losing that connection, the more my pain increased. In sessions, I started banging my head again. This angered her. I began to resent Emily, who, I felt, was responsible for the pain, and, by extension, the behavior that angered Marybeth. Sometimes I slapped my face, to slap away Emily.

"What was *that* about?" Marybeth would ask.

I would hear chastising in her tone and flee behind a chair in shame. Crouched on the floor in child's pose, I protected my head with my arms and made no answer.

At home, I found relief from the pain by letting myself descend into what felt like a psychotic labyrinth. I spoke aloud to people who weren't there. Objects changed size, including parts of my own body. I lay on the floor, unable to move my arms or legs, welcoming the paralysis that gave me a time-out from being and feeling. This was similar to what had often happened before, except now I understood why I had always been able to get unparalyzed and into a normal head the instant something required me to, like a ringing phone. It was because of the MPD/DID: specifically, a part of me—an alter—I came to call AlmostVivian.

AlmostVivian was like a built-in administrator. She made sure I got dressed in the morning and left for work. When I started growling sotto voce on the train anytime someone accidentally touched me, she changed my three-mile commute to an above-ground walk. As soon as I arrived at my office, she made sure whoever was out went back in. Then she stepped aside to let Vivian become dominant. Unencumbered by knowledge of Inside, Vivian was able to chair meetings about the design of new computer systems, and, on weekends in the library, help panicked students find materials for their overdue papers. Unlike the Overview-me, who simply observed from a birds-eye perspective, AlmostVivian was an essential player, interacting, influencing, and steering.

As my Inside life grew increasingly chaotic, AlmostVivian had to do triage. Essentials were laundry, so I would have something to wear to work, and taking out the garbage, to prevent roaches. Nonessentials were going through the mail and paying bills, vacuuming, hanging up clothes, and unpacking grocery bags. One day, making my way through layers of mail, clothing, and bags—some empty, some not—to get to the window, I heard a crunch. I realized I had stepped on a framed artistic print, still in its brown paper wrapping, that Susan had given me months before. Looking around the room as if for the first time, I was shocked at the scene. Until then, I had been so focused on getting through each minute that I hadn't noticed the condition of my apartment.

Throughout this time, I continued to write letters to the Atmosphere Marybeth and leave them with her doorman. They were about Emily, and the hard time AlmostVivian was having, and about an 18-year-old I now called Lisa, whose craziness I welcomed, because it obliterated Emily's pain.

The understanding Marybeth I wrote to was so different from her in-person version that I was surprised anew each time I saw her. She didn't like it when I referred to Emily or Lisa by name. I got the feeling she believed that if I did have MPD/DID, the way to cure me was to ignore the alters and force me to be a unified person—and if I didn't have it, she needed to rid me of the delusion.

"You're not like Sybil!" she spat one day.

It was as if she had thrust a knife into my heart. As if who I was wasn't acceptable.

The pain lasted only seconds before AlmostVivian took control. "I *know* I'm not like Sybil," I said in a stronger voice than I had ever used with Marybeth. "I'm like *me*. And I can't be the way you want me to be." I took a breath. "I need to take a few weeks off from coming here, so I can figure things out."

For the first time since I'd known her, Marybeth looked stunned. "I'm worried that you won't come back."

"I'll call you in three weeks," I said gathering my things.

ON THE WALK HOME, I felt light. I had extricated myself. I would use the time to write Marybeth a long letter explaining why, from my point of view, our relationship had deteriorated. I wanted her to realize that some things she had said were hurtful and despite her once assuring me she wouldn't drop me she had. The adult-me had long wanted to tell her that, but each time I walked into her office, my insides got rearranged, and I became like a little child, unable to keep hold of what the adult-me wanted to say.

Two mornings later, however, as I was walking to work, my lightness gave way to grief, and I started to cry. I knew it was Emily, bereft at having lost Mommybeth. With a mile and a half to go, Almost-Vivian let it happen. I would be fine once I got to work. I always was.

But when I was a block away, tears were still running down my cheeks. "Don't worry, Emily," I heard myself say aloud. "I'll find you a mommy this afternoon. You don't have to cry anymore." I watched one of my hands reach in front of me to take the other, then felt the squeeze. The tears stopped.

By the time I entered the lobby and flashed my ID at the guard, AlmostVivian had formulated a plan: two hours to finish the program specs that were due that day, a half hour in the corporate library perusing the *Directory of the American Psychological Association*, a half hour at the pay phone in the lobby. I didn't want to change therapists permanently. I just wanted a foster-therapist to help me get through these three weeks.

Looking through the *Directory*, I wondered how to tell whether the people behind the names had experience with MPD/DID. Then I remembered Sarah Slagle, my roommate's doctor at Einstein, 20 years before. She'd always had a smile and a soft-voice hello for me when I saw her in passing. AlmostVivian felt that voice and smile were more what Emily needed right now than someone who understood MPD/DID. I found her number and went to the pay phone.

The first miracle was that I didn't get her answering machine. The second was that her voice hadn't changed. The third was that she remembered me.

I explained that I wanted help figuring things out in my hiatus from the therapist I'd been seeing the past four years and was planning to return to. That was OK with her, and we made an appointment.

"There's one thing I need to know now," I said. "Will you still let me come if I'm more than one person?"

She didn't ask what I meant. She just said yes.

WITHIN A MINUTE OF RE-MEETING SARAH, I felt at home and knew I'd made the right choice. When I described my situation, she asked whether I wanted her to talk to Marybeth. I told her I did.

The second time we met, she told me she and Marybeth had had a long conversation.

"And?"

Sarah hesitated. "She asked whether I would be your therapist."

"What?!"

Sarah held me with kind eyes. "She asked me to let you know something she'd been keeping from you."

That sounded creepy, yet the way Sarah leaned in was reassuring, as if she knew what she was going to tell me might hurt and wanted to do it as gently as possible. I hardly knew her, but I trusted her. "What is it?"

Marybeth was having surgery the following week, something she'd known about for months. What I had perceived as her harshness in trying to force me to think and feel a certain way had been her effort to get me to a place where she felt I could stand on my own while she was gone.

"So she means temporarily," I said.

"No. Permanently."

Emily's pain shot through me. I clutched my chest and began rocking back and forth.

"I know it's not what you wanted," Sarah said.

"What did you tell her?" I whispered, becoming still.

"If it was OK with you, it was OK with me."

I looked at Sarah in her dark-colored dress with a brooch pinned on the front, so warm she could have been Marmee in *Little Women*. There were a few comforting lines radiating from the corners of her eyes, and her short brown hair flopped forward like silk when she bent down. I didn't want to leave Marybeth, but Marybeth didn't want me. Sarah had known Dr. Welch. Somehow, that made a difference.

"OK," I said. "But she should have asked *me* first." ▪

CHAPTER 34

Believing, Doubting

"THIS MESSAGE IS FOR EVERYONE," Sarah said into my cassette recorder while looking into my eyes, "to let you know I'm right here, and I'm not going away, and I still have half the string."

Emily tucked her head and smiled shyly. The babies on the bottom level squirmed with content, and my insides felt satisfyingly full. Sarah spoke a moment longer, then pressed STOP.

The wording of this end-of-session routine had evolved over the year I'd been seeing her. She used to say, "to let you know I *will be right there*." That upset me. *Will be* implied a break in time during which we would be apart, and *there* referred to a place away from me. I needed to feel she was with me continuously.

The next part of the routine was standing at the door together.

"Bye, Sarah," I said to the mommy I called by her first name.

"Bye, Vivian."

"Bye, Dr. Slagle," to the doctor.

"Bye, Vivian."

"Bye, Sarah," ending with the mommy.

"Bye, Vivian."

I turned the knob—it was important that *I* do that, so I didn't feel she was getting rid of me—and slipped out, taking with me the image of her kind face. By the time I walked through the lobby of her building and reached the street, she had made a seamless transition from in-person Sarah to Atmosphere Sarah. If our connection faltered before I saw her again, I had her voice on my cassette. It helped, too, that early on we had cut a piece of string in two. One piece resided in her wallet, the other in mine.

For the past year, Sarah had been providing me with a place where I felt welcome. My inside "family," feeling safe here, had come forward one by one: the few I'd been aware of when I was seeing Marybeth, and some who were new to me, though not entirely—more like shadow presences I'd been peripherally aware of coming into the light. One of those was Wendy, a precocious, chatty six-year-old whose main job was to protect Emily. She told Sarah her name came from Wendy in *Peter Pan*.

Early on, I described my internal structure to Sarah as consisting of three levels: top, middle, and bottom. The top level—Emily, Wendy, Vivian, AlmostVivian, others—interacted with the world. Sometimes they communicated among themselves, not always harmoniously. When I'd first realized I was multiple, I knew about the

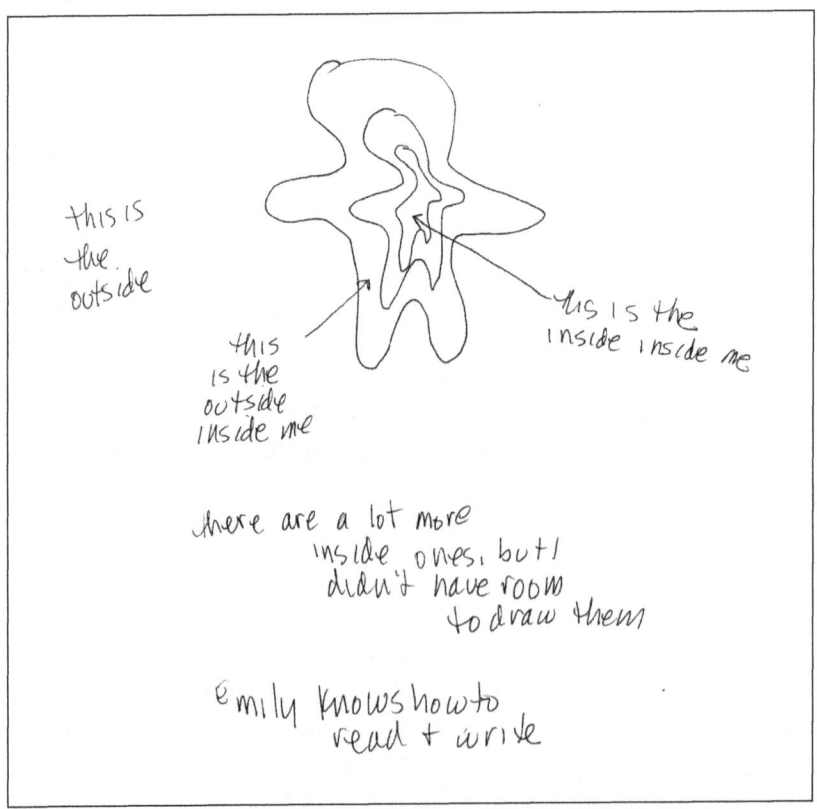

top level only, so I didn't call it the top level. Then I "discovered" the middle and bottom levels. The bottom level consisted of a cluster of babies more or less alike. In sessions they were alternately drawn to Sarah, locking eyes with her silently to pull her in, or they grunted, whimpered, and howled. Sometimes they got paralyzed, and AlmostVivian would have to signal Sarah with eye blinks that I couldn't move. The middle level was a mass of beings who lived in a menacing place where it was hard to breathe, and they had to constantly fight gravity to avoid being pulled into quicksand.

I'd also described to Sarah the difference between disembodied Atmosphere people and "real" people who walked around in skin containers. Other therapists had known about the Atmosphere, but Sarah was the first I told about having two versions of her: real and Atmosphere. I felt that the Atmosphere, while unlike anything I had read about in my research, was connected to the MPD/DID, but I didn't know how. I simply added it to the many things about multiplicity I had yet to understand, still not considering it could indicate something else was going on, too.

Sarah didn't seem put off by any of this, but she had no experience treating MPD/DID and was happy to read the articles I brought her. I vacillated between believing the diagnosis and feeling it was so outlandish it couldn't possibly be true, doubts I shared with Sarah. When I came across a recently published book, *Diagnosis and Treatment of Multiple Personality Disorder*, I bought two copies and gave her one.

Written by Frank W. Putnam, a psychiatrist at the National Institute of Mental Health, it was intended as a guide for therapists, but in places I felt it was specifically about me: when he wrote that "infant or small child personalities frequently curl up in fetal positions, crawl on the floor, or huddle in corners"; or described "alterations in sense of body size or body parts... or the experience of being outside of one's body and watching one's self from a distance"; or noted that multiples frequently test their therapists to determine whether they are trustworthy. He talked about magical thinking; about changes in voice, speech, and language; about "the lack of a firm 'now' against which to measure what is past and what is present." I was particularly interested to read the section on etiology, or causes. While sexual abuse was often a factor, so were other types of trauma, emotional as well as physical.

Putnam confirmed what I had come to understand from my other reading: the partitioning mechanism of MPD/DID is helpful to a child who lacks other means of escaping a distressing situation. It turns into a liability when she becomes an adult and no longer needs to keep knowledge and feelings sealed off in order to survive. He seemed approachable, and I decided to write him a letter.

I told him about my hospitalizations, my time in the halfway house, my jobs, and my devastation the year before when my then therapist didn't want to see me anymore.

> *I am not exactly like the generic patient you describe. I do not lose time or have amnesia. I never wake up in strange places not knowing how I got there. I have continuity. (Occasionally things that I know are recent seem far away and remote, but I always know what they are.) I want to know whether, given the differences, you think I could have MPD. This may sound strange, but it is very important to me to know, for two reasons. One is to know there is hope that I can get better. The other is so I can know that, although my previous therapist got annoyed at some of my behavior, she was only that way because she didn't understand how I was inside, not because I am a disgusting person.*

When I showed the letter to Sarah, she suggested I add more about how I was, as most of what I'd written was about how I *wasn't*. So I wrote about Emily, who was six and had a lot of pain in the center of her chest. And Lisa, who was 18 and the only one of us who was crazy. Lisa sometimes got a little dangerous, as in suicidal, I wrote, but she would never do anything because most of us wanted to live and we wouldn't let her. Wendy was "the back side of Emily." She was also six but didn't have the same pain. Sometimes Emily dissolved into GhostGirl, who was two-dimensional and lived under the hall staircase in the house on 20th Avenue. There were other people: Vivian; AlmostVivian (who was writing this, I explained), TheOneWhoCursesCars, Dorothy, TheGirlOfTheDeadLeaves, TheGirlWithBuckTeeth, the babies, TheOneWhoTellsSarahWhatToDo, TheOnesWhoLiveInTheBlackHole...

> *Sometimes we are empty, and no one is there. It is like being in neutral. Sometimes more than one of us is there—sometimes as many as three. Sometimes we feel the other people very strongly, and we know they are there... Other times, it*

seems preposterous, and we can't imagine that is what is going on. It seems as if we are wasting our time being in therapy, and we can't even imagine ever being upset. It seems like a big fake. We are not sure of anything. I think we are afraid of what you will say either way. If you said we don't have MPD because we don't have amnesia, we would lose hope of getting better. If you said we do have MPD, that would make it too official, and while it would be comforting, it would also be frightening. This is in spite of the fact that we were the first to have realized it, not any of our therapists. This is in spite of the fact that sometimes we know it is true and don't need your confirmation. Other times, even if you said it was true, we probably wouldn't believe it. It is a little mixed up.

Sarah mailed the letter, along with a cover note on her official stationery, saying she was my therapist, had no previous experience with MPD, and we both found his book helpful.

Putnam's reply arrived a few weeks later. At first I was disappointed. It was brief, addressed to Sarah, not me, and didn't specifically answer my question. But Sarah said I could infer his answer, because he had given her the name of the psychiatrist Lily Blum, who headed a peer-to-peer MPD study group for professionals in the New York area. He'd also written, *Ms. Conan might be interested in* Many Voices, a journal by and for people with MPD published in Ohio. I wrote away for a subscription.

When my first issue arrived, I was amazed to read things I could have written myself: about alters who were children, becoming attached to your therapist, denial and disbelief, how to deal with internal chaos while you had to work or interact with family and friends. Like a dog who spots another dog in a sea of humans, I was excited to have found a community.

At the same time, I was glad it was a remote community, comprised of people I knew only through their writing, artwork, and by-lines such as *Star, who lives in Jennifer*. I conceived of them as more unstable than I was, apt to switch without warning and behave bizarrely in public. I might have been a bit crazy, but I was never over-the-top.

Then, through Sarah's contact with Dr. Blum, I learned about a support group that convened monthly at a school in Manhattan. The prospect of actually meeting another multiple was both alluring and scary.

I ARRIVED AT THE SCHOOL EARLY and, peering into the support-group room, saw only one woman. She was in jeans and a T-shirt, setting up chairs. If I entered, I'd be alone with her. What if a random movement of mine triggered a flashback and caused her to switch? She might perceive me as dangerous. What if she threw a chair at me in self-defense?

"Would you like some help?" I asked from the doorway.

"That would be great," she said.

I had just spoken to someone with multiple personalities! She had answered! I assisted with the chairs, thankful she didn't know the injustice I had done her in my mind.

The meeting was equally humbling—I hadn't expected it to be orderly. The moderator, herself a multiple, opened by reading the guidelines. They included:

- Address your comments to the group as a whole, not to any individual member.
- Do not give advice.
- Alters are welcome, as long as they respect the guidelines.

I related to almost everything that was said: about therapists; shame; whether, and with whom, it was safe to share your diagnosis; ways of dealing with a switch when you were in public. If someone's voice or demeanor changed while he or she was sharing, the group continued to listen respectfully. Throughout the two hours, I felt so shaky I didn't trust myself to say anything, or even to relax into my seat. When it was over, I left before anyone could speak to me, but I knew I would return.

After a few more meetings, however, I began to feel a difference between myself and the other people. I didn't consider myself a "survivor," or see my parents as "perpetrators." There was a lot of talk about incest—everyone but me seemed to have been a victim—but no mention of anything like the Atmosphere. Still, there was enough of a fit to keep me coming back.

MEANWHILE, SARAH WAS CONSULTING privately with Dr. Blum. I loved her for caring enough to do this. Dr. Blum asked Sarah to ask me to make an annotated list of my alters and draw a map showing how they were organized.

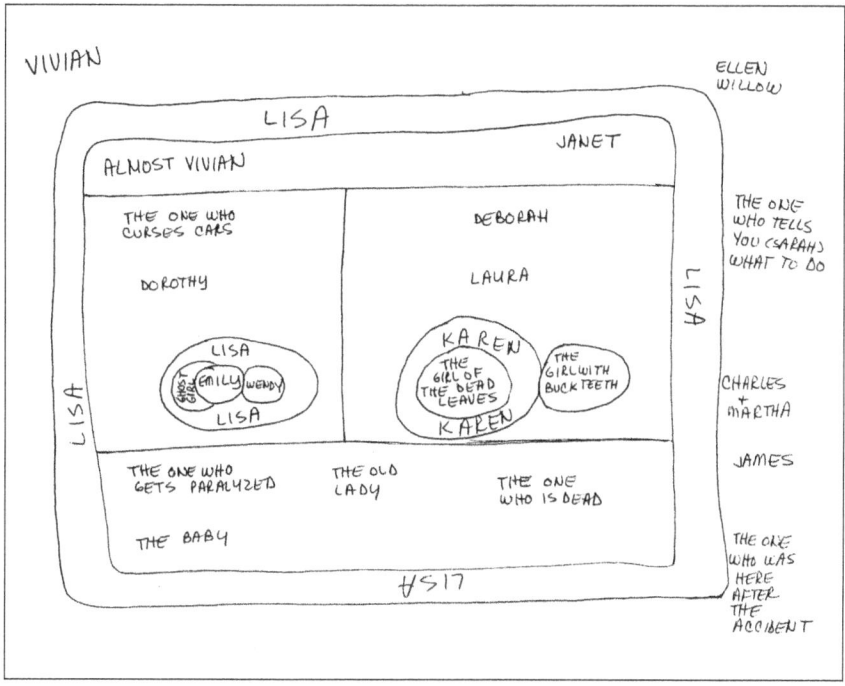

As I created the map, I was surprised to realize how many of us Lisa encased in her sphere. I had thought AlmostVivian would be more encompassing, but reading the words appearing on the screen when I typed the annotations, I saw that AlmostVivian was *the only one of us who is not real. If we get better, she will be the only one who will disappear and not exist anymore.* I wrote that she was an administrator whose job was to make sure we stayed safe (didn't bang our head too hard) and stayed alive (didn't commit suicide). It was also her job to make sure the wrong ones of us didn't come out at inappropriate times or in inappropriate places and that we looked normal, had a place to live, got where we had to be on time, brushed our teeth, and went to bed at night (this was one of her hardest jobs).

> *None of us likes her, but we need her in order to live. We don't dislike her. It's just that she doesn't have a lot of patience for us. Sometimes she is mean to Emily, especially when Emily's neediness gets too big. Other times, she is nice to Emily. But even when she is nice to her, it isn't because she likes her. It is just so she can get Emily less upset and keep things going.*

About Lisa, named for the mentally ill girl in the book and movie *David and Lisa,* I wrote she was the only one of us who thought of herself as beautiful and sexy. She had first come into being at my Sweet Sixteen party. She hadn't had a name then, but as I'd felt my shoulders straighten and heard my voice become more assured, I'd had the sensation of another presence taking over my body. In the years since, it had been Lisa who dressed fashionably and dated men, sleeping with them so Emily could have someone to hold her.

Lisa could be lots of different ways, I wrote. Sometimes she was fine, and sometimes in a lot of pain.

> *It is other people's pain, but she doesn't know that; to her, it feels like her own.*

If someone else felt depressed, trapped, or desperate, Lisa got dangerous or crazy. Then all the feeling was in Lisa,

> *and whoever was having a hard time before is not there so much anymore. Lisa blots out everything else. That is how she saves us.*

Lisa also had plans for how not to live anymore. If any of the others felt trapped by life, or got desperate because there was no way out, they became calmer because they knew Lisa had a way to end things.

> *She keeps us safe by getting dangerous. (Just knowing we can do something makes us more secure and peaceful, and then we don't have to do it.)*

The only trouble with Lisa's saving us by getting crazy or dangerous was that sometimes it could go too far.

> *All the times we were in the hospital, it was because of Lisa. AlmostVivian took her there because she (AlmostVivian) couldn't control things anymore.*

About Wendy, I wrote:

> *She is usually perky and lively and cheerful (but not always). Don't mess with Wendy. If you do, you will wake up*

the one who doesn't want us to talk to you. Wendy knows things she's not supposed to know. She is too grownup for a little girl. Be careful of talking too deep to Wendy.

While I included information on who some of the alters were named after, I didn't say how I had first come to know what those names were because I'd never thought about that. It seemed as if the names had just been there, already established. Handing the map and annotated list to Sarah, I explained that it was the top level only. The middle and bottom levels were too amorphous to draw.

After Sarah sent my map and annotated list to Dr. Blum, I yearned to meet this woman who was advising her in my treatment. Sarah arranged an appointment for me.

I TOOK PAINS DRESSING for the session—I wanted Dr. Blum to like me—and settled on a pink sweater, black pants, a bracelet, and dangling earrings. Walking into her office, which was in the garage of her suburban house, I felt beautiful in an Ophelia-like way. Also nervous. I could hear my heart beating.

Dr. Blum was in her fifties, with an unpretentious manner that put me at ease. The first thing she asked was, "Who are you?" A copy of my map and list was on her desk.

I had never identified myself to an outside person as other than Vivian, even if Vivian wasn't who I felt like inside.

"Lisa," I said.

A rush of surprise at my boldness. The thrill of being recognized, as Dr. Blum wrote *Lisa* on a lined pad. She explained that whoever walked into the session should be the one who left at the end. If there were switches in between, it was Dr. Blum's job to get Lisa back. I wondered how she planned to do that when I couldn't switch at will.

Dr. Blum popped a cassette into her recorder, saying she would give it to me at the end of the session so I could give it to Sarah, then directed me to a recliner. She dimmed the light, but I could still make out the shelves of children's games lining the walls. Something for alters of all ages, I thought. I couldn't see her face, but I could see her hand, poised over her pad.

"Is there anything special you want to tell me?" she asked.

Feeling she would understand everything about me, I let go of Outside and permitted myself to descend.

The next day, transcribing the tape for Sarah, I was surprised to hear not only regular talking, moans, and nonsense syllables, but stretches of silence. What had been going on inside had felt loud and exhausting, yet now I couldn't remember the content. *Unintelligible*, I wrote in many places. Not much for Sarah to go on.

At one point, I heard a skirmish and remembered that a geyser-like feeling had sprung me from the recliner to a corner on the floor. Dr. Blum had been on the floor beside me in an instant, pad and pen in hand.

"Where are you?" she asked.

"I don't know." It was a young whisper.

"You don't have to be afraid," Dr. Blum said, her voice now that of someone talking to a child. "You're safe here."

I was transcribing only what I heard, so I didn't write that it was as if I'd been split in two. One part was a little girl; the other, the Overview-me. The Overview-me saw that Dr. Blum had recognized the switch. No therapist had done that before. The Overview-me saw, too, that Dr. Blum was taking notes, even as she was talking in a reassuring voice. It was as if she were two people also: Atmosphere-like, able to see who I was inside, and un-Atmosphere-like, having to write things down to remember.

Dr. Blum spoke calmly for a few minutes. Listening to the tape, I didn't feel she understood the mixture of pain and fear that had gotten me to the floor, but she did realize something big had happened. She asked me to return to the recliner, which I eventually did. The tape didn't include the last few minutes, when Dr. Blum requested that Lisa come out. I was so turned around inside I couldn't get Lisa back, but I pretended to, and Dr. Blum appeared satisfied.

I saw Dr. Blum for several more sessions, one of which Sarah came to also, to observe. Each time, I was struck by their differences. Dr. Blum was technically expert, but she rarely made eye contact. It was as if she were dissecting me according to a manual. Sarah held me with her eyes and saw my soul. She responded intuitively to whatever age or emotion I was feeling at the moment, much the way a mother responds to changes in her child. When Sarah stopped her consultations with Dr. Blum, saying Putnam's book was a good-enough guide for her now, I wasn't sorry. ∎

CHAPTER 35

Being Seen

ALONG WITH MY GROWING ATTACHMENT to Sarah came jealousy of anyone or anything that took her attention from me. At first I was afraid to let her know how possessive I felt, but as I grew more secure, I became bolder.

"Your office is nothing but a subway car," Wendy accused, eyeing the bulging appointment book on her desk. At the start of each month, it was stuffed with bills she handed to each patient as she saw them. "One passenger gets off, another gets on. You really don't care about them."

"That's not true," Sarah said in her soft, melodious voice. "I care very much."

"You might want to mail our bill," Wendy suggested. "Some of us don't know we pay you. If they did, they wouldn't be able to come here."

"I can certainly do that."

"And you might want to hide your appointment book before we arrive."

"Shall I do that now?"

"Yes."

I turned so I wouldn't see where she put it.

BECAUSE SARAH'S IN-PERSON version was so much like her Atmosphere version, any indication that I was not her sole concern made me feel she had abandoned me. Once, when I had to change my session to the day she saw patients in her suburban home, I noticed photographs of her sons in the den she used as an office. The hole in my chest hurt so much I couldn't stay in the room, even after she turned the frames around so their faces weren't showing. We continued that session in my car—my territory, not hers.

Sarah had quickly become the most important person in my life. In addition to my fear that something would take her focus from me, I feared I would lose her to a catastrophe. If she said she would call at 9:00 p.m. and didn't call until 9:15, I was sure she had died or someone in her family had been in an accident. One way or another, she was no longer available to me. To ward off my worries, I went to elaborate lengths to shield myself from any indication that she had a life apart from me. I avoided seeing the patient before me leave by appropriating an alcove off to the side of the waiting room, where Sarah knew to look for me. I protested if there was any change in her appearance, like a haircut, and a whole session might be taken up with her convincing me she was still the same Sarah.

Once, at the beginning of a session on a warm June day, Sarah yawned.

"Are you tired?" I asked, worried she wouldn't be able to pay attention to me.

"Not that I know of," Sarah said.

Perhaps she wasn't getting enough air. "You can turn the air conditioner back on." She usually shut it off for me because I didn't like the noise.

"It's fine the way it is. Why don't you finish telling me about the meeting at work and your award."

I had been excited about that when I walked in. Now my only concern was keeping hold of Sarah. "I don't mind if you turn it on."

"It's really all right. Try to get back to what you were telling me."

I tried—I wanted to cooperate—but it was half-hearted. Still, we closed the way we always did, with three goodbyes at the door.

On my way to work the next day, I dropped off a letter in Sarah's office. The first part, written an hour after I saw her, was by Emily:

> *Your mommy says goodbye to you at the door with a smile and a kiss and love in her face so you can go into the street and cross the street and go to school and you know she will be there when you come home....*

Several pages followed, written early the next morning by the Overview-me:

> *One version of you (the in-person version) has form. You are made of flesh and bones and you have skin that covers you and you have a frame that you can hang clothes on. You are a physical person. We can see you and hear you. The atmosphere version of you is not at all that way. You permeate the air and the molecules that surround us....*

I wrote that different ones of us had different needs. Some took comfort in knowing where she was and what she was doing. Others needed to have the Atmosphere so strongly that any knowledge interfering with her presence in the Atmosphere was a threat, even something as simple as a yawn. The letter concluded:

> *I hope you understand and can help us with this. I think you can, or we wouldn't be writing about it to you. We love you so much—we love the in-person version of you—because we never had an in-person person before who was like you. We had lots of atmosphere people before who were like you. But no in-person one.*

ON MY THREE-MILE WALK to work, I often stopped at several pay phones to leave messages. "Sarah," a young voice might say. "It's seven-forty-two on Monday morning. We're over here on Madison and Fifty-first. The pain in my chest is bad again. It's from Emily. She needs to cry, but she can't. Lisa's a four right now, and it keeps going up. And a man with an attaché case bumped into us on Fifty-seventh when he ran to make a light. Not on purpose, but it started TheOneWhoCursesCars, and we can't stop her. She just goes on and on. Please don't forget me. Bye for now. Bye, Sarah... Bye, Sarah... Bye, Sarah...."

I paused after each "Bye, Sarah" to give her time to respond "Bye, Vivian," the way we said goodbye in her office. I told her the hour and minute, as well as my location, so when she came back in time to be with me she would know exactly how to find me. The "four" let her know how dangerous Lisa was on a scale of one to ten.

If I had a session after work that day, Sarah might say, "I received three messages from you this morning." The me in her office wasn't the me who had left the messages and didn't care to discuss them. Still, whoever did leave them needed to have the confirmation.

IN THIS AND COUNTLESS OTHER WAYS, Sarah provided me with an infrastructure. There wasn't much movement forward during therapy, but that had been OK when what I needed most was the stability of a home for my insides. By the time I'd been seeing Sarah three years, however, AlmostVivian realized we were depending on her the way we used to depend on Valium, and the therapy had no direction. She discussed this with Sarah, as well as with a friend from the support group. My support-group friend suggested that Sarah consult with her therapist, Jeffery Smith, who had MPD/DID experience. Sarah was agreeable. She also understood my wish to meet Dr. Smith before she did.

A DOOR OFF THE WAITING ROOM opened and a man of medium height came out, fiftyish, balding, in a button-down shirt with an open collar and rolled-up sleeves. "Hello. I'm Dr. Smith," he said in a voice at once welcoming and professional.

"I'm Vivian Conan," I said.

In contrast to Sarah's cozy, vintage-looking office, Dr. Smith's was no-frills but comfortable: a bookcase and couch, two upholstered patient chairs flanked by end tables, and a chair next to his telephone table for him, all in shades of gray and brown. We took seats opposite each other.

I told Dr. Smith that I loved Sarah but felt she responded to each situation or crisis as it came, without having an overall plan. He nodded every so often, his eyes never leaving me. There was a solidness about him, and from his occasional questions, I felt he saw me as a unique person, not a generic MPD/DID patient. My initial stiffness gave way to ease, and I found myself going in a direction I hadn't planned.

"I stole a cookie this afternoon," I said. "One of the big ones that come individually wrapped. I didn't walk out of the store with it. I never do. I'm afraid of getting caught. I just eat it while I'm shopping, and by the time I get to the cash register, it's gone."

"Somebody really wanted someone to give her a cookie," Dr. Smith said.

His understanding made me suddenly shy. I lowered my gaze and my body curled into itself. "Mish *kah*-na *min*-nah," I whispered.

"Hello," Dr. Smith said, as if we hadn't been talking before.

I lifted my eyes but couldn't speak.

"I'm Dr. Smith, and I'd like to know you. Do you have a name?"
I shook my head no.
"How old do you feel?"
I shrugged and lowered my eyes again.
"That's OK. You don't have to talk. I'm glad you felt safe enough to come. This place is for you."

The Overview-me noted how different this was from Sarah. When I'd told her I stole a cookie, she'd said, "You *stole* a cookie?" But this man, whom I had just met, knew that to Inside, cookies were a comfort you shouldn't have to pay for. They were something a grownup was supposed to give you. Also, whenever Sarah sensed I had switched, she finished whatever she was saying, even if it wasn't relevant to the one of us who was there at the moment. Only after she had completed her thought would she ask, "Are you someone else?"

"No," I would say. "I'm me."

"But are you the one who was just here?"

It was as if Sarah understood MPD/DID intellectually but didn't fully comprehend what it was like to live with multiple parts who perceived the world in different ways. She was on the outside looking in at us. Dr. Smith was inside *with* us.

It was thrilling to be seen now, both for the cookie and the switch. Sometime toward the end of the hour, when AlmostVivian took control of the session, she asked Dr. Smith whether we could see him again after he spoke with Sarah. We made an appointment for the following week.

"I have one question," he said when it was time to leave. "Is there anyone in you who doesn't want to live?"

No one had ever asked one of us to report on others. "Lisa, sometimes, but she's not dangerous right now."

He nodded.

SARAH WAS WARM and accepting, not put off by my neediness, and I felt I couldn't live without her. She was the first woman Emily pined for who returned Emily's love. At the same time, having experienced what it was like to be seen and acknowledged by Dr. Smith, I was reluctant to give that up. For a year, I saw him whenever Sarah went on vacation. After that, with their agreement, I began seeing them both on a regular basis, paying for it by continuing to work seven days a week. By then, I was calling him by his first name.

JEFFERY AND BABY-ME SAT CLOSE together on the floor. She attached to him with her eyes. In the silence, her hand rose toward his face. It hesitated, deciding, then glided back to briefly brush her own cheek. Toward his again, measuring the space between them, getting nearer, but still not daring to make contact.

"It's OK to touch," he said softly.

She wanted to but was afraid of confirming what she was beginning to know—that he was a person apart, bounded by skin. Her scream shattered the quiet. Her hand dropped, and a convulsion wracked her body. Saying nothing, he continued to anchor her with his eyes. The tremors stopped and she grew calmer, her hand floating up to begin another cycle of exploration.

After several more attempts, she summoned the courage to touch. His skin felt warm, soft, but more solid than the air her hand had been traversing. A new awareness seeped into her. He remained still. The unbroken connection of their eyes was the only thing that let her know she was OK. She withdrew her hand. Jeffery's eyes receded and became reabsorbed into the Atmosphere that returned to surround her.

This sequence, repeated in many sessions, usually ended with an abrupt takeover by AlmostVivian, who would begin talking about something unrelated. "I have to get to work early tomorrow, because my team is meeting with the actuarial department to discuss specs for the new system." But one day, while the magic of the moment still hung in the air, a realization began to coalesce: the Jeffery I was looking at, a solid form in a physical body, was the same as the Jeffery whose invisible presence surrounded me in the Atmosphere.

"I know who you are," a young voice said aloud. "You're Jeffrey: J E F F R E Y."

"That's not how you spell my name," he said. "It's J E F F E R Y."

Wendy popped out. "Why are you telling us that now?" she asked angrily.

"I didn't want you to find out later and be surprised."

"It doesn't *matter* how you spell it. Something was happening, and you ruined it."

"I'm sorry," he said. "I guess I needed to be seen."

She had no idea what that meant. Nor did she care. She glared at him.

"Is there any way I can fix it?" he asked.

"You have to buy us a cookie. And you have to pay for it with your own money."

I was shocked to hear those words coming from me—more shocked when he said OK. He locked his office, and we went out.

In a nearby store, Wendy giggled when Jeffery pulled his wallet from his pocket. It was such an un-Atmosphere thing to do. Her giggle was tinged with the nervousness of those underneath, who couldn't understand how someone who was able to see your insides could know about credit cards.

SARAH AND JEFFERY were more or less the same in the Atmosphere, but there was a difference in how I perceived them in person. Sarah never tried to hide who she was, and little by little, I came to know she was married and had two school-age children. She had a sailboat. She was in the process of writing an essay on Emily Dickinson from a psychological standpoint. She had a subscription to the opera. She was active in her church.

About Jeffery, I knew nothing except that besides his private practice, he ran an alcohol rehab clinic. He wore a wedding ring, but that seemed so incongruous with the rest of him I discounted it. I couldn't imagine him talking to someone else, let alone living with anyone. To me, he had no existence outside his office.

I had a relationship with two Sarahs: Atmosphere Sarah and in-person Sarah. When I locked eyes with her in a session, I felt I was drinking in the love of a real-life mommy. I had a relationship with only one Jeffery: the Jeffery who existed in the Atmosphere. When I locked eyes with him in a session, I was getting something even more fundamental than love: I was confirming my existence.

Outside of sessions, when I had more perspective, I surmised that what was happening with Jeffery had to do with the way infants perceive the world. I began doing research again, this time on child development. I read about how babies become aware that they are separate beings, how they attach to their caregivers, and how they learn about object permanence—the concept that people and things exist even when they're not visible.

I saw that in some ways, the Atmosphere was like an infant's experience of the world. A newborn has no idea she exists as a separate person, that the boundary of her body is her skin. She is aware only of a primordial ocean of feelings and sensations in which she and everyone and everything are intermingled and merged. She cries when she is hungry, and milk arrives in her mouth. She cries when she is wet, and she becomes dry. She doesn't know whether the relief results from something inside herself or outside herself. She doesn't even know she has a self.

I read that as the baby begins to realize she and her mother are separate beings—at around six months—she becomes anxious, because she hasn't yet learned that people and things can exist when they are out of sight. Her mother leaves the room and it's as if her mother is gone forever. The peekaboo game helps the baby learn this isn't so.

I felt validated by this research. Though the timing was off—I was 50, not an infant—what I was experiencing had been written about. That was enough to make me feel less strange about my wordless exploratory sessions with Jeffery. I didn't try to figure out anything more or question why it was happening. I didn't even think it was something that needed to be "cured."

Not until several years later would I learn that Jeffery believed the cause of my MPD/DID was attachment trauma. He felt that unless my attachment issues were addressed first, more specific MPD/DID work—getting individual parts to become aware of the others and getting all parts to work together rather than against one another—would not be effective. He thought that in order to heal, I had to have an Atmosphere-like experience with a real, flesh-and-blood person. To that end, he tried to make himself as much like the Atmosphere as possible. This meant being as closely attuned to what I was feeling and experiencing as he could. It also included being available for phone calls outside of sessions, not letting me know anything about his personal life, and trying to be consistent, even in his clothes. When he saw that I got upset if he had on different socks, he tried to remember to wear the same ones on days I had a session.

While I didn't understand Jeffery's methodology at the time, I did make the connection between the Atmosphere and the way babies develop. I gave him and Sarah copies of relevant pages from articles and books—by D.W. Winnicott, Mary Ainsworth, John Bowlby, and Margaret Mahler—but didn't discuss them. The me who did the research was not the me who showed up for sessions. Sarah let me know, however, that Jeffery was impressed I'd managed to find the pioneers in the attachment-and-separation field. I hadn't known they were pioneers. I had simply done a subject search, but I felt proud.

"Of course I did," I told her "I'm a librarian." ■

CHAPTER 36

The Left Back Burner

I CALLED MY FATHER a few days after he left Brooklyn for a six-month snowbird stay in Florida. "How do you like your apartment?" I asked. He had rented it sight unseen.

"It's OK, but they have all these complicated appliances to cook your food."

"You mean a stove?"

"Yes."

The 74th Street apartment still had the original gas stove Papoo installed when he built the house in 1926. If the Florida stove had required a wooden match, my father would have had no problem lighting it. He didn't seem too concerned, though. "I bought some oranges," he said. "They don't have to be cooked."

At 83, he had decided to remain in the States for his customary winter sojourn. My mother, 76 and still working for the Social Security Administration, had always visited him in Europe on her vacations. This year, she would go to Florida. When I spoke to her on the phone—once or twice a week—she might say, "I had a letter from Dad. He says hello." "Hello back," I'd reply, without asking for more details.

Two months after my father left, I went down to Florida for a long weekend to visit a friend. I called him to say I was an hour away and would like to see him. He worried that he had no place for me to sleep. Once I assured him I didn't need one, he was enthusiastic about my coming.

His condo was in a gated community for seniors, landscaped with palm trees, tennis courts, and swimming pools. I parked my rental car and knocked on his door.

"Hello, Viv," he said, pleasure spreading across his face. We hugged.

He was thin and slightly more stooped than I remembered, wearing tan shorts, a sleeveless undershirt, and old running shoes with cutouts to accommodate the bumps on his toes. His sparse white hair was wispy, his knees knobby, and there were a few growths on his face and shoulders.

He showed me around: kitchen, bedroom, living room, dining alcove. His paddleball racket and a chartreuse tennis ball were on a chair, alongside a white sunhat, the brim softened by many washings. On the table were a deck of cards, a newspaper folded open to the bridge page, and, next to his eyeglasses, little pieces of paper with columns of handwritten numbers. On another chair were additional pieces of paper, also with numbers.

In the kitchen, on the otherwise empty counter, were three large sweet potatoes, uncooked, and a jar of vitamins. On the left back burner of the stove was a small, empty pot.

"Do you want some lunch?" my father asked, opening the refrigerator. It contained only a bottle of Mazola corn oil and two bowls covered with plates, each on its own shelf.

"I already ate," I said. "I see you figured out how to use the stove."

"Yes, but I can't cook the potatoes. They don't fit." He pointed to the small pot.

"Don't you have other pots?"

"No."

It was hard to believe a furnished apartment came with just one pot. I opened the cabinet under the counter and found a blender, a coffee maker, and a trove of pots and pans of all sizes.

I pieced together what had happened. My father, overwhelmed by the unfamiliar kitchen, had simplified his life by selecting one small pot, stowing away the rest, and forgetting they existed. Somehow, he had figured out how to use the left back burner of the stove. With his one pot and one burner, he cooked one item at a time: brown rice, or lentils, or sweet potatoes. By chance, the potatoes he bought before had always been small, but yesterday's were too large for the pot. It hadn't occurred to him that he could cut them.

"You can cook them in here," I said, putting a large pot on the stove.

"Where'd you find that?"

"In the cabinet. Or you could bake them."

"Bake?"

"In the oven."

"I don't have an oven."

"You do." I opened its door.

He looked at me in bewilderment.

I pierced the potatoes with a fork, slid them onto the rack, and set the temperature to 400. On top of the stove, I put up a large pot of lentils, and another of rice. My father watched me as if I were Aladdin, marveling that everything was cooking at the same time.

Beneath my busyness, I was aware that this was a new turn in our relationship. My father had always imposed his own method for doing things on the rest of the family. Now, he was vulnerable enough to allow me to help him. That made me feel closer to him, almost maternal.

While the food was cooking, we chatted, and I learned more about his life here. There was a free bus that made stops within and outside the community. He had spent a long time deciphering the printed time schedule, then made two simplified lists: one that pertained only to the stop closest to his condo; the other, to the stop at the supermarket. But a few days before my visit, the community had switched its contract to a new bus company. The handwritten papers on the chair were from the old schedule; those on the table, the new.

I felt an unfamiliar respect for my father. The study skills he had honed over a lifetime—memorization and repetition—which I had found oppressive as a child, were allowing him to remain independent despite his slowly advancing dementia. After World War II, his little pieces of paper had helped him prepare for the high school equivalency exam; and, after the launch of Sputnik, to learn Russian, chemistry, and physics—he'd been hoping to land a science translator's job for the government but never did. Today, his papers were helping him get to the supermarket.

When the food was cooked and cooling on the counter, my father wanted to show me the fitness center and tennis courts, so we went for a walk. Along the way, a man greeted him and asked whether I was his daughter.

"He was lost this morning," the man said. "I helped him find his apartment."

After the man left, my father explained that he'd been out walking and hadn't known how to get back. He didn't seem upset by this. It was just another event that eventually had a satisfactory conclusion. I felt this was more serious than the pots, though, and made a mental note to let my mother know. Yet I was also amused, remembering the dictum my father used to follow: never ask anyone for directions unless they're wearing a uniform.

He was in a good mood, and we went on to the clubhouse. At the bulletin board, he pointed out a flyer for bridge games, saying, "No matter where you go, if you play bridge, you'll always be able to meet people. If you want to take a course, I'll pay for it. They probably have one at the Ninety-second Street Y."

I was amazed he still remembered the 92nd Street Y. Touched, too. He had rarely given presents. All through the years, my mother had been the major breadwinner and gift-giver. The gentle man he was today had probably been there all along, but he'd been so worried about preventing every imaginable disaster that he had often been harsh in protecting us. Having lost his ability to worry about the future, he was softer now, even sweet. I was sorry about the dementia but glad for the new relationship it was allowing.

"Thanks for the offer," I said, though I knew I wasn't going to take a bridge class. "I'll check out the catalog for the Y when I get home."

Back in his apartment, I found some large bowls for the lentils, rice, and potatoes, and put each in the refrigerator on what I presumed was its assigned shelf.

"I'm leaving these out," I said after I washed the pots, "so you can use them."

I wrote down directions for operating the other three burners and put signs on the knobs and handles. We did several walk-throughs, which included turning each burner on and off. My father thanked me for the miracle of the food, and we hugged goodbye.

On my return to New York, I reported to my mother, then reverted to keeping up with my father through her, except for one call I made to him a few weeks later. He still remembered the food I had cooked and thanked me for it again but had no recollection of the pots or the oven. I gathered that all but the small pot on the left back burner had promptly disappeared into the cabinet, wiped from memory.

MY FATHER DIED TWO YEARS LATER, in October 1993, in a nursing home in Brooklyn. With my large extended family sitting in the chapel pews, I read the eulogy:

> His fierce love for me and my brother often made him take harsh measures to insure that we followed what he felt was the proper path: learning, preparing for the future, and having the right values. He never tired of teaching and drilling us. This was tedious at best, terrifying at worst. Now that I am older, I can see that everything he did was motivated by a desperate love and caring.

Those words were for the audience, and intellectually I believed them. But for a while my memories were more of my father's harshness than the mellowness he had shown in Florida. I had been surprised a few years before when Sarah asked why my mother hadn't considered getting psychiatric help for him. "They did have medication at the time," she said. I felt Sarah didn't understand the tyrannical hold my father had on us. He had been a gale that pummeled us to the left and right as we each tried to steer our own course in isolation, unable to band together and support one another. No one thought in terms of a diagnosis. Years later, going through my mother's journals after her death, I would learn that when I was in elementary school, she had tried to get my father to go with her to marriage counseling, but he had refused. I would also learn that Papoo had been the only one in my family to break the noninterference code, telling my mother that if she got a divorce, he would help her financially. She opted to stay married because she didn't want to be without a husband.

IT WAS NOT UNTIL FOUR YEARS after my father's death that I had enough distance from him to become curious about what he had experienced as a youth and what had shaped him. All I knew about his parents was that they were from Russia and had both died by the time he was 18, so he'd had to work to support his younger brother and sisters: my Uncle Fifi, who we went to see occasionally on the other side of Brooklyn; and my Aunts Gussie and Rachel, who we visited in the Bronx every Thanksgiving.

No one in my father's family told stories, the way everyone in my mother's did: about how an inspector on Ellis Island put a chalk mark on Nona's coat because she had an eye infection and Papoo rubbed it off and brought her to his line so she wouldn't be sent back to Greece; about how Aunt Diana was born at home prematurely in the middle of February, and Papoo saved her life by wrapping her in wet blankets and putting her in the oven with the door open.

I knew only two things about my father's childhood, learned years apart. When I was a teenager, he told me each block in his Lower East Side neighborhood had a stickball team, and he was captain of his. In tournaments, his block always won. "The champs," he said proudly. Years later, when the New York Public Library transferred me to the Seward Park branch on the Lower East Side, my father could barely contain his excitement as he told me he went to Seward Park High School.

Aunt Gussie, his only sibling still alive, was 84 and still mentally sharp. I asked her what she remembered.

She said their father was an iceman and had to strap huge blocks of ice to his back and deliver them up many flights of tenement steps. His back always bothered him, and he wore a special support girdle, which she helped him lace tight every morning. Their mother was a good cook but couldn't walk much because her feet were always swollen. For two years after their parents died, the four children lived by themselves, with neighbors looking in on them. When, at 16, Rachel married, the other three split up, with my father going to Brooklyn to live with someone Gussie referred to as "Bobbi's mother."

I recalled that three or four times over the years, at weddings and funerals of people I didn't know, a shapeless woman emerged from the crowd to tell me my father had lived in her mother's house after his parents died. I felt slightly repulsed each time and tried to escape from her and her musty old world as quickly as I could. Now I would have liked to talk with Bobbi, but she was dead.

I remembered that my cousin Hazel, Uncle Fifi's daughter, had once done family-tree research. At the time, I wasn't feeling warmly toward my father and didn't care to know what she'd found. She lived in Massachusetts, and we hadn't spoken in years.

"Our fathers' father's name was Samuel," Hazel said when I phoned one day in early September, "but he was sometimes called Aaron. Their mother's name was Frieda."

My father's parents had names.

Hazel told me Samuel had come to America from Russia in 1900; his wife, in 1905. Several Lower East Side addresses traced the family's moves to different apartments. Death certificates revealed that Frieda had died of pancreatic cancer in 1927; Samuel, of "general cancer" a year later. Hazel knew where they were buried—Montefiore Cemetery in Queens, less than an hour's drive from my house—but she had never been there. She even gave me the grave locations: Samuel in Block 90, Row 8R, Grave 2; Frieda in Block 90, Row 4L, Grave 9. I decided to go that weekend.

EVERY PIECE OF EARTH except a narrow center path was filled with closely spaced graves. The somber majesty of these legions of the dead seeped into me, and I felt peaceful counting rows: 8R for Samuel. I ignored the R, because I didn't know what it meant, and stopped at eight. With a mixture of excitement and trepidation, I began making my way across the row, stepping into ankle-deep ivy and pushing bushes aside to read inscriptions. There were 20 graves in the row, ten on each side of the path, but no Samuel or Aaron.

Thinking I hadn't understood the layout explained to me by the woman in the cemetery office, I decided to look systematically at all 200 graves in the Block. There were ten rows, twenty graves in each: beloved sons and husbands, loving wives and daughters, some stones with an inlaid porcelain photograph of the person lying beneath. I tried pulling the ivy off those that were overgrown, but the stems clung fast and I came away with only a handful of leaves. I managed to clear just enough to see that it wasn't Samuel or Frieda, then moved to the next. My fingernails were stained green, my eyes itched, and I started to sneeze.

Then, pulling back the branch of a sapling, I saw it:

> *Our Dear Father*
> *Samuel Cohen*
> *Died December 14, 1928*
> *Age 54 Years*
> *FATHER*

For a moment I stared, not moving or feeling. Then I started to slip back in time, retaining my 55 years while my father got younger.

His hair was no longer gray but the curly black I remembered as a child. Together, we glided back to before my birth and stopped when he was 19. I felt a surge of warmth for this vulnerable young man whose father had just died. I thought of the young men I cared about today. My nephew, a senior in high school, serious about soccer, applying to colleges, needing his father at the same time that he acted nonchalant and independent. My cousin's sons, devastated when their father died in a plane crash.

All at once, I felt the depth of my father's loss. I understood that he had wanted to prepare me to survive any similar loss. I loved him that moment as I never had before. I loved my newly found grandfather, too: the Grandpa whose lap I had never sat on; the father who tried to take care of his four children after his wife died, then got sick himself. In the Jewish tradition, I picked up a small rock and placed it on top of his gravestone.

Now I began searching for Frieda, finishing my inspection of all 200 stones. When I didn't find her name, I decided to return to the office.

My Volkswagen Golf was parked in a narrow lane barely the width of one car. I was opening the door when a gray Lexus pulled up behind me. A well-dressed, elderly man got out. His passenger, an elderly woman in a fur coat, remained in their car. The cemetery layout was complicated. Feeling that there would be less chance of getting lost if I returned the way I had come, I explained that I wanted to back out.

"Too bad," the man scowled. "I have an unveiling at ten, and I'm not moving." It was ten after ten.

I was shocked at his tone but said nothing. I would drive forward and check the map for a different route to the office. I was just turning the ignition key when a black Ford Escort pulled up in front of me, head-to-head. I decided to walk. It would take more than 20 minutes to get there and back, and by that time, the unveiling might be over.

I had taken only a few steps when the Lexus man approached me. He pointed to the Escort. "That car is going to back out. You drive forward and turn right, so I can go straight through."

"That's fine with me," I began. "It's exactly what I wanted—"

"Don't *answer* me!" His face contorted with rage. "Just get in your car and *drive!*"

I stood still, stunned.

"GET IN!" He pounded my door with his fist. His companion watched from behind her window.

AlmostVivian thought it best not to answer him. He was clearly in a state where he couldn't listen to reason. But anger bubbled up from Inside. "Don't you touch my car!" I growled.

He took a step toward me. "I'll touch whatever I want."

AlmostVivian was back. I opened the door and got in. The man slammed it shut, then hit my fender with his fist. Hard.

Feeling like a little girl, I started to cry. I turned on the ignition and tried to depress the clutch pedal. My foot was trembling and I couldn't get it down.

Suddenly, I was angry again. I *hated* this man. I wanted to punch his ugly, twisted face. I hated my father, too, with the fury-veins standing out on his temple like thick, red cords. I hated him for beating Brownie on the nose with a rolled-up newspaper when he barked. I hated him for raging at me whenever the phone rang after 8:30 at night, as if I should have been able to predict it and stop it. I hated him for not letting me watch the TV program on Abraham Lincoln my teacher assigned for homework. Most of all, I hated him because I felt powerless.

The Ford Escort backed out. Leg still shaking, I got the clutch pedal down, eased my car forward, and turned right, leaving the way clear for the Lexus man.

The office was crowded, with a line that circled around to the plants on the window side. I took my place at the end of it. A man had joined the woman behind the counter, and each was helping someone locate a grave.

I was furious again, alone and isolated, not connected to anyone or anything. Nor did I want to be. I hated every single human being on earth, including these people waiting in line. I hated my father most. For screaming because heat came from the radiators when he wanted the room to be cold. For ranting about my cousin when he was practicing the drums.

Every so often more people entered. I began taking in snatches of their conversations. They were strangers sharing confidences, talking about visiting their dead relatives each year around Rosh Hashanah. They exchanged advice: the best route to the different cemeteries, where to park. They were in their forties, with designer running outfits and Brooklyn accents. They were in their eighties, with canes and European accents. In my mind, I shared my own cemetery story with them, and I began to feel connected to humanity.

My turn. The woman confirmed that Frieda's location was the one I had. About Samuel, she shrugged when I told her I had found him in a different spot. But I came away with a helpful clue: L and R meant the left and right sides of the center path.

When I got back to the plot, the cars were gone, and there was only the calm solitude of the dead. It soothed me. After carefully counting the specified number of rows and stones, I stopped in front of one that said:

My Beloved Wife
And Our Dear Mother
Fannie Cohen
Died April 26, 1927
Age 47 Years
WIFE

I had seen this stone before but passed it by because it hadn't said *Frieda*. Now I looked at it carefully. Hazel has said April 27. It was too close to be a coincidence. I called her on my cell phone. She told me the 1910 census listed the name as Fannie, though other records, including the 1920 census, listed it as Frieda.

I looked at the grave a long time, willing my grandmother to become real. But my anger still lurked near the surface. *Beloved Wife*. I sat on the ground and put my fingertips to the stone. It was cool and slightly gritty. *Our Dear Mother*. I brushed away some plant debris and pressed my palm against the marble. Dear Mother, who held my father when he was a baby and smiled into his eyes. I traced the grooves of the inscription. Dear Mother, my Grandma Fannie, who set the table for dinner when Grandpa Samuel came home from work with his hurting back. Dear Mother, who got sick and died, and my father didn't have a mother anymore. A tear slid down my face. Feeling an unaccustomed peace, I placed a rock on Fannie's gravestone.

Back in my car, I sat awhile with the window open, savoring the stillness. Then I tuned the radio to WQXR and pulled away. ▪

PHOTO ALBUM: 1966–1997

Photo Album: 1966–1997 ▪ 359

Out on pass from Albert Einstein Hospital to be Maid of Honor at Susan's wedding, wearing a dress I made in occupational therapy (April 1968)

A photo-booth portrait I took while living at a halfway house after leaving Albert Einstein Hospital (1969)

With my mother at my brother and sister-in-law's Manhattan apartment (1973)

Issuing a temporary library card to Isaac Asimov at the New York Public Library's Columbia branch when I was Branch Librarian (1976)

On a lake in Harriman State Park, NY, wearing a favorite T-shirt (Summer 1977)

Relaxing on a friend's patio in Manhattan (July 1980)

Photo Album: 1966–1997

My father at age 80, playing chess in a local park (August 1988)

With my father in the Coney Island nursing home where he spent his last months. My mother brought him a newspaper every day. (1993)

No matter what was going on inside me, at MetLife (above) or any other job, I was always able to pull myself together and perform. (1994)

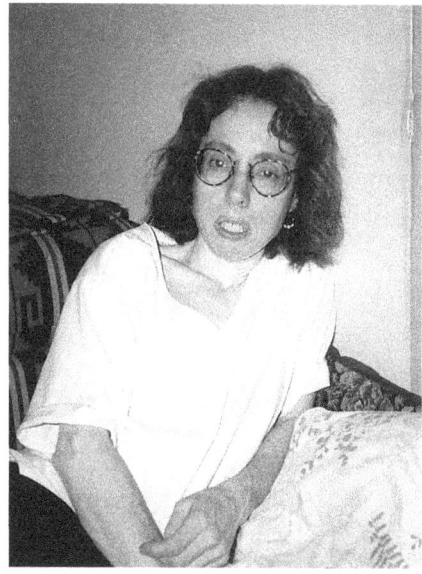

My therapist Sarah took this photo when the babies who usually stayed hidden inside me emerged. (May 1994)

PART SEVEN

HEALING

CHAPTER 37

The Saddest Present

"DO YOU GOT ANYTHING TO TELL ME?" Wendy asked, her custom at the start of a session. It was late October, 1998. I looked at Jeffery trustingly, expecting his usual *No*.
"Yes," he said softly, reluctantly.
"What is it?" Not Wendy's confident voice, but someone's who felt she was about to be dropped.
"I'm going to be away from December sixteenth to January fifth."
Three weeks. A long moment of silence. Then Wendy again. "You know dose doll-babies I cut up with scissors a few years ago? I need to see them."
Jeffery lifted the couch seat and rummaged through the storage chest beneath. That was where he kept my blanket and pillow, crayons and drawing pad, what made his office my special place for four hours—two double sessions—each week. I looked away, not wanting to see what else he stored there.
Hearing the lid close, I faced him. He handed me a small paper bag. I turned it upside down and tiny plastic body parts fell to the floor.

ALMOST VIVIAN HAD BOUGHT the dolls several years before, when I was still seeing both Sarah and Jeffery. It was during the time the babies on the bottom level were coming out often in sessions, alternately moaning and screaming. I listened and was amazed, because I didn't feel any torment. Sometimes I tried to stop the sounds by choking the babies in me, putting my hands around my neck and squeezing so tightly I coughed. Jeffery would pry my hands off so I could breathe, telling me to let the sounds happen, that even though I didn't know what they were about, someone in me did, and eventually I would, too.

But outside of sessions, I felt their neediness coursing through my veins, a hunger and yearning that could never be satisfied. I was sure that monster neediness would repel Sarah and Jeffery and I would lose them forever. I hated the babies and wanted to bash them out of me. I needed Sarah and Jeffery to know about the hate. It was too big for me to handle alone. On the walk home from work one evening, AlmostVivian got the idea of using dolls instead. She stopped at a toy store and bought their entire stock of miniature plastic babies, 12 of them. Each was about four inches tall, sealed in its own cellophane package, with dimples and blue eyes.

In my next session, which was with Sarah, I took the dolls and a pair of sharp scissors from my backpack. Laughing diabolically, I held the closed blades like a dagger and plunged them into a doll's stomach. "I'm going to *kill* you!" I said, as I began cutting through the waist. It was a voice like that of TheOneWhoCursesCars but raging at the Inside babies instead of Outside people. The plastic was hard, and the scissor loops dug into my fingers. I kept cutting. When the doll's body was severed, I pulled on her head. It came off with a popping sound. I tossed the three pieces aside and attacked the next doll.

At the same time that one part of me was gleefully plunging scissors into the guts of dolls, another part was aware of Sarah, sitting silently on the floor with me. As if I were in her head, I knew she was uncomfortable. I also knew it troubled her to be uncomfortable, because she felt that as a therapist, she should understand and accept what I was doing. I didn't want her to be uncomfortable. I needed her to talk in her gentle Mommy voice and look at me with the soft eyes that were ordinarily filled with love for me. I needed her to understand the desperation behind my lunatic laughter. But the more I butchered the dolls, the more uncomfortable she seemed.

Suddenly I felt dirty. Unacceptable. Sarah was good and pure. She believed in God and went to church. I stopped cutting, threw everything back into the paper bag—the three dolls I had mutilated, the nine still sealed in cellophane, the scissors—and stuffed the bag into my backpack. For a minute I looked at Sarah, not saying anything, trying to win her back with my eyes. She regarded me dubiously.

I felt my face get soft and my body relax. Then I heard Emily's whisper. Young, trusting, shy. "Sarah?"

Sarah cocked her head and looked at me from a different angle.

"Sarah?" I whispered again.

The warmth came back into her eyes. "Emily?"

I slid my hand toward her along the floor. She took it in hers, and we locked eyes. "Hi, Sarah," I said.

"Hi, Emily." She smiled kindly at me. All was well again.

The next day, in my session with Jeffery, I continued the massacre.

"Somebody's really angry at the babies," he said.

Once I saw I didn't repulse him, I let go, stabbing and cutting. "Now you're going to *die*!" I growled.

Theoretically, I knew this killing spree wouldn't free me from the babies. I also knew I was supposed to embrace and care for them, because they were part of me and needed to heal. But I didn't *want* them to be part of me. Shrieking and giggling, I dismembered all but one, then stopped. If I destroyed the whole lot, how would I get them back when I was ready for them to heal? I tossed the last cellophane-wrapped doll to safety on the other side of the room, then snatched one of the severed heads off the floor and cut it into tiny slivers.

SEVERAL YEARS HAD PASSED since then. The bottom level was less dominant, and I less needy. I had forgotten about the dolls until now, with Jeffery's three-week absence looming. Looking at the body parts on the floor, I knew I had to fix the most broken baby—the one with her head in slivers—before he left, so I could take her home and care for her myself while he was away.

"Do you got any glue?" Wendy asked.

So began our routine for the next few weeks. At the beginning, middle, and end of each session, I glued one sliver of the baby's face in place, allowing time for it to set, all the while joking about my pediatric trauma unit. It was painstaking work. I wouldn't let Jeffery help but was glad he was there, watching each piece make the baby more whole.

I also asked questions.

"Are you going to be in another time zone?"

"Yes."

"What airline are you taking?"

"I think it's Tower."

I had been expecting something like United or American. Those flew to many places in the United States. Tower went mostly across the Atlantic Ocean. Best not to ask where. "Make sure you're careful."

"I'll be very careful."

Things could happen even if he was careful. Dr. Welch died while he was on vacation in Europe. "Are you going to come back?"

"Yes."

In our last session before Jeffery left, I worried that I wouldn't be able to hold onto the reality of his existence for three weeks.

He said some of us knew he existed when I couldn't see him. Others didn't. "You need to set up a bucket brigade, so the ones of you who do know can pass the information to the ones who don't."

I liked that idea and sprawled on my stomach, crayons in hand, to draw 21 tiny buckets. I cut them out, wrote one date on each, and heaped them, like a pile of multicolored confetti, on top of the mended baby. She had scars on her face that would never go away, but she was whole.

Jeffery drew me a coupon: two stick figures, big and little, him and me, holding hands. There was a dotted line connecting their hearts, and a border around the whole picture.

"Is dat border because you and me are in the same world together, even if you can't see me and I can't see you?"

"That's exactly right."

"And even if you're in a different place, you're still the same person?"

"That's exactly right. I'm me, and I never change on the inside, even if I wear different clothes, or my voice sounds different, or I'm in a different place."

When it was time to leave, I put everything into my backpack: mended baby, paper buckets, coupon. As I stood in the doorway, I realized Jeffery's office would be empty for three weeks. That was scary. I hoped he wouldn't die.

Atmosphere people never died. People in bodies did.

"Be very careful," I whispered.

He nodded and waved.

We said goodbye three times and I backed out, holding him with my eyes until I closed the door.

FOR THE FIRST TIME since Jeffery started becoming more of a flesh-and-blood person than an Atmosphere person, all of us believed he existed, even though he was away. Every few days, we mailed a letter to his office, along with the cutout paper buckets for the days that had passed since the previous letter.

On the day he was scheduled to fly back—three days before my session—I visualized him in his body. *He orders a drink when the flight attendant comes down the aisle. He rests it on his tray table while he reads a magazine. He gets on line for the bathroom.* All day, I listened to the radio—for plane crashes. I worried that he wouldn't be able to land because of the snow, even though most of it was in the Midwest.

The phone rang late that evening.

"Hi, Vivian. It's Jeffery. I'm back." We had prearranged that he would call.

"Thank you for telling me," I said, and we hung up.

I played his words over and over in my head. Was his voice different? Was he the same person?

Tuesday came at last. To avoid seeing the patient before me leave, I walked through the waiting room to hide in the kitchen, as had long been my custom. Soon I heard the first in the usual sequence of sounds. The door to his office. Next, the hall door. He or she was gone. Now the noise of the sliding-door closet in the waiting room. I peeked out. He was standing in front of the closet. In a body-shape. Jeffery, yet not Jeffery. He took off his shoes and put on another pair. So that's where he hid the new ones that upset me. I knew I should step back, because he would pass the kitchen door on his way to the next sound: the bathroom. But I ran into the waiting room.

"I saw you!" I laughed, jumping up and down. "I saw you go into the closet and change your shoes."

Jeffery looked momentarily surprised. Then he smiled, a wide smile that deepened the crinkles in the corners of his eyes. "Hi, Vivian."

"Are you really back?"

"Yup. It's me." His smile got bigger.

He's obviously happy to see me. I'm glad he's happy. I'm devastated he's happy. His happiness is proof that he wasn't with me in the atmosphere all along. I hate him. I love him. I hate him. I punched him in the arm.

Still, he smiled.

"So, how are you?" I said, a little girl trying out sophisticated talk. It sounded funny. I giggled and tried another phrase. "Nice to see you." *Oh my god. That's what you say to someone who has been away.* The scary words kept tumbling out of me. "How was your trip? It's been a long time." He smiled. I wanted to cry. I punched him again and giggled some more.

I tried to frame him in a familiar context, but nothing fit. He wasn't the Atmosphere Jeffery, because he didn't know everything I thought and felt and did while he was gone. Yet he connected eyes with me in the old way. But he was in a physical body. And his body had probably been across an ocean. Could the Jeffery who smiled at me now be continuous with the Jeffery who had waved goodbye three weeks ago?

I spent the entire session trying to merge the before and after Jefferys. I looked for the mole he used to have on his forehead. It was still there. Most of all, I kept checking his voice and eyes. The old Jeffery was in both. Yet I couldn't settle and never got to tell him all the things I had saved up. I left feeling empty and cheated.

When I got home, I wrote a letter that I mailed the following day.

> *You think you came back, but you didn't. Your smile came back, but not your insides to our insides... You can't expect to take up from where we left off....*

OVER THE NEXT FEW MONTHS, as Jeffery's presence in the Atmosphere continued to fade, the entire Atmosphere began to lose potency. Though Sarah and Marybeth were still in it, their essences were weak, not enough to sustain me. There were major upsets over minor events. Jeffery forgot to call when he said he would, or he remembered to call but his voice was ever-so-slightly hurried; either way, I was sure he hated me and I had lost him forever. Jeffery wore a new sweater; this evidence that he went to a store or received a gift meant he was gone from the Atmosphere and I had lost him forever. Jeffery changed my session from Fridays to Thursdays so his weekends could begin earlier; it was clear I was a burden to him and had lost him forever.

With each incident, I felt betrayed anew. "I HATE YOU!" the angry ones screamed. The hurt ones whined. "You said you would call, and you *forgot*. You shouldn't *say* something if you can't *do* it." The abandoned ones became paralyzed and mute. Each time, Jeffery reassured me that I hadn't lost him and he hadn't changed. Only my perception of him had changed. Each time, I would feel better. Until the next time.

The more Jeffery became real as a flesh-and-blood person, the more self-conscious I was about the nonsense syllables and noises that had seemed natural and acceptable before. But I was unable to talk about Inside concerns in regular English words, so I filled long stretches of my sessions with prattle about Outside happenings: my boss was being fired; the traffic on the way to his office had been horrendous. All the while, Inside yearned for the kind of connection I used to have with the old Jeffery.

I brought a computer to a session and found I could type what I couldn't say out loud. Jeffery answered either by typing back or talking, depending on what I indicated I wanted. This became our new method of communication. Often, I didn't know what I was going to say until I saw the words appear on the screen. It was as if they flowed from my fingertips, bypassing my brain.

One day, I wrote about what I considered Jeffery's shortcomings as a skin-container person, and how much I missed his Atmosphere version. I finished typing and handed him the computer. When he lowered his eyes to the screen to read, I took the opportunity to scrutinize his body. Who was this person trying so hard to reach me? I looked for things that would make him real and found them in comforting imperfections: a small hole in his sock, one unruly gray hair sticking out of his thick black eyebrows, an ink spot on his shirt pocket. He typed something, then held out the computer to me.

> I'm a skin person, but I'm a lot more like an atmosphere person than what you think of as a skin person. Because you think of a skin person as somebody who drops you. Somebody who breaks the connection with you. I'm not the kind of skin person who does that.

I looked up to see a sincere face that matched the words. His eyes met mine and held them, and I felt a tiny bit of the connection I used to feel with the Atmosphere-like Jeffery. At the same time, I was aware that he was not in the Atmosphere. The eyebrow hair was still sticking out.

ONLY WENDY COULD REPORT in out-loud words about anything that mattered to Inside. Before I had this new conception of Jeffery, she used to appear just at the beginning of sessions, a scout checking for potentially dangerous skin-world manifestations in the otherwise Atmosphere-like Jeffery. But with Jeffery rarely in the Atmosphere anymore, Wendy now stayed out for most of the session, a lone soldier on the front line, and no one else got a chance to be with him. At first, because Wendy was perky and chatted freely, Jeffery thought I was adapting well to my new perception of him.

"Wanna hear a joke I heard on the radio?" Wendy asked one day in her saucy little-girl voice.

"Sure," Jeffery said.

"What's the difference between an HMO and the PLO?"

"I give up."

"You can negotiate with the PLO."

Wendy was delighted when Jeffery laughed.

"I know a joke, too," he said.

Jeffery had never told us a joke before. Atmosphere people didn't joke. "What is it?" she asked, trying to maintain a cheerful voice.

"How can you recognize a happy motorcyclist?"

"I give up."

"He's the one with dead bugs on his teeth."

Wendy managed the required giggle, but there was an earthquake Inside. Jeffery had violated a boundary, crossed further into skin territory than Wendy could protect us against. Her giggle stopped abruptly and she punched him in the arm. "You're not supposed to tell jokes," she said angrily. "Only *we're* allowed to tell jokes."

His face turned serious. "I'm sorry. I won't do it again."

"And don't smile! Don't act glad to see us when you first come in." She punched him in the other arm. "That's just to make it even," she said in a more gentle voice, "so your arms will be balanced."

We had had the conversation about smiles many times. Jeffery knew we saw his smile as proof that he was seeing us for the first time after a break. If he had been in the Atmosphere, there wouldn't have been any breaks. "It's good to remind me," he said.

I DID KEEP REMINDING HIM—about his smile, his tone of voice, his mannerisms—in an attempt to preserve what little remained of the Atmosphere. I still needed it for time-outs from the real world, though it wasn't as soothing as it used to be.

Atmosphere people were no longer pure essences, so completely mingled with mine that I never felt self-conscious about anything I did. Now they were separate, looking down on me from someplace near the ceiling, where they hovered in invisible bodies. "Alone" in my apartment, I was embarrassed when I pulled my pants down to sit on the toilet, because they could see me. Once, when I was cooking fish, I opened the window to get rid of the smell—not for me, but for them. I felt foolish whenever I did things like that, yet I kept doing them.

The only times I felt satisfyingly connected to Jeffery were when we had toast, my ultimate comfort food. He let me keep supplies in his kitchen: a toaster on the counter, a loaf of artisanal white bread and a stick of butter in the refrigerator. We developed a ritual of having toast at the beginning and end of each session. "Breaking bread together," Wendy called it. She was usually the one who ate with him, chatting, using big words, playfully comparing the designs his bites and hers made in our slices. Jeffery and I may have been separate people, but we were having the same sensations of taste, smell, and crunch.

FOUR MONTHS AFTER his Tower Air Christmas vacation, in the last week of April 1999, Jeffery and I were sitting on the floor in the kitchen at the start of a session.

"Do you got anything to tell me?" Wendy asked.

"Yes."

I stiffened and waited.

"I won't be here next Thursday."

I felt a stab. "Did you forget it was my birthday Friday?" We had planned to celebrate during our Thursday session. The stab went so deep, I couldn't even punch him. I inched backward until I felt the wall behind me, then slumped forward, head between my knees.

"I'm sorry," Jeffery said.

He did sound sorry. I looked up to see him sitting cross-legged on the mat.

"I *hate* you!" screamed an angry voice. "You forgot my *birth*day," whispered a devastated one. I punched his arm several times. He pressed his arms into his sides but didn't flinch.

It suddenly struck me that all this was ridiculous. My body would be 57 next week, and I was carrying on like a three-year-old having a tantrum. Jeffery wasn't an Atmosphere that had deserted me. He was an ordinary human being, the kind you might see in the supermarket, but a very wonderful human being. It was rare that he missed a session. He must have something he really needed to do, and I was making it so difficult. Part of me was still upset. Another part felt a surge of love for him.

While one voice was whining, "It was gonna be my *birth*day," another voice, grownup and calm, interrupted with, "Wait. I think it's time to give you a present."

Jeffery looked at me quizzically. I reached for my computer and began typing.

> ...When you are a baby, you would never think of giving your mother a present, because your mother just IS. She is part of you and you are part of her. But when you get a little bigger, you realize your mommy is a separate person, and she can get glad at you, and she can get mad at you. That is very scary. Now you have to do things to make her like you, or you will use her up. When you realize you are supposed to buy your mother a present for Mother's Day, you cross into a whole different dimension. You lost something you will never get back.

I passed the computer to Jeffery. He read. But before he could type an answer, I took it again and continued writing.

> We never thought of you as someone we needed to give a present to. But last weekend, something made us know that now we did. We remembered when you used to say you needed to be seen. And we knew you would be seen if we gave you a present. So we walked up and down the booths of the Columbus Avenue crafts fair, and then we saw a very special puzzle box with a secret compartment... When we were packing up the shopping bag to come here tonight, we put the box in, and we were very depressed about it. Then we forgot it was there—until we just got so upset when you asked us to change the session next week when it is our birthday. We realized we were right. It's time to give you a present. It's the saddest present we ever gave. But it's also a very nice present.

I handed the computer to Jeffery. This time, when he finished reading, I reached inside the shopping bag and passed him a small package wrapped in white tissue paper. Jeffery held it in his hand and looked at me, as if he didn't know what to do.

"Open it!" I commanded.

Rigid with anticipation, I watched him unwrap the layers of tissue. When at last he held the round box in his hand, he still didn't say anything. He just turned it over slowly, examining the top, the bottom, the side. But I saw that he was admiring the graceful streaks of dark brown grain running through the blonde wood, polished as smooth as satin.

"Take it apart," I instructed. "The side piece first."

He fingered the side, then slid it up. It came off in the shape of a crescent moon. He slid the top off sideways to reveal another cutout piece underneath. I watched his face and was thrilled to see his appreciation deepen as he lifted the last piece and discovered the hidden compartment, lined with dark brown felt. It was a truly magical box, small enough to fit in the palm of your hand, large enough to hold a secret.

"Thank you," he said, looking up. "It's a very beautiful box."

I felt powerful—and grownup. I had given Jeffery a present that made him happy. I had let him know I saw him. But underneath, a deep sadness started to roll over me. Before it completely engulfed me, Wendy, always close to the surface, popped out. "I think it's time to have some toast," she said gaily.

"Good idea," Jeffery agreed. ■

CHAPTER 38

Object Permanence

I KNEW IN JUNE THAT JEFFERY would take another three-week vacation at the end of July. Whenever he'd been away in the past, all I had allowed myself to ask was, "Are you going to be in another time zone?" and "Are you taking a plane?" But things were different now. Jeffery was gone from the Atmosphere more than he was in it, and if I didn't know where he was, he wouldn't exist at all.

I began asking questions in the beginning of July and quickly established that he wouldn't be in another time zone and wouldn't be taking a plane.

"So where *are* you going?" I asked as we sat facing each other from our usual places on the carpet.

"This is a big step," Jeffery said. "Are you sure you want to know?"

"Yes!" The conviction in my voice belied my trepidation.

He hesitated a few seconds. "I'm going to New England."

The words bounced around Inside. For some of us, *New England* was more specific than *away*, which was where Jeffery had always gone before. For others, it was a lump of stuck-together states, not specific at all. And what would he be doing in New England? Staying at a bed-and-breakfast? Visiting friends? Family? Some of us wanted to know. Others dreaded the knowledge.

Wendy, listening from Inside, saw that this was going to be a difficult interrogation and popped out to act as go-between. "New England is a lot of places," she said. "Which one are you going to?"

"First I'm going to Block Island," he said slowly, as if weighing each word.

"Block Island?" Wendy's voice was quick, matter-of-fact. "Is that in Rhode Island?"

"Yes."

"How long does it take you to drive there?"

Jeffery looked uncomfortable. "I don't go by car."

"How *do* you go?"

"By boat."

"By ferry? Where do you take it from?"

He looked more uncomfortable. "I don't take a ferry."

"Do you got your *own boat*?"

"Yes," Jeffery said sheepishly, as if admitting a transgression.

There were rumbles from Inside, but Wendy felt we could handle more. "Is it a sailboat or a motorboat?"

"A sailboat that has a motor on it."

"Where do you park it?"

Jeffery pivoted to reach for one of the index cards on his telephone table. He wrote something, as if not saying it out loud would soften the blow, then placed the card facedown in front of me. I turned it over and saw one word: Stonington.

"That's where Sarah parks her boat!" Wendy accused.

This had to be more than coincidence: Jeffery and Sarah, my current and former therapists, who hadn't known each other before they knew me, owned sailboats and kept them at a boatyard in the same town in Connecticut. I remembered an exchange Jeffery and I had had several years before, when he'd inadvertently said something that let me know he'd been on Sarah's boat. Until then, I'd thought he and Sarah spoke to one another only when they conferred about me. It had been upsetting to find out they did things socially.

"Did you have your own boat that time you went on Sarah's?" Wendy asked.

"No."

"You got it afterward?"

"Yes, but I already knew how to sail."

"That doesn't matter. You got the idea to get a boat from seeing Sarah's boat?"

"Yes."

"You never would have known Sarah if it wasn't for us. So, indirectly, you got that boat because of us."

"I guess you could look at it that way."

This was a new concept: I could make a difference in Jeffery's life. I had only a moment to savor it before Wendy realized something else. "Is that where you go every weekend when you leave early on Fridays? On your boat?"

"Yes."

The jolt from this information was too strong for Wendy to deflect. Someone punched Jeffery twice in the arm, as hard as she could, then turned toward the wall and sulked.

Jeffery spoke to her back. "Just because I go someplace else doesn't mean you lost me." She studied the gray carpet and tried not to listen. "It's true that I do other things, but that doesn't mean I forget you." She poked the tight loops, dug out a piece of lint, rolled it between her fingers. "I'm always connected to you by the invisible strings that stretch from my heart to yours."

Inside, huddling beneath the protective sulk, was listening intently. First, only the tone of his ever-gentle voice penetrated. Then they heard the reassuring words. Soon, someone felt safe enough to venture out.

"If you go far away," came a tiny voice, "the strings will break."

"They're special strings," Jeffery said, still talking to her back. "They're very strong and never break."

"Can they stretch across the water?"

"Yes."

"And they stay good even in a thunderstorm?"

"That's right."

After a few more questions, it was almost time for the session to end. As if on cue, Wendy reappeared. She spun around to face Jeffery, caught his eye, and smiled. "I think it's time to have some toast," she said.

"Good idea."

I ARRIVED AT THE NEXT SESSION with two AAA maps: one of Connecticut, Massachusetts, and Rhode Island; the other of Maine, New Hampshire, and Vermont. All the New England states.

"I want you to mark the places you're sailing to," I said, handing Jeffery a red felt-tipped pen. Then, taken aback at my brashness in ordering him around, "Is that OK?"

"Yes." He glanced at the maps, laid one aside, and picked up the other. "This is all we need."

I was relieved. If his wanderings could be contained within the borders of one map that could be neatly folded, maybe this wasn't going to be so bad.

For the rest of the session, Jeffery and I pored over the map. He drew a red line through the blue water from Stonington to Block Island and marked it *Day 1*. A line from Block Island to Cuttyhunk, Massachusetts. "That's Day Two," he said and wrote *Day 2* alongside it. *Day 3* was to Martha's Vineyard, *Day 5* to Nantucket....

This set the pattern for each of the sessions in the remaining few weeks. Every Tuesday and Thursday, immediately after toast in the kitchen, we went into Jeffery's office and I took the map out of my backpack. "Day One is from Stonington to Block Island," he said. I ran my finger over the first red line. "Day Two is from Block Island to Cuttyhunk." I slid my finger over the next. I was like a child who demands the same bedtime story night after night and protests if one word is different in the telling.

In our last session, I gave him snacks I bought at the health food store: fat-free pretzels; Almondina cookies, the kind we sometimes ate together in sessions; blue corn chips. They were for his boat, so he would think of me when he ate them. I asked whether I could take home the mug I drank from when we had toast, and he went into the kitchen to get it.

"Will you send me a postcard?" I asked and was immediately sorry. Jeffery wasn't good at remembering. If he said yes, then forgot, it would be worse than if I hadn't asked. He did say yes. I told myself not to count on it.

When it was time to go, I put the mug and map into my backpack. "Please don't forget me," I said as I slipped my arms through the straps.

"I won't," Jeffery said solemnly.

We walked through the waiting room to the hall door. "And don't forget to wear your hat," I said, locking eyes with him.

"I won't."

"Bye, Jeffery."

"Bye, Vivian and Wendy and Emily and everyone else."

"Bye, Jeffery."

"Bye, Vivian and Wendy and Emily and everyone else."

"Bye, Jeffery."

"Bye Vivian and Wendy and Emily and everyone else."
Still holding his eyes, I backed out and closed the door.

I WROTE A LETTER to Jeffery almost every day he was away, sometimes more than one. I wrote from my MetLife desk, from my apartment in the city, from the weekend bungalow I was renting in the Hudson Valley. I mailed each letter in the post office the day I wrote it, even though I knew he wouldn't get it until he returned.

> *Monday, August 2, 1999. We miss you. We are not used to missing anyone. People usually exist, or they don't exist. They exist if we see them. They don't exist if we don't see them. That way it is easier. You never miss anyone. But now we know you exist, even though we can't see you. So we miss you.*

> *Saturday, August 7, 1999. I'm at the river now. There is the sound of the water slapping against the rocks, but you can't hear it. Maybe it is the same as the sound of the water slapping against the side of your boat, but I think it is a little different. The rocks are not smooth. They have bumps and grooves and jagged edges and smooth edges. But your boat is all smooth. Probably. Unless it has a lot of barnacles on it. But you probably keep it very clean. So the sound of my water slapping against the rocks isn't exactly the same as the sound of your water slapping against your boat, but at least you know a little what it is like.*

> *Saturday, August 14, 1999. I hope you read this letter before we see you, because you need to know NOT TO SMILE.*

WHEN JEFFERY CAME BACK, he did remember not to smile, and his voice sounded the same. But he had a tan.
In the past, he had sometimes returned from a weekend with a tan. I had never known where he'd been, so though his tan upset me, it was no different from his wearing a new shirt. Those upsets rarely lasted more than the 15 or 20 minutes it took for me to berate him for his transgression, and for him to reassure me that despite the outward change, he was the same. But now I knew where the tan had come from, and nothing he said could

convince me he was still the same. It was as if I realized for the first time that Jeffery really *had* been away.

When I couldn't talk to him, or even type, because I wasn't sure who he was, Wendy came out and acted as decoy. She had toast with him, playfully examined the light patch on his wrist where his watch hadn't let the sun penetrate, and chatted about all the Outside things we had done in his absence. In response to her banter, Jeffery relaxed his vigilance. He forgot not to smile. The more he smiled, the worse Inside felt—and the more Wendy prattled.

When I got home and couldn't see the tan or the smile, I was able to transform him back into the Atmosphere Jeffery and write him a letter.

> *All those places he's going to now that seem so new to us, they really aren't new. Probably he was going to places all along. We just didn't know about it. It's the same way that babies don't know their mommy goes to work, or to the supermarket, or to the beauty parlor. Or to anyplace else she goes. All the baby knows is that sometimes mommy isn't there, and then she is there. The baby doesn't know what mommy does in the in-between times. The baby is lucky, because the baby is not capable of knowing, so the facts can't hurt her. But if the baby knew her mommy has a whole other life that doesn't involve her, she would be devastated.*

OVER THE NEXT FEW WEEKS, I became even more sensitive to the slightest change in Jeffery or his office: a new shirt, a different arrangement of magazines in the waiting room, a new brand of paper towels in the bathroom. I was upset if he didn't draw his drapes closed exactly the way they were last time. I monitored not only his tone of voice but the rate of his speech. If his words came out ever-so-slightly faster, I was sure he was in a hurry to get rid of me.

I began leaving him phone messages throughout the day, keeping him up-to-date on what I was doing every minute, so I wouldn't vaporize into nothingness. "Hello, Jeffery, I'm working in the library tomorrow. I'll be driving up the parkway, but if there's a lot of traffic, I'll switch to the highway. Just so you know I might be on either road."

Things went on this way for several weeks, until one day in September, when we were sitting on the mat in the kitchen at the beginning of a session.

"My mother's doing OK," I said.

"Was there something wrong with her?" Jeffery asked.

"You didn't check your messages yesterday," I whined, "or you would have known. I went with her for her eye operation."

I was afraid as soon as I said it. Since his return, Jeffery had patiently listened to my barrage of phone messages, and also to my in-person complaints about his paper towels, his drapes, his clothing, his magazines. I waited for a change in his expression or voice that would tell me I had gone too far and had lost him forever.

But when he spoke, it was in his usual gentle tone. "Channel One is always on," he said, looking at me steadily with his kind, hazel eyes, "and it doesn't depend on time or space. So it stretches and it reaches, and it's always touching you directly from my heart. And I can always feel it connected to me."

Doesn't depend on time or space. Directly from my heart. The words reverberated Inside.

"Channel Two is the one that catches me up with where you are and what you're doing." He was sitting very still, but his eyes were alive, holding mine, and his words began to fill the hole inside me, oozing soothingly into all the nooks and crevices. "And since Channel One is independent of time and space, I don't need to know exactly where you are or what you're doing. You're connected to me and you exist no matter what."

There was an enormous explosion Inside, as I finally understood.

I FELT CERTAIN THAT AFTER this breakthrough, things would be different. So when I found myself getting upset about what I now saw as petty grievances—Jeffery got a haircut; there was a new lamp in his waiting room—I was too disappointed in myself to notice the more subtle change. Yes, those things still upset me, but not nearly as much as they used to, because the ones of us who understood about the channels explained them to the ones who didn't, and we were able to calm ourselves.

As the intensity of my upsets decreased, I began to wonder about Jeffery's life. Before his sailing vacation, I had tried to ignore the many clues that he had one: the time he explained that he was temporarily without an answering machine because he had given his to his son; the day I saw his wife's name and their home address on the subscription label of a magazine in his waiting room. Each discovery had caused a disturbance that lasted more than a month.

But now it was safe to know about his life. Knowing would no longer cause me to lose the Atmosphere Jeffery, because the Atmosphere Jeffery had already faded considerably. Knowing was essential, because it would make his flesh-and-blood replacement more real. I didn't want definitive answers, though—no official facts—so I didn't ask questions. Instead, I reviewed clues. Jeffery had been on Sarah's boat. Jeffery had lived in a house until a few years ago, when he had moved into the big apartment building with the fake waterfall in front (I found that out by driving to the address on the magazine label). Jeffery had once cancelled a session because "I have to teach a class." Jeffery had a cat that sometimes meowed when he was on the phone with me.

I knew Sarah never sailed alone, so there had probably been four people on her boat the day he sailed with her: Sarah and her husband; Jeffery and his wife. Jeffery had probably given his son an answering machine because his son was old enough to move out of the house. Perhaps he went away to college. Maybe after his son moved out, Jeffery didn't need a big house anymore, so he moved into the waterfall apartment.

For two months, I juggled clues and embellished scenarios. Then, in early December, I asked what I thought was a safe question—whether Jeffery would be going away for Christmas.

"I'm not going away," he said, "but I'll be taking a few days off."

After my distress at this information subsided, I thought about the implication. If Jeffery was taking time off even though he wasn't going anyplace, it must be because he wanted to be with his family in the waterfall. Now I had to know what that family *really* consisted of, especially the children. Was there more than one? A son wouldn't be so bad, but what if there was also a little girl? What if he loved her more than he loved me? I didn't think I could stand that.

This was a hard question to ask, and I kept postponing it, until I woke one morning and realized it was already December 15.

At 9:00, sitting at my desk at MetLife, with people carrying briefcases and coffee hurrying past my cubicle, I cupped my hand over the phone and whispered to Jeffery's answering machine. "Hi, Jeffery. This is Vivian. They need to know how many children you have. They need to know before they see you tomorrow. Please leave a message on my home machine. Thanks. Bye."

I hung up and tried to work, but all I could do was shuffle the pages of a report from one hand to the other and manage a wan smile whenever anyone popped their head into my cubicle to say hello. Every ten minutes, I dialed my home number to check for Jeffery's message.

It came at 11:40. "Hi, Vivian. There're three of them, and their names are Carol, and Mark, and Gary. One girl and two boys. So bye for now. Bye, Vivian... Bye, Vivian... Bye, Vivian."

Three! How old were they? It was 1:30 before I got the courage to leave another message. "What are their ages?" was all it said.

His return message came at 4:30. "Hi, Vivian. Carol is thirty years old, and Mark is twenty-eight, and Gary is twenty-three."

I was relieved. Though my body was 57 years old, Jeffery's children were like grownups to the children inside me, and I wasn't jealous of them. I went to sleep that night more relaxed than I had been in months. But the next evening, as I was getting ready to leave for the session, I realized Jeffery might have grandchildren.

I left him a message. "Are there any grandchildren? Please answer before six-thirty."

The phone rang at 6:25. I didn't pick it up but listened through my answering machine. "Hi, Vivian. No, there are not any grandchildren. None at all."

Whew! I grabbed my car keys and flew down the stairs.

Though things weren't as bad as I had originally thought, I was nervous when I rang Jeffery's bell at 7:15. For me it wasn't as if he had had children all along. It was as if he had just gotten them. This drastic change in his life might make him act differently toward me. I walked through the brightly lit waiting room and slipped into the darkness of the kitchen, where I paced from refrigerator to sink to stove.

At 7:30, the familiar sound sequence began. Door opening, voices in the waiting room, hall door slam, a few minutes' silence. The squeak of the bathroom door, a shorter silence, toilet flush, another squeak, and finally the click of the waiting-room fan being turned off. I stopped pacing and stood rigid.

The kitchen door opened, and there was Jeffery's silhouette. It had the same shape it always did. I turned on the light so I could see his face. He looked the same, but his voice might be different. I wasn't yet ready to find out, so I beckoned him in with my finger, then sat on the edge of the mat. He sat opposite, all the while holding me with the steady eyes I knew so well.

We sat without moving or talking, but many questions and answers flew between his eyes and mine, and after a few minutes, I was almost sure he was the same Jeffery. Still, I needed confirmation.

"Who are you?" I asked.

"I'm Jeffery," he said softly. "I'm the one you know, the one who loves you."

"Was it OK that we asked you all those questions?"

"Yes."

We sat in silence again, but this time it wasn't a testing silence. It was a peaceful one. Soon, the miracle of it all began to fill me up. When it was so big that I couldn't hold it anymore, I reached into my backpack, took out my computer, and began typing.

> When you think something is going to be the end of the world, you have to avoid it, or it will kill you. But in order to ignore it, you have to set up a lot of walls in you, and then you can't be here all the way because there is always something that says this is off limits, even to think about. We worried that the facts would take you away from us. But they didn't. And that is the most amazing thing about all of this. You are still you. You didn't change. And you can still know us even if there are other people and all of that.

I handed Jeffery the computer. He read, and then we sat quietly, looking into each other's eyes, and I saw that this was just as big for him as it was for me. ▪

CHAPTER 39

Windchill

IN AUGUST 2001, I INVITED my 86-year-old mother to visit me for the weekend in the country house I was renting for the summer. On our first evening there, I was in the kitchen drying dishes, when she walked in and said, "On Yom Kippur, before you ask God for forgiveness, you're supposed to ask the person you wronged. So I'm asking. Do you forgive me for all the bad things I did when you were growing up?"

This took me by surprise. Our conversations usually consisted of news exchanges, telling each other about places we had been or errands we had run. I didn't want more give-and-take beyond that.

"Yeah, I forgive you," I said, dabbing a stray drop on a cup.

"That doesn't sound like forgiveness."

Her voice was one I'd never heard before. It was vulnerable. Looking up, I saw an earnest face that scared me. I wanted to bolt.

"I forgive you," I repeated, meeting her eyes.

"That still doesn't sound like forgiveness."

Suddenly I realized what a risk my mother was taking, and that she was in pain. I had the power to take it away or make it worse. I put down the towel, hugged her, and said, "I forgive you."

She hugged me back, saying, "Now I know you mean it."

I wasn't sure how much I did mean it, though I was glad she thought I did, because I felt I ought to mean it. But in the months that followed, I felt more peaceful than I had in a long time. My mother had given me a gift. She had acknowledged that the things she'd said and done had really happened and she knew they'd been hurtful.

I recalled a conversation I'd had with her seven years before, shortly after my father died. We were in my car, on a three-hour drive to a family picnic on Long Island, when she began talking in a stream-of-consciousness review of her life: about her parents, her marriage, her career, her regret that she hadn't learned social skills when she was young. Among other things, she said she had once thought of asking a judge to order my father to stop making Marvin practice the piano. I wanted to ask why she hadn't, but she had already moved to another topic, and I didn't want to interrupt.

My chance had come a year later, when we were sitting in a restaurant and the conversation turned to my father. I mentioned the beatings Marvin used to get when he was practicing the piano and asked what had stopped her from going to a judge.

"Jack never hit Marvin when he practiced," she said.

What? "So why were you thinking of going to a judge? What's so terrible about making Marvin practice the piano that a judge would consider stopping it?"

She had no answer.

Now, in the months after my mother's question about Yom Kippur and forgiveness, I wanted to understand how she had come to be the person she was. I felt lucky she was still alive. With my father, I hadn't been ready to know him until after his death. When I asked whether she would share her recollections with me—I said it would help me understand my own problems—she was more than willing. She seemed to welcome the chance.

Our main mode of communication was letters. I would write a question and leave room on the page for the answer. She would fill it in and mail it back in the self-addressed envelope I provided.

She also sent me some journal pages she had written when I was growing up. Mixed among the handwritten sheets was one that was typed, the draft of the letter she never mailed to the judge.

> Not only does he force him to play, but he accompanies the playing with vocal shouts of disapproval and on occasion hits Marvin.... I'm sure Marvin would accept even one hour readily as contrasted with four. Is it possible to settle this with my husband without the children losing respect for his authority? I would not like to diminish his authority in the eyes of the children.

I also learned about my mother's life and experiences from the stories she told me whenever we ate out, which was every week or two. One day, I asked about her first marriage and found out her husband of three years had left her for her girlfriend.

I visualized my mother as a young woman feeling the pain of abandonment and lost love. "How long did it take you to get over it?" I wanted to know.

"I never got over it," she said.

I was stunned. The marriage had ended more than 60 years before.

She said she married my father several months after she met him, more because she thought it would please her mother than out of any feeling of romantic love. My father hadn't wanted a party, so they went to a Justice of the Peace.

"Did you go on a honeymoon?" I asked.

She said they spent their first night in my father's furnished rented room on the Upper West Side of Manhattan. The next morning, he suggested they go to a country hotel in New Jersey for a few days. They took the bus without calling to make a reservation. An hour later, they arrived to find only one room available. They had just registered for it, when another couple without a reservation drove up. The other couple expressed such disappointment that my father, without consulting my mother, offered to relinquish the room. Though disappointed herself, she didn't protest. She thought my father was probably glad of the excuse to save money and return to their room in Manhattan.

What I found most interesting was her recollection of their first major fight. It was on a weekend, she said, when she was a few months pregnant with me, and the issue was heat. Home alone—it was my father's Saturday rotation at the post office—she was preparing to take a bath. It was chilly, so before she went down the hall to the shared bathroom, she closed the window in their room and turned on the radiator. She was back in bed, relaxing with a book, when my father came home. He began screaming that it was too hot. Stunned, my mother watched him open the window, then pull off his clothes. Ten minutes later, when he was still yelling, she said she was going for a walk. He made no move to stop her.

She turned onto Broadway to find herself in the midst of couples on their Saturday night out. Cold, but not wanting to go back for a jacket, she passed a movie theater and bought a ticket, just to be in a warm place. Sitting in the darkness, she cried as she watched Bette Davis in *The Little Foxes,* half paying attention to the story, half reviewing her options. She considered leaving him... But she was going to have a baby... By the movie's end, my mother had resolved to stay married, and she returned to their room. Neither of them talked about what had happened.

I asked why she hadn't known my father got upset about heat before. She said that was the first chilly day since their marriage.

For some reason—maybe because her story had been so specific—I wanted to verify it. My parents were married on July 4, 1941, and I was born on May 7, 1942. I calculated that she would have been a few months pregnant with me in the fall of 1941. I looked at microfilm of *The New York Times* to determine the first day that had a temperature drop, which did turn out to be on a weekend. Then I found the *New Yorker* movie listings for that date, and *The Little Foxes* was, indeed, playing on the Upper West Side at that time.

About my birth, my mother said, my father wanted to name me Delores, but she had wanted Vivian. He conceded when she argued that Delores meant sadness and Vivian meant life. I was to be Vivian Ann, for Nona, whose Greek name, Hanoula, translated to Anna. After the then routine ten-day hospital stay and a subsequent week in Nona and Papoo's house without my father, my mother brought me home, which was an apartment in Knickerbocker Village on the Lower East Side of Manhattan. The next morning, my mother told me, she was proudly nodding to neighbors as she pushed my carriage through the courtyard when my father commandeered it, forcing her to walk to the side. From that moment on, he was in charge of everything, and I was the focus of his attention. She said she felt jealous and insignificant and soon began to resent me.

On each of my visits, my mother asked to be forgiven "for not being nice to you when you were growing up." She said she was still coming to terms with that. I told her I did forgive her and asked whether she felt it.

"I haven't forgiven myself," she said. "I wasn't thinking of you. I was just thinking of me."

"You were trying to survive."

"Yes, that was it." She seemed relieved at my explanation.

My mother was becoming a person I could relate to, and I found our conversations healing.

O N A BLUSTERY WINTER DAY six months before my mother's question about forgiveness and Yom Kippur, I heard a radio announcer explain the concept of windchill. Your skin surrounds your body, he said. And just over your skin, between you and the rest of the world, is another layer, a coating of air a fraction of an inch thick. That layer, heated by your body, is warmer than the rest of the air. It insulates you. When a gust of wind blows the layer away, you're not insulated anymore, so you feel colder, even though the actual temperature hasn't changed.

That was astounding. You didn't end at your skin but extended out a bit. It meant that while Jeffery wasn't loose in the Atmosphere, he wasn't stuck in his skin container, either. He could radiate.

In my next session, with his permission, I hovered my hands over the bald top of his head. I felt the heat. He said he felt heat from my hands, too. I experimented. How far away could I get and still feel Jeffery's "windchill." Less than an inch. Even so, it was something.

Our start-of-session routine changed after that. Now, when Jeffery came to get me in the kitchen, I would whisper, "Can I feel your windchill?" He would sit still while I held my hands over his head until I felt some warmth, usually within a few seconds. Only then did we have toast.

T HOUGH I HAD LIVED with the Atmosphere most of my life, not all my parts had been aware of it. Of those unaware, some, like Ellen Willow and the babies on the bottom level, were never without the Atmosphere, so they didn't realize there was another way of being. Others, like super-competent Vivian, didn't need the Atmosphere because they got along fine in the outside world. Still others did not get along well in the outside world but had non-Atmosphere ways of coping with whatever was upsetting: TheOneWhoCursesCars (anger); Lisa (becoming suicidal, taking drugs, sleeping around); TheGirlOfTheDeadLeaves (depression).

The parts of me who did know about the Atmosphere were the ones who were aware of both worlds: Atmosphere and real. Some, like AlmostVivian and Wendy, had the difficult job of maintaining the Atmosphere illusion for the ones who didn't know any other world and couldn't exist without it.

Jeffery was the only one of my therapists who realized how much the Atmosphere had structured my existence. Long before he explained his strategy to me—that in order to heal, I had to have an Atmosphere-like experience with a real person—he had been consciously trying to create a safe holding environment in his office and to hide, as much as possible, any of his real-world manifestations he knew would upset me. But it was primarily Jeffery's near-perfect understanding of how I *felt* that made him seem Atmosphere-like.

The more I sensed that Jeffery understood how I felt, the more his Atmosphere and real versions seemed to merge, and the more I held him to a higher standard than other real people. If he made one small "mistake"—if I saw a check peeking from his shirt pocket—I felt such a searing pain that I punched him. Jeffery never said it was trifling that he had a check in his pocket, because he knew it wasn't trifling to me. It meant this space we were in together was not exclusive. Another patient had been here earlier and had paid him with a check. He would say, "Oops," as he stowed the check in a drawer, and for the rest of the session, through the magic of dissociation, I was able to not-know it existed.

Whenever Jeffery made a mistake, while part of me berated him, another part was aware that it was a luxury to be allowed to express my anger and to have it taken seriously. It was as if there were three of us there: Atmosphere Jeffery, flesh-and-blood Jeffery, and me. As always, Atmosphere Jeffery understood how devastated I was. But now, the flesh-and-blood Jeffery understood, too. With each successive mistake and its resolution, the two Jefferys moved closer together. Atmosphere Jeffery was becoming incorporated into skin-container Jeffery.

With Jeffery progressively fading from the Atmosphere, my life became simpler, because there were fewer things I had to keep hidden from myself to maintain the Atmosphere illusion. Even parking my car was easier. There were two parking areas for Jeffery's building: one in front, which was invariably full; and one in back, which usually had space. Jeffery ordinarily parked in back, and because I used to get upset whenever I saw his car—a reminder that he drove away and did other things—for years I arrived at least half an hour early and waited in front for someone to pull out. Now I wasn't bothered when I saw his car—it was reassuring, because it meant he was here—and I parked in back.

MY NEW RELATIONSHIP with Jeffery spilled over into my relationships with other people. I became aware that they, too, had a windchill layer. Not everyone, only those who were genuine and nice. I didn't hover my hands near their heads but felt a connection just by talking or sitting across from them in a restaurant.

I no longer felt like a two-dimensional imposter walking around in the real world trying to appear as if I belonged. I was three-dimensional, a bona fide member of the club, entitled to connect directly with other members. People who didn't know anything about the Atmosphere or MPD/DID noticed the change. My cubicle-mate at work said, "You seem different lately. More sparkly." Like most of my family, my sister-in-law, Mara, knew I was in therapy but not my diagnosis. "It's much easier to talk to you now," she said. "You're more connected." People commented on how "vibrant" I seemed, how "good" I looked. My receptiveness toward my mother and my wish to understand her were part of this change, too.

It was as if I had awakened from a long sleep to a world bright with possibilities. I had a ready-made set of friends and relatives I had been halfway plugged into for years. Now I was ready to plug in all the way. I began going to lunch with people from work. I lingered at the end of my writing workshop to talk with the other students. At family gatherings, I was less inclined to carry around platters of hors d'oeuvres and serve the coffee—ways of avoiding intimate conversation—and more inclined to sit and talk with my cousins and their children. I began meeting my old friend Susan for dinner and trading emails with Linda, who now lived in Florida.

THE WORLD FELT NEW and fresh. I was glad to be alive and wanted to celebrate. I would be turning 60 in May 2002 and decided to throw myself a huge party in a restaurant. I would invite everyone in my new world, the outside world, who was important to me: those of my aunts and uncles still alive; my cousins and their children; my brother and sister-in-law; my three nephews, Jesse, Matthew, and Jordan; my old friends Susan and Linda; my new friend Judy; coworkers; friends from my writing workshop; neighbors from my summer rental.

When I told my mother, she said, "If you had gotten married, I would have made you a wedding, so I'd like to sponsor this party. You do the planning, and I'll help you financially."

I mailed save-the-date notices to over 100 people, then yo-yo'd from elation to worry that no one would come. "They'll come because it's you," Jeffery said. I wanted to believe him, but he was biased.

Though I couldn't tell my guests, the celebration was for two of us: the me who was 60; and Emily, the me who was six. Until then, Emily's sadness and timidity had caused us many difficulties, and the others resented her and treated her as an outcast; they felt she was holding us back from participating in the world. But we were slowly coming to appreciate Emily, to realize she was the one who held in safekeeping all the human feelings the rest of us had missed for so long. She was the behind-the-scenes reason we were able to feel real now and connect with Outside people.

I looked for party clothes in Lord & Taylor. The 60-year-old me wanted something sophisticated. Emily wanted a pink dress with ruffles or flowers. We compromised: a white linen pants outfit with blue embroidered flowers above the hem of the blouse. Emily liked it. Vivian liked it. We bought it.

Emily wanted to wear flowers in her hair. We took her down to the flower district, where she chose a blue silk snowball, to match the embroidery on the blouse. During a session with Jeffery, she pulled out the tiny parts of the flower and glued them onto a plastic headband. Jeffery helped by setting up the glue gun. The next week, he sat with her while she strung two bracelets of small, pastel-colored beads, to match the colors of the flowers on the invitation.

THEY DID COME. From Brooklyn, Manhattan, the Bronx, and Westchester. From Long Island and New Jersey. From California, Virginia, Maryland, Massachusetts, Missouri, Pennsylvania, Oregon, and Florida. Over 100 people, from toddlers to 90-year-olds.

They danced. They ate. They talked. The waiters circulated with drinks and bruschetta, then set up a buffet of salmon, chicken, pasta, grilled corn, grilled asparagus, and mashed potatoes. The tuxedoed pianist—a long-lost second cousin from Papoo's side who I rediscovered when one of my writing friends wrote a piece about him—played Rogers and Hammerstein show tunes and music of the '50s and '60s. The children, off in an alcove, entertained themselves with the goodies Emily had packed in individual bags for them:

colored construction paper, a box of markers, beads, a deck of cards, extra-long pipe cleaners in many colors.

Just when it seemed I couldn't be happier, Susan passed out song sheets and everyone sang, to the tune of "The Candy Man," her lyrics about all the wonderful things Vivian was: creative, helpful, a good friend, a loving daughter, a great aunt. It felt strange at first, as if I were listening to my own eulogy. But as one verse followed another, I began to relax. I looked out at all the people singing to me and realized I had a different connection with each of them. Then I stopped thinking and let their blended connections wash over me while I swayed with the music.

After the song, 100 people sang "Happy Birthday" to me, waited while I made a silent wish—that I would be comfortable in the world—then applauded when I blew out the candles on my cake. It was like a fairytale, and I was the princess.

IN THE DAYS FOLLOWING THE PARTY, I still felt the glow. I read what people had written in my guestbook. I had the pictures developed. I felt reborn into the world—connected, entitled.

"You could say the skin world is a minefield," I said to Jeffery, "but if you learn how to tiptoe correctly, you could have a good time."

Had this world been out there all along, and I just never knew? ■

CHAPTER 40

The Same Dog

A FEW MONTHS AFTER THE PARTY, my love affair with the Outside world came to an abrupt end. Everything slid back into gray scale. I began hurrying out of my writing workshop again and avoiding other social interactions. I could tell from their clipped hellos and tight smiles that people I had recently begun to reconnect with didn't understand why I was pulling away. I didn't understand it either, so I couldn't explain. I felt disconnected from myself as well, as if everyone in me except Wendy had vanished. Not integrated but disappeared.

Though I had often felt isolated in the past, I'd been used to it, the way I imagined you get accustomed to living with the limitations of a chronic illness. But now that I had tasted connection, my isolation seemed like a cruel joke. Every night I went to sleep hoping I would wake to my sparkly, connected self.

Months went by. A year passed. I stopped hoping. I got out of bed each morning only because I had a routine to follow: library job three days a week—I no longer worked at MetLife, having taken early retirement—writing workshop one day a week, session with Jeffery one day a week.

The library allowed me the safety of talking to people with a script.

"May I help you?" I asked the woman who approached the reference desk.

"My son has to write a paper on the military press, and he asked me to get him some books and articles."

"Sure." I culled a list of books on war correspondents from the catalog and showed her how to use ProQuest to find newspaper and magazine articles.

With each smile and thank-you from these strangers, I felt just enough warmth to confirm that I was still human.

Most distressing was the loss of Jeffery. I couldn't find my way to him, even when he was sitting next to me. On the few occasions that I hovered my hands above his head, I felt the heat but not the deep-down, satisfying connection I used to feel. Jeffery said that was because of my protector parts.

"You have to take a risk," he said, week after week. "You have to let the protectors out so I can talk to them and find out why they don't trust me."

I thought Jeffery was off-base. I didn't mistrust him, and I didn't believe there were protector parts of me who did. At the same time, I thought he must be right, as he had usually been in the past.

Session after session, I tried to find the protectors. Sometimes I let my fingers wander over my computer keyboard while I watched for them in the words that appeared on the screen. Other times I sat silently, hoping they would surface on their own. Or I turned out the light and hid under a blanket. Or asked Jeffery to leave the room for a few minutes. I also tried meeting him outdoors; we would walk in the small nature preserve near his building. The more I tried, the more I felt like a failure for not being able to do what Jeffery—and I—felt I should do: produce the protectors.

The only one of us who could connect with the skin-container Jeffery was Wendy. Before the Atmosphere crumbled, Jeffery had automatically known everything that happened to us every minute of every day, without anyone having to tell him in words. His knowing was what had made us feel real even when we weren't in his physical presence. But now, if no one told him in words, he wouldn't know; and if he didn't know, we wouldn't exist. In sessions, Wendy talked about seemingly inconsequential things in a valiant attempt to keep him on the line.

"We ate out with The Lady"—my mother—"and Aunt Mollie last Saturday. There's just one restaurant we can go to when Aunt Mollie comes because the waiters don't get upset when she yells at them for filling her water glass more than halfway. She's afraid she'll spill it. She's ninety-three." While she talked, Wendy monitored Jeffery's face to make sure his attention wasn't wandering.

Because she felt responsible for holding everything together during sessions, Wendy stayed out longer and longer, until, eventually, she monopolized all our time with Jeffery. The only way he knew about anyone else's concerns was through her reports.

"We parked our car three spaces over from yours, and they looked in your window." Wendy cocked her head and scrutinized Jeffery's face for signs of disapproval. None. Safe to continue. "They saw the Benjamin Moore color chart on your back seat."

"That's right," Jeffery said.

It was a simple statement, but Wendy was pleased. His tone reassured everyone Inside he wasn't angry that they'd peered into his car. And it wasn't such a catastrophe that he had something so un-Atmosphere-like as a paint chart, because it didn't seem to have changed him. She had done her job.

The rest of us saw that Jeffery was fond of Wendy. She could kid around and make him smile. The more Wendy stayed out, the more everyone else felt cut off from him. And the more they felt cut off from him, the more they felt cut off from the rest of the world. It was as if we needed Jeffery's light to shine through us in order to be real and human. He did shine his light on Wendy, but no one else could absorb it. Wendy understood that.

"As long as I'm here," she said during one session, "no one else can get a chance to be with you. And when we leave here, they're going to feel worse disconnected."

"Maybe you could go Inside for a while and let someone else out," Jeffery said.

"You want to get rid of me!" Wendy threw a mock punch. She was hurt, even though Jeffery had merely echoed what she'd said.

"I don't want to get rid of you." His face was serious. "But it might be good to give someone else a chance."

I knew that wouldn't work. I'd never been able to produce anyone on demand. Switches happened by themselves. But Wendy wanted to please him. "If I go, can I come back later to have toast with you?"

"Yes."

"Can I come back even before toast?"

"Yes."

"OK. I'll try." Wendy smiled ruefully. She waved. "Bye."

"Bye." Jeffery waved back.

We sat in silence. A door slammed down the hall. The radiator creaked. I didn't know what I was waiting for, but if I could relax maybe something would happen.

Nothing did. All I was aware of, besides the building noises, was Wendy, peeking out from Inside like a mother hiding behind a parked car to watch her child walk to school. I tried to empty my mind so whatever needed to happen would happen. It was like trying not to think of the word *elephant.*

"It's not going to work," Wendy announced in a loud voice after two minutes that seemed like 20. "I'm all you're going to get."

WHILE WENDY WAS CAPABLE of connecting with Jeffery, she never came out in public to make connections with other people. She was specialized and could talk only to grownups who felt parental toward her—like Jeffery, and Sarah before him. We felt they saw her as an endearing child, articulate and precocious. But to Outside people, we were 61, not six, and Wendy would have embarrassed us. Even in Jeffery's office lately, we were embarrassed by her singsong voice and lapses of grammar, characteristics we had never noticed before. Jeffery said we were aware of them now because we were becoming more co-conscious. That was supposed to be a step toward getting better, but it was making things harder for us.

Then, one evening in the fall of 2003, I ate out with old friends from my writing workshop. I spent a wonderful two hours listening to these women talk about their families and friends, their careers, health, and ideas for new projects—writing and otherwise. There was no script, just talking from the heart mixed with real listening and caring. As I sat at the table, not sharing anything of my own but feeling satisfyingly connected, I longed to talk about the disconnect that had taken over my life. It wasn't until three of us were lingering over coffee and tea that I felt safe enough to begin.

I didn't have to give them much background, because they knew from the workshops that I was writing about healing from mental illness. "I'm finding getting better to be almost as hard as being sick, but in a different way," I said.

They listened the same way they had listened to everyone else, as no Outside person except Jeffery had ever listened to me before. They didn't say things like, "You seem fine," or "It'll pass." They talked as if my concerns were as legitimate as any of the more concrete issues aired around the table earlier, as if everyone goes through a rough period sometimes, and this was mine.

It was the first time I had dared to speak to ordinary Outside people—they weren't therapists or in a support group—about Inside happenings. And it was the first time I had explained all this to anyone in an adult voice. Amazingly, these ordinary women heard me. On the walk home after our goodbyes, I felt as if a door had opened, just a crack, but enough to let me glimpse a new way of being.

A few days later, one of the women emailed to tell me of an idea she had gotten from *The Artist's Way* by Julia Cameron that she thought might be helpful: write three stream-of-consciousness pages each morning when you first get up, without censoring yourself or lifting your pen from the paper, even if what comes out is, *I don't know what to write today,* or *I have to take my shoes to the shoemaker.* My friend thought the process might help me feel more connected to myself. I thought it was worth a try.

You weren't supposed to show the morning pages to anyone, but if no one knew what I had written, it would be too much like being on the Island of the Blue Dolphins, so I asked Jeffery whether I could email them to him every day. He hesitated—I knew he was worried about being inundated—then said we could try it if there was a chance it would help me break through this impasse. I told him I also needed him to reply. His answers could be just a sentence or two, confirmation that I wasn't throwing a bottle into the ocean.

The morning writing, as I came to call it, had an unexpected benefit: It gave me a way to communicate with Jeffery as an adult about my disconnect, something I couldn't do in his office. Though the idea was to write with pen or pencil, I used a keyboard. I would sit on my bed, inches from the treetops outside my fourth-floor window, the sunshine visible but not yet intrusive—it didn't reach my side of the street until afternoon—feeling as if I were at a séance. Like a medium receiving messages, I would watch words appear on the screen.

> Who are the people we are supposed to have relationships with? People in our class. The people at the library. People we have known for a long time, yet who have all become new for us. How do you start over in a new culture? How do immigrants who come to America make it? I think immigrants have it easier, because they have enclaves where they stay with people from their old culture, where everything is familiar and comfortable. We have no place like that....

I emailed the writing to Jeffery as soon as I wrote it, then monitored my email all day for his reply. This kind of communication, with a built-in wait, was new to me: Jeffery was no longer in the Atmosphere, so he wouldn't know the content until he read it.

His reply came late that evening.

> The crux of feeling strange, insecure, hiding, is that the world outside is a dangerous place. It really isn't. The danger is from the distant past. Wherever you find yourself, there are good people who will like you, so the world is really hospitable. Yes, there are always a few who aren't so good, but they can be avoided.

These back-and-forths helped me understand my situation intellectually but did little to change the way I felt. Then, one day, during a morning writing, I remembered something I had read in a biography of Helen Keller about people who have been blind from birth or a very early age and have their sight restored as adults. Suddenly thrust into the visual world, they have a hard time adjusting. I realized my disconnect had more to do with what the formerly blind went through than it did with the protectors. Relieved to have an explanation that felt right, I combed the library for literature on the experience of the formerly blind. My research led me to *An Anthropologist on Mars* by Oliver Sacks.

In it, Dr. Sacks wrote about Virgil, blind for 40 years before he had an operation that could possibly restore his sight. The surgeon removed the bandages the next day, asked Virgil to open his eyes, then waited for his response. Virgil opened his eyes but didn't speak. Only when the surgeon prompted him with, "Well?" did Virgil say he could see. Much later, he explained that he had opened his eyes to a blur of color and shapes he couldn't decode. He had no idea one of the shapes was a person until the surgeon's mouth moved when he said, "Well?"

Dr. Sacks could have been writing about me. In his blind world, Virgil had no visual conception of space, distance, shape, or perspective. In the Atmosphere, I had little conception of things like chronological time, which has past, present, and future. I didn't comprehend skin-world continuity, that someone is still the same person even when he wears different color clothes or is in a different mood.

And I didn't understand that if you wanted someone to know something, you had to tell him—that he wouldn't know automatically.

I brought Dr. Sacks's book to a session. As usual, Wendy took over as soon as I walked into Jeffery's office, so the adult who had come to this understanding through the book and the morning writing couldn't explain it for herself.

"When Virgil opened his eyes," Wendy said, sitting cross-legged on the carpet opposite Jeffery, "he just saw a bunch of colors and shapes. All mixed together."

"Of course," Jeffery said. "He couldn't differentiate the figure from the ground."

"You don't have to get so technical! Go to the head of the class!" Jeffery smiled.

"There was another blind man who had a dog," Wendy went on. "When he got his sight back, he knew the shape he was petting was his dog. But then the dog turned sideways to walk across the room, and his shape looked different. And the man thought it was a different dog, even though he knew it had to be the same dog."

"Oh," Jeffery said, in a tone that showed he got it.

Wendy was satisfied, and the rest of us, listening from Inside, were relieved. Now maybe he would be able to help us.

READING ABOUT the newly sighted also helped me understand why I had felt so good when I first lost the Atmosphere, and why, a year later, I began to feel disconnected and isolated in the real world. A newly sighted person might bump into things in a familiar place, but when he shuts his eyes and uses his blind ways of navigating—counting the number of steps to the top of the stairs—he does fine. After a while, though, he loses the ability to revert to his blind ways. He can't return to the blind world, but he doesn't yet possess all the concepts and skills necessary for living in the sighted world.

I, too, was in limbo. For the first year after I lost the Atmosphere, I had been able to re-enter it now and then. It happened automatically, whenever the real world became too hard to navigate. But the Atmosphere wasn't the same as it used to be, because I no longer had two versions of people I knew personally. Jeffery wasn't in the Atmosphere anymore. Instead, it was populated with people I'd never met, like Oprah, and Richard Kluft, whose articles on MPD/DID I had read in the clinical literature. While their in-person versions didn't know me, at least their Atmosphere versions did. Now I couldn't return to even that watered-down Atmosphere, but I hadn't yet mastered all the concepts and skills necessary for living in the real world.

Limbo explained why I felt disconnected from other people, but not why I felt disconnected from myself. I was still missing a piece of the puzzle. While Jeffery and I tried to figure out what it was, life was getting more difficult, both in and out of sessions. I was now painfully self-conscious whenever I spoke to people, whether it was to Jeffery or any of my friends, relatives, or coworkers. I felt like a fledgling person, unsure of what to say or do even in situations where I used to feel confident.

Wendy was still the only one of us who felt comfortable with Jeffery. In sessions, she was out most of the time, reporting as faithfully as she could on what the rest of us were thinking and feeling. But the more she talked, the more someone Inside was embarrassed by her singsong voice. One day, my hand swooped out and slapped my face.

"Don't do that," Jeffery said. "Why did you hit her?"

My shoulders shrugged.

"They think I talk like a baby," Wendy said. "It embarrasses them."

"I like the way you talk," Jeffery said.

"*You* do, but no one else does. You know, I think we still have MPD. Do you think we do?"

It was strange to hear Wendy's voice, which I heard as not-mine, express my thought. Yet it wasn't that I didn't know I had MPD/DID. It was more that I didn't acknowledge or remember it all the time, and then something like one part of me slapping another happened to remind me.

"Yes," Jeffery said.

"That explains a lot," Wendy said. "And you know what else? I think there are some of us who never had the Atmosphere. Or even knew about it."

"There are ones of you who were always able to make connections in the skin world," Jeffery said. "All along, you had times when you did feel connected. In the library. In your writing class. With your nephews. But during the times you felt disconnected, you didn't know about the times you were connected."

"So why can't the ones who could make connections before let us feel connected now?"

"I'm not sure. That's something we still have to find out."

AS THE MORNING WRITING went down one path, doubled back, then took another, I realized I had gone through a major internal shift apart from losing the Atmosphere. I still had MPD/DID—a fact I had almost lost sight of in the cataclysmic change of losing the Atmosphere—and my internal players were still the same, but their influence in the overall mix was different. Wendy remained dominant in therapy, but outside of sessions, there had been an upheaval in the way I perceived the world, a jump from a child-dominated orientation to an adult one. One morning I typed:

> Another thing that is upsetting lately is waking up and finding yourself middle-aged, 61 going on 62. What happened to the rest of your life?

I wrote many paragraphs about the distinction between event time and perception time.

> If you lose event-time, you don't know certain events took place. We know events that took place. But most of the time, we perceived them through a 6-year-old lens. When we were at a party, all dressed up the same grownup way everyone else was, we looked grownup, but we really weren't. So we weren't able to participate in the conversation as an equal. We were always on the periphery of life. Now, all of a sudden, we feel entitled to participate in adult conversations. That part is nice. But it was too much of a leap... losing 55 years of perception-time and waking up in a world you have to get used to.

Jeffrey wrote back:

> Yes, losing 55 years is very big. As recovery progresses, the little ones begin to grow, but there is much that has been lost, and the older ones have to grieve for the time they have lost.

It helped to know he got it, but I couldn't grieve on demand. The next morning I wrote:

If your mother dies, people understand, and they give you sympathy. If you are mourning for the lost years of your perception, no one understands, so you can't mourn in public, and you can't get sympathy.... Maybe we have to sit shiva for ourselves. For the ones of us who never got a chance to live the missing years. To mourn them and talk about them for a certain period of time, the way you do in the Jewish religion. But when you sit shiva, lots of people come around to visit with you, and bring you food, and let you cry with them and laugh with them. You can't sit shiva by yourself.

GRADUALLY, I BEGAN TO REALIZE what the missing puzzle piece was. Besides Atmosphere/real-world limbo, there was child/adult limbo. It wasn't a coincidence that losing the Atmosphere and suddenly growing up had happened at the same time. When the Atmosphere faded, I was still predominantly a six-year-old. On the surface, I had task-specific adults who went to work, class, and some social events, but except for the few Prague Spring years immediately before my breakup with Mike, I never had a through-and-through, all-purpose adult. Now, in my new landscape, I was forming real—not just surface—connections with Outside people. I needed somebody who could relate to them. So I had created a 60-year-old—a personality who arrived fully grown—to deal with the world I found myself in. To give her dominance, I'd had to push aside all the parts I had come to think of collectively as me, to ignore any hint that I still had MPD/DID.

Understanding that made things a little easier. But I still felt like a stranger to myself, and I felt Jeffery wasn't the same person I had known before. I didn't know how to relate to him. A children's picture book, *Farfallina and Marcel,* helped me make sense of it all. I kept a copy in Jeffery's office and often asked him to read it to me at the end of a session.

It's the story of the friendship between Farfallina, a caterpillar, and Marcel, a gosling. When they play hide-and-seek, Farfallina hides on a low leaf, because Marcel can't climb, and Marcel hides behind a nearby tree, because Farfallina moves slowly. One day, Farfallina says she doesn't feel right, and she climbs a tree. Marcel waits for her below. Days pass, and still Farfallina doesn't come down.

Marcel finally leaves. A long time later, when Marcel has grown into a goose with large wings and a long neck, Farfallina comes out of her cocoon as an orange butterfly. Farfallina and Marcel don't recognize each other, but one day they start a conversation and find out they each feel sad about losing a friend. As they begin to do things together, they feel they have known one another a long time, even though they think they just met. Eventually, they discover they are the friends they thought they had lost. They look different, but they're still the same inside.

As Jeffery read, Wendy would lean in to turn the pages, and others of us peeked out to look at the pictures.

"So even though you're Skin," Wendy often said at the end of the story, "You're still the same Jeffery who was in the Atmosphere. Right?"

"That's right," he would answer.

We would lock eyes with him for a moment, and I'd start to feel a connection, to know he was there inside himself, the way he used to be. It felt good, but scary. I couldn't hold it.

"I think it's time to have toast," Wendy would say in her perky way, and, leaving the book on the floor, we'd go into the kitchen.

Our toast ritual had evolved. When it first began, I always made Jeffery's the same as mine. But as he became more of a real person, I saw, from little things he said, that he didn't like his toast the way I did. I preferred mine crisp, with lots of crunch. He liked his less well done, with soft insides. So now, I took his piece out first and left mine in a little longer. We were separate people. ▪

CHAPTER 41

My Mother's Keeper

THE PHONE CALLS CAME at all hours that spring of 2007.

From my 92-year-old mother's aide: "Your mom just hit me with her cane."

From 97-year-old Aunt Mollie: "Please tell Beckie to stop screaming in the hall."

From Mollie's aide: "Please don't let Beckie come down here anymore. She's upsetting Mollie."

From my cousin Robert, Mollie's son: "Vivian, you gotta do something. Your mother's waking up the whole building."

It was my mother's calls that disconcerted me most.

"Vivian, this is your mother. I don't know where I am. I may be up near Peekskill. I don't know the name of the town." Her voice was calm as she imparted all the information she believed I would need to help her. "I thought I would be able to get a train to take me home to Brooklyn. But they tell me, or the one that's powerful tells me, that I am in— She says I will go to my house if I want to, but she doesn't tell me how to do it or why to do it."

"You *are* in your apartment," I said. "Look to your left. Do you see the picture of Nona and Papoo?" I explained that she had fallen, and the woman with her, "the one that's powerful," had been there for a month, to help her with things like dressing, going to the toilet, and cooking.

"I don't need help dressing or in the toilet," my mother said, "and I can go to a restaurant when I'm hungry."

After the first few calls, I realized that with no short-term memory, my mother didn't know she wasn't as capable as she'd been before. And her apartment probably didn't seem like home because a stranger—someone who had come into her life too recently to enter her memory bank—was sleeping in the living room. I began saying things like, "Wherever you are, I'm going to know how to find you." That sometimes calmed her.

My mother's decline had escalated dramatically that year, since the day in March when she'd fallen and also, my brother and I found out subsequently, had a heart attack. In the year leading up to that March day, the worst had been her short-term-memory loss and three other falls, two of which resulted in concussions and severe bleeding from face and scalp wounds. Each time we'd gotten home from the emergency room, she'd been adamant. She did *not* want an aide. Though she lived alone in her apartment, she wasn't alone in the building. Robert lived directly below her, and Aunt Mollie and her aide were downstairs in what used to be Nona's apartment. So after I stayed with my mother in Brooklyn for a day or two, I went back to Manhattan and resumed my life.

Except for the falls, it had been a relatively peaceful year for my mother. I spoke to her every day and visited weekly, when I would help her write checks to pay her bills. In other ways, she was self-sufficient. She walked to the supermarket on 20th Avenue, to the bank on Bay Parkway, and to the JCH for the daily seniors' lunch with her cronies at Table 2. She sorted through each day's junk mail, setting aside the holistic catalogs in case she wanted to send for something, tearing off the address labels from the others before adding them to the recycling pile. She had breakfast at McDonald's daily, and at least once a week she ate dinner out, usually with me, sometimes with my brother and Mara. She always insisted on paying and gave us a little extra for ourselves because, "It shouldn't cost you anything to visit your mother." Every evening at 7:00, she went down to Aunt Mollie's apartment, and they watched *Jeopardy* and *Wheel of Fortune*. At 8:00, she went upstairs to bed.

It had been a good year for me, too—a renaissance of sorts. The limbo era was finally coming to an end, and the moments I felt like a foreigner in the real world were now the exception. No particular event marked the turning point. One day I just noticed I was relaxed with people. My MPD/DID, while not gone, was more contained. During sessions, I was sometimes dismayed to hear a child's voice coming out of my mouth, but, otherwise, Inside didn't interfere with my daily life.

I was working as a librarian part time, singing in a choir, attending writing workshops, and volunteering at SeniorNet, where I taught computer skills to older adults. I felt like a full participant in these activities, not an outsider, and was making new friends. Though I hadn't gone on any dates for more than 15 years, Jim and I had maintained contact and spoke frequently.

I was also addressing the 25-year mess in my apartment, not merely stacking everything into neat piles only to watch them erupt a few days later when I searched for something. This time, I was starting at the bottom, reorganizing my closet, drawers, and filing cabinets, throwing out things I didn't need. When all was in order, I planned to buy new carpeting, hire someone to wash the windows, and invite people for my first dinner party since the breakup with Mike 26 years before.

Best of all, after some fits and starts, the rapprochement I was having with my mother was flourishing. I had come to genuinely appreciate her. She was caring of others, dignified, undemanding, and grateful for the attention I was showing her. "It's love at second sight," she said to me one day in a restaurant. "I'm so lucky you still want to be with me." When I said goodbye after my weekly visits and began the drive back to Manhattan, I would see her in my rearview mirror, waving from the doorway at the top of the stoop. Always, when I got home, there would be a message on my answering machine with the words she couldn't say in person. "Vivian, it's six-thirty now. I hope you have a safe trip home. And thank you for being with me, Vivian. It's a pleasure to have you, and it's a pleasure to be your mother now. 'Cause I know sometimes I used to be nasty to you, but now I'm not. And I love you. And thank you, thank you, thank you. Bye-bye, Vivian."

My only complaint to Jeffery was that I couldn't *feel*. I was always in neutral, with no highs or lows. He said that was because some parts of me were progressing at a different rate than others. In order to allow those who were getting along in the Outside world to flourish, I had to squash down anyone who lagged behind. He supposed that was Emily. His theory sounded plausible. I hadn't felt Emily's pain or longing in a while. Nor had I done any arts-and-crafts projects, and those had always been Emily's—hours when I had been happily absorbed sewing or stringing beads. Jeffery suggested I nurture Emily by allowing myself more time for crafts, so, in February, when one of my cousins told me she was involved with an arts retreat weekend in the country, scheduled for July, I decided I would go.

I hadn't yet sent in my deposit when my mother had the March fall that changed her life and mine. Not only did her dementia instantly become full-blown—possibly from one concussion too many—but she was so weak from the heart attack and the vast amount of blood she lost from her head wound that she could barely stand. The ER resident felt she should be admitted so her heart could be monitored. But over the course of our 12-hour stay—my brother joined me for the last six—my mother became progressively more agitated, not remembering she'd fallen, not understanding where she was or why she had to remain on the stretcher and use a bedpan when she wanted a regular toilet. My brother and I, feeling she would only become more upset as an inpatient, brought her home and hired a sleep-in aide.

At first, my mother seemed to welcome the aide's help, but after a week or so, when she was able to walk again, very unsteadily, she screamed when the aide wouldn't let her leave the apartment in the middle of the night to go to work. To escape from her, my mother would go down to Aunt Mollie, yelling the whole way because the woman she was trying to get rid of accompanied her on the staircase to prevent her from falling. She shrieked so much that Mollie started locking her out.

I was the one all the parties on 74th Street called when the house seemed about to detonate, not my brother. My phone became an instrument of torture, triggering an adrenalin spike every time it rang. When I couldn't troubleshoot by talking, I cancelled whatever I had scheduled—work, SeniorNet, dinner dates, therapy sessions—and drove to Brooklyn, a ride that took anywhere from 45 minutes to double that, depending on the time of day. Those drives were in addition to my frequent nonemergency trips: to take my mother to the doctor, to enroll her in an adult daycare program, to bring food, even to do the laundry—she was so wobbly, I was afraid she might fall if her aide left her to go to the washing machine in the basement.

I concluded each visit by taking my mother out to eat, our custom, which she still expected. But our dining excursions no longer gave me pleasure. The mother I had so recently found had been replaced by someone who couldn't make eye contact or have a regular conversation. When we got back from the restaurant, I helped her up the stairs and into a chair in the living room next to her aide, then began the goodbye process.

"I'm going now," I said, kissing her cheek.

"Why are you leaving me with a stranger?"

I explained who the woman was. My mother wrote it down. Again I said goodbye. Again she asked, I explained, she wrote. After several more iterations—between each, she hobbled from room to room with her walker, unable to settle—I felt the boundary between us dissolve and her confusion seep into my own brain, as if I were the one struggling to fit my perceptions into a reality defined by others. Each time, when I closed the apartment door behind me and walked through the hall to the street, I felt like a mother leaving a distraught child in kindergarten.

I began to get myself back as soon as I got into my car. This was my territory: my seat cushion, my maps, my radio stations. I checked the traffic report to determine the best route home, then connected my MP3 player and turned on my recording of *Heidi*. Children's stories, the only ones I could listen to lately, calmed me better than the tranquilizers Jeffery had recently prescribed at my request, pills I was hesitant to take too often because I drove a lot, and also because I was afraid of becoming addicted. A message was invariably waiting for me when I got home. "Vivian, I can't leave a message after the beep, because I need to talk to you. I am a prisoner in my own house, and I need *you*, Vivian, to help me get out...."

I would call to say I had just been with her—she had no recollection of my visit—and explain who the woman in her apartment was. I waited while she asked her aide for a pen and paper so she could write down what I said, then hung up, knowing she would probably call again in a few minutes.

I began sleeping with my eyeglasses on, and also the light, ready to spring into action at a moment's notice. I no longer read the newspaper, watered my plants, paid my bills. The mess in my apartment grew worse. I rarely took showers or cooked; I picked up snacks at convenience stores and ate while I hurried down the street.

In the midst of all this, I forgot that my 65th birthday was approaching until Marvin and Mara invited me out to dinner. Their call seemed to come from another planet, a place where my mother was background, not foreground, and people made restaurant reservations. I had no way of navigating to that world. But the date was a week away, an inconceivable amount of time in my minute-to-minute existence, so it was safe to say "That would be really nice."

When the day came, I still didn't realize the dinner, set for 7:00 at a restaurant near my apartment, was imminent. That afternoon, driving to Brooklyn on yet another emergency trip, I felt I was in a Category 5 hurricane, trying to rescue the only other survivor, my mother, when it was likely we would both perish.

While the Driver me, free of any distress, kept the recommended three-second distance from the vehicle in front of me, I let out howls so deep they grated my throat. As I listened from someplace outside myself, I realized it had been several years since I'd heard them. The MPD/DID was no longer in remission. That wasn't so bad. It would help me get through this. The howls gave way to whispered nonsense syllables. "Ah-*lee*-kah. No kish-*mah*-nee." I wondered what they meant. My throat felt raw. I worried I was getting sick, until I remembered the howls. "Mah nish-ta-*nah*." That one I recognized. The start of the Passover question: *Why is this night different from all other nights?*

I turned on my recording of *The Wizard of Oz,* read by the same grandfatherly narrator I knew from *Heidi.* We were up to the part where the Scarecrow and the Tin Man were carrying a sleeping Dorothy out of the poppy field to safety. I listened with a child's heart, thoroughly engrossed. At the same time, with an adult's mind, I came to a new appreciation of the story. Dorothy, the Scarecrow, the Tin Man and the Cowardly Lion were the original support group.

I wished I had a support group. Marvin helped with one-time things—removing the door from my mother's room so her walker could fit through; buying a microwave oven and arranging for cable TV installation, items the aide expected—and he also took my mother out to eat every two weeks. If I asked him to do something specific, he would, but he couldn't give me emotional support, and that's what I needed most. I wouldn't find out until many months later that he was dealing with distressing issues of his own.

A few blocks from my mother's house, I turned off the story to give myself time to switch from someone who needed care to someone who could give it.

During the next few hours, I took my mother to the doctor, got her a prescription for a different antipsychotic, and filled it at the pharmacy. We went out to eat. She said she lost her purse in some building in Peekskill—would I drive her there to search for it? I knew it would do no good to tell her Peekskill was 60 miles away, she hadn't been there in years, and her purse was probably at home, so I drove her up and down some Brooklyn streets, inquiring whether this or that looked like the place. Each time, she said no, go a few more blocks. After ten minutes, I convinced her to continue the search tomorrow. I brought her home, gave her aide instructions about the new medication, and went through the goodbye process.

When I arrived at my apartment a little after 6:00, there was a message from my mother on my machine. I phoned her back. She wanted to call the police because it was getting late and my father wasn't home yet. When I couldn't convince her he'd been dead for 14 years, I told her I would make some inquiries and get back to her.

"Thank you," she said in a relieved voice, and we hung up.

My head and every muscle ached, as if I had the flu. I put on my nightgown and got into bed, intending to call my brother and sister-in-law and say I was sick. But before I could pick up the phone, an internal taskmaster sprang me out of bed and into the shower, my first in a week. I dried off, rummaged through my drawers for a clean blouse, then dressed it up with dangling earrings, a beaded rope necklace, and a black satin shawl. Soon I was hurrying down Broadway on the 15-minute walk to the restaurant, threading my way through people carrying attachés, paper-wrapped flowers, and Citarella specialty food bags. I threw my shoulders back and checked my reflection in a store window. Good. I didn't look out of place.

Marvin, Mara, and my 27-year-old nephew, Jesse, were already seated when I arrived. It was good to see them.

"Sorry I'm a little late," I said as they rose to kiss me.

After we placed our drink orders, they gave me a Peace Lily plant that had two delicate white flowers. "Thank you," I said, genuinely pleased.

TWO MONTHS AFTER the March fall-cum-heart-attack, my mother fell again. Her aide came out of the bathroom to find her on the floor in a pool of blood that was flowing copiously from her right hand. She had apparently tried to catch her balance by reaching for a nearby shopping cart, but as she dropped to the floor, her hand slid over the metal manufacturer's label, and she sliced off a half inch from two fingers, bone and all.

After inpatient surgery at Lutheran Hospital in Brooklyn, my mother had no recollection of the fall or her injury and didn't understand why her hand was bandaged or why she was forced to stay in bed. I don't think she even knew she was in a hospital. The aide who had been with her at home was with her here, too. When the aide couldn't stop her from trying to pull off the dressing, the nurses, competent but overworked, tied her wrists to the bedrails.

For a week, my mother alternated between howling for hours, trying to get free, and being medicated into a coma-like stupor. Each of her shrieks rent my heart on my daily visits, and the heavy breathing of her drugged sleep made me feel I was in that bed myself, trying to fight my way out of a Thorazine sinkhole. At the same time, like a bear defending her cub, I held off the hospital social worker, who wanted my mother discharged to the first nursing home that would take her, regardless of its reputation; the good ones all had waiting lists and said even if they didn't, they wouldn't accept someone with a "behavior problem" like my mother's. I arranged instead for her to be transferred to Beth Israel Medical Center's state-of-the-art geriatric psychiatry unit, hoping they could devise a psych-med cocktail that would leave my mother calm without being so medicated she couldn't open her eyes. My brother and I agreed that when she left Beth Israel, she should go to a long-term nursing home, not back to her apartment.

Far from being in a renaissance, I now walked around with a jagged boulder embedded in my heart. It was there when I smiled and said, "May I help you?" to a library patron; when I walked past the outdoor café on the way to my garage, stifling the moans that floated out on my breath as if they were part of my metabolism; when I washed tea mugs in my kitchen, sobbing without restraint, hoping the sounds traveling through the exhaust vent to other apartments weren't identifiable as me. This was what I'd been longing for, I told myself: the ability to feel. Now I had it, and it was overwhelming. Still, I wouldn't have wanted to return to my nonfeeling state. For the first time in a long while, I felt real.

Something else good was happening: I discovered I could talk to people about what was upsetting me. Unlike my mental-illness difficulties, which made others feel uncomfortable and want to keep their distance, my problems with my mother made them come closer. Nearly everyone, it seemed—library colleagues, writing friends, singers in my choir, people I was still in touch with from my old MetLife job—had an aging-parent story of their own or knew someone who did. All it took was a mention of my mother for them to open up to me. I had never before felt part of the collective human experience. It was as if my mother were giving me a gift. I had lost her, but that loss was propelling me the last way out of the long, dark, limbo tunnel and giving me life in the real world.

I FOUND A PARKING SPACE in front of Jeffery's building, turned off the motor, and glanced at the clock. 3:47. Thirteen minutes until our session. As I felt my muscles go slack, I realized how tense I'd been. It made sense, considering everything I'd crammed in today. I'd driven my 20-year-old nephew, Matthew, and all his gear to the camp bus in the Bronx for the start of his summer counselor job. I dropped off two more bags of my mother's clothes at the nursing home in another part of the Bronx so they could be labeled with her name and future room number: 541. I returned to Manhattan, left my car in my Upper West Side garage, and took two crowded trains to Beth Israel on the East Side to see my mother. Then I took two trains back, retrieved my car, and drove here.

Tomorrow, my mother would be discharged from Beth Israel. I hadn't told her she would be moved to a nursing home, only that she was "going to leave this hospital." I didn't know how much she understood. For my sake as well as hers, I hoped it was little. It was hard enough for me to grasp that she would never go back to the house on 74th Street her father had built in 1926, when she was 12, the house she had lived in for most of her 92 years.

A bird landed on a branch of the tree that shaded my windshield. I took a deep, three-part yoga breath—belly, ribs, chest—hoping to enter the serenity of the world outside my window. Something in me opened. I started to cry, jammed back the tears, and got an instant headache. I fished through my backpack for water and aspirin, swallowed three, then pulled out my phone to leave Jeffery a message. Usually, if I didn't want to wait indoors, I said, "I'm walking in the forest," meaning the nature preserve near his building, and he joined me for our walk-and-talk loop. Today, I said, "I'm in my car. It's parked in front, a little to the left."

A yellow school bus pulled up, red hexagon stop sign springing out. I checked the clock—4:02—then watched through my windshield as a small boy with a too-big backpack got off and ran into his waiting mother's arms. The stop sign retracted. Seconds later, the bus, the boy, and his mother were gone.

This idyllic landscape was a farce. So was Jeffery. He thought I had a life ahead of me, seemed not to grasp that since I turned 65 I was a senior, just like my mother, and it was only a matter of days before I followed her into decline and dementia.

My only hope was that I still had MPD/DID, that someone existed within me who wasn't old and decrepit. If I didn't have MPD/DID, if this was who I was permanently, I might as well be dead. Jeffery said there was no question I still had it. He said it explained how, while I believed all I did was lie in bed unable to move, I'd really been quite busy: I'd used the three weeks my mother had been in Beth Israel to visit nursing homes in Brooklyn, Manhattan, and the Bronx; and I'd resisted accepting any, despite pressure from Beth Israel's social worker, until I found one that had a good dementia unit *and* an available bed *and* was only a short drive from my apartment so I could visit often. He said it explained how, at the same time that I felt my life was over, I'd actually been connecting with people in a very real way.

Intellectually, I knew Jeffery was right. I had done these things. They amazed me, because I didn't feel anyone else in me, least of all someone capable—and I didn't feel a connection with anyone in the real world. I couldn't even cry anymore.

A shadow darkened the air. I turned my head to see Jeffery's face in the passenger window. I pointed to the seat next to me. He got in, adding his presence to my space without disturbing it by talking.

I would have liked to stay like that forever, communing the way we did when he was still in the Atmosphere, but there was only so much that skin-container Jeffery could intuit. If I wanted him to know what I was feeling or what had been happening since we last spoke, I'd have to talk.

"Tomorrow my mother will go to the place she'll be in for the rest of her life," I said.

Jeffery's nod unleashed me, and I felt a tear slide down my cheek. Ignoring it, I lowered my eyes and continued in a steady voice. "She doesn't scream anymore, and she's not asleep all the time, but she can't make eye contact, and I can tell she's agitated inside. I wouldn't mind if she were delusional. It would be fine if she thought she was in Europe, or that my father was still alive, as long as she was peaceful. But I don't think she'll ever be peaceful again." I looked up as a new idea gave me hope. "Could this be from the medication?"

"It's possible," Jeffery said. "I don't know."

That wasn't the answer I wanted. "What a horrible state to live in," I said, my voice quavering.

Another tear rolled down. Jeffery lifted his hand to brush it away. I checked him before he reached my face. Only five minutes ago, I couldn't feel anything. I didn't want premature comfort that would stop my sorrow and make me dead again. He understood and pulled his hand back. I loved him for this.

"She's not the mother I knew anymore," I said. "I'm in mourning for someone who is still living."

We sat in silence, his eyes on me, mine looking through the window at a leaf on the ground. Then I began to sob, grief pouring out of me like lava. At the same time, from someplace outside myself, I observed how satisfying it was to cry if you were with someone who understood, and I noticed that I wasn't self-conscious about my twisted face or dripping nose.

When I stopped heaving, I pulled a tissue from my pocket. Gently, Jeffery took it from me, and I let him wipe my face.

We eventually moved the session to his office. When it was over, at my request, Jeffery walked me back to my car. He got into the passenger seat for our goodbyes.

"Bye, Jeffery," I began, locking eyes with him.

"Bye, Vivian."

"Bye, Jeffery."

"Wait." He looked away.

I took in a breath and held it. He had never interrupted the three-time goodbye sequence before.

"There's something we forgot to discuss."

"What?" I whispered, drawing back against the door.

"Next Wednesday is July Fourth. I could see you another day."

An executive me took over, told him Monday or Tuesday would be OK. He said probably Tuesday at 8:30 in the evening, he would call me. I knew he wasn't sure because he didn't have his calendar with him, but I didn't like to think about his calendar. I still didn't like knowing he had other things scheduled besides me.

"Can we start over?" I asked.

"Sure."

We locked eyes, and this time, the goodbyes went smoothly. A few seconds after the last "Bye, Vivian," he broke his gaze, then got out to stand on the corner and lift his hand in a wave that froze, like a photograph. Part of me still thought Jeffery stayed that way until I saw him again. Another part knew he went about his life in the intervening week. A barrier between the two parts allowed me to preserve the nonmoving Jeffery. He was like my home. I could never go out into the world—to work, the store, the hospital—if I didn't have an apartment to come back to, four walls holding not only my furniture, but my essence. As long as Jeffery stayed right there, I could do whatever I had to do tomorrow and the rest of the week.

I waved back, and the Driver me pulled away. Someone wanted to look in the rearview mirror to see Jeffery with his hand in the air. Someone else said not to. Though he knew how important this was and wouldn't cross the street and go into his building while I could see him—we'd done this many times—what if he forgot? I didn't look. A moment later, I turned right at the light, out of danger.

Another minute, and I was on the parkway. My cell phone rang. A call from the Beth Israel social worker, I thought, as I adjusted my hands-free earbud, but it was Jeffery.

"Eight-thirty next Tuesday is good," he said.

"Why didn't you leave a message on my home machine?" I tried to control my panic.

"I wanted to tell you right away, so you wouldn't think I forgot."

Now you're not on the corner!

"Oh," he said, as if he just realized it. "I'm sorry."

"Can we do it over?"

"Good idea."

"Bye, Jeffery," I whispered while the Driver kept driving.

"Bye, Vivian."

"Bye, Jeffery."

"Bye, Vivian."

"Bye, Jeffery."

"Bye, Vivian."

I hung up quickly, before I could hear a click from his end that said he was no longer in the rearview mirror.

As my insides settled, I thought how lucky I was to have him. And he was right. I did still have MPD/DID. Otherwise, I could never believe he was standing on the corner at the same time that I knew he was not on the corner. I saw, too, that the Atmosphere had returned—not completely, but enough to let me believe something as preposterous as Jeffery remaining in suspended animation all week. This may have been a relapse, but it was OK. MPD/DID and the Atmosphere were old friends, come back to help me through this stressful time. ■

CHAPTER 42

Water Doesn't Flow Uphill

"I'LL JUST TAKE FIFTEEN MINUTES to get there," I said to Jeffery. "I hope you'll say yes."

My mother had been in the nursing home for five days. I thought things would magically get better the instant she arrived—she would participate in activities and blossom. Instead she slept most of the day in the common room and was jittery when awake. Still unable to separate myself from her, I felt her lethargy, confusion, and agitation in my own body, not only on my daily visits but all the time. Neither of us was doing well.

Jeffery was partially back in the Atmosphere, but not enough to automatically know everything I was experiencing. He'd often said he could understand things through my talking about them, but I still wasn't used to that way of communicating. If he actually visited my mother, I told him, he would see how she was, and, by extension, how I was.

"If you think that's the best way to spend our time together, I would go," he said.

When we arrived, we found my mother standing with her walker near the nurse's medication cart, drinking from a paper cup. She held it out to me.

"Vivian, what's this?" she asked, as if I'd been with her all along.

"Hi, Mom. It looks like apple juice." I tried to hug her. She was stiff and didn't hug back.

I introduced Jeffery as "my friend," and the three of us walked at my mother's slow pace to her room, which she didn't know was hers, despite the framed photographs of her relatives on the wall and her coverlet from Brooklyn on her bed. She talked but couldn't make eye contact or have a regular conversation, and her face was tense. I tried to read her 90th birthday book with her: the compilation of remembrances from everyone in our large family. It appeared to have no meaning for her. She wanted to get-up-sit-down-go-someplace-she-didn't-know-where. Jeffery didn't say much. We left after 15 minutes.

On the drive back, he was silent.

"What do you think?" I asked.

"It's a nice place. It's clean and doesn't smell like urine."

"What do you think about my *mother*?"

He didn't answer, and I began to wonder whether he'd heard me. Then he said, "There are some things in life you can't do anything about."

Was he talking to himself or me? "What do you mean?"

"There are some things you can't change." His voice sounded hollow.

He's more affected by my mother than I am, I thought with shock. I tried to revive him, saying, in as upbeat a voice as I could, "At least she's not tied to her bed anymore."

"Yes."

Back in his office, with an hour left of our double session, Jeffery again said there were some things you couldn't change.

"I need to talk to you about my mother," I said, "but you can't help me the way you are."

I wasn't angry. When he was solid, I could pout if he disappointed me, but now I felt abandoned. Retroactively. Throughout the past three months, Jeffery had said he understood what things were like for me, but he hadn't understood until he saw for himself. Talking, the skin-world way of communicating, didn't work well.

"Maybe when you're away in August, I'll look for a grief counselor, one who specializes in mourning for people who are still living," I said. "I don't even know whether such a thing exists. Or maybe I'll join a support group for dementia caregivers."

Jeffery pulled a volume from his bookcase and held it out to me. *The 36-Hour Day*. "I already looked at this in the library," I said, handing it back. "I don't want a book. I want a live person."

"You have me."

"No, I don't. You're strange."

"I know." He met my eyes. "I'm sorry."

It didn't occur to me until months later that he might have had a similar experience in his own life. All I knew was that Jeffery was supposed to be my rock. He wasn't supposed to crumble.

THE ARTS WEEKEND in the country was to start two days later. My mother was far from OK, but she was being cared for by a remarkably compassionate staff at the nursing home, and my brother would be around for emergency calls. I decided to go.

I registered for watercolor landscape painting, then settled into one of the rustic cabins that ringed the lake. Except for my cousin and her husband, I knew none of the 70 people there.

There were three other students in my workshop. The first morning, the instructor gave a 15-minute talk about how landscapes were masses of color and shading. In a series of mountain ranges, for instance, the farthest away always seemed lighter, the closest, darker. To be balanced, a painting should contain four types of masses: light, average-light, average-dark, dark. It should also contain bold accents in the lighter parts. He demonstrated how to squeeze dabs of paint from tubes onto the pallet in a rainbow sequence, and how to wet the paper before we began. That was it. The rest was painting.

All my life, I'd had to be the best at whatever I did. It was the only way I knew to connect with real people and get them to like me, especially teachers. I had never been good at drawing or painting, and in the watercolor workshop two of the students were accomplished artists. There was no chance I could be the best. I found that liberating. With nothing to strive for, I could relax.

The other beginner and I soon began talking. First, it was only about our paintings. "Does this look like average-dark?" But by the end of the first day, I had told her about my mother and found that she had a mother situation, too, and siblings who were trying to work out the sharing of her mother's care.

Life was easy, slow, and the conversation, both serious and mundane, was unscripted. One of the accomplished artists, overweight, talked about her health and diet, and I saw that everyone had problems, even if they were good at something. I felt accepted in this group. People liked me for me, not my perfect artwork. I could even laugh when the instructor looked at my painting of the lake and said, "Water is always horizontal. It doesn't flow uphill." Leaning over my shoulder, he took my brush and drew one line that made everything look right.

JEFFERY AND I BEGAN our first session after the arts retreat with a walk in the nature preserve. I told him I thought my mother was depressed. She kept her eyes closed most of the day, even when she wasn't sleeping.

"I wonder whether she would be less depressed at home," I said.

"That's not an option." Jeffery's voice was uncharacteristically clipped.

"I *know* it's not an option!" I wanted to punch him. Instead, I kicked a tree. "I'm talking hypo*thet*ically."

"I get it."

He probably did, but part of me kept wanting to punch. At the same time, another part saw clearly, as if I were a textbook example, that this was how a baby must feel when he hits his mother because he needs something from her, but she can't figure out what it is and nothing she tries works. I told this to Jeffery.

"That's exactly right," he said.

As soon as we got back to his office I took out my computer, now my preferred method of communication with him.

> There are some things he has a hard time handling, so he can't help us with them.

I often referred to Jeffery in the third person when I wrote, as if I were telling a Jeffery who understood about a Jeffery who didn't.

I passed the computer to him and waited while he typed, then handed it back to me.

> The last part of that sentence is the tragic one. I can have a hard time and still be close enough to be able to help you, but you assume I am totally useless to you at that moment. When we say things aloud, that helps me, and I am more likely to be able to go back and handle it.

I looked up at him for a second, then began typing.

It's a little scary. He's not solid for some things, and
he is solid for others. It means we have to be wary of
him. We can count on him partially, but not all the
way. We don't know where to put our feet—where the
ground will hold us, or where it will fall through from
our weight.

Jefferey's answer:

To some extent, talk is the way to determine that.
I don't always give the true answer, but often, by
talking, we can make it OK.

Talking. The skin way of communicating. Something imperfect I wasn't yet used to.

A FEW SESSIONS LATER, Jeffery and I were again typing, still the best way I had of staying in an adult mode with him. I wrote that I'd been thinking about how he was there for me sometimes but not all the time, and I realized that's how real people were. They weren't perfect, like the Atmosphere, but they could still be pretty good. *Partial* was a characteristic of the real world. I was learning how to piece together all the partials to get something that could sustain me the way the Atmosphere had. I typed a question.

Does everyone in the skin world live in this partial way?

I passed him the computer. A moment later he passed it back.

When you see people comfortable, you imagine they
must be comfortable on an Atmosphere level, and
they're really not. They're comfortable on a partial level.

I put down the computer. "That's so tricky," I said aloud. It was Wendy's voice.

"Partial feels like settling," he said, speaking in response to my talking, "but actually, what you're settling for is what everybody takes for granted life has to offer. And it's just mediocre in comparison with the Atmosphere, because the Atmosphere is purified and ideal, and compared to that, regular life is a step down. But for everybody else, it's just what life is made of."

"Are you saying everybody feels this?"

"No. Most people don't feel a step down at all, because they've just grown up knowing that people are the way they are, which is partial. And if they ever had something like the Atmosphere, it was so early in their life that they don't remember it and they lost it a long time ago."

"If they don't feel it, they don't know what they lost. I know, because I had something better." Still Wendy's voice.

"The key thing about the Atmosphere," Jeffery said, holding my eyes, "is that you can have a total, complete connection, and that makes you feel very cozy and warm and safe. Compared to that, the partial meeting of two human beings feels like a disappointment. There's something similar with people who have addictions, because they experience levels of comfort or satisfaction or relaxation or even pleasure that are beyond what's normal to experience. So when they give up their drugs, it feels to them like the life that's satisfying to everybody else is not very satisfying."

Jeffery, as usual, did not talk down to Wendy. It was as if he assumed there was an adult there, too, listening from Inside. This was one of the things I loved about him. Now, from an adult point of view, I thought about what he said, though when I spoke, it was still with Wendy's voice.

"How do they get used to it?" she asked.

"At first it's disappointing, and then gradually they recalibrate, and the small pleasures and levels of comfort that other people experience begin to feel pretty good to them."

"So you change your standards. You settle for less, and you think it's just as good. How horrible." Wendy's voice, but with an adult understanding behind it.

"Life has high points and low points." Jeffery made wavy motions with his hand, as if drawing a cardiogram in the air. "You're always going up and down, and you feel good at the high points and pretty bad at the low points. But the high points, compared to the Atmosphere, aren't really very high at all. They're quite low, actually."

"Are you partial?" An adult voice this time.

"Yes, but it doesn't seem like it, because that's what life is like."

"In what way are you partial?"

"Partial in that the connections aren't perfect, and I'm seen some of the time, but not all of the time."

"You need to be seen to feel good?" This was a new understanding for us. An adult understanding.

"Yes, but I don't even imagine being seen perfectly all the time."

"Do I see you enough?" Wendy's voice again. Only she would have dared ask what we all wanted to know.

"Oh yes, you do. Yes."

I let out a sigh-laugh of relief. At least if I saw him, he wouldn't desert me.

"HER SKIN DOESN'T LOOK RIGHT," I said to the man in the copy shop a month later. "Is it possible to tone down the red?"

"I already did." His face was stony. "It's the best I can do."

"That's my mother." I tried to hold back tears as I pointed to the picture above the *Happy New Year* greeting. "She's ninety-two and in a nursing home. It's the Jewish New Year, and she's sending this to all her family and friends. I want it to look good, so they'll know she's OK."

Expression unchanged, he took the sheet and walked back to his machine.

I had been camera-stalking my mother on my daily visits, snapping her in the rare moments when she was awake and doing something normal: eating an ice cream pop, stringing colored wooden beads at a table with other residents, sitting on the patio. I needed to show the world—and myself—that she hadn't disappeared into a black hole. My plan was for her to sign each of these New Year cards herself. The surgery that closed the ends of her shortened fingers with skin flaps had been three months before, and they had healed cleanly. Yesterday, I had put a pen into her hand to see whether she could write her name. She could.

The man placed another sample in front of me.

"Much better. Thanks," I said. "I need thirty."

Face still somber, he disappeared behind his machine again.

After what seemed like forever, he approached the counter with a small pile. "It's twenty-eight fifty plus tax, but you can give me twenty-five."

His still immobile face belied his words, and it took a second for his generosity to register. "Thank you so much!"

With the barest of nods, he rang up the sale and handed me a receipt.

When I walked out of the store, my entire inner world lit up, as if the ends of a broken circuit had come together. This was exactly what Jeffery had been telling me: If you take a risk by showing people what you need, they'll usually respond positively. I headed home feeling a bond with everyone in the street. They might have been strangers, but they all had potential.

A few blocks from my apartment, I paused in front of a flower stand, drawn to a bunch of tiny pink blooms. I hesitated. They would only add to the clutter in my apartment, which had grown worse now that I was emptying out my mother's apartment. Better wait until I straightened up. But that could take months, and these particular flowers were tugging. I took out my wallet to pay for them, feeling a smile rise from deep within me and spread across my face. I knew that smile. It was Emily's, whenever I let her get something she wanted.

As I walked home with the flowers in my right hand and the cards in my left, it struck me that I was a member of the sandwich generation, caught between looking after a child and an elderly parent. I liked knowing I could take care of both. I was part of the real world now, with all the rights and responsibilities that came with citizenship. ∎

Epilogue

I AM SOMETIMES ASKED what healing looks like, whether there was a breakthrough moment, what became of all the people in me, whether I'm integrated, what the goal of therapy is.

While most of my parts are blended, I still have traces of MPD/DID, and the Atmosphere occasionally resurrects itself, particularly when I'm under stress, but neither is a major factor in my life anymore. There was no breakthrough moment. At some point, I simply became aware that I had crossed from feeling like a person with a mental illness to feeling like an ordinary person who happens to have a few problems. I can't say exactly when the change occurred—the process was gradual—but I can say it has made an enormous difference in the way I relate to people. I am fully present and sure of my right to be among them as a member of the same species.

The Atmosphere was more isolating for me than the MPD/DID. Though the attachments I had in it were perfect, I much prefer the imperfect connections I have with real people. And I have come to appreciate a new emotion: loneliness. The Atmosphere had shielded me from my dread of being on the Island of the Blue Dolphins, where there was no hope of ever finding another person. Now, I don't feel dread. I feel lonely. There is hope in being lonely. It means people are out there, and I can find them if I make the effort.

Because it took so long to get the proper diagnosis and treatment, I never married or had children. I miss that. But I am lucky to be the aunt of three wonderful nephews, a grandnephew and grandniece, and to have a network of warm cousins.

I also feel privileged to have been able to care for my mother. The nursing home eventually weaned her off all psych meds, and she spent a peaceful two and a half years there before dying at 95. On my daily visits, we went to the coffee shop, sat outside, or stayed in the common room. I felt good that I had been able to bring her in for a soft landing, that I was managing her pension income and paying her bills, and that I could intercede with the nursing home staff on her behalf. I especially felt good that her face lit up whenever she saw me in the doorway. Until my mother's last years, I had never experienced what it was like to be responsible for the welfare of another human being. It was a lot of work but immensely gratifying, her final gift to me.

I continue to work part time as a librarian, and to sing in a choir that has become like another extended family. I have also volunteered with Girls Write Now, an organization that pairs underserved high school girls who want to write with female mentors who are writers. For seven years I mentored two lovely young adults who have now moved on to college and jobs, and who probably don't know I get as much from our ongoing relationship as they do. And I have made deep connections with fellow students in my writing workshop. When they ask questions—"You refer to other people as humans. Did you feel human yourself?"—their motive is not to pry but to clarify. They are figuring out what I am trying to say and helping me say it better. I do the same for them.

I continue in therapy; I still have some young parts, and there are things about the real world I have yet to learn. But it is no longer the main event of my week, and it is no longer desperate. I don't see the goal of therapy as integration, or even being completely free of magical thinking. I see it as being comfortable in the world in whatever state I'm in, as long as that state doesn't interfere with interacting in a satisfying way with other people. Losing the Atmosphere brought me to a place where most people start therapy. I am fortunate that Jeffery is able to adapt to the changing me. He addresses the problems I currently have, which are more like those of patients whom therapists sometimes refer to as the "walking wounded" or the "walking worried." At the same time, he knows where I came from, so when I have an occasional relapse, he understands what is happening and is able to ensure it is short-lived.

Perhaps what has changed most is that I like my life. For years, I was able to get through each day only by telling myself that if things got so bad I couldn't stand them, I would kill myself. I can't pinpoint the exact moment that changed. I didn't even know it *had* changed until one day a number of years ago when I was in the dentist's office and he wanted to schedule my next six-month appointment. Until then, I was never certain I would be around in six months but made the appointment to humor him. This time, I realized I had every intention of keeping it. ▪

PHOTO ALBUM: 1998–Present

Photo Album: 1998–Present • 435

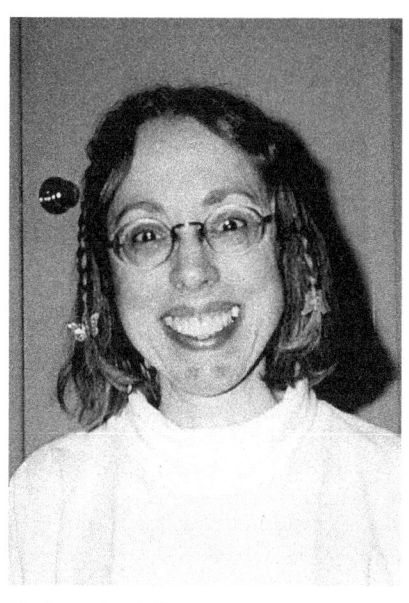

My therapist Jeffery took this photo when Wendy, a precocious six-year-old in me, was dominant. (Spring 2001)

My friend Susan was included in all my family's celebrations, including this Hawaiian-themed Bar Mitzvah. (May 2001)

My mother, Bea, 86, and Aunt Mollie, 91, at the same Hawaiian-themed Bar Mitzvah (May 2001)

With my lifelong friends, Susan (left) and Linda, at the 60th birthday party I threw for myself at a Manhattan restaurant (May 2002)

Marvin and me with my mother at the party we held in a Brooklyn restaurant to celebrate her 90th birthday (December 2004)

With my mother in a cousin's backyard on Long Island shortly before her health took a sharp downturn (Spring, circa 2006)

In the day room of the Bronx facility I found for my mother when Marvin and I had to move her to a nursing home. Note the two missing fingertips on her right hand, the result of a fall in 2007. (Circa 2008)

Taking the air outside my mother's nursing home (August 2008)

Linda, Susan, and me at our 50th Brooklyn College reunion (May 2014)

At work in a library in Westchester County (September 2018)

In St. Louis, about to accept a writing award from the American Jewish Press Association (June 2019)

Afterword

Retracing the Human Journey of Attachment

Jeffery Smith, MD

LOSING THE ATMOSPHERE IS MORE than an account of living with multiple personalities. In telling her story, Vivian opens a window onto the drama of early attachment: how, during our first three years, we become connected to our caregivers and, through those connections, gain awareness of ourselves and begin to forge the capacity to cope with strong emotions.

The best way I have of understanding Vivian's Atmosphere is to think about the experience of birth. After existing in the insulated, warm, muffled environment of the womb, humans are suddenly ejected into a world with loud sounds, sharp sensations on the skin, and cold air. The shock must be enormous. Now imagine a protected child like Vivian facing the emotional equivalent of birth. The Atmosphere was ever-present, existing in the form of molecules intermingled with hers, so there was total, immersive contact. This womblike protection kept her from ever experiencing aloneness. Any fear was met with a reassuring presence; emotional pain was instantly understood and thus barely felt. After years of being surrounded by this protective Atmosphere of benevolent beings with no needs of their own, constantly attuned to the feelings of one small girl, she is suddenly subjected to the harshness of raw emotions.

Losing the Atmosphere is about encountering for the first time fear, pain, and separateness. We have all gone through these very experiences but so long ago that they lie beyond the reach of memory. Because Vivian's self was split into separate parts, and because some parts were shielded from these universal experiences until adulthood, she is able to give a firsthand account of a journey we all make on the way to becoming attached and emerging as social beings.

WE OWE MUCH OF OUR UNDERSTANDING of the importance of attachment and the human interactions that foster its development to John Bowlby. In a 1952 World Health Organization report on the needs of homeless children in postwar Europe, he called international attention to a problem everyone who worked with them knew to be real: children denied a chance to form attachment bonds to a mother or primary caretaker during their first years of life suffered irreparable damage. Though severe physical or sexual trauma is more commonly the cause of dissociative identity disorder (DID), or multiple personalities, what made Vivian split into distinct parts was attachment trauma.

When we started our work together, she displayed several patterns of insecure attachment. While part of her was very capable of forming emotional bonds, other parts were so shy and ashamed that they avoided interacting with people. There were also parts shielded from outside contact. Still others felt constantly unreal, and one, in particular, was in perpetual search of a mommy. In ***Losing the Atmosphere***, we see previously sequestered parts of Vivian begin to traverse the developmental stages of becoming attached. As this evolution occurs, adult parts of her are able to describe emotional events that resonate with deep, preverbal memories of our own experience.

The Atmosphere and attachment are the subjects of Vivian's story, but DID also plays a role. Dissociation results from the mind's innate ability to split off parts of experience to protect the self from overwhelming emotion. It is far more common than many people, even experts, realize. When we see victims of a disaster staring blankly and going through the motions of whatever they must do, we are witnessing people who have dissociated their feelings. Emotion has been split off from consciousness, leaving them aware of only the bare facts. There is survival value in this: it permits us to do what we must when our emotions would otherwise be overwhelming. Not until later, when conditions are more favorable, will these same people be in a position to face their feelings and heal from the trauma they have endured. Dissociation is the mind's natural way of protecting us from feelings that go beyond our capacity for coping. This splitting can last a matter of hours, days, or decades. When, at last, dissociative barriers evaporate in therapy or another supportive milieu, feelings kept out of consciousness come back unchanged from when they were first sequestered. Memories of traumatic events return with the full intensity of the emotions that could not be dealt with at the time, but now in a context of safety and healing.

In Vivian's case, the traumas were not the typical ones of child abuse. Her parents loved her, but they treated her in highly unusual and unpredictable ways from the beginning. Repeated attachment traumas placed barriers in the way of her normal need to form warm, safe emotional connections with her parents. Instead, at moments of overwhelming fear and pain, parts of her emerging self were split off by dissociation. The splits enabled some segments of her self to be sheltered from the trauma, leaving more robust but less feeling aspects of her personality open to experiences of day-to-day living. Over time, these segments gelled into more clearly defined personalities, as well as a multitude of very young fragments. In effect, significant parts of Vivian were frozen in time and place, protected from the influences of experience and consciousness, but also isolated. It was as if major parts of her being were locked in time capsules, unchanged from when they were split off from the mainstream of her development. Thus, it was possible for the surface Vivian to go to school, have friends, become a teenager, and enjoy growing up in a large extended family without revealing or having awareness of her inner selves.

I HAVE DESCRIBED DISSOCIATIVE BARRIERS as if they were simple, all-or-nothing walls keeping parts of the self from consciousness. They are actually more complex and varied. Barriers can be partial, allowing some aspects of dissociated experience to "leak" through. Leaks can be multidirectional or one-way. The flashbacks of war veterans are an example of walled-off experience leaking into consciousness. Healing comes only when the barriers are dismantled. Until that happens, flashbacks can continue indefinitely, causing great distress to the person who suffers from PTSD.

With Vivian, the dissociative barriers were partial and variable. This is what allowed a thoughtful and self-aware young girl to look in the mirror and "know" that there were Atmosphere beings observing her every movement, empathically attuned to every feeling she might have. The importance of the partial permeability later on was that it allowed the very articulate adult parts of her to be our therapy guides in the world of the younger parts. Internally, much awareness was shared. Nonetheless, as is typical in DID, there were distinct parts who would suddenly pop up with distinct voices, mannerisms, and attitudes.

By the time I first met Vivian, she had already identified a number of parts of herself with some of the classic categories: a caretaker, a defender, an administrator, children. But it soon became apparent that DID was not the main problem. Attachment was. Our work together illustrates what I have come to think of as the four principles of attachment.

THE FIRST IS: *To exist, you must be seen.* Obviously, you can exist physically if no one sees you, but there is something fundamental about being human that can't happen without the experience of seeing ourselves through the eyes of another person. This part of the work with Vivian started at what she called "the bottom level," populated by vaguely differentiated preverbal babies. They made strange cries and moans, but most of all they needed to attach to me through our gaze. Eye contact was a life-giving connection for them. Over many months, these dormant beings began to "crawl out of the grave," the metaphor an older Vivian used to describe their return from oblivion.

The principle behind this phase of her treatment could be restated as: *To gain consciousness of one's own existence, one must be seen by another.* This is true, but what the babies in Vivian gained was more than consciousness. Mostly without words, they gained the connection they needed in order to begin to explore and experience. Before they emerged in treatment, they were much like orphan babies deprived of human contact, who, unable to grow physically or emotionally, often die.

According to Bowlby and other attachment researchers, human infants have a powerful drive to establish empathic connections, to have the sense that their caregiver understands their feelings. The infants who do best developmentally are those whose primary caregivers accurately understand their emotions and, in a calm way, reflect back to the child what is happening. At first this is through eye contact and tone of voice. The babies in Vivian needed exactly that, and, as they did connect, they began to grow.

THE SECOND PRINCIPLE IS: *Until a feeling is understood by another, it will be too big and too frightening to cope with.* Contemporary attachment researchers and theorists have increasingly focused on the role of the primary caregiver in affect regulation—that is, keeping feelings at a level of intensity that will not overwhelm the child. A mother who correctly understands and reflects back the child's experience helps the child modulate her feelings to a level she can bear. As this exchange is repeated, the child builds confidence in being able to cope with emotions and gradually doesn't need her mother as much.

This principle was illustrated early in Vivian's therapy. Whenever there was a strong sense of connection with me, she would experience a pain in her chest. Gradually, we came to realize that these were times when a part of her, a child named Emily—the closest to the original core self—was "waking up" and experiencing a longing for a mother. What brought her to life was the possibility of being understood empathically. That was all she needed. Any attempt on my part at active comforting would make Emily go back into hiding because she read it as my intolerance of her feeling state. I learned that she simply needed me to be a witness while she was experiencing the pain. Over time, she became better able to tolerate the feeling and more able to be close to the surface, or even present. While the Atmosphere, too, had soothed her feelings by providing an empathic witness, it had done such a good job that she hadn't learned to tolerate feelings, but only to conjure up the Atmosphere's enveloping safety.

The Atmosphere consisted of a mixture of imaginary people and people Vivian actually knew, like therapists and teachers. As she explains, the people she knew had two versions: in-person, which she described as being in a "skin container," and Atmosphere. What she called "betrayals"—times when the actual person's behavior was inconsistent with his or her caring and understanding in the Atmosphere—were always attributed to the skin-container version. Real people have feelings and needs, are restricted to a single place, and don't always understand.

The need to have feelings understood by another was what drove Vivian, as a child, to create the Atmosphere, though she didn't do it consciously. She experienced the Atmosphere as a collective of loose molecules mingling with hers in the air, a benign presence that was in constant emotional contact with her. While their substance mixed with hers, she retained her identity. It was not a merger, but a bath of connection. The Atmosphere people saw everything she experienced and understood the pain she endured. They were soothing, omnipresent, and attentive, with none of the disadvantages of real people, especially ones like her parents.

As long as the Atmosphere was constantly available, there was no need for parts of Vivian to cope with the vulnerability of real-life connections or the overwhelming intensity of raw emotions. Why go through the painful experience of learning to trust? The skills of relating, or creating and maintaining connections with real people who have needs of their own, were of no value as long as the Atmosphere was there.

But the Atmosphere was a fantasy, and fantasy isn't real. As our relationship strengthened, parts of Vivian that had relied on the Atmosphere began to rely on her relationship with me, her therapist. When it worked, the realness of that connection was even more satisfying for her than the Atmosphere. But unlike the Atmosphere, I was not totally consistent.

HEINZ KOHUT, A PSYCHOANALYST known for his "self psychology" theory, believed that breaks in empathic connection are often the events that produce therapeutic gains. This was the case in my work with Vivian. She had an exquisite sensitivity to what she perceived as a wandering of my attention, and she worried that I would become distracted and lose interest in her. (Note how closely this matches the ways her mother would lose interest in her or suddenly turn on her.) I tried to avoid breaks in connection, but they inevitably occurred, either because my attention did wander, or because some event—like my forgetting to turn off the ringer on my office phone—betrayed the fact that I had a life apart from her.

Ultimately, when things like that happened and reality poked through the illusion, it was therapeutic, but only in moderation. At first, almost any failure of connection, even the hint of a possible failure, would cause Vivian to switch to a state in which I was of no importance to her. Her voice would go flat, as if I were a stranger. This worked to protect the part of her that was in danger, but it also prevented us from establishing further contact until we had laboriously worked through the painful event. It was only in the no-man's land between the skin and Atmosphere worlds that there was room for each catastrophe of connection to be processed.

The first time I fully understood the pervasiveness of the Atmosphere was about five years into our work together. On her way to a session, Vivian called from her cell phone to say she'd had to take a detour because of the snow and was lost. I told her to "turn right at Scarsdale Ford." She arrived at my office 15 minutes later looking stricken. My directions had revealed, beyond any doubt, something part of her still did not know: I had an existence outside of the office. I was taken by surprise. While parts of Vivian knew I must have such a life, my practice of not making references to outside activities or other patients had allowed other parts of her to maintain the illusion that between waving goodbye at the end of one session and greeting her at the start of the next, I remained motionless, standing in the doorway. Until that day, no reality had contradicted her assumption. Vivian's multiplicity had silently been at work protecting those parts from this awareness.

Usually when there was a connection break, it took until the next session or longer to repair the damage. What helped was for both of us to understand exactly what had happened. Vivian had to overcome her discouragement, and I had to let go of any defensiveness and acknowledge my role. Only then could we go forward. Some breaks were small, some large, but each time, she was like a turtle going into its shell. Any move to force a quick resolution would make the situation worse. Repair had to come through patient understanding, empathy, and acknowledgement.

Very slowly, these failures in connection and our work to repair them helped Vivian build her ability to cope with feelings and to accept the loss of more of the Atmosphere version of me. On the other hand, her gains were limited by the dissociation that had saved her in her early life. She was still able to distance from her emotions by switching. Her self-protection was automatic and involuntary, even though she would complain of its consequence: that she did not feel like a three-dimensional person. What was missing was emotion.

THIS BRINGS US TO THE THIRD PRINCIPLE of attachment: *Internalizing a sense of the constant presence of the other is what allows us to tolerate aloneness.*

The time between sessions had always been a problem. The more Vivian relied on the real, in-person version of me, the more she required tangible indications that I continued to exist outside our sessions and was still interested in her. She couldn't take it for granted. We experimented with phone messages, actual (hard copy) letters, coupons to keep during periods of my absence, even voice recordings. Inevitably, within a few hours of a session, her sense that we still had a connection would disappear and she would revert to depending on the Atmosphere.

What she had trouble with is *object permanence*, that is, the ability to maintain some kind of internal representation of mother or a primary caregiver even when she or he is not there. Normally, this develops gradually during the first few years, subject to disruption with stress or prolonged absence. Exactly what the child internalizes is not known. It could be the mental image of the mother, or it could be something less concrete, such as a very basic sense that the world is a safe place. Whatever is internalized becomes part of the child's permanent psychic apparatus.

Vivian had no need to internalize the Atmosphere. Being constantly available, it remained external. As a result, she did not internalize the feeling of connection that normally softens the experience of being alone and enables us to weather separations. Instead, her mind used dissociation to shield parts of herself from awareness that any separation had happened. A number of years into our therapy, I knew Vivian had begun to internalize something of our ongoing relationship when she first dared to speak of "next time," implicitly acknowledging that there would be a period of separation.

THE FOURTH AND LAST PRINCIPLE of attachment is this: *The ability to integrate both positive and negative sides of our concept of a needed person allows us to know we are still lovable, even when we have made the other person angry or when we are angry with them.*

For many years, part of Vivian remained at a two-year-old level of development, maintaining two separate sets of relationships. The first was for when things were going well, with a perfect Vivian and a perfect other. The second was for times of conflict, with a bad Vivian and an angry other. But Vivian's experience was different from what usually occurs—the eventual integration of these two sets of relationships—because the bad Vivian and angry other could be isolated and split off from consciousness. In this way, the anger, pain, and fear that would normally accompany difficult times did not contaminate the pure positive feelings that were vital to her emotional survival.

Melanie Klein, a child psychoanalyst best known for her object relations theory, hypothesized that children do not experience the *good self* and the *good other* as part of the same mental schema as the *bad self* and the *bad other*. One of the great developmental achievements of the third year of life is the knitting together of these two states, allowing us to love and feel loved even in the midst of conflict. Observers such as Margaret Mahler, a psychoanalyst who studied the development of emotional separation and individuation, have chronicled how the "terrible twos" are the battleground on which integration of good and bad images of self and other are—or are not—achieved. The hallmark of adults who lack this integration, and cannot cover it by dissociation, is oscillation between idealizing and vilifying those they care about most.

Vivian's multiplicity and ability to dissociate allowed parts of her to bypass this process for many years. It was not until she began letting go of the Atmosphere, in which there is only good, that she had to confront good and bad in the same relationship. As long as she had an Atmosphere version of me and other important people in her life, a problem between us could easily be solved: when the in-person version was not OK, she would revert to the perfectly attuned Atmosphere version. But as the Atmosphere version of me began to fade and not be available, a failure of attunement was more of a problem. Vivian would go to desperate lengths to preserve a positive relationship. When that failed, she would dissociate to a state in which I hardly existed, the same as she did when she perceived a wandering of my attention. In this way, she was much like the avoidant children described by John Bowlby and Mary Ainsworth, another attachment pioneer. She would treat me as if she had no need for me and I meant nothing to her. This would last until we were able to re-establish "perfect" attunement by my coming to realize what had gone wrong and regaining my empathic connection.

OVER SEVERAL YEARS, Vivian made the transition to relying increasingly on our real, in-person relationship for a sense of connection with me. As she did so, the Atmosphere became less available, even when she needed it. When this first happened, Vivian was like a two-year-old realizing that Mom isn't perfectly in sync with her wishes. Her feelings combined devastation with anger and hopelessness. Even the formidable intellectual grasp of her more mature parts was barely able to soothe the upset. Today, at a point beyond the end of the book's narrative, she is fully engaged in our relationship and no longer avoids dealing directly with anger and disappointment when there is a break in attunement. She has learned to cope with the universal human problem of having conflict with a person you absolutely need and being afraid that somehow your anger will destroy a vital relationship.

As Vivian worked to acquire what many of us take for granted—becoming comfortably, securely attached—the phase she used recurrently was, "No child left behind." By this, she acknowledged that dissociation had allowed her to protect, but also to isolate, parts of herself. Even as she is moving toward deeper and more satisfying relationships in the real world, there are a few parts of her that remain in a developmentally younger state. As each of these parts goes through the process of losing the Atmosphere, she must experience the emotions of fear and distress all of us confront in becoming fully attached. For this reason, Vivian's recovery resonates with the experiences that, for the rest of us, are embedded deep in our preverbal memory. Somewhere in the core of our being, we all know the fragility of human connection and instinctively relate to her life-and-death drive to be seen. ▪

Jeffery Smith, MD, is the author of *Psychotherapy: A Practical Guide* (Springer, 2017), *Getting the Most from Your Therapy* (Libentia, 2016), and *How We Heal and Grow: The Power of Facing Your Feelings* (Libentia, 2014).

Acknowledgments

THIS BOOK WAS 25 YEARS IN THE MAKING. My original intention was to write a magazine article about how hard it is to live in the world when you have MPD/DID. To that end, I enrolled in a Writer's Voice workshop called "The Personal Essay," taught by Bettina Drew. It was Bettina who suggested I write a memoir.

When Bettina moved on, I found a home in Charles Salzberg's "Advanced Nonfiction" course, offered through New York Writers Workshop, where I remained for the long haul. No amount of thanks can express my gratitude for the help and support Charles provided. Not only did he shepherd me through draft after draft of chapter after chapter, but he created community. Charles nurtures writers of all ages, writing styles, and subjects. Through him, I have become part of a network of writers that extends well beyond the classroom.

It was in Charles's workshop that I met the three authors who have become my other writing family: Chaya Deitsch, Sally Hoskins, and Sally Koslow. I continue to look forward to our biweekly pick-apart-each-other's-writing sessions laced with camaraderie. My thanks and appreciation also to the many other friends I have made throughout the years in Charles's class, too numerous to name here. I treasure our relationships.

One consequence of writing a book for 25 years is that the manuscript tends to sprawl. Helen Zelon and Bettina Drew made helpful suggestions for cutting it down along the way. When I finally reached the end, enter editor extraordinaire Dawn Raffel, my Maxwell Perkins, who whittled it down further and gave my story shape.

Deep thanks to my agent, Diane Stockwell, who championed my book from the start, buoying my spirits through more glowing rejections than I care to count. I eventually found a warm welcome at Greenpoint Press, where, with infinite sensitivity and good humor, Editor Gini Kopecky Wallace gave the manuscript its final polish, fact-checking and pointing out places that needed clarification. Design Director and Business Manager Robert Lascaro not only did beautiful, meticulous work on the cover, the photos, and the physical look of the book, but supervised the entire production process, including printing and distribution. Greenpoint's Treasurer-and-more Robbie Tucker made the business end of things understandable and easy. And Charles Salzberg, Editor-in-Chief, creates an environment that makes miracles possible with a shoestring staff of four.

Last but definitely not least, a huge thank you to my wonderful family: my brother and sister-in-law, my nephews and their partners and children, and several generations of cousins and their families. Thank you for your love and support, and for the feeling of belonging I get just from knowing you're all there. I'm so glad you're in my life.

About the Author

VIVIAN CONAN is a writer, librarian, and IT business analyst who lives in Manhattan. A native New Yorker, she grew up in a large Greek-Jewish clan in Brooklyn, graduated from Brooklyn College, and holds master's degrees from Pratt Institute and Baruch College. Her work has appeared in *The New York Times*, *New York* magazine, *Lilith*, *Narratively*, and *Ducts.org*. She received a 2007 fellowship in Nonfiction Literature from the New York Foundation for the Arts and a 2019 Simon Rockower Award from the American Jewish Press Association. Vivian sings with the Peace of Heart Choir, which performs free for communities in need, and has mentored teenage writers as a volunteer with Girls Write Now. **Losing the Atmosphere** is her first book.

Learn more at **VivianConan.com**.

www.ingramcontent.com/pod-product-compliance
Lightning Source LLC
Chambersburg PA
CBHW031129160426
43193CB00008B/77